PRACTICAL THEOLOGY

PRACTICAL THEOLOGY

Perspectives from the Plains

Edited by

MICHAEL G. LAWLER
&
GAIL S. RISCH

CREIGHTON UNIVERSITY PRESS
Omaha, Nebraska
Association of Jesuit University Presses

Library of Congress Cataloging-in-Publication Data

Practical theology : perspectives from the plains / edited by
Michael G. Lawler & Gail S. Risch.
    p. cm.
  Includes bibliographical references.
  ISBN 1-881871-36-3 (hard).-- ISBN 1-881871-37-1 (pbk.)
  1. Theology. I. Lawler, Michael G. II. Risch, Gail S., 1951-

BR118.P72 2000
230--dc21

                                        00-020116

EDITORIAL

Creighton University Press
2500 California Plaza
Omaha, Nebraska 68178

MARKETING &
DISTRIBUTION
Fordham University Press
University Box L
Bronx, New York 10458

Printed in the United States of America

We dedicate this book
to our students at
Creighton University

Contents

Theology and the University

Michael G. Lawler

This is a book of practical theology which originates in the Theology Department of a Catholic University situated on the Great Plains. It is shaped
by three influences: the Plains, the University, and Theology. Its origin on
the Plains does more than give the book a title; it also shapes it, as place always does. Place differs from space to the extent that space is neutral and
place is shaped by personal and communal experience and meaning. Place
is where we locate our sense of deepest meaning, from where we interpret
the present and envision the future. The authors represented in this
collection are all Christian theologians living and working on the Plains,
and sharing the life of the intellect and spirit characteristic of the Plains.
That spirit, most frequently described as down-to-earth and honest, is a
good spirit for doing Christian theology where the basic truth is of a God
who revealed Mystery in an incarnated, down-to-earth way. That spirit is
evidenced here as theologians reflect on and write about not only the
theological truths that make up the Christian tradition but also how these
truths are incarnated, made down-to-earth, in their lives and the lives of
their local and global neighbors. The diversity of their reflections and conclusions, on church, authority, gender, the environment, and even gambling,
mirrors the breadth and length and height and depth (Eph 3:18) of the
Mystery-God whose truth they seek individually and communally.

It is standard for a book of essays to have a theme, and this one is no
different. It's theme, however, is not a *content* which each theologian comments on from a different theological perspective; it is rather a theological
method followed in each essay. That method, in general, is the traditional
theological method of faith seeking understanding; in specific, it is individual and communal reflection rooted in the sacred space-time of the Plains.
The authors offer their reflections to all students, young and old, who seek
God down-to-earth in their lives.

1

THEOLOGY AND UNIVERSITY

Along with place, two other influences shape this book: the university and theology. The connection between theology and university began in the thirteenth century when the first great universities—Paris, Oxford, Cambridge, Bologna—were founded, all of them Catholic, all of them chartered by the Church to an academic freedom unconstrained by the state. There was no discussion about theology's place in the university; it was taken for granted. Theology, the highest form of knowledge and truth, and therefore the Queen of the Sciences, belonged and flourished in the universities. The theology practiced in those early universities, which came into its ascendancy with Cyprian and Augustine, Lombard, Aquinas, and Bonaventure, and was later reformed by Luther and Calvin, Schleiermacher, and Barth, was rooted in a principle of authority. That authority was itself rooted in the belief that God has been definitively revealed to humankind in the life, death, and resurrection of Jesus of Nazareth, and that revelation is both preserved and continued in the Christian Churches. In such a climate, theological truth was not something for men and women to discover, still less to create, but something given to them in the tradition of the Churches, especially in that sacred written tradition called the Bible, believed to be the very word of God. And who would dare challenge the word of God?

But times and givens have changed. The Reformation and the French Revolution transformed the great universities from Catholic to secular, and the Enlightenment made the assumptions inherent in earlier beliefs subject to critical questioning. Critical questioning is dialectical, not single-visioned; it rigorously considers the pros and cons of a question, develops coherent arguments, and situates answers on a broadly accepted intellectual canvas. It is epitomized best, perhaps, in Descartes' radical doubt and Kant's critical philosophy, and it demoted theology from its privileged position as Queen of the Sciences to its present precarious position on the outer margins of the Humanities. The re-establishment in the nineteenth century of the Belgian University of Louvain as a Catholic university and the establishment of some two hundred and thirty Catholic universities in the United States ignited a modern debate about the place of theology in the modern university. Neither focus nor space permits me to rehearse that debate here.[1] In this brief introduction, I have no wish to re-enthrone theology as Queen of the University. I wish only to show that critical theology, in the sense explained above, has a rightful place among the disciplines that comprise the modern university.

My argument for inviting theology into the university has two theses: the university needs theology and theology needs the university. Before either of these theses can be explicated, however, careful definition is demanded, for both university and theology are bedeviled by charlatans.

When I say *university*, I intend that third, higher level of learning which follows on high school. On that third level, students and teachers are engaged, not in teaching and learning rote truths and committing them to short-term memory until they can be tested and forgotten, but in rigorously critical thinking about the truths, ideas, institutions, theories, and practices that have abounded and continue to abound in human space-time. Those truths, ideas, institutions, theories, and practices are, of necessity, philo-sophical, scientific, cultural, historical, literary, artistic, political, legal, and economic. A university is the home of the highest intellectual activity. It is concerned primarily and directly with the cultivation of the intellect, and only secondarily and indirectly with liberal, scientific, professional, or religious education. To claim the name *universitas*, an educational institu-tion where all human truth is openly and fairly discussed, evaluated, dis-covered, and welcomed, an institution must include, again of necessity, discussion, evaluation, discovery, and welcome of that universal human truth which is religious and theological. That is part of what I intend when I claim that the university needs theology.

The university is a place where the various disciplines of higher learn-ing converge, in the sense that they meet, critically challenge one another, and emerge from the challenge with a mutually enhanced understanding of not only their own positions but also the positions of others. After too many years struggling for convergence in universities on three continents, I am no longer naive. I know that, however true that statement is in theory, it is not nearly so true in turf-protection practice. There is too little conver-gence, too little contact among faculties, too little mutual dialogue and challenge between them, leaving all of them diminished. Religion and theology, its intellectual offspring, can be denied their place in the universi-ty convergence; many modern universities are instantiations of that posture. They cannot, however, *pace* discredited nineteenth-century scientific rationalism, be *successfully* denied their place in the university conver-gence. Where it is excluded, history demonstrates, some other discipline usurps its role, with ludicrous results: space travelers report no sign of God in the heavens, creationists deny incontrovertible fossil evidence in un-necessary defense of a young earth, groups of terrified believers expect the arrival of the resurrected Jesus in a spacecraft on March 1, 1998 (He refused to conform to such ludicrous expectation). Where good, rigorously critical theology is excluded, bad, uncritical theology flourishes, for men and women continue to raise the ultimate questions which provide the data of religion and theology. In asserting that the university needs theology, I am asserting only that the academic discipline of theology is the one best suited to analyze that data in a critical and informed way.

How is this theology I speak of to be understood? There has been no substantive change in the definition of theology in the Western tradition since Augustine-influenced Anselm. Theology is *fides quaerens intellectum*, faith seeking understanding, or, in Karl Rahner's twentieth-century explication, "the conscious effort of the Christian to hearken to the actual verbal revelation which God has promulgated in history, to acquire a knowledge of it by the methods of scholarship and to reflect on its implications."[2] Theology is not open-ended, no more than biology or economics is open-ended, so that whatever anyone names theology or biology or economics is admitted to the category. Theology is not just any reflection someone chooses to name theology. Theology is faith seeking an understanding that is achieved at the end, not at the beginning, of a process of critical, methodical, and systematic questioning of the data of faith and revelation. It is precisely because it is a rigorous, intellectual questioning that theology needs the university, the place where the cultivation of the intellect takes precedence over all ideology.

Since theology is the conscious effort to hearken critically to God's revelation, a question arises: what does God reveal when God reveals? The answer, as boldly stated by the Second Vatican Council, is that God reveals Godself.[3] God does not reveal knowledge about God; God does not reveal conceptual propositions describing God; God reveals Godself and invites humans into graceful fellowship. To speak loosely, as if God were an object alongside other objects in the world, the object of revelation is not a set of doctrinal or theological propositions. The object of revelation is not an object at all, it is a subject, an ultimate, divine subject-Mystery which humans name in their limited language *God*. That language, and its limitations when describing any subject, human or divine, raises other questions.

The formal object of theology, to repeat for emphasis, is not a set of propositions or truths. It is the transcendent, holy Mystery that grounds and provides the horizon for all existence.[4] Theology is about ultimate and ineffable Mystery, not about ultimate *words*, however inspired, not about ultimate *propositions*, however solemnly defined. The words and the propositions are necessary; they are all that humans have to symbolize the holy Mystery. They are necessary, however, not to define and to set limits to the Mystery, but to provide images and symbols signposting the way to the Mystery and inviting, even demanding, further questioning on a journey to understanding and truth that approaches its goal, as a long tradition of mystics, philosophers, and theologians have taught us to see, only asymptotically. That asymptotic quest for religious truth is called theology.

Theology and theologians bear a burden their co-religionists should share but have long forgotten or, perhaps, in their fascination with facile words, have never known. That burden was famously phrased by Augustine of Hippo: *Si cepisti, non est Deus* (if you understand, it is not God you understand).[5] After a lifetime of intellectually rigorous theology, in the context of what he took to be the most inspired of divine revelations, Aquinas agreed. In this life, though humans can know *that* God is, they can never know *what* God is.[6] That is the burden theology brings to the university, a search for truth that leads not to definitive certitude about the Mystery that surrounds and embraces humans, and therefore manipulation and control, but to insight and understanding, and therefore appreciation of the Mystery. In the university theologians share their burden with others of equally limited insight. The Heisenberg Uncertainty Principle, which states that the more accurately we determine the position of an electron the less accurately we can determine its momentum, and vice versa, was formulated in the search for an understanding of physical reality.[7] It applies also, even more so, in the search for understanding of reality that transcends the physical. The more women and men think they have literally positioned and described God the more they have missed the reality of God, not because of some temporary and ultimately curable human ignorance but simply because God *is* Mystery.

Though etymologically theology (*theou-logos*) is discourse about God as biology (*biou-logos*) is discourse about life, methodologically it is done by believers seeking understanding of the very foundations of their own lives and the lives of their global neighbors. It is, therefore, a human and humanistic discipline. The faith that seeks understanding "includes knowledge of a saving event, confidence in the word of God, man's [and woman's] humble submission and personal self-surrender to God, fellowship in life with Christ, and a desire for perfect union with him beyond the grave. Faith is man's [and woman's] comprehensive 'Yes' to God's revealing himself as man's [and woman's] savior in Christ."[8]

God is Creator, Father, Revealer, Savior, ultimate, absolute, infinite, Trinity. These theological words and the concepts they articulate symbolically, along with a myriad others I need not enumerate here, make up the language of religious experience. They derive, it was assumed for centuries, from the interpretation and articulation of that experience. But the critical analysis of social, cultural, and historical contexts that takes place in the university warns that it is too simplistic to assume that, to uncover the meanings embedded in theological language, all we have to do is to isolate that part of human experience that is *religious* experience. Such an approach assumes a three-stage model of relationship between individual experience and its social, cultural, and linguistic contexts. There is: first, raw individual experience; second, the sensation, imagination, and conceptualization of that raw experience; third, the communication to others through language of that sensed, imagined, conceptualized, and judged-to-be-true experience. The problem with that three-stage model is embedded in the first stage: there is no such thing as raw, uninterpreted experience.

Language is at work on all three levels of experience, imagination and conceptualization of experience, and communication of experience. At each level experience is not only interpreted but also literally created and shaped by the language which names it. Without language, we would not experience at all; experience would simply lie beyond our grasp. That is true for all human experience, and it is even more true *a fortiori*, as the philosophers say, for any experience of Transcendence and holy Mystery. Religious experience, whatever else it may be, is never raw, pre-conceptual, pre-linguistic experience.

In our language, words like 'God,' 'creator,' 'faith,' 'revelation,' 'salvation,' 'transcendent,' 'mystery,' and the meanings embedded in them, create and shape our religious experience. It is more accurate to say that culture and language provide the foundation for religious experience than to say that religious experience provides the foundation for religious and theological language. Naming something, experience for instance, not only gives it a name but also draws it out of its objective isolation into subjective relationship with the namer. Naming anything alters it by construing it in relation to us.[9]

Theologians are not in the business of simply handing on truths, concepts, words, stories, and propositions; they are in the business of formulating, and thereby creating, religious and theological truths, concepts, words, stories, and propositions. Their activity results in the creation of both signposts to the ultimate truth of the Mystery they believe surrounds and grounds humankind and the present religious experience in which that Mystery may be discerned.[10] Professors of theology are different from professors of religious studies, specifically in their level of commitment to the truths they examine. Theologians seek understanding of doctrines they believe to be true: their methodology starts with doctrine accepted as true and seeks deeper understanding of it. Professors of religious studies approach religious doctrine in a neutral, non-committed way: their methodology starts with doctrine as sociological fact abstracting from any truth claim. "There is but one God," Jews, Christians, and Muslims believe. Theologians ask what that proposition means in human lives; professors of religious studies acknowledge that is what Jews, Christians, and Muslims believe but do not ask whether it is true or not. Religious studies "is not aimed at persuading students to adopt any religious or ethical position";[11] theology is. "The study of religion does not in the first instance determine the truth or otherwise of a faith or ideology";[12] theology critically does. Theologians believe the truths they question. It is, in fact, precisely because they believe them and wish to formulate the present meaning in them that they raise critical questions about them. The belief and passionate commitment that characterize all theologians will be evident in all the authors that follow.

Because theologians are in the business of rigorously examining what they believe to be true, they must also be in the business of rigorously examining the tools they use, and that is another reason why theology needs the university. It is in the university that the standard tools of theology, namely, culture, history, experience, words, images, concepts, rituals, stories, and propositions are critically examined by philosophers, historians, anthropologists, sociologists, psychologists, geneticists, linguists, physicists, and a host of others whose conclusions can help theologians achieve critical understanding. This is especially true in the Catholic university dominated by the Catholic assumption that all truth is one. The Vatican Congregation for the Doctrine of the Faith argued that theologians, to fulfill their task in the church, must understand the meaning of revelation, must utilize philosophical concepts, and must consult the "human sciences" to understand better revealed truth.[13] I add only that the best place to do this is in the university, the place of the highest and most rigorous intellectual examination.

If human experience does not become *religious* experience without the influence of literally creative theological and religious language, neither does religious and theological language have any real meaning without the experience it images, conceptualizes, and symbolizes. Unless it is rooted in experience, filled with experience, responsive to and illuminating of experience, theological language is empty of meaning and quite useless for anything other than the mantric repetition of words assumed to be true. The teaching and learning of words uncritically accepted as true is not a task for any discipline in the university. The university's task is the critical questioning of words and concepts, rituals and propositions, not to prove them false, though this can and has happened, but to discover if they are meaningful articulations of experience and can, therefore, sustain present and future faith. Put more plainly, the teaching of catechism by rote is not a task for theologians in a university. The theological task is not the uncritical handing on to memory of unexamined words and concepts. It is the handing on to personal faith of words, concepts, and propositions that have been subjected to critical examination and have been found to be still-adequate articulations of the experience of contemporary believers seeking ultimate truth in their lives.

John Wain, not the swashbuckling Duke of Hollywood but an English literary critic of the 1960s, wrote the following:

> To write well means far more than choosing the apt word or the telling arrangement of syllables … it is a matter of feeling and living at the required depth, fending off the continual temptation to be glib and shallow, to appeal to the easily aroused response, to be evasive and shirk the hard issues. It is a matter of training oneself to live with reality…. This is a large claim; if what I am saying is true, the artist is better, stronger, braver, more perceptive, than the ordinary person. I shrink from my own meaning, for who can enjoy making such a claim, with the responsibility it involves?
>
> If the responsibility is great, and the risk of ignominious failure greater still, the reward is in proportion. An author, if he is big enough, can do much for his fellow humans. He can put words into their mouths and reasons into their heads; he can fill their sleep with dreams so potent that when they awake they will go on living them…. There, at the center, are the artists who really form the consciousness of their time; they respond deeply, intuitively, to what is happening, what has happened and what will happen and their response is expressed in metaphor and symbol, in image and in fable.[14]

I make no apology for the lengthy citation, for while Wain was speaking of artists, I am thinking of other denizens of the university, theologians, philosophers, and scientists. There is a creative center in every culture; it is only from that center that women and men can be influenced; and to work from that center does make peculiar demands upon a thinking person. At that center critical thinkers drink deeply of the fact that reality is always, and of necessity, *present* reality. However much tradition may be handed on to them from the past, thinkers can never be content with that past tradition, for their duty is not only to pass on tradition but also to pass it on interpreted and made down-to-earth in present reality, thereby assuring its future. They have, therefore, to open themselves to the newness of present reality, and they have to react to the newness creatively so that what comes to them from the past can be verified as meaningful in the present, or simply discarded. Not only individual theologians must inhabit the center of present reality but also religious communities, not to yield to it uncritically but to dialogue with and respond to it creatively. Any religion that shirks this dialogue, that ignores present reality and its creative center and chooses to walk into the future looking only backwards at its past, fails in its mission to the present revelation of God and the present faith of its adherents. Such a religion is inevitably doomed to banishment from the center of life to the irrelevant margins. There are signs that the absence of the Christian churches from the contemporary center has led large numbers of Western Christians to conclude to their total irrelevance.

In the long run, none of this is anything more than a specification of the Catholic principle of incarnation and sacramentality. Incarnation means that God has come down-to-earth, that the gulf between God and humans has been overcome; sacramentality means that, since God has come down-to-earth, humans can catch glimpses of God in human reality. At the center of reality, in Hopkins' vivid metaphors, there is "the dearest freshness deep down things" where "the Holy Ghost over the bent world broods with warm breast and with ah! bright wings." The Catholic Church has confessed that "the church has always had the duty of scrutinizing the signs of the times and of interpreting them in the light of the gospel" so that, "in language intelligible to each generation she can respond to the perennial questions which men [and women] ask about this present life and the life to come, and the relationship of the one to the other."[15] The language intelligible to each generation is precisely the language taught and learned in its fullest critical scope in the university. I am arguing that only when its theologians take their place in the university, only when they engage in the rigorous intellectual life of the university, can any religion claim to be in possession of all truth and any university claim to be *universitas veritatis*.

THEOLOGY IN THE CATHOLIC UNIVERSITY

The ultimate source of every Christian theology is the holy Mystery communicated to men and women in revelation, especially in the revelation incarnated in the Christ. That holy Mystery, Hauser explains, is embedded in our world as Spirit and can always be discerned in our lives with a little prayerful care. A more proximate source of theology, Christian theologians commonly say, is the Bible, "the word of God in human language."[16] Christians do not, of course, *believe in* the Bible; they believe in God and in the Word God sent down-to-earth to be its life and light (John 1:4). They believe, too, they know nothing about this Word apart from what they read in the New Testament, and therefore Christian theology cannot but include the study of that Testament and of its implications for past, present and future Christian life. There are, however, a number of necessary caveats here.

The first caveat is already suggested in the above description of the Bible, "the word of God in human language." Inasmuch as the word of God in the Bible is articulated in *human language*, its meanings are inescapably tied to that language and to everything that shapes it in human space-time. Several essays in this book call attention to things that undeniably shape human language. Wright highlights and insightfully reflects upon a common anthropological theme, namely, the importance of place, which shapes human experience, encodes it symbolically, including in language, and stores it in the memory called tradition. Place, therefore, geography if you like, will always be an important consideration for a theology which seeks to understand not only what a tradition teaches but also what it meant for the believers who created it and what it continues to mean for the believers who hear it today. Theologians, whether they would interpret the sacred texts of the Bible or the theological texts of the religious tradition, attain "the true goal of their work only when they have explained the meaning of the ... text as God's word for today."[17] The place which shapes and encodes this collection is the Christian Church on the Plains.

Place is not the only thing that influences human language, and so a second caveat. The meanings of language derive from and are embedded in a social system. When a speaker or writer and a hearer or reader share the same social system, understanding may follow. When they do not share the same social system, when they come from different social systems, especially from systems widely separated in space-time, even if they appear to share the same translated words, non-understanding or misunderstanding is the more likely outcome. Malina and Simkins explore the implications of this social fact for reading both Testaments. Language and gender, they argue respectively, derive their biblical meanings from the social systems of an ancient place and time in which they were written, not from the modern American system in which they are read. Even the Bible, word of God in words of men, is necessarily bound to the place, the societies, and the social systems in which it originated. Adequate, insightful, even fair understanding of the Bible, therefore, the Pontifical Biblical Commission teaches, requires "as exact a knowledge as is possible of the social conditions distinctive of the various milieus in which the traditions recorded in the Bible took shape."[18] The beginning point of every explanation of the biblical texts as God's word for today, the true goal of every reading of the Bible, is the uncovering of the social system in which the text is embedded. Calef draws on the social system operative in the early church to bring the contemporary church the good news that brave and competent women were an essential part of its life and mission and to suggest that it should continue to be so today. Hamm focuses on the Hebrew roots of the biblical text to construct a *theo*-logical theory of environmental justice and to heal a quite unnecessary cleavage between creation and redemption theologies.

There is a third caveat, historicity or the influence of history. The Congregation for the Doctrine of the Faith pointed out in 1973 that difficulties with the teaching of the Church sometimes arise "from the historical condition that affects the expression of revelation."[19] Those difficulties arise from what we discussed above, namely, the fact that language is tied to social system and social system is not the same in all of human space-time. The language used, therefore, for any given doctrine will not be equally expressive or meaningful in every time, in every place, and in every circumstance. No theology derives from "Olympus or from Sinai as thunderbolts from heaven but rather proceeds from the earnest and open inquiry of perplexed human beings who operate on the assumption (always open to critical scrutiny) that decisive clues to the meaning of our life on earth are present in the Christian mythos."[20] Theological inquiry operates not only in a specific place but also in a specific time and it is shaped by both that place and that time. Schultenover applies this notion of historicity to the doctrine of the church, drawing on the Kuhnian category of paradigm to illustrate the multiple models of church that have been employed in history. O'Keefe applies it to models of exegesis, references the allegorical exegesis of the Fathers and the historical-critical exegesis of the moderns, and argues that neither necessarily needs to be superseded by the other. Reno employs a philosophical variation to assess the contribution of the recent Lutheran and Catholic Joint Declaration on the Doctrine of Justification. The same paradigmatic approach could be used for the on-going understanding and assessment of any Christian teaching.

Though the Bible is undoubtedly the foundational Christian text, it is not the only Christian text. There are other "texts," "symbols, rituals, events, witnesses,"[21] which also embody Christian teaching. Mueller examines two such texts, two important Christian witnesses, Francis of Assisi and Ignatius of Loyola, to discern from their lives the way to become a peacemaker. Both Francis and Ignatius, indeed every saintly witness-text, make it clear that Christian theology and doctrine present a radical challenge to Christian action. It is never enough for Christians to profess belief in Christ, they must also make that belief real in practice by living a life in accord with their belief. This call to Christian action is embedded proximately in the *prophetic* character of initiation into Christian life and ultimately in the gospel of Christ. "Not everyone who *says* to me, 'Lord, Lord,' shall enter the kingdom of heaven, but he who *does* the will of my Father who is in heaven" (Matt 7:21). The will of the Father, Francis and Ignatius, and countless other Christian saints, argue, is a will to Peace.

Cyprian, the third-century bishop of Carthage, gave voice to the theological principle that putting on Christ in baptism is meaningless unless it is followed by a Christ-like life. If we have put on Christ, he writes, "we ought to go forward according to the example of Christ."[22] John Paul II, the twentieth-century bishop of Rome, agrees: "communion gives rise to mission, and mission is accomplished in communion."[23] Fleming, Bergman, and Salzman continue that Christian tradition of practical theology around concerns that currently exercise the inhabitants of the Plains. What should be the attitude of the Christian to gambling now sweeping the Plains like a plague, dragging thousands down into the mire of debt and bankruptcy? What should be the attitude of Christians toward their ecological connection to creation, the social and natural environment, currently groaning in such pain from human greed and plunder? What should be the proper relationship between the teaching authorities of the Catholic Magisterium and adult Catholics seeking to be faithful to their God, their Christ, and their Church? Should it be a way of mutually distrustful excommunication or the Christian way of mutually trustful peace? This practical theology continues the gospel and theological tradition that insists that being a Christian makes moral demands in every area of one's life.

The questions in the preceding paragraph raise a final consideration for this brief Introduction. In contrast to Protestant theology, which tends to be done in isolation from any ecclesial context, Catholic theology is done out of and on behalf of a church. The theologians in this collection all take seriously the character of this church as a faith-community, even when they are critical of it and call it back to the gospel in the present.

It is not overstating the case to say that theology exists for the sake of the community of faith, though the statement needs explanation. To assert that theology exists for the sake of the church is in no way to ignore or diminish the personal responsibility of the theologian. It is simply to explain that personal theological responsibility extends not only to oneself but also to the community called church. To do theology, to reflect on what I believe in order to understand it better, implies there is something I believe. That something is a theological word addressed to me and demanding a response from me, and that word comes to me from the community of faith to which I belong. When I reflect on the word, and when I articulate it in the present, in either the unchanged form in which I received it or a changed form more attuned to and, therefore, more clearly understood today, I articulate it not only for myself but also for the church from which I received it. The theologian is not the author of the belief on which she or he reflects; it is received from the past and from the community which mediates that past. When a theologian reflects on belief in the present, she or he has responsibilities not only to herself or himself but also to the past and to the community which remembers and mediates the past.

Christian theology comes out of the past. The earliest theology, that of the first followers of Jesus who reflected on the meaning for them in their space-time of his life, death, and resurrection, was formulated in a set of written documents that later came to be called sacred scripture. That scripture drew its original authority from the universally-acknowledged apostolicity of its writers, but it also received ongoing interpretation and elaboration as the community of faith which originally *received* it as scripture moved forward in history and sought to hand it on as theology interpreted for the present.[24] The church, and the theologians who function out of the church and on its behalf, have always understood that the theology they receive from the past, and the text that is the privileged locus of that theology, are to function as conveyor not only of *past* but also of *present* meaning. The theological effort to receive past meanings and to make them meaningful in the present necessarily involves theologians in the task of interpretation. That interpretation is specifically the interpretation of a past that continues to make the present meaningful and, therefore, allows the community of faith to move forward with hope and confidence into the future.

The concern of theologians is with not only a received community and personal past but also a meaningful personal and community present and future. Such is the concern of the Plains theologians represented in this book. They offer to their churches and to their fellow believers the outcome of their concern and reflection, the Christian past taken seriously and made meaningful in the present. They invite those churches and those believers to move forward into the millennial future determined to continue the Christian mission of bridging the gulf between God and humans and continuing the incarnation, the down-to-earthness, of God in the world.

NOTES

1. Those who wish to consider that debate can consult the following works: K.D. Hartzell and H. Sasscer, eds., *The Study of Religion on the Campus Today* (Washington, DC: Association of American Colleges, 1967); Ninian Smart, *The*

Phenomenon of Religion (New York: Seabury, 1973); David R. Griffin and Joseph C. Hough, eds., *Theology and the University: Essays in Honor of John B. Cobb, Jr.* (Albany: State University of New York Press, 1991); Francis Schussler Fiorenza, "Theology in the University," *Bulletin of the Council of Societies for the Study of Religion*, 22 (1993), 34-39; Theodore M. Hesburgh, ed., *The Challenge and Promise of a Catholic University* (Notre Dame: University of Notre Dame Press, 1994).

2. Karl Rahner and Herbert Vorgrimler, *Concise Theological Dictionary* (London: Burns Oates, 1965), 456.

3. *Dei Verbum*, 2.

4. See Karl Rahner, *Foundations of Christian Faith: An Introduction to the Idea of Christianity* (New York: Seabury, 1978), 44-89; "The Concept of Mystery in Catholic Theology," *Theological Investigations* IV (London: Darton, Longman, Todd, 1966), 36-76; "Observations on the Doctrine of God in Catholic Dogmatics," *Theological Investigations* IX (London: Darton, Longman, Todd, 1972), 127-44.

5. Augustine, *Sermo 52*, 1, 16, PL, 38, 360.

6. *Summa Theologiae*, 1, 3, preface; see also *Expositio in Sancti Pauli Epistolas*, *Opera Omnia* XIII (New York: Misurgia Publishers, 1949), 15.

7. Werner Heisenberg, *Physics and Philosophy* (New York: Harper and Row, 1958) and *Physics and Beyond* (New York: Harper and Row, 1971).

8. Juan Alfaro, "Faith," in *Sacramentum Mundi: An Encyclopedia of Theology* (New York: Herder, 1968), II, 315.

9. See David Power, *The Eucharistic Mystery: Revitalizing the Tradition* (New York: Crossroad, 1992), 277-83.

10. See Second Vatican Council, *Dogmatic Constitution on Divine Revelation*, n.2.

11. Claude Welch, "The Function of the Study of Religion," in Hartzell and Sasscer. *The Study of Religion on the Campus*, 9.

12. Ninian Smart, *The Phenomenon of Religion*, 11.

13. The Congregation for the Doctrine of the Faith, "Instruction on the Ecclesial Vocation of the Theologian," 10, *Origins* 20 (1990), 120.

14. John Wain, *Sprightly Running: Part of an Autobiography* (London: Macmillan, 1962), 263-64.

15. Second Vatican Council, *Gaudium et Spes*, 4.

16. Pontifical Biblical Commission, "The Interpretation of the Bible in the Church," *Origins* 23 (1994), 500.

17. Ibid., 497.

18. Ibid., 506.

19. *Mysterium Ecclesiae*, *Acta Apostolicae Sedis* 65 (1973), 396-408.

20. Theodore W. Jennings, Jr., *Introduction to Theology* (Philadelphia: Fortress Press, 1976), 4.

21. David Tracy, *Blessed Rage for Order: the New Pluralism in Theology* (New York: Seabury, 1975), 15, n.5.

22. *De Bono Patientiae* 9, PL 4, 628.

23. *On the Lay Faithful*, 32.

24. See Karl Rahner, "The Development of Dogma," *Theological Investigations* I (London: Darton, Longman, Todd, 1965), 66; also "Current Problems in Christology," Ibid., 149-50.

A Sacred Sense of Place:
Reflections on Being at Home on the Plains

Wendy M. Wright

> This place,
> the utterness of this place,
> the singleness of this place,
> this place is part of the body of God.[1]

As United Flight 580 makes its final descent into Omaha's Eppley Airport and I have buckled my seatbelt and put my tray table into its upright position, I strain over my seatmate's shoulder trying to locate familiar landmarks: the nipped off oxbow curve of the Missouri river that formed decades ago to become Carter Lake, the Cathedral's twin spires that top the highest of the gentle hillocks rippling westward up from the Missouri's banks, the jutting prominence of Woodman Tower that forms the axis for the modest cluster of high-rise office buildings and provides what Omaha has of a city skyline.

This city on the plains, a century ago one of the great gateways of America's westward migration, has been home to me now for a dozen years. In the scores of times during the last decade that I have reentered this place, my sense of indeed returning "home" has grown in depth and clarity. In fact, it has taken the better part of those years to begin to apply the term "home" with all its rich, complex resonance at all to Omaha.

If, as poet-philosopher Gaston Bachelard suggests, home is "our corner of the world," a "nest," a "first cosmos," my sense of being a nestling hovering over a womb-like refuge, circling to make a descent that will return me to a longed for spiritual, affective, and locational habitation, is quickened.[2] My eye may seek the landmarks focused by flight 580, but my heart hones in the direction of two other locations: the block-long neighborhood of 36th Avenue and the Platte River which runs southeast just to the west of the city. It is in these two places that my sense of home is most focused.

The idea of home is as ancient, complex and varied as human experience itself but I find the thought, articulated by cultural anthropologists, that places capture experience and store it symbolically, a powerful one that corresponds to my own intuition. Place differs from mere space to the extent that experiences shape them meaningfully. For human beings the ultimate place of experience is the body. We store our memories in muscles, mind, and cells. Beyond this, we store our memories in external places of intimate habitation. Thus home is the penultimate place of experience. Home is the place where we locate our sense of deep meaning garnered from the past. Home is also the platform from which we interpret the present and envision the future.[3]

But it is not merely my personal experience that gives meaning to a place, for places store the memory of earlier inhabitants. That memory is encoded in the landscape itself as well as through narrative traditions passed on in written and oral form. A true sense of a place involves the natural environment, the cultural environment, my personal perception of the place, shaped by my sense of individual and collective identity, and the experiences I gather as I dwell in this place. Home then is that place that is crowded with the activity and aspirations of all the organic life that has and does concentrate in that specific locale and is perceived by myself to correspond to my most primal identity.

The first of the places that I call home is the block on which I live. In an older section of the city, (as age is calculated in this region so late settled by immigrants of European descent), mine is a street defined by its shortness and by its modest, older family dwellings sheltered by a profusion of towering, mature trees. Our own house, located just south of the center of the block on its east side, is a circa 1920s two-story, whose original wood exterior is now covered with yellow vinyl siding and whose interior, catacombed by flights of staircases leading to the various floors, reveals the various stages of the house's life. Within the house are demarcated the activities of its various inhabitants. Original hardwood floors, now well worn and in need of refinishing; pine paneling added in the attic fifteen years ago by the young boarder fresh out of the military who kept himself busy fixing the place up; the newest coat of "wheat" semi-gloss latex wall paint, ours, layered over his flat white paint, layered over the forest green paint preferred by the elderly widow who had deeded the house to her boarder, layered over a faded flowered Victorian wallpaper applied by unknown residents.

The changing configuration of my own family over the last decade is evidenced in the house as well. A basement storage area has been refurnished to provide a guest bedroom space for eldest daughter, now home from college only at holidays and summers, leaving her long-time attic bedroom free for her youngest sibling to move, from the tiny nursery alcove that was his up to the attic, freeing the alcove as an office for parents who have hitherto done their taxes at the kitchen counter and stored essential documents in the piano bench in the living room.

Sheltering the house on the southeast side is the generous embrace of a magnificent black walnut tree of uncertain age and ancestry. Its heavy presence hangs over the cluster of peonies, a row of fence-hugging hedges, and thin graceful silhouettes of the redbud trees we have planted. Our house is both distinct from yet clearly reminiscent of all the other houses on our block. A few sturdy red brick structures punctuate a neighborhood of wood framed homes representative of what local architectural historians call variously the "prairie box," "craftman's bungalow," "California bungalow," or "foursquare" style.

The current residents on the block include several elderly widows and older couples who raised their many children here in this heavily Catholic city, persons who have seen the parade of infants become young people leave and empty the neighborhood of children, only to see again a new generation of families move into the pleasant, modestly priced houses with roomy yards and plenty of bedrooms. Others who live here are those newer young families whose offspring streak joyously from lawn to lawn during the months of summer. There is a smattering of single people here as well, a fiftyish rural transplant who wears a hunting cap and drives his ancient pickup down the street at the leisurely speed of five miles per hour, raising his forefinger off the steering wheel in neighborly greeting, and several mid-life career women seen chiefly going in and out of their doorways at rapid pace to corporate meetings.

36th Avenue is the sort of neighborhood where people walk their own dogs, plant their own tulips, and comment appreciatively on their neighbors' new roofing and disapprovingly on their negligent summer lawn care. These are descendants of varied ethnic populations that first settled this city a century and a half ago, Italians, Poles, Czechs, Bohemians, Irish, Germans, a smattering of Scandinavians, and a later small contingent of Hispanics and African-Americans, drawn by the lure of homesteading, the advent of the Transcontinental Railroad, or the opportunities of the cattle industry.

This undistinguished block-long neighborhood is where my heart hones as I descend into Eppley Airport. But that honing has a wider scope as well. For none of us truly inhabits a place by simply occupying space. Cultural geographers have posited that dwelling in a place inevitably involves a participation in its customary behavior or "habitude."[4]

Habitude provides a distinctive ethos to this place. As a native of the metropolitan, multicultural sprawl of Los Angeles, I feel that Omaha is a "big small town," not only because of its size of one-half million, but because people here, especially in the old Cathedral neighborhood just west of downtown, behave the way smalltown Midwest inhabitants do. Many of the families on my block can boast connections with the area for several generations. I will never forget my amazement, the year we moved in, at discovering that our installation of a backyard swing set attracted a considerable audience of neighborhood residents, not all of them children, hanging over the back fence and exchanging pleasantries about the ramifications of our installation to their environment.

The economic range of households on our block spans the lower to mid-middle class. These are insurance company employees, supermarket checkers, banktellers, managers of Venetian blind manufacturing plants, word processors, radiology technicians, and retired navy midshipmen. The 36th Avenue annual summer block party unfailingly features a keg of beer, homemade deviled eggs, a greenbean and mushroom soup casserole topped with chow mein noodles, and squirt gun drenchings by grade-school aged children. Culturally conservative, these middle Americans maintain a certain historically grounded populist spirit. Most are church-going, outspokenly moralistic, unspeakably generous, and protective of those they consider their own.

The habits of being of these people who dwell on this formerly tallgrass prairie, despite the fact that most of them earn their living in urban blue or white collar jobs, are the habits of persons whose consciousness is formed by being workers of the earth. Conservatism, preservation, pragmatism, a certain skepticism about innovation, about ways that are too fast, too "citified," or too divorced from all that is settled, stable, and good: these are the values of an agricultural people whose survival is linked to the survival and fruitfulness of the land. Midwestern religiosity is similarly of this conservative strain.

From the air I can glimpse beyond the city limits to the wide expanse of country that bioregionalists name the Dissected Till Plains, the far western fringe of what was natively the tallgrass prairie just east of the Great Plains. In fact, unlike most of the aerial landscapes visible on both coasts of this continent, the region above which my plane hovers, with the exception of the city itself which spreads out for several miles, is basically rural and thinly populated. One can drive fifteen minutes north, twenty minutes south, and thirty minutes west from my downtown Omaha house and be in open country, most of which is under cultivation but much of which feels liminal and interstitial.[5]

When I conjure up home, after the 36th Avenue neighborhood, it is this open countryside that recommends itself for my contemplation. Especially I find myself focused on the Platte River which slices a silver-green liquid swathe through the land in a southeasterly direction just west and south of town. The Platte is in my mind as both a carrier of deep cultural memory and the unique feature of landscape that defines for me the experience of genuinely dwelling in this particular place.

The headwaters of the Platte are discovered to the far west in the mountainous regions of Wyoming and Colorado where the North Platte and the South Platte respectively originate. These two waterways converge midstate to form the Platte. Its movement is eastward as it carries water off the eastern slopes of the Continental Divide across the gently descending plains to the Missouri where the channel widens and the waters course southward to union with the Mississippi and the Gulf of Mexico. A corridor of human movement, the Platte River basin has been, especially in the last century, a carrier of persons westward. The Great Platte River Road was the major corridor of American expansion during the era of the pioneers. It was a wide, flat, dry expanse of land that provided, in mountain man James Clyman's 1824 estimation, "as firm a road as any in the Union or even in the world."[6] Platte, in fact, is French for "flat" and is the translation French explorers made of "Nebraska," the Oto Indian name for the shallow braided river that extends 1,000 miles in length and is bordered on both sides by wide, dry, passable tracks of land.

Along this naturally available westward route surged vast numbers of people. Some were traders, trappers, teamsters of Clyman's ilk. Others were stagecoach drivers, Pony Express riders, and station keepers. Still others were soldiers, occupants of the many military outposts that dotted the treeless expanse of the plains. Some were explorers like Lewis and

Clark, foreign observers like Englishman Richard Burton, or American writers such as Francis Parkman and Mark Twain. Most were emigrants, persons whose principal objective was to cross the continent in ox or horse drawn canvas covered wagons in search of a better life, whether it be in the form of the gold fields of California, the silver mines of Colorado, or the farms of Oregon. Some even came seeking salvation. Along the Platte corridor in 1848, the refugee church of Jesus Christ of the Latter Day Saints, under the charismatic leadership of Brigham Young, surged westward. They spent what Mormon sacred history calls "The Long Winter" encamped in what is now Omaha's northeast sector. Their martyrs, felled by the ferocity of the winter elements, lie buried now in the Mormon Cemetery. The remains of other martyrs litter the Platte River trail as well, both Native American and emigrant, casualties of the sorry clash of cultures out of which modern America was born.

Knowledge of the American westward movement with its mythic images of wagon trains and hardy pioneers was mine long before I ever set foot on Midwestern soil. It was part and parcel of an American education in my grade school era. If school Thanksgiving festivities were always recognizable by the paper Pilgrim hats and Indian headgear we constructed, so end-of-the-school-year pageants always featured the fourth-grade class dressing up pioneer fashion, girls in gingham dirndl skirts and pioneer bonnets, boys in overalls and plaid farm work shirts.

O don't you remember sweet Betsy from Pike?
Who crossed the tall mountains with her lover Ike.
With two yoke of oxen, a tall yeller dog,
A big Shanghai rooster and one spotted hog.
Singin' 'Goodbye Pike County, Goodbye for a while.'
We will come back and see you when we've panned out our pile.

Our singing gave voice to the nation's sense of Manifest Destiny. We patterned out the country's westward trekking to square dance rhythms. On our imaginations were etched images from Laura Ingalls Wilder's *Little House* series long before it was sentimentalized into a television program. Young Laura, sunbonnet dangling in unladylike fashion down her back, hair flung wild with the force of prairie wind; her family's frantic search for baby Carrie lost in the endless acres of impenetrable tallgrass; the grim, gaunt survival of the long, hard winter; the enticing torrents of Plum Creek that seduced and nearly carried Laura away.

For all the nationalistic romance of my youthful sense of this middle prairie region of the continent, for all the fanfare which made the westward movement a part of an American civil religion, there was always an undercurrent of foreboding, hardship, and danger that surrounded the prairie myth. I will never forget the starkness of Ole Rölvaag's novel, *Giants in the Earth*, was part of my high school English curriculum. There was not only the hardy, peripatetic traveler who passed through the prairie, there were also the ones who settled to farm the land. Some, like the Ingalls, came claiming American identity. Others were immigrants. Forever etched on my spirit is the haggard figure of Rölvaag's pioneer widow poised at the doorway of her sod house as her sanity gradually leeched out into the bleak prairie spread before her.

This sense of the thinly veiled cruelty of this land was enforced by my choice of reading material upon arriving in Omaha in 1987. Willa Cather, claimed by Nebraska as one of its own authors, wove unforgettable word-tapestries of the immigrant prairie pioneers: Alexandra, the Bohemian mistress of the wild and often unyielding land, the bullet-riddled bodies of the ill-fated lovers Marie and Emil clasped in a last embrace, their inchoate yet expansive flight into what-might-be clipped by the narrowness of a provincial culture.

All these presences inhabit this place, their cultural memory made new through literature, oral tales, and museum displays. They are linked to me through our shared experience of this land. Although now it is altered by modern construction, this land still maintains its inexorable hold on its human inhabitants. The horizon-to-horizon expanse of the cloudless, eggshell blue sky; "Nebraska blue," I call it. The fierce, icy grip of winter winds coursing from the northwest across the plains. The constant, subtle shifting of the Platte River from one season to the next, its slow, undramatic meander setting the pace for a Midwest culture as austere beneath as it is congenial on the surface.

Despite the fact that for most Americans, swathed as we are in the illusory veil of technological mastery of our environments, the natural landscape is perceived as mere backdrop or scenery to the air conditioned, steel-girdered, jet-propelled enclosures that are our lives, the fact remains that environment shapes our subjectivity.[7] Contemporary theologians have explored this process, noting the way in which the natural world-habitat and the cultural milieu-habitude, play a central role in shaping our perception of the holy.[8]

Environments are not interchangeable and our sense of that which perdures, sustains, and animates created life, especially our immanent sensibility of that sustenance, is shaped by the terrain we inhabit. Perhaps it is a truism to say that religious intuitions and our varied senses of the manifest form of sacred appearance correspond to landscape. Yet how could the vast, silent stretches of the Arabian deserts give rise to anything but Islam, that iconoclastic celebration of the vast grandeur of the unknowable God? Why else was it that psycho-historical biographer Eric Erickson confessed that his great work on Mahatma Gandhi was, in fact, a transposed exploration of the spirit of Francis of Assisi because he had written it when on sabbatical in the Umbrian countryside? And why else, after many years of careful study of the life and writing of St. Francis de Sales in California, when I received a grant to actually visit his Alpine homeland of Savoy, did I truly grasp his spiritual vision?

What might be the aspects of divine presence communicated through the typography of the plains? Perhaps phrases such as these hint at an answer: spaciousness, vastness, breadth, width, austerity, semi-aridity, harshness, emptiness. "Epiphany," a contemporary poem by Pem Kremer captures this sense of the relation between the shape of the land and the shape of God.

Lynn Schmidt says
  she saw you once as prairie grass,
  Nebraska prairie grass;
  She climbed out of her car on a hot highway,
  leans her butt on the nose of her car,
  looked out over one great flowing field,
  stretching beyond her sight until the horizon came:
  vastness, she says,
  responsive to the *slightest shift of wind*,
  full of infinite change,
  all One.
  She says when she can't pray
  She calls up prairie grass.[9]

One lives surrounded by a sense of a fierce and lonesome beauty here on the plains. One lives as well with a sense of the unpredictability of the climate. Always there is the wind, welcome in the wilting humidity of a summer's afternoon, fearsome in the icy grip of a winter storm. Yet beneath the fickle weather is the solidity and constancy of the earth itself, the material embodiment of what Thomas Merton termed "the hidden ground of love."[10]

Nebraska is not the place I originally called home, nor has it been easy to feel that I am genuinely at home here. It was only after a decade of actually being in residence that any interior sense of deep homecoming accompanied my returnings, that I could look out of an airplane window and sense that unmistakable faint release of tension in the region around my heart that signaled arrival at a place of origins. Since then, the complex, layered quality of experiencing a place to which one is not native as home, has fascinated and perplexed me. It has occurred partly on the level of natural habitat, partly on the level of cultural environment, partly on the level of personal and familial life. The stage of life at which I find myself has something to do with it as well as my sense of religious identity.

Southern California is the place where I was born. The metropolitan sprawl of central Los Angeles, in the districts between Hollywood and downtown, including Silver Lake, Griffith Park, and Echo Park, were home for twenty-six years. But the specific memories of those years do not radiate for me with a numinous sense of home, although they were good years and, especially in terms of my family of origin, fond ones. That numinous radiance emanates from a town further north on the California coast, Santa Barbara, where some of my most pivotal life-commitments were made. I dwelt in the city hovered over by the mythic presence of Saint Barbara for ten years during my graduate school training. A conversion to the Roman Catholic church, meeting and marriage to the man who was to be my life partner, the initiation of deep friendships with academic and spiritual mentors, the life-changing experience of first becoming a mother, these and other memories mark Santa Barbara as the place I most easily call home.

When I moved from there, freely and with a sense of those commitments calling me to a new place, it was not those specific personal memories that provoked a sense of grief. It was the loss of the landscape itself. And that landscape included not merely the specific geographical features of Santa Barbara but those of the entire Southern California region. My mother used to call it "the Mediterranean climate." I feel it viscerally in the form of color, air, light, and topography. Nowhere else were those elusive olives and burnt sierra hillsides, that dusky, adobe soil, the infinitely rich palette of somber grey-greens dotted with magenta bougainvillea blossoms.

Nowhere else was there the electric orange burst of poppies on a chalk grey field of dusty miller. Nowhere else that unmistakable sense of being cradled between the coarse, tar-flecked sands of the Pacific shore and that arid, low-shrubbed range of hills. Nowhere else smelled of salt-sea air wafted in over groves of pungent eucalyptus.

For a few years after I left Southern California, I missed friends and family. For a bit longer, I pined for the informal, leisurely lifestyle that the climate affords. A dozen years later, I still find myself startled into tears at an unexpected encounter with a jacaranda tree, an oak-lined walkway, a cut hydrangea blossom on display. To be on Southern California soil is to elicit a flood of personal memories but, even more inarticulately, it is to stand once again on the land from which I come. It is to stand on holy ground.

To possess a spiritual sense of place is, in part, to be sensitized to its deep history. A place may throb with sacred presence because something holy happened there, because it is the location of a sighting, or the unfolding of a prophetic life. But places may also be sensed as sacred simply because they exist. As we bring to them a contemplative attitude, they may become numinous. By contemplation I do not mean here a technically defined state of advanced prayer as was described in the writings of a Teresa of Avila or a John of the Cross. Rather I am using the term in the older, looser way it was used by many of the church fathers. Contemplation was for them a simplified, whole seeing. Contemplation in this sense tends towards wordlessness and the simplification and unification of thought, feeling, and desire. A contemplative attitude is an attitude of deep receptivity, of allowing oneself to be entered, reformed, and remade. One approaches reality, both the external and internal facts of existence, not as a problem to be solved but as a mystery into which to live fully.

To possess a contemplative ear is to cultivate a listening awareness that allows one to hear what is beyond one's current range. To possess a contemplative eye is to see what is by running the heart's tentative fingers over the terrain of the real. To see and hear in a contemplative mode is to see and hear in that wonderful way that refuses to yield to categorization or reductionistic analysis. Where wind is wind, the beating of a heart is the beating of a heart, but where wind and heartbeat have never genuinely been heard and seen before. To possess a spiritual sense of place is to be alive to "the isness of things."[11]

It has taken the better part of the dozen years I have resided in Nebraska to begin to feel anything akin to a sense of home and, as with my sense of Southern California, it is the powerful lure of the natural landscape that convinces me that I am indeed at home here. The stretch of the Platte southwest of Omaha provided my first, and still primary, sense of the distinct bioregion in which I now dwell.

My favored points of entry into the long meander of the Platte are two short stretches of riverbank located a mile apart near Venice, Nebraska. Just beyond and before "The Merchant of Venice," a half-century-old wood farmhouse that now serves as a roadside stop for antique-hunters, there are country roads leading to the left and right. The first of these guides you through the ranger station that marks the entry of Two Rivers State Park. After purchasing a day pass, you drive through the curlicue of gravel paths that loop around a small fishing lake, several groves set aside for picnickers, a cluster of retired Union Pacific cabooses converted into summer cabins, and recreational vehicle hook-up sites, until you find yourself at a dirt clearing which provides parking space for visitors wishing to spend a summer's day by the river. Wide sheltering torsos of cottonwoods dwarf the few bathers who loll on the scrubby grass veneered with a thin layer of cotton wisps.

Before you is the Platte, perhaps a quarter mile wide here, shallow as rivers go. Depending on the season, it is reached by finding a temporary foothold along the muddy, ever-shifting sand that will not tangle you in an underwater trap of accumulating driftwood, jutting rocks, and sink holes. If you find a foothold where the shifting riverbed sets high, you can wade out to the river's middle where the bed rises up above the water level, forming sandbars of varying lengths and shapes. In fact, when the water volume is low, usually in mid- to late-summer, from the shore the river appears to be more sand than water, a crazy quilt of streamlets stretched over a blanket of grey silted earth.

The second point of entry to the river is entered by taking the right-hand country road, a brief quarter mile around the bend to the retreat center operated by the Sisters of Mercy. Once on the property, you pass behind the pale green wooden one-story structure that contains a half-dozen rooms for retreatants, venture out through the "St. Francis Peace Forest," an incipient grove of variegated trees trying to establish a foothold in the sandy soil, pass down a winding path cut through the low underbrush to another part of the river bank, where the current might be slow and the water shallow enough to wade in. Here is found the great felled carcass of a cottonwood which provides a rough barked pier onto which the intrepid, crouched explorer can climb, hands clutching the remains of limbs, to arrive at a seated lookout from which the full expanse of the Platte's meander is visible.

I am not a stranger to bodies of water. Growing up in Southern California, the Pacific was a constant presence and more recent family hiking ventures have allowed familiarity with Rocky Mountain streams. But the Platte is utterly other as water goes. For one thing, its faces are legion. Only in summertime does it smile and beckon so graciously. Autumn's dipping temperatures make viewing the subtle fall color changes delightful from the bank, but the water by that time is dark and chill. Winter brings deathly cold. Chunks of ice float downstream in masses of pale gray slush. Its January palette ranges from drab whites through ash and stone grays to steely blue. Spring returns a pastel blush to the water's surface, but runoff from distant mountains often cause the Platte to swell and rise, creating fast moving currents that can carry an unsuspecting swimmer to a swift death.

Mid-summer provides the window in time through which you can enter to become an intimate participant in the Platte's mysterious life. Then you can wade in the water. This is like no other experience I know. From the footholds on the bank you step into the deeper channels cut by the water's momentum along the edges of the channel. The sand beneath your feet is dense, shifting, and forms a treacherous underwater terrain pockmarked with invisible rises and depressions, making each step toward the river's center a fearsome adventure. It is easy to lose your balance and suddenly find yourself collapsed into an underground sinkhole or pulled every which way by small swiftly forming whirlpools. But once you have eased away from the riverbank, calmer water at the river's central course allows you a rare experience. Summer days in Nebraska are muggy and hot and the Platte's flowing waters are cool. Sandbars jut up steeply and you emerge quickly from a full body immersion onto a sand bar where water is lapping only around ankles and feet. As you walk, the immersion lessens and deepens, making you keenly aware of the moving lapping line on calf, thigh, wrist, and shoulder blade, the changing threshold where moisture gives way to the tender brushes of warmed air.

A few hardcore sunbathers generally brave the entry ritual with lawn chairs hoisted safari style on their heads then lay themselves out on a convenient sandbar to toast under the low lying sun. You can theoretically travel down the Platte on foot for miles, swimming lazily between the maze of sandbar islands that undulate up and down upon the surface, trekking over stretches of damped down, foam flecked sand. Except for the occasional intrusion of a motorized pontoon boat, human sounds are absorbed by the musical slip-slapping at her shores and the dense, almost desert silence of a sultry sun-drenched atmosphere hovers above the ribbon that is the river.

The late poet Denise Levertov has observed that in the past few decades, especially in America, there is an increasing affinity between the way we experience and speak about nature and the way we experience and speak about the sacred. As this affinity grows, she says, the affinity between poetic and religious discourse deepens.[12] This, I think, is a true observation. We are increasingly sensitive to the sacrality of the earth, growingly aware in our sciences of the mysterious and miraculous biosystem and cosmic reality of which we are a part. As a contemporary culture we are edging more and more toward a perception of the divine as primarily immanent. More and more we are inclined to reverence the natural world. We take off our shoes and declare the place on which we stand "holy," not because the fiery apparition of a distant deity has singed and left this place smoldering but because we are awakening to an unacknowledged shared grief at the possible destruction of the intricate complex and fragile environment in which we dwell. A recent publication, filled with the exquisite poetry and prose of modern American writers, is an example of this phenomenon. Its title, *The Sacred Place: Witnessing the Holy in the Physical World*, sums this truth up well.[13]

Perhaps such a poetic apprehension of place might be thought to take one well beyond traditional Christian theological concepts of the relation between God and world, creator and creation, eternity and time. Certainly, a generation ago the genre of nature writing, which like landscape painting has long been a feature of the American aesthetic imagination, was a literary enterprise distinct from theological or devotional literature. If the created order was featured in such writing it was generally as a reminder, allegory, or metaphor of a higher, more spiritual order of reality. However, some contemporary theology has bridged the ancient dualism between the natural and supernatural that has characterized Christian thinking over the centuries. Witness Sallie McFague's *Body Of God*, Rosemary Radford Ruether's *Gaia and God* or Denis Edward's *Jesus The Wisdom of God*.[14] Further, much present-day literature that falls under the rubric spirituality, while it is sometimes informed by or derived from historic religious traditions, including Christianity, often moves beyond traditional theological concerns to probe the planet for a sense of luminous presence.[15]

A poetics of place has not been entirely absent from the Christian heritage, however. Perhaps this tradition is best exemplified by nineteenth-century Jesuit poet Gerard Manley Hopkins. Hopkins may have been a genius unacknowledged among his contemporaries but his fundamental theological vision, which sadly he tended to repudiate late in his life under the influence of a spiritual asceticism that deemed his contemplation of nature as antithetical to the claims of the spirit, was not idiosyncratic but very much in keeping with the Christian humanism of his Jesuit roots.

A fundamental axiom of the Christian humanism that was the sixteenth-century seedbed of the Society of Jesus, is that one gains access to the divine precisely through the created order. In other words, the world, especially the human person, is fashioned in the divine image and likeness. While original sin is acknowledged as marring that image, humans are nonetheless perceived as capable of growing toward the fullness of their original nature. Thus all that is most human, reason, will, imagination, as well as the arts, literature, and philosophy we fashion, can be trusted, when rightly exercised, to give us true glimpses of God. Similarly, the natural world itself is seen as a window, translucent to the eye focused by prayer and discipline, through which the numinosity of divine life might be viewed. The finite in all its forms is thus our gateway to infinity, gateway without which we could never perceive divine life. Finitude and infinity are seen to be so intimately linked that they are essentially inseparable. Thus each particular instance of the created order, each person, place, leaf and rill is luminous in its own unrepeatable beauty. Each has what Hopkins called a distinctive "inscape."

> The world is charged with the grandeur of God.
> It will flame out, like shining from shook foil;
> It gathers to a greatness, like the ooze of oil
> Crushed....
> There lives the dearest freshness deep down things;
> And though the last lights off the black West went
> Oh, morning, at the brown brink eastward springs—
> Because the Holy Ghost over the bent
> World broods with warm breast and with ah! bright wings.[16]

I have come once again to that small retreat house on the banks of the Platte just north of Highway 92. It is late August and I realize, of the many times I have visited this place, that I have never managed to be here so late in the summer season for the roadsides are festooned with black-eyed yellow sunflowers, flora I do not associate with the place. It is a quiet day, a break in scheduled programming that makes operation of the center possible, when closet solitaries like myself can come, wander, pray, sleep, and be bothered by no one. I rise early and venture out onto the property that borders the river. The place is littered with memories of the last decade. As I walk across the grassy field on my way to the riverward path, I pass a wooden placard that bears the names of donors instrumental in creating the Peace Forest, a project of my husband's while he was director of a small local non-profit justice and peace organization. A tinge of sorrow reminds me of his later ill-fated history with that organization. A perusal of the donor list brings to mind the deep history of peacemaker in this place. I conjure up the visage of Fr. Markoe, a Jesuit priest who, in the 1940s well before the civil rights movement had gained momentum, founded the Omaha student DePorres Club whose aim was the promotion of racial justice.[17] A sideways glance at one of the planted trees that have survived brings to mind my elderly father, now five years gone, in the presence of his grandchildren, his hat shielding him from the stifling heat and ferocious prairie wind, his foot bearing down on the lip of a shovel. He, the WWII conscientious objector, the life-long peace activist, at the end of his life engaged in the never-ending generative performance of seeding the ground for new life, his sapling peace tree next to him cradled in the small arms of his pre-school aged granddaughter.

The narrow path cleared beneath the cottonwoods winds around a small pond. As I clear a familiar corner, I am startled by a new sight: the low-hung morning sunlight backlights a vast sea of gossamer-thin spider webs draped like party decorations about a wide field of tallgrass, each web's unrepeatable intricate pattern hung with thousands of tiny glistening lanterns, rain drops from a late nights' thunderstorm waiting to be vaporized by the greater coming light of the sun.

The cottonwoods are heavy with leaves whose greenness longs to give way to yellow and brown. The damp warming air is alive with sound: the fat, lush rustling of late summer leaves teased by the wind, a cacophonous symphony of insect sounds—how I wish I knew enough to distinguish the cicadas, crickets, the various species of frog! As I round the edge of the lake I recall a morning half a decade ago, when the fall of my foot was the only sound for miles, and the cottonwoods were bare, gray-black silhouettes arching in embrace over the bright icy glare of the path made pillowy by a three-foot snow fall. My footprints, calf-deep, piercing deep hollows into the virgin snow. Grateful to be alive on this still solitary walk, I gingerly fingered the fresh surgical wound pierced beneath the bandage wrapped around my throat.

At the next bend, I am reminded with a smile of an early spring morning, as a weary winter temporarily retreated and the sweet poignant wafts of new grass arose, when in a wild soul-weary impulse of desire for renewal, discovering a sun-flooded clearing shielded behind the brush, I stripped down to the barest hint of clothing and stretched out on the earth, letting shafts of spring light and a flood of tears burn and wash away the sins and sorrows of the previous year.

This place on the Platte is the earthen vessel in which are carefully contained layer after layer of sacred sensing. It, with the river that borders it, the city east of it with its block-long neighborhood, has become the place I call home. A decade of my personal sacred story is encoded on this landscape. Each time I come here it is both the same and always new. Each time there is a surprise: brown woolly caterpillars inching their way across the asphalt on the country road, the late evening apparition of a lone heron wading lakeside, a playground of chatty squirrels scampering up and down the cottonwood trunks, cheeks stuffed with seeds and acorns for winter storage. Each time I come a new layer of knowing, a new piece of the unfolding story of life is celebrated and prayed, stored for a time when remembering will be all there is. When the finite will render itself so transparent, infinity alone will remain.

NOTES

1. "This Place" from "Eden's Promise: A Song Cycle," text by Wendy M. Wright, music by Martin Willet, copyright 1995, HarvestSong Music, Omaha, NE.

2. Gaston Bachelard, *The Poetics of Space* (Boston: Beacon Press, 1959), 4-5, 91.

3. Katherine Platt, "Places of Experience and the Experience of Place' in *Longing For Home*, ed. Leroy S. Rouner (University of Notre Dame Press, 1996), 112-27.

4. John B. Jackson, *Discovering the Vernacular Landscape* (New Haven: Yale University Press), 91.

5. A five minute drive east takes one to the Missouri River and the Iowa border.

6. Quoted in Merrill J. Mattes, *The Great Platte River Road: The Covered Wagon Mainline Via Fort Kearny to Fort Laramie* (Nebraska State Historical Society, 1969), 10.

7. Belden Lane, *The Solace of Fierce Landscapes: Exploring Desert and Mountain Spirituality* (New York: Oxford University Press, 1998), 9.

8. Ibid., 10.

9. In *Cries of the Spirit: A Celebration of Women's Spirituality*, ed. Marilyn Sewell (Boston: Beacon Press, 1991), 255.

10. Merton used this term first in 1967 in an address at Smith College in Massachusetts. It appears later throughout his letters. Cf. the collection edited by William H. Shannon, *The Hidden Ground of Love: The Letters of Thomas Merton on Religious Experience and Social Concern* (New York: Farrar, Straus & Giroux, 1985).

11. I have used this term in my *Sacred Dwelling: A Spirituality of Family Life* (Leavenworth, KS: Forest of Peace Books, 1994), 181ff. For a further exploration of this contemplative attitude as experienced in everyday life, see my article, "Living Contemplatively" in *The Merton Annual*, 10 (1997), 59-76.

12. Denise Levertov, *New and Selected Essays* (New York: New Directions, 1992), 4-6.

13. W. Scott Olsen and Scott Cairns, editors, *The Sacred Place: Witnessing the Holy in the Contemporary World* (Salt Lake City: University of Utah Press, 1996).

14. Sallie McFague, *The Body of God: An Ecological Theology* (Minneapolis: Fortress Press, 1993); Rosemary Radford Ruether, *Gaia and God: An Ecofeminist Theology of Earth Healing* (San Francisco: Harper and Row, 1992); Denis Edwards, *Jesus The Wisdom of God: An Ecological Theology* (Maryknoll, NY: Orbis Books, 1995).

15. Perhaps the most able chronicler of this poetics of sacred place is Douglas Burton Christie. See his article "The Literature of Nature and the Quest for the Sacred" in Olsen and Cairns, 65-177; "Nature, Spirit and Imagination in the Poetry of Mary Oliver" in *Cross Currents* (Spring 1996), 77-87; "Mapping the Sacred Landscape: Spirituality and the Contemporary Literature of Nature," *Horizons* 21 (1994), 22-47; "Living Between Two Worlds: Home, Journey and the Quest for Sacred Place," in *Anglican Theological Review*, LXXIX: 3 (Summer 1997), 413-32.

16. "God's Grandeur," in *Poems of Gerard Manley Hopkins*, ed. W. H. Gardner and N. H. MacKenzie (Oxford: Oxford University Press, 1970), 66.

17. The club was named for Martin de Porres, the mulatto saint from Peru who had a special sensitivity to the poor and marginalized.

Three Theses for a More Adequate Reading of the New Testament

Bruce J. Malina

While the majority of Americans resident in the eastern third of the country still share a pre-Lewis and Clark mentality, calling Indiana and Ohio the "Midwest," those who live in the "breadbasket" know that the center of the country is to be found in the Great Plains region. Of the "nine nations of North America" (Garreau 1981), the central region of the United States is distinctively characterized by wide open expanses, extraordinary agricultural fertility, exceptionally low population density, and wide temperature extremes, all of which affect the way people live and think about their geographical location in the country and their social location in the nation and cosmos. The region is a culture area, with a distinctive cultural geography (see Duncan and Ley 1993). Scholarship produced here can quickly shed the blinkers forced upon the selective inattentiveness of researchers in other parts of the country. I would hope that the following essay is a case in point.

This essay is about the meanings attributed to the modern English words "Jew," "Christian," and "Gentile" as equivalents to the meanings of the first-century A.D. Mediterranean words that they translate in historical study. I begin by specifying two presuppositions: the first about how language works; the second about Mediterranean social institutions in antiquity.

One of the significant principles of contemporary biblical interpretation informed by the social sciences is that words derive their meanings from the social systems in which they are used. For sociolinguists, language is considered a three-tiered affair (see Halliday 1978). Concretely, language consists of squiggles and sounds. At a slightly higher level of abstraction, these squiggles and sounds are learned to be patterned or sequenced squiggles and sounds. Socially shared patterns of markings and soundings constitute the wording level of language: words, sentences, paragraphs, and the like. Finally, the wordings in their concrete form of squiggles and sounds mediate meanings. What is the source or origin of the meanings? Since they make sense to other human beings, the meanings mediated through wordings and concretely realized in squiggles and soundings come from the social system of the speaker or hearer, writer or reader. For example, the wording pattern concretely realized in the markings "Round Steak" derives its meaning from the slaughterhouses, butcher shops, market meat sections, and cooking habits of our everyday U.S. world. A sign stating "Round Steak only $1.99 per pound" would not be mistaken for the name of a movie or the cost of entry to the theater. Nor would it be mistaken as an ad for lumber, cement, crayons, or an airline ticket. Without our habits of butchering and beef preparation, along with our monetary system and weights and measures, the sign would be confusing at best, meaningless at most.

The point is that words, including "Round Steak," have their meaning from a social system. When speaker and hearer or writer and reader share the same social system, understanding is highly likely. However, when speaker and hearer or writer and reader come from different social systems, past or present, misunderstanding or non-understanding is the rule. Humans demonstrate a propensity to perceive the patterns they are used to even where there are none (see Johnson 1978: 3-7). To deal with the "blur" that happens in situations of misunderstanding or non-understanding, hearers and readers most often supply information from their own social systems to make up for what they are missing in the communicative interaction. While this procedure makes alien hearers or readers inconsiderate, such persons are often unaware of the cultural or temporal distance separating them from the speaker or writer.

This, of course, is especially true of readers of ancient documents like those in the Bible. Without adequate exposure to the social system of the alien authors of those books, one can only interpret in terms of one's own socialization. Consider the situation of a large numbers of U.S. students who study French or German or Japanese wordings and believe they are learning French or German or Japanese meanings. The same is true of professional and non-professional biblical interpreters who study Hebrew, Aramaic, and Greek wording, without giving a thought to the social systems of the past that endowed these wordings with meanings. The situation is aggravated by biblical translations allowing "Do-It-Yourself" readers to assume they can understand what they are reading since it is in

English. English wordings realizing U.S. meanings now have a biblical stamp of approval. In sum, if meaning in language derives from social systems, to understand documents from the past in an accurate and considerate way, one must know the social system in which those documents were produced. Otherwise misunderstanding or non-understanding is inevitable (see Malina 1991).

A second presupposition behind the considerations that follow is that in antiquity there was no free-standing religion or economics as we experience them today. In antiquity, both religion and economics were embedded in the two focal and explicit social institutions of the pre-eighteenth-century world, kinship and politics. There was domestic religion and political religion, just as there was domestic economy and political economy. To think of ancient religion and economics apart from their domestic and political matrices is inaccurate and inconsiderate (see Malina 1986; 1994; Hanson and Oakman 1998).

Kinship is about "naturing" and nurturing human beings.[1] When economics and religion are embedded in kinship, the value objects involved with provisioning the group as well as the group's relation to the general order of existence will be formulated in kinship symbols and kinship terminology. These value objects are self, others, nature, time, space, and the deity(ies). In domestic religion, religion will be "kinified." Kinship roles, obligations, and expectations express prevailing religious roles, obligations, and expectations. Kinship roles such as father, mother, children, brother, sister, slave, ancestor, patron, or client; obligations such as honor and obedience, respect and remembrance; and expectations such as debts of obligation (loving kindness), mercy, group attachment (love) are some of the terminology of religion. In the domain of domestic religion, we read of the God or gods of the ancestors, the God of Abraham, Isaac, and Jacob, or ancestral places of worship and pilgrimage, of household altars and household sacrifices such as the Passover, and the like. The hearth in the whole Mediterranean culture area was a symbol of family life, since light like life could not be created but only handed on from some sacred source. Hearth and table behavior, therefore, were always religious. Kinship groups included the local family and the extended family or clan, *beth ab* and *mishpaha*, *oikos* and *familia*, *domus* and *gens*. In advanced agricultural societies, we find fictive kin groups in the form of a range of associations, generally marked by the central kinship activity of eating a common meal.

Politics is about effective collective action.[2] When a social group gives evidence of a political institution, such as a monarchy or a *polis* (Hellenistic city; see Rohrbaugh 1991), then economics and religion will be likewise "politified." Political roles, obligations, and expectations give form to religious roles, obligations, and expectations. Political roles such as chief, king, lord, subject, warrior, citizen; obligations such as civic duties, taxes, tithes, military service or corvee; and expectations such as covenant obligations, obedience, and compliance are part of the terminology of religion. In the realm of political religion, we read of God or gods as warrior, of a heavenly city, of a god of heavenly armies, of various civic virtues deified, of temples and altars for political sacrifice, and of such feasts as Sukkoth and New Year marking the fortunes of the body politic. The *polis* or monarchic central place had a perpetual light, Hestia, Vestal Temple, perpetual Temple lamp, marking the life of the political religious body. Hence central temple(s) and political life were always religious. Just as the sight of individual animate beings indicated its inner light, pointing to its life, so too the household light and the temple light symbolized the life of the respective entities. Death pushed out life, as darkness pushed out light. To affirm life and to restore life in face of death was the scope of that ritual behavior called sacrifice (see Malina 1996). Since life was believed to derive from the deity in antiquity, behavior relative to life was always religious. Since religion was embedded in kinship or politics, sacrifice likewise will be kinship or political in some form or other.[3]

In sum, the meanings of biblical terms derive from the social systems at the time the biblical documents were written. In those social systems, religion was embedded in kinship and/or politics. In such a situation, unless economic or religious benefits could be converted into kinship or political advantage, such benefits would be socially meaningless and unnoticed. Thus in antiquity, "religious" conversion of any sort had to yield kinship or political advantage.

THESIS ONE: THERE WERE NO JEWS
OR CHRISTIANS IN THE NEW TESTAMENT PERIOD

An initial, but fundamental, problem underlying inquiry into Jewish and Christian relations in antiquity is terminology. Almost invariably, the words "Jew" and "Christian" are made to bear the freight of contemporary conceptions, themselves weighted down with a millennial array of redefinitions. To speak of Jews and Christians in antiquity requires, first of all, a description of these words to allow for temporal and cultural distance from modern usage. This is acutely necessary since, as previously noted, the meanings realized in language derive from the social systems of speakers and hearers or writers and readers. To be a considerate reader of the documents of antiquity, the modern reader will have to enter the alien social system of the ancient writers.

It might appear a bit unsettling, but the fact is there were no Jews or Christians in antiquity in any modern sense of these words. Persons designated by these labels today have little in common with the ancient Mediterraneans called *Christianoi* or *Ioudaioi*. The reason for this is that all forms of modern Christianity are rooted in Christendom, the political religion of the Roman Empire, initiated by Constantine and his Council of Nicea (325 A.D.) and legalized by Theodosius in 381 A.D. The many forms of the Jesus movement that led up to Christendom were Israelite fictive kinship groups with a fictive kinship or domestic religion.

The same is true of all forms of contemporary Jewish religion. All modern Jews and their Jewishness are rooted in the scribal Pharisaic or ben Zakkaiist invention of the Israelite kinship-religion articulated in the Babylonian Talmud and related writings. It was only with the ben Zakkaiist emphasis on the *Mishnah* or Second Torah, the formation of a rabbinic order, and the composition of the Talmud as focus of norms that a formal break between Pharisaic Judeans and other forms of Judaism, including Jesus groups, was distinctly perceptible (5th cent. A.D.). When one strand of Jesus-group ideology was transformed into official political religion by Theodosius, heretical groups were no longer heretical, the viewpoint of fictive kinship religion, but traitor groups, the viewpoint of political religion. Just as there were no Christians before the fourth century A.D., so there were no Jews in any readily recognizable modern sense before the fifth century A.D. The Jews of the Talmud, like the Jews of today, refer in fact to those whose kinship-embedded religion is that of the ben Zakkaiist, rabbinic, scribal Pharisaism of the Double Torah, written and oral.

While there are a number of reports of Judeans in conflict with Jesus-group members (Eusebius, *Historia Ecclesiastica*), so long as various Jesus-group authors considered Judeans to be heretics, there really was no parting of the ways between Jesus groups and Israelite groups before Constantine. Neusner was quite right in denying any early parting of the ways between so-called Judaism and Christianity before the fifth century

A.D., since it was only then that Christian and Jewish ideologies emerged in rather different institutional configurations. "The characteristic and definitive traits of the Judaism we call 'rabbinic' only came to the surface in the fifth-century documents produced in the aftermath of the cataclysm of the fourth century" (1995: 282).

The Greek term *Christianoi* means "Messianist" and is found initially in the New Testament documents as a denigrating designation by Antiochean outsiders (Acts 11:26; see 26:28). When it occurs in 1 Peter 4:16 ("to suffer as a Christian") the term serves to label Jesus adherents as members of a political religious association, like the other Judaisms of the period (see Elliott forthcoming, *ad versum*). Yet, with the destruction of the Jerusalem Temple in 70 A.D., all Jesus groups transformed into fictive kinship associations, even if outsiders considered them political dissidents. In conceptualizing the qualities and ideologies of the groups that follow the experience of Jesus of Nazareth, therefore, it is best not to designate them "Christian" groups. They were more properly Jesus groups of various kinds. During Jesus' own activity in Galilee and Judea, he recruited a political religious faction to proclaim theocracy in Israel; he announced "the Kingdom of Heaven." After Jesus' crucifixion and his being raised by God, his former faction emerged as a reconstituted political religious group, looking forward to his coming as Messiah with power. Yet early on, this political religious group splintered into a number of fictive kinship-religious groups. The original reconstituted political religious Jesus group gave up its political aspirations, it seems, with the final expulsion of all Judeans from Jerusalem in 135 A.D.

Given the nature of the story told in the New Testament documents, the term *Ioudaios* occurs rather frequently. In those documents, it seems this word is best translated *Judean*, that is, of or pertaining to the people living in the region called Judea. The term had an ingroup and outgroup sense. For the ingroup, members of the house of Israel, Judean was opposed to Galilean and Perean. The regions of Judea, Galilee, and Perea designated where members of the house of Israel were located in the Roman province of Syro-Palestine. For the outgroup, however, Judean meant any member of the house of Israel, since Israel's central place was Jerusalem in Judea. Hence outside Palestine, a Judean was a member of the house of Israel; in Palestine a Judean was a person from Judea.[4]

Nearly all Bible translations use the English word *Jew*. This latter translation is misleading, to say the least, since it would have readers apply meanings from today's social systems, and lead them to think that Jews of today are identical to or related with Jesus' contemporaries. This is historically inaccurate. In antiquity *Ioudaios* meant "of or pertaining to persons whose origin traces to Judea," hence Judean. The map of the Mediterranean in antiquity was nothing like today's map. There was no Turkey or Greece or Israel or Italy or any other nation state. There was only the central city of Rome that exerted political hegemony over the cities, towns, and villages of the Mediterranean. This was called the Roman Empire. The Empire absorbed all sorts of peoples known by geographic origin. As with animals, first-century Mediterraneans categorized persons in terms of their place of origin.

To see the difference translation can make, consider Matthew's gospel for example. It is quite apparent that in Matthew, the word *Ioudaios* means only *Judean*. It designates a member of a segment of a people, called "Israel" in Matthew, deriving from a certain place after which that group is named, *Ioudaia*. The opposite of *Judean* in Matthew is *Galilean*, while both together, including "Judea beyond the Jordan" (19:1; also 3:5; 4:25), make up *Israel*. The opposite of Israel is non-Israel, the peoples other than Israel, the rest of the peoples of the world, "Gentiles."

To read the document called Matthew with historical accuracy and fairness, the author's social niceties have to be respected. Thus, since Jesus is born in Bethlehem of Judea (2:1. 5) he is sought after as king of the Judeans (2:2). From the outset, Matthew contrasts Judea with Galilee (2:22). John appeared not in the Jewish desert but in the Judean desert, the desert located in Judea (3:1); Jerusalem and all of Judea, not all the inhabitants of Jewishland, came out to him (3:5). Jesus is clearly not from Judea but from Galilee (3:13; 21:11) by whose sea (4:18; 15:29) significant events took place. Similarly a large crowd from Jerusalem and Judea came out to Jesus (4:25). Again, we are told Jesus went to the hill country of Judea, not of Jewishland, beyond the Jordan. He warns that those in Judea, presumably Judeans, will have to run to the hills when their central city will be attacked (19:1). In the passion account, we find out that non-elites knew Jesus as "Jesus the Galilean" (26:69), something unknown to the Romans who label him, despite protest, as king of the Judeans (27:11. 29. 37), clearly a wrong designation, even if ironic. Eventually the authorities of Israel mockingly, yet correctly, call him "King of Israel" (27:42), the people to whom, as Matthew previously has told us, Jesus in fact was sent. Finally the locals, Judeans, tell the story of the tomb (28:15). On the other hand, for Jesus' execution, some who followed Jesus from Galilee found themselves in Judea (27:55); and it was in Galilee (28:7. 10. 16; see 26:32) that the final commissioning takes place.

The point is further underscored by Matthew in that Jesus' own people is called Israel (Matt 2:6) as in the commissioning of Matt 10:5b. Joseph is directed to go into the land of Israel, not Judea or of the Judeans, (2:20-21). Jesus' favorite name for his people in Matthew is Israel (8:10; 9:33; 10:6. 23; 15:24. 31; 19:28; 27:9).

In the story of Jesus, *Ioudaia* refers exclusively to the region called Judea and its population and locale. Further, for Matthew even the word "Christian" is an anachronism. Thus contrasts such as Jew and Christian, Christian Jewish, or Jewish Christian all befoul adequate and accurate interpretation of Matthew and the rest of the New Testament. The commission in Matt 10:5b is to Israel alone, "the lost sheep of the house of Israel." A question worthy of Matthew, and of John, is that of the relation of Judeans to Israel (see Malina and Rohrbaugh 1998). It is not unlike that of the relation of Israel to non-Israelites. As later noted, there is no reason to believe the final edict in Matthew, to make disciples of all nations (Matt 18:16), meant anything other than Israelites of all nations.

THESIS TWO: THERE WAS NO JESUS GROUP
MISSION TO THE GENTILES IN ANTIQUITY

Ethnos is the Greek word translated "Gentile" (from Latin: *gens*, a birth-related people) or "a people" and, quite anachronistically, "nation."[5] The Greek word was used to express a range of meanings. Liddell-Scott offer company, body of men, race, tribe, nation, people, caste. Moulton-Milligan give province (outgroup, outsiders of city), category (of people), class (of priests), association (of grave diggers), collegium. In ancient Israelite writings, "Gentile" (Heb. *goy*, Gk. *ethnikos*) was an Israelite ethnocentric and often ethnophobic[6] term for all other peoples of the world apart from Israel. It essentially meant "non-Israelite," and bore a range of emotional freight that only ingroup/outgroup oriented societies can muster for the outgroup. Thus the collocation "Judean and Gentile" referred to all human beings from the Israelite ethnocentric perspective. Romans used a similar phraseology when they spoke of "Romans and Barbarians." Barbarians meant uncivilized people, like Parthians or Scythians, Middle Eastern peoples who live between the two vast Empires of antiquity, Rome and China (see Morgues 1998).

Romans considered Israelites to be barbarian as well, a viewpoint that caused Philo of Alexandria to bristle (*Embassy to Gaius* 215; see Wallace and Williams 1998: 33-70). The normal opposite of Barbarian, though, was Greek, which meant civilized, speaking the common Greek language, knowing Greek civic institutions, embracing Greek values, schooled in Greek rhetoric and the Greek classics, and the like.[7] Paul's phrase "Judean and Greek" is probably best translated "Traditional Israelites and Civilized Israelites." After all, Paul's main audience was of Israelite origin with a sprinkling of non-Israelites. The phrase is not about ethnicity since there was no "Greece" at the time, and non-Israelite members of Jesus groups were "unnatural" personages (Rom 11:24 "grafted contrary to nature"). Rather, Paul's letter to the Romans shows that the church at Rome was predominantly Israelite in membership, a fact now adequately demonstrated by Mason (1990) and Nanos (1996). Their conclusion is further confirmed by the material evidence which points to early Jesus groups in Israelite quarters of Rome, namely, Trastevere and Via Appia near the Porta Capena.

Consequently, if "mission" means going to non-Israelites with a view to "converting" them to one's own form of Israelite religious ideology, there is no evidence from antiquity of a mission to the Gentiles, either on the part of the wide assortment of Israelite groups, whether Jesus groups or other Judean groups (contra Hahn 1965; Jeremias 1967; and many others since then). There is simply no proof that either Jesus or Jesus' early disciples had any intention of a mission to the Gentiles. Why should the God of Israel care about Gentiles? Israel's traditions did not suggest any options for a Gentile mission. In the whole New Testament discussion about going into non-Israelite regions of the Mediterranean, there never is any appeal to a statement by Jesus of an outreach to non-Israelites. It stands to reason that those discussing relations with non-Israelites who approached Jesus group members did not think Jesus offered them anything. Once God raised Jesus, however, and called some non-Israelites, some core group members of the reconstituted Jesus movement seem to have sought clarification for the event in Israel's scriptures. Sanders has collected a set of views about Gentiles available from these Scriptures:

There are at least six discernible, although often overlapping predictions about the Gentiles in the end-time within the biblical prophets, all of which are repeated somewhere or other in later Jewish literature. It is perhaps worth noting that four of these occur in Second Isaiah. The lists are not intended to be exhaustive:

> 1. The wealth of the Gentiles will flow into Jerusalem: Isa. 45.14; cf. Isa. 60.5-16; 61.6; Micah 4.13; Zeph. 2.9; Tobit 13.11; 1QM 12.13 f.
>
> 2. The kings of the Gentiles will bow down, and the Gentile nations will serve Israel: Isa. 49.23; cf. 45.14, 23; Micah 7.17 (lick the dust), 1En. 90.30; 1QM 12.13f. (quoting Isa. 49.23).
>
> 3. Israel will be a light to the nations; her salvation will go forth to the ends of the earth: Isa. 49.6; cf. Isa. 51.4; Isa. 2.2f.; Micah 4.1. It accords with this that the Gentiles may be added to Israel and thus be saved: Isa. 56.6-8; Zech. 2.11; 8.20-23; Isa. 45.22; Tobit 14.6f.; 1En. 90.30-33. Here we should include also the one passage which predicts a mission to the Gentiles, Isa. 66.19.
>
> 4. The Gentiles will be destroyed. Their cities will be desolate and will be occupied by Israel: Isa. 54.3; cf. Ben Sira 36.7, 9; 1En. 91.9; Baruch 4.25, 31, 35; 1QM 12.10.
>
> 5. As a supplement to the theme of destruction we may add predictions of vengeance and the defeat of the Gentiles: Micah 5.10-15; Zeph. 2.10f.; T. Mos. 10.7; Jub. 23.30; Ps. Sol. 17.25-27.
>
> 6. Foreigners will survive but will not dwell with Israel: Joel 3.17; Ps. Sol. 17.31. (Sanders 1985: 214).

Obviously Israel's sacred writings contained Micah 5 as well as Micah 4, and there are also harsh statements in Second Isaiah. Gentiles can be accepted provided they submit to Israel; thus many passages listed as indicating the salvation of the Gentiles in fact refer to their military defeat and subjugation.[8] Surely Jesus and his first followers had to know these biblical predictions of the sure destruction of Gentiles.

One of the surest proofs that Jesus' career is to be seen within the general context of Israelite prophetic revivalism is that the movement which he initiated spawned no Gentile mission during his lifetime. The same is true for the reconstituted Jesus faction after Jesus' resurrection; no non-Israelites were involved. Jesus proclaimed a new theocracy for Israel and saw his task as preparing the house of Israel for living in this theocracy. His "gospel" was the theocracy, nothing more, nothing less, and involved the ancestral God of Israel seeing to the social well-being of his chosen people. Like Israel's prophets of old, Jesus' focus was political religion, religion articulated in terms of the political institution and its structures, roles, and values. As political religion, the Jesus movement focused on God's power on behalf of God's people, and not all people.

Furthermore, it is only the political religious aspect of the Jesus movement that can account for some Jesus group members expecting Jesus to come with power, as Messiah for Israel. "Messiah" is a clearly Israelite specific, political religious role. From the viewpoint of the ideology that marked the Jesus movement group, Matthew's gospel, and John in its own way, are the best reflection of the political religious hopes that undoubtedly traced back to Jesus himself.

The impression of a mission to the Gentiles seems to derive from the way Gentile group members began to read the New Testament, notably after Constantine (see below). If we adopt a first-century Israelite perspective and read the New Testament, what we find is the following. For all Israel, the focal approach to the ancestral God of Israel was the political religion institutionalized in the Temple, its personnel and its prescribed behaviors, sacrifice, prayer, lights, and the like. Judeans spread around the Mediterranean kept contact with this political religion by means of their common ancestral story and customs, the Temple tax and infrequent pilgrimages. The political religion of the Temple was the defining *sine qua non* of Israel. After Jesus' death/resurrection, Jesus-group members reconstituted his political-religious faction and began to proclaim him as Israel's Messiah to come with power soon. This, of course, was something that those holding power in the political religious institution were not happy to hear. The reaction was the usual violence characteristic of political institutions. It was the good news of Jesus as Messiah soon to come that had to be spread among all Israelites. As Galatians indicates, Peter and colleagues took this news to regions of Judean ascendancy, largely in Syria, while Paul took the news to the synagogues that were to be found among largely non-

Israelite populations of the Eastern Mediterranean (apart from Egypt; Gal 2:7-8). The new focus on the forthcoming Messiah displaced concern for Temple worship and its personnel. Whatever else Paul's collection might mean, it meant that instead of collecting the Temple tax among emigre Judeans, it was more fitting to collect funds for the Jerusalemite Jesus groups (Rom 12:13; 15:25-26; 1 Cor 16:1; 2 Cor 9:1, 12).

Early on, however, a small number of non-Israelites asked to join Jesus groups. In Acts we read of an Ethiopian (8:26-40) and a Roman centurion (10:1-8) joining Jerusalem groups; Paul speaks of a few others. The coming of these non-Israelites and the reluctance on the part of Judeans both in Jerusalem and in non-Israelite cities triggered a reassessment of the meaning of Jesus' being raised by God. The outcome was a recasting of a political religion agenda in favor of a fictive kinship religion agenda. Jesus' resurrection was in fact a new revelation of God, with Jesus like the Mosaic Burning Bush. Jesus is no longer Israel's forthcoming Messiah, but rather cosmic Lord of all peoples. With the Roman destruction of Jerusalem in 70 A.D., this fictive kinship religion perspective gained the ascendancy. Jesus groups expanded by networking among Israelites, kept their ideology almost exclusively in an Israelite idiom, but were willing to abandon Judean customs considered barbaric by most peoples of the time, circumcision, food regulations, Sabbath observance, and avoidance of outsiders. By the time of the Council of Nicea in 325 A.D., there were some 880,000 members in main-line Jesus groups. Until that time, the vast majority of members had their origin in the house of Israel (similarly Stark 1996; Hopkins 1998).[9]

THESIS THREE: THERE IS NO
ANTI-SEMITISM IN THE NEW TESTAMENT

Social scientific approaches to the New Testament make it increasingly bewildering to find people arguing about "anti-Semitism" (sic) in the New Testament (e.g., Runes 1975; Sandmel 1978; Freudman 1994, and many others).[10] In point of historical and cultural fact, the New Testament writings are definitely ethnocentric, and the *ethnos* in question is Israel.[11] All Biblical documents are ethnocentric; they are all written from the perspective of Israelite authors writing for Israelite audiences. If the New Testament is anti-anything, it is anti-Gentile.

Americans were irate when the Ayatullah Ruhullah Khomeini dubbed the U.S. "the Great Satan." Yet these same Americans attend church services where they hear Matthew's gospel in which the greatest insult is to be called "Gentile " (cf. especially Matt 5:46-47; 6:7-8, 32; 18:15-17, see Sim 1995). This is what these Americans are. Selective inattentiveness to Israelite ethnocentrism in the New Testament seems to be due to total American or Gentile ethnocentrism, treating the Bible and the world as though it were for non-Israelites. Thus non-Israelite Bible readers read, for example, about "the meek inheriting the (holy) land" and refer it to the land distribution in general, or about the calamities striking the "land (of Israel)" in the scenario of Revelation 4-11 and take it to mean the whole earth. For a historically accurate and considerate reading of the New Testament, it is important to realize that all the documents of that collection and their protagonists were ethnocentric and anti-Gentile to a greater or lesser degree. They were little interested in the other peoples of the world apart from Israel.[12]

EITHER/OR PERCEPTION

Given the social perceptions of antiquity, this could not be otherwise. Until the middle of the seventeenth century A.D., perception was always in terms of *sic et non*, "yes or no," "for or against," "hot or cold," "either/or" (Lloyd 1966; Gigerenzer, et al. 1989). Indifference or neutrality were so much out of the question that those who were not against us may be presumed to be for us. "He that is not against us is for us" (Mark 9:40; Luke 11:23 and Matt 12:30). Furthermore, on the social level, to be indifferent or lukewarm was a real insult in the Mediterranean. It implied a denial of the status of the person to whom one is indifferent, a repudiation of another. "I know your works, that you are neither cold nor hot. Would that you were hot or cold. Thus because you are lukewarm and neither hot nor cold, I am going to vomit you out of my mouth" (Rev 3:15-16). Americans believe it is perfectly proper to be indifferent to somebody; indifference has no negative implications. Indifference is not neutral for a Mediterranean; it is an expression of arrogance and conceit, hence it is essentially hostile. Such behavior would be interpreted as a challenge to honor by an arrogant and hostile competitor (Triandis and Vassiliou 1972: 315-16). People were "rich or poor"; a "middle class" was out of the question.

These "either/or" constructs take on social reality in the perception of human beings as members of ingroups or outgroups. The ingroup/outgroup perception of social reality was characteristic of Europe at least until the seventeenth century, and is quite central to the Mediterranean even today. Its ramifications for Bible study have been immense.

Without a doubt, all of Israel's sacred writings, perhaps apart from Job, come from ingroup-oriented Israelite authors and/or groups. All of the New Testament and its single documents come from first-century or early second-century Mediterranean ingroup-oriented, Israelite authors and/or groups. After all, Jesus groups formed the first Palestinian-rooted form of non-Temple Israelite religion, kinship religion. After the destruction of the Jerusalem Temple in 70 A.D., Jesus groups were followed in this by ben Zakkaiists, scribal Pharisaic groups that remained largely reclusive. After that destruction, Jesus groups claimed to be true Israel (Matthew's gospel) or the only real Judeans (Rev 2:9).

All the documents derive from and witness to cultures in which ingroup/outgroup perception is a fundamental category of assessment. Some consequences of this: first, it is obviously true that there cannot be any anti-Semitism in the New Testament. This nineteenth-century category for "anti-Jewish" is anachronistic when applied to the first century A.D. There were no Jews or Christians in the New Testament in any modern, contemporary sense of the word.[13] Since the dialogue between personages represented in the documents and the authors of the documents themselves takes place among members of the house of Israel, within Israelite society or with positive reference to Israelite society, it would be simply silly to designate such interaction as anti-Semitic.

Second, it is obviously true that when both the dialoguing partners derive from Israelite society, and one of the partners is judged by the gatekeepers to be "like a non-Israelite" for whatever reason, the outcome is not "anti-Semitic." Otherwise ancient scribal Pharisees and not a few modern Jews would all be "anti-Semitic" for their criticism of Jesus and the Jesus movement groups.[14] Third, it is equally true that, when Israelites have or gain the ascendancy within a defined area perceived in terms of ingroup/outgroup, documents defending the ingroup nourish and express strong feelings against non-Israelites, often rabidly so (e.g., Matthew; see Hruby 1969; Sim 1995).[15] This is not surprising, since ethnocentrism is part and parcel of the Jewish tradition, a replication of ideological exclusivism (see Novak 1983).

CONCLUSION

The foregoing considerations lead to an obvious conclusion. When reading ingroup/outgroup documents, interpretation will always follow from the reader's social location and the consciously or unconsciously chosen point of view. Gentile Christians reading ancient Israelite documents will think they were written for modern Gentile Christians and modern Jews reading Israel's ancient writings will think they are for them (see Harrington 1998).

Consider two examples. First, consider the message of Matthew as exclusively Israelite (for an overview of the social location of Matthew, see Vledder 1997: 117-167; Sim 1995: 19-21; Cuvillier 1997 would make Matt 15:21-28 the key to the gospel). Historically the work echoes with recollections of the political religious, Israelite-specific dimension of the Jesus movement, specifically in the "many" over against "all" statements in the Synoptic tradition. To put those statements in their proper social location in Matthew, for example, one must read "many in Israel." Thus:

"Enter by the narrow gate; for the gate is wide and the way is easy, that leads to destruction, and those who enter by it are many [in Israel]" (Matt 7:13).

"On that day many [in Israel] will say to me, 'Lord, Lord, did we not prophesy in your name, and cast out demons in your name, and do many mighty works in your name?'" (Matt 7:22).

"I tell you, many [in Israel] will come from east and west and sit at table with Abraham, Isaac, and Jacob in the kingdom of heaven" (Matt 8:11).

"Truly, I say to you, many [Israelite] prophets and righteous men longed to see what you see, and did not see it, and to hear what you hear, and did not hear it" (Matt 13:17).

"But many [in Israel] that are first will be last, and the last first" (Matt 19:30). "The Son of man came not to be served but to serve, and to give his life as a ransom for many [in Israel]" (Matt 20:28; Mark 10:45).

"For many [in Israel] are called, but few are chosen" (Matt 22:14).

"For many [in Israel] will come in my name, saying, 'I am the Christ,' and they will lead many [in Israel] astray" (Matt 24:5).

"And then many [in Israel] will fall away, and betray one another, and hate one another. And many [Israelite] false prophets will arise and lead many [in Israel] astray" (Matt 24:10-11).

"For this is my blood of the covenant, which is poured out for many [in Israel] for the forgiveness of sins" (Matt 26:28; see Mark 14:24 who lacks the explicit expiatory motif).

"But they found none, though many [Israelite] false witnesses came forward" (Matt 26:60).

"The tombs also were opened, and many bodies of the [Israelite] saints who had fallen asleep were raised, the holy city and appeared to many [in Israel]" (Matt 27: 52-53).

"There were also many [Israelite] women there, looking on from afar, who had followed Jesus from Galilee, ministering to him" (Matt 27:55).

Even Matthew's death predictions point to an intramural, intra-Israel conflict:

"From that time Jesus began to show his disciples that he must go to Jerusalem and suffer many things from the elders and chief priests and scribes [of Israel], and be killed, and on the third day be raised" (Matt 16:21).

Similarly, "the whole world" refers to Israel in the whole world:

"And this gospel of the kingdom will be preached [to Israel] throughout the whole world, witnessed by all peoples, and then the end will come" (Matt 24:14).

"Truly, I say to you, wherever this gospel is preached [to Israel] in the whole world, what she has done will be told in memory of her" (Matt 26:13).

After all, the good news of the forthcoming theocracy that Jesus proclaimed was directly about Israel and Israel's political religion. Now what of Matthew's explicit *ethnos* replacement in 21:43: "Therefore I tell you, the kingdom of God will be taken away from you and given to a people (*ethnos*) producing the fruits of it." In context this passage is addressed to the chief priests and Pharisees of Israel, who perceived "that he was speaking about them" (Matt 21:45). In context, the threat is directed to chief priests, and the term *ethnos* clearly means a group, caste, company of men, body of men, that would take the place of the present chief priests, as in Isa 66:18-21 where all Israel will be gathered from among the nations and ferried in honor to "my holy mountain in Jerusalem." Among these "some of them I will take for priests and for Levites, says the Lord" (Isa 18:21). It was only after Gentiles in various Jesus-related movement groups began to read Matthew and take such statements in their own ethnocentric framework that the scope of Jesus' mission gets reconfigured, first for rather small Gentile house-churches, then for Constantinian political religion.

Further, as political religion with God as focus of a forthcoming theocracy, what God wished of his people Israel was its commitment on his behalf, known variously as "faith" or "obedience." The final edict in Matthew (28:16) ostensibly speaks of "making disciples of all peoples"; again, I do not use the term "nation" because its present denotation emerged only in the eighteenth century A.D. (see Anderson 1991). Yet in the Matthean ethnocentric context, to make disciples of all peoples is to seek out Israelite residents among all ethnic groups, that is, make disciples of Israelites found among Gentiles.[16] After all, there is no indication in the whole document that Gentiles are anything other than outgroup. The perspective is one of Israel and all other peoples of the world, of Judeans and foreigners, as in Acts 2:5: "Now there were dwelling in Jerusalem Judeans, devout men from every ethnic group under heaven." It was obviously to Israelite colonials spread among all other ethnic groups that information of God's forthcoming Jerusalemite theocracy had to be spread.

Another example. Given the existence of the Jewish religion from the fifth century A.D. on, a book like Joshua is a charter for Jews to effect a *herem*, that is, a Gentile holocaust, against any non-Jews whose land Jews wish to take, whose property Jews wish to appropriate (see Rolwing 1994: 107-188; on the Jewish slaughter of all Christians in Yemen in 524, see Beaucamp et al. 1997). Thus Joshua sanctions stealing, plunder, and destruction of non-Jews for Jews, by Jews, and on behalf of Jews. If the book be read as a Christian book, with Joshua the prototypical Christian, and the outgroup being pagans (including Jews as a type of pagan; see O'Donnell 1979), the result would be what happened in Germany. I am not saying that this is the only cause of what happened in Germany, but it is indeed the only ideological source for what happened in Palestine against the Christian and Muslim Palestinians. Similarly, the Deuteronomist had been put to work as ideological underpinning of South Africa's apartheid (see Deist 1994).

The really pertinent observation here is that ingroup/outgroup documents, when read anachronistically and ethnocentrically, in terms of good guys (ingroup) and bad guys (outgroup), will produce negative results for whoever plays the bad guy, or outgroup, role in the story. At the concrete level, all depends on who are the good guys in society using the story and who plays that role in another time and place. Consequently, if a Christian takes the bad guy/good guy, ingroup/ outgroup story, and puts Jesus in the ingroup and Jesus' opponent Judeans in the outgroup, and then puts non-Israelite Christians in the same ingroup with Jesus as in the post-Constantinian church, the result is a story in which very "Semitic" authors insist that Jesus dies for the world, meaning Gentiles. For the historical analysis of Jesus, the Jesus movement, and incipient Christian movement, there seems to be no evidence until Nero for postulating any conflict outside of Israelite society. Ingroup/outgroup members were all of the house of Israel or connected to it.

In sum, Christian anti-Semitism, meaning unwarranted[17] anti-Jewish attitudes and behavior, emerged in the world of Christendom almost three centuries after the formation of Jesus groups, with the emergence of the Jewish religion. It would be anachronistic to retroject modern anti-Semitism to the New Testament; it is just as anachronistic to speak of a Judaeo-Christian tradition before the nineteenth century A.D. (Cohen 1971). After all, if Jews and Christians lived apart during the period of Christendom, it is impossible for any "tradition" to develop at all. On the other hand, if we stick to the level of doctrine and ideology, we might make a better case for a Muslim-Christian tradition since for both Jesus is born of the Virgin

Mary, is sent by God as Prophet, is now with God, and will come again to mark God's final judgment of humankind. All of these central features common to Islam and Christianity are totally denied by the Jewish tradition.

Perhaps modern Christians and their recent Reformation theories of Scripture and inspiration would do well to reflect on the words of an ancient bishop of Haran, the town from where Abraham departed for Canaan:

> Were it not for the Gospel, we would not have acknowledged Moses to be from God. Rather, on reflection, we would have vigorously opposed him. Likewise, we have acknowledged the prophets to be from God because of the Gospel. It is not on the basis of reason, since we have acknowledged them because Christ has informed us that they are prophets. Also, because we have knowledge of Christ's whole economy, and having read their books and discovered that they had previously described his whole economy just as he accomplished it, we have acknowledged that they are prophets. At this point in time we do not acknowledge Christ and his affairs because of the books of the prophets. Rather, we acknowledge them because of Christ's saying that they are prophets and because of our own recognition that his economy is written in their books (Theodore Abu Qurrah, Bishop of Haran d. 9th cent. AD; Griffith 1992: 165).

SOURCES

Abulafia, Anna Sapir
1985 "Invectives against Christianity in the Hebrew Chronicles of the First Crusade." 66-72 in Peter W. Edbury, ed., *Crusade and Settlement*. Cardiff: University of Cardiff Press.
Anderson, Benedict
1991 *Imagined Communities: Reflections on the Origin and Spread of Nationalism*. London: Verso.
Banks, Kathleen
1998 "An Open Letter to Fundamentalist Ministers from a Member of a Christian Fundamentalist Church." *Washington Report on Middle East Affairs* 27 (July/August), 82, 95.

Beaucamp, Jöelle, Françoise Briquel-Chatonnet and Christian Robin
    1997 "Chrétiens et martyrs dans l'arabie heureuse." *L'Histoire* No.
        207, 66-69.
Beck, Norman A.
    1997 *Anti-Roman Cryptograms in the New Testament: Symbolic
        Messages of Hope and Liberation*. New York: Peter Lang.
Bowersock, Glen W.
    1988 "Palestine, Ancient History and Modern Politics." 181-91 in
        Edward Said and Christopher Hitchens, ed., *Blaming the Victim:
        Spurious Scholarship and the Palestinian Question*. London/ New
        York: Verso.
Cohen, Arthur A.
    1971 *The Myth of the Judeo-Christian Tradition*. New York: Schocken.
Cuvillier, Élian
    1997 "Particularisme et universalisme chez Matthieu: quelques
        hypothèses à l'épreuve du texte." *Biblica* 78, 481-502.
Deist, Ferdinand E.
    1994 "The Dangers of Deuteronomy: A Page from the Reception
        History of the Book." 13-29 in F. García Martínez, A. Hilhorst,
        J.T.A.G.M. van Ruiten and A.S. van der Woude, ed., *Studies in
        Deuteronomy: In Honour of C. J. Labuschagne on the Occasion of
        His 65th Birthday*. (Supplements to *Vetus Testamentum* 49) Leiden:
        Brill.
Del Valle, Carlos
    1997 "La Prière de la polémique: la bénédiction des hérétiques." *Revue
        des Études Juives* 156, 191-94.
Duncan, James and David Ley
    1993 "Introduction: Representing the Place of Culture." 1-21 in James
        Duncan and David Ley, eds., *Place/Culture/Representation*. Lon-
        don/New York: Routledge.
Dunn, Geoffrey D.
    1998 "Tertullian and Rebekah: A Re-Reading of an 'Anti-Jewish'
        Argument in Early Christian Literature." *Vigiliae Christianae* 52,
        119-45.
Elliott, John H.
    Forthcoming *1 Peter: A New Translation with Introduction and
        Commentary. Anchor Bible*. New York: Doubleday.
Feldman, Lewis H.

1993 *Jew and Gentile in the Ancient World: Attitudes and Interactions from Alexander to Justinian*. Princeton: Princeton University Press.

Freudman, Lillian C.
1994 *Antisemitism in the New Testament*. Lanham/New York: University Press of America.

Garreau, Joel
1981 *The Nine Nations of North America*. New York: Avon.

Geertz, Clifford
1966 "Religion as a Cultural System." 1-46 in Michael Banton, ed., *Anthropological Approaches to the Study of Religion*. New York: Praeger.

Georgi, Dieter
1995 "The Early Church: Internal Jewish Migration or New Religion." *Harvard Theological Review* 88, 35-68.

Gigerenzer, Gerd and Zeno Swijtink, Theodore Porter, Lorraine Daston, John Beaty, Lorenz Krüger
1989 *The Empire of Change: How Probability Changed Science and Everyday Life*. Cambridge: Cambridge University Press.

Gloger, Yoesh (the Priest)
1991 *Jesus Mishegahs: The Jewish Christmas Book*. New York: Gloger Family Books.

Griffith, Sidney H.
1992 "The Gospel in Arabic: An Inquiry into Its Appearance in the First Abbasid Century," *Oriens Christianus* 69 (1985) 165 [126-67], in Sidney H. Griffith, *Arabic Christianity in the Monasteries of Ninth-Century Palestine*. Brookfield VT: Variorum, 1992.

Hahn, Ferdinand
1965 *Mission in the New Testament*. trans. Frank Clark (*Studies in Biblical Theology* 47). Naperville, IL: Alec R. Allenson.

Halkin, A. S.
1952 *Moses Maimonides' Epistle to Yemen: The Arabic Original and the Three Hebrew Versions*. New York: American Academy for Jewish Research.

Halliday, Michael A. K.
1978 *Language as Social Semiotic: The Social Interpretation of Language and Meaning*. Baltimore: University Park Press.

Hanson, K. C. and Douglas E. Oakman
1998 *Palestine in the Time of Jesus: Social Structures and Social*

Conflicts. Minneapolis: Fortress.

Harrington, Daniel J.
  1998 "Is the New Testament Anti-Jewish? The Need to Develop a Sense of History." *Irish Theological Quarterly* 63, 123-132.

Hopkins, Keith
  1998 "Christian Number and Its Implications." *Journal of Early Christianity* 6,185-226.

Horsley, Richard Λ.
  1994 "The Death of Jesus." 395-422 in Bruce Chilton and Craig A. Evans, eds., *Studying The Historical Jesus: Evaluations of the State of Current Research*. Brill: Leiden.

Hruby, Kurt
  1969 "L'amour du prochain dans la pensée juive." *Nouvelle Revue Théologique* 91, 493-516.

Jeremias, Joachim
  1967 *Jesus' Promise to the Nations*. trans. S. H. Hooke. Rev. ed. (Studies in Biblical Theology 24) Naperville, IL: Alec R. Allenson (rev. of 1958).

Johnson, Allen W.
  1978 *Quantification in Cultural Anthropology: An Introduction to Research Design*. Stanford: Stanford University Press.

Koester, Helmut
  1994 "The Historical Jesus and the Historical Situation of the Quest: An Epilogue." 535-45 in Bruce Chilton and Craig A. Evans, ed., *Studying The Historical Jesus: Evaluations of the State of Current Research*. Brill: Leiden.

Lauterbach, Jacob Z.
  1970 "The Attitude of the Jew towards the Non-Jew." 159-206 in his *Studies in Jewish Law, Custom and Folklore*. New York: Ktav.

Lloyd, G. E. R.
  1966 *Polarity and Analogy: Two Types of Argumentation in Early Greek Thought*. Cambridge: Cambridge University Press.

Malina, Bruce J.
  1986 "Religion in the World of Paul: A Preliminary Sketch," *Biblical Theology Bulletin* 16, 92-101.
  1991 "Reading Theory Perspective: Reading Luke-Acts." 3-23 in Jerome H. Neyrey, ed., *The Social World of Luke-Acts: Models for Interpretation*, Peabody, MA: Hendrickson.

1994 "Religion in the Imagined New Testament World: More Social Science Lenses" *Scriptura* 51, 1-26.

1995 "Early Christian Groups: Using Small Group Formation Theory to Explain Christian Organizations." 96-113 in Philip F. Esler, ed., *Modeling Early Christianity: Social-Scientific Studies of the New Testament in its Context.* (Proceedings of the Second International Congress on Social Sciences and New Testament Interpretation, St. Andrews, Scotland) London: Routledge.

1996 "Mediterranean Sacrifice: Dimensions of Domestic and Political Religion." *Biblical Theology Bulletin* 26, 26-44.

Malina, Bruce J. and Richard L. Rohrbaugh

1998 *Social Science Commentary on the Gospel of John.* Minneapolis: Fortress.

Mason, Steve

1990 "Paul, Classical Anti-Judaism, and the Letter to the Romans." 181-223 in D. J. Hawkin and T. Robinson, eds., *Self-Definition and Self-Discovery in Early Christianity.* Lewiston, NY: Mellen.

Millar, Fergus

1983 "Empire and City, Augustus to Julian: Obligations, Excuses and Status." *Journal of Roman Studies* 73, 76-96.

Moehring, Horst

1984 "Joseph ben Matthia and Flavius: The Jewish Prophet and Roman Historian." *ANRW.* II 21.2, 864-944.

Morgues, Jean-Louis

1998 "Rome et la Chine: le partage du monde." *L'Histoire* No. 218 (Feb. 1998), 25-26.

Nanos, Mark

1996 *The Mystery of Romans: The Jewish Context of Paul's Letter.* Minneapolis: Fortress.

Neusner, Jacob

1995 "Was Rabbinic Judaism Really 'Ethnic'?" *Catholic Biblical Quarterly* 57 (1995), 281-305.

Novak, David

1983 *The Image of the Non-Jew in Judaism: An Historical and Constructive Study of the Noahide Laws.* (*Toronto Studies in Theology* 14). Lewiston, ME: Mellen.

O'Donnell, James J.

1979 "The Demise of Paganism." *Traditio* 35, 45-88.

Pilch, John J.
   1997 "Are There Jews and Christians in the Bible?" *Hervormde Teolo-
       giese Studies* 53, 119-25.
Reminick, Ronald A.
   1983 *Theory of Ethnicity: An Anthropologist's Perspective*. Lanham/
       New York: University Press of America.
Rohrbaugh, Richard L.
   1991 "The Pre-Industrial City in Luke-Acts: Urban Social Relations."
       125-49 in Jerome H. Neyrey, ed., *The Social World of Luke-Acts:
       Models for Interpretation*. Peabody, MA: Hendrickson.
Rolwing, Richard J.
   1994 *Israel's Original Sin: A Catholic Confession*. San Francisco:
       Catholic Scholars Press.
Rufinus of Aquileia (345-410 A.D.)
   1997 *The Church History of Rufinus of Aquileia: Books 10 and 11*.
       trans. Philip R. Amidon, S.J., New York/Oxford: Oxford Univer-
       sity Press.
Runes, Dagobert D.
   1975 *Let My People Live!* New York: Philosophic Library.
Sanders, E. P.
   1985 *Jesus and Judaism*. Philadelphia: Fortress, 1985. On Gentiles,
       212-22.
Sandmel, Samuel
   1978 *Anti-Semitism in the New Testament?* Philadelphia: Fortress.
Schonfield, Hugh J.
   1937 *According to the Hebrews*. London: Duckworth.
Sim, Donald C.
   1995 "The Gospel of Matthew and the Gentiles." *Journal for the Study
       of the New Testament* 57,19-48.
Stanley, Christopher D.
   1996 "'Neither Jew nor Greek': Ethnic Conflict in Graeco-Roman
       Society." *Journal for the Study of the New Testament* 64, 101-24.
Stannard, David E.
   1996 "Uniqueness as Denial: The Politics of Genocide Scholarship."
       163-208 in Alan S. Rosenbaum, ed., *Is the Holocaust Unique?
       Perspectives on Comparative Genocide*. Boulder, CO: Westview.
Stark, Rodney
   1996 *The Rise of Christianity: A Sociologist Reconsiders History*.

Princeton: Princeton University Press.

Triandis, Harry C. and Vasso Vassiliou

1972 "A Comparative Analysis of Subjective Culture." 299-335 in Harry C. Triandis et al., *The Analysis of Subjective Culture*. New York: Wiley Interscience.

Veyne, Paul

1989 "'Humanitas': Romani e no[i]." 385-415 in Andrea Giardina, ed., *L'uomo Romano*. Bari: Laterza.

Vledder, Evert-Jan

1997 *Conflict in the Miracle Stories: A Socio-Exegetical Study of Matthew 8 and 9*. JSNTSS 152. Sheffield: Sheffield Academic Press.

Wallace, Richard and Wynne Williams

1998 *The Three Worlds of Paul*. London/New York: Routledge.

Witherington, Ben

1998 *Grace in Galatia: A Commentary on St. Paul's Letter to the Galatians*. Grand Rapids: Eerdmans.

NOTES

1. To paraphrase Geertz (1966:4), kinship is a system of symbols which acts to establish powerful, pervasive and long-lasting moods and motivations in human beings formulating conceptions of value objects involved in naturing and nurturing people and clothing these conceptions with such an aura of factuality that the moods and motivations are perceived to be uniquely realistic.

2. Again, paraphrasing Geertz (1966:4), politics is a system of symbols which acts to establish powerful, pervasive and long-lasting moods and motivations in human beings formulating conceptions of value objects involved in effective collective action and clothing these conceptions with such an aura of factuality that the moods and motivations are perceived to be uniquely realistic.

3. This is not all that confusing. When U.S. persons meet in the U.S. and inquire about their respective nationalities, they invariably give the country of origin of their immigrant ancestors. Should the same U.S. persons be together in another country, and should a local person ask them what is their nationality, they would all respond "American, from the U.S." What counts is who is asking about their nationality.

4. Most modern scholars treat the term *Judaism* as though it referred to a socially disembedded, free-standing, religious institution. This is totally anachronistic for antiquity. Rather the term *Judaism* in the Greco-Roman world refers to

the ideology, customs, and behaviors of persons who derive from Judea. Withering-ton (1998: 98), for example, believes that Maccabean writings are a form of self-description by Israelites who used the term *Ioudaismos* to indicate that they followed "a Torah-true Jewish (sic) lifestyle and belief system," as opposed to Israelite Hellenists (see 2Macc 2:21; 8:1; 14:38; 4Macc 4:26).

5. "Nations" in the modern sense arose only in the eighteenth century A.D. (see Anderson 1991). At times, the plural of *ethnos* (*ethnē*) is translated "pagans." The word "pagan" (from the Latin: *paganus*, a rural peasant, a rustic) was applied by Christian elites to label non-Christians, including Judeans, only in the fourth century A.D. (see O'Donnell 1979).

6. "Ethnophobia" characterizes Israelite attitudes toward the other peoples of the world during the Greco-Roman period of antiquity. Tacitus, for example, claimed that "toward every other people, they (Judeans) show only hate and enmity" (*Histories* 5.5.1). Ancient Israelite documents evidence Judean abhorrence of the pervasive quality of Hellenism and its universal scope, the range of gods and goddesses unconcerned with human behavior, the openness to all foods, laws relating to property, the practice of physical body integrity, concern for political religion. Outbursts of Judean hostility were frequent in Alexandria in 38 A.D., Jerusalem in 66-74, 117-18, 132-35 A.D., in Rome in 45 A.D. (for more examples, see Stanley 1996).

7. "With the spread of Greek culture and Greek rule across the eastern Mediterranean, a 'Hellene' came to mean someone who spoke flawless Greek and embraced Greek culture and institutions, regardless of national origin" (Stanley 1996: 113). In the first century A.D., Rome, like other empire builders of antiquity, considered its empire as the only central political power in the world. There was no civilized, humanized world apart from Rome. People did not come under Roman rule or Roman oppression. Rather to be Romanized was to be civilized, immersed in worldwide, Hellenic civilization. Veyne has noted: "Republican Rome, that people who had as its culture that of another people, Greece, did not feel this culture as strange, but simply as civilization. Likewise, in the Empire and outside its frontiers, Greco-Roman civilization was civilization itself; one did not Romanize or Hellenize, one civilized" (1989: 411).

8. At best for Gentiles, there were attitudes like those of Zeph 3:8 which combined the threat to judge and destroy all other peoples of the world with the promise to assimilate them. For an instance of multivalenced attitudes, one may cite Sib. Or. 3.489-808, which deals successively with the historical vicissitudes of empires, with the messianic era, and with the final consummation. There are dire predictions of the destruction of non-Israelites of any sort because of their presumed idolatry and sexual immorality (e.g., 3.517f.; 669-72; 761), coupled with the hope that many will turn to God on Israel's terms, worship him, and share Israel's salvation (3.616).

9. The impression that most Jesus group members after the second century were of non-Israelite origin derives, it seems, largely from the fact that a number of philosophers did indeed join Jesus groups as single, unattached individuals in search of a way of life. Justin of Samaria, Clement of Alexandria, Athenagoras of Athens, Tertullian of Carthage were such non-Israelites. All of the "Apostolic Fathers" were undoubtedly of Israelite origin. So were the majority of ordinary Jesus group members who became aware of Jesus groups through networking in Judean quarters of Mediterranean cities.

10. "Anti-Semitism" is of nineteenth-century coinage (1881 in *OED ad verbum*), used as a euphemism for "anti-Jewish." Historians are becoming increasingly more insistent that there were no "Jews" in the first-century Mediterranean since, as previously noted, all modern forms of the Jewish religion emerge in the fifth century A.D. (for example, see Miller 1992:193-4; Horsley 1994:398-399; Koester 1994:541-543; Pilch 1997). It is equally clear that there was no single form of Second Temple Israelite ideology, often called "Judaism," in the first century A.D.; rather there was a wide range of various Torah-based and Temple-focused groups and associations in Israel (see Georgi 1995; Dunn 1998).

11. The term "ethnocentrism" was coined by William Graham Sumner in 1906: "Ethnocentrism is the technical name for this view of things in which one's own group is the center of everything, and all others are scaled and rated with reference to it."

12. The works dealing with attitudes of Judeans toward Gentiles in antiquity (e.g., the early work of Lauterbach 1970 and the recent massive essay by Feldman 1993) sound rather sanitized when read alongside the *Toledoth Jeshu* (Schonfield 1937). For a critique of the apologetic and/or propagandistic tendency among Israeli scholars dealing with this area, see Moehring 1984 and Bowersock 1988.

13. As previously noted, one of the significant principles of historically oriented biblical interpretation is that words derive their meanings from the social systems in which they are used. Now take the truism that "Jesus was a Jew." If the word "Jew" derives its meaning from our contemporary social systems, then the statement makes no sense whatsoever. After all, all forms of Jewish religion trace back to the Talmud, itself rooted in the Mishnaic tradition deriving from Yohanan ben Zakkai at the end of the first century A.D., some sixty or seventy years after Jesus. To call Jesus a Jew would be much like saying Jesus was a Catholic Christian or Peter was a Pope. Modern Christianity can be traced back only to Christendom, the political religion emerging with the assimilation of the largely Israelite Jesus movement groups by the post-Constantinian Roman Empire. It was likewise in the period after Constantine that the Jewish religion emerged.

14. Modern Jews label Jews who criticize Israel or deny the uniqueness of the Holocaust, for example, as self-hating Jews (see Stannard 1996). The same would have to hold for Israel's Old Testament prophets like Isaiah, Jeremiah, or Ezekiel. Of course the question is who is the self-hating "Semite," the prophet or the people

against whom the prophet inveighs?

15. A first indication of this are the anti-Roman cryptograms in the New Testament (see Beck 1997); then there is the synagogal cursing of apostates, applied in scribal Pharisee circles to Jesus group members, and later on to all Christians (see Del Valle 1997) down to modern times (Banks 1998). The highlights of the Jewish anti-Gentile tradition can be easily traced (see, e.g., Abulafia 1985; Beaucamp et al. 1997; Gloger 1991; Halkin 1952).

16. To some this may seem farfetched, yet all depends on the speaker's social location and subsequent frame of reference. Several years ago I was at an Israeli bond sale, at the close of which the Israeli speaker said he had now to visit other Americans since this was his first stop. Of course, the "other Americans" meant solely "other Jewish Americans." While this is no proof, it does demonstrate how Matthew's making disciples of all peoples, in context, means Israelites among all peoples.

17. I would emphasize the word *unwarranted*. Note how Rufinus describes Jewish behavior in Jerusalem at the time of Emperor Julian:

Now such was his refined cunning in deception that he even deluded the unhappy Jews, enticing them with the sort of vain hopes that he himself entertained. First of all, summoning them to him he asked them why they did not sacrifice, when their law included commandments for them about sacrifices. Thinking an opportunity had come their way, they answered, 'We cannot do so except in the temple in Jerusalem. For thus the law ordains.' And having received from him permission to repair the temple, they grew so arrogant that it was as though some prophet had come back to them. Jews came together from every place and province and began to make their way to the site of the temple, long since consumed by fire, a count having been assigned by the emperor to push forward the work, which was pursued with all earnestness and financed both publicly and privately. Meanwhile they insulted our people and as though the time of the kingdom had returned threatened them harshly and created them cruelly; in a·word, they behaved with monstrous arrogance and pride" (Rufinus *HE* 10:38; Amidon 47).

Gender and the Body
in Ancient Israel

Ronald A. Simkins

THE SYMBOLIC BODY

A fundamental insight from anthropology is that the human body serves as a symbol of society in a wide variety of cultures. The microcosm that is the body replicates the powers and dangers of society, its complexities and boundaries. Dietary restrictions or sexual taboos, for example, are not mere vestiges of an earlier, less enlightened era, although they may become this. They correspond to social concerns regarding the composition of the family, relations between different communities, and control of property. The physical body, what it can eat, and with whom and when it can have sexual relations, is thus perceived according to the structures of society. In the words of Mary Douglas,

> The body is a model which can stand for any bounded system. Its boundaries can represent any boundaries which are threatened or precarious. The body is a complex structure. The functions of its different parts and their relation afford a source of symbols for other complex structures (1966: 115).

As a symbol of society, the body functions both as a model *of* society and as a model *for* society. The social perception of the physical body serves to justify and reinforce the social system. The biblical dietary laws, for example, replicate the dangers to Israelite society represented by deities other than Yahweh, and thereby reinforce Israelite monolatry. The body social is perceived as a macrocosm of the body physical. Again, according to Douglas:

The social body constrains the way the physical body is perceived.
The physical experience of the body, always modified by the social
categories through which it is known, sustains a particular view of
society. There is a continual exchange of meaning between the two
kinds of bodily experience so that each reinforces the categories of
the other (1970: 65).

For the people of ancient Israel this analysis can be extended further.
The body also served as symbol of the world at large, the totality of the
physical and social world of the people's experience. This was possible
because they perceived the physical world as a bounded system with
features analogous to the body, and the body as rooted in and symbolic of
the structures of the social world. The body thus mediated the symbolic
relationship between the social and the physical world. As a result, the
people's experiences of the physical world shaped their perception of their
bodies, which thereby shaped their perception of society. Their physical
bodies and social experiences in turn further reinforced their perception of
the world.

The thesis that I will argue in this paper is that this complex symbolic
relationship between the body and the social and physical world formed the
basis of the ancient Israelites' understanding of gender. Gender represents
the ongoing social construction by which a society defines, fundamentally,
the biological human differences in sexual reproduction, what constitutes
"male" and "female," and the means by which it delineates the normative
patterns of behavior which embody these differences, how males and
females should act. It is a social understanding of the body. The ancient
Israelites' perception of their sexual, procreative bodies was shaped by
their experiences of the natural world, particularly in subsistence agriculture. Their understanding of their bodies was determinative of their gendered social roles and the gendered structures of society.

SOCIAL CONSTRUCTION OF GENDER

In the biblical tradition, the ancient Israelite understanding of gender is
expressed most clearly in the Yahwist creation myth (Gen 2:4b-3:24). The
social patterns of behavior between men and women are outlined in
normative form, and the cultural meanings which are embedded in these

patterns are made explicit through the metaphors and structure of the myth. The Israelite understanding of gender is presented in this narrative through a metaphor that compares the bodily process of procreation to agriculture, and is symbolized by the structural wordplays between *ha'adam* and *ha'adamah* (2:7) and between *'ish* and *'ishshah* (2:23), and by the social roles instituted for the man and the woman (3:16-19).

The garden narrative begins with the creation of the man (Gen 2:4b-17). The Yahwist begins the narrative in typical Near Eastern fashion by describing that which was absent at the time of creation: The earth was a dry, sterile desert with no pasturage or field crops. The Yahwist then gives the reason for the earth's sterile condition: Yahweh had not yet sent rain on the earth, and there was no man to cultivate the soil. Therefore, in order to provide someone to work the soil, and thereby bring vegetation to the dry, barren earth, Yahweh God formed the man (*ha'dam*) from the dirt of the arable land (*ha'adamah*). The wordplay between *ha'adam* and *ha'adamah*, presented as masculine and feminine forms of the same word, attests to the man's relationship to the land. Having his origin in the soil, the man is dependent upon the arable land from which he was taken. Yet the arable land is also dependent upon the man if it is to be anything more than a barren desert, for the man must till it and sow seed in it to produce vegetation. For this reason the man was created.

Scholars have long noted that the creation of humans from dirt or clay is a common ancient Near Eastern metaphor. What has not been noticed, however, is the cultural understanding of creation in which this metaphor is rooted. In the Mesopotamian creation myths the fashioning of clay served as a metaphor for gestation during pregnancy. In the myth of Atrahasis, for example, Enki's treading of clay and Belet-ili's pinching off of fourteen pieces in order to create humans are juxtaposed to a description of the process and rites of childbirth. In Egypt the rain-headed Khnum, to whom most scholars have compared Yahweh's creation of man, fashioned humans out of clay on his potter's wheel. But as several hymns to Khnum make clear, the ancient Egyptians also attributed to Khnum the necessary and critical task of forming human fetuses during gestation. His work and skill as a potter served as a metaphor for his activity in the birth process.

In the Genesis creation myth, the forming of the man from the dirt of the arable land should be interpreted as a metaphor for the man's birth from the land. Yahweh acts as a potter by forming the human fetus in the womb of the earth (compare the similar image evoked in Ps 139:13-15). Then

Yahweh acts as a midwife by delivering the man out of the ground, breathing into his nostrils the breath of life. The male *ha'adam* comes from the female like a fetus from its mother. The wordplay between *ha'adam* and *'ha'adamah* establishes the relationship between the man and the arable land to be like a child and his mother. On who impregnated the earth, the father of ha'adam, the narrative is silent. Yahweh might be assumed, but the birth process has been abstracted to include only the depiction of gestation and parturition.

With the creation of the first woman, Yahweh takes a different course of action (2:18-24). Being unable to form a suitable helper for the man from the land, Yahweh takes one of the man's ribs in order to build an individual who corresponds to the man. By creating the woman, Yahweh introduces differentiation into the human species. Humans can now be distinguished as man (*'ish*) and woman (*'ishshah*), or more properly, as husband and wife, for the terms used are explicitly social in orientation. The specific gendered social role of each individual, however, has not yet been outlined. At this point in the myth the Yahwist simply notes that their social roles find fulfillment in the institution of marriage (2:24).

The relational pattern established between the man and the woman in this part of the myth is complex. Phyllis Trible has argued that both the man and the woman have their origin in a non-differentiated human creature, *ha'adam*, and thus represent complementary parts of humankind (94-105; compare the critique of Lanser). But the man, *'ish*, is identified with *ha'adam* throughout the myth. Moreover, the woman is taken *me'ish*, "from the man,' just as the rib is taken *min ha'adam*, "from the man," suggesting that the woman has her origin from the man and is thus dependent upon the man. Yet the wordplay between *'ish* and *'ishshah* also suggests a complementary relationship between the man and the woman. The man, *ha'adam*, is called *'ish* in order to emphasize the unity of substance between himself and the woman, *'ishshah*. Although the animals and the birds shared with the man a common origin *min ha'adamah*, "from the arable land," no helper was found who corresponded to the man. His naming of the creatures distinguishes them to be unlike him. The man's recognition of the woman as *'ishshah*, therefore, signals her correspondence to him. She is a suitable helper.

Although the myth's description of the woman's origin from the man suggests that she is dependent upon the man, the nature of this dependency is not explained. Moreover, the basis for this dependency, that the woman comes from the man, appears to be contrary to nature. According to the current scientific understanding, procreation entails the joining of the man's sperm and the woman's egg in conception, each contributing half of the needed genetic material, within the woman's uterus where the resulting embryo, develops until parturition. However, this knowledge is less than a century old, and clearly was not possible in the world of ancient Israel. The ancient Israelites understood the "facts" of procreation differently, and these "facts" are symbolized in the myth by the woman coming from the man. Although the man is born from the "female" land, the woman is dependent upon the man for her existence. The myth structures this ambiguous relationship between the man and the woman, symbolized by the wordplay between 'ish and 'ishshah, in reflection of the mutually dependent relationship between ha'adam and ha'adamah. The specific dependencies of this relationship remain to be articulated.

The pivotal episode in the garden narrative focuses on the woman's dialogue with the serpent and her and her husband's subsequent eating of the forbidden fruit of knowledge (2:253:7). By eating the fruit, the human couple become like God knowing good and evil. The knowledge of good and evil, probably a merism for universal or cultural knowledge, is what distinguishes the human couple from all the other creatures that Yahweh created from the land. Through knowledge the man and woman gain the potential for culture; the human couple become creators like God.

The specific way in which the human couple's newly acquired knowledge makes them like God is indicated by the context. The episode frames the man and woman's acquisition of knowledge with references to their nakedness. Before they eat the fruit, the human couple are naked and have no shame or "do not shame each other." The implication is that the man and the woman are sexually unaware. Without knowledge they are like children unacquainted with the significance of their bodies, and so their nakedness means nothing to them, their public nakedness does not impugn their self-worth. After they eat the fruit, however, the man and the woman know they are naked and they appropriately cover themselves. The human couple are now aware of their sexuality; their nakedness has significance to them; and therefore they cover their genitals. They display shame, guarding their public reputation, so that they will not be perceived as acting like a shameless person, a person without honor. The fruit of knowledge has made the human couple like God, and their similarity to God is symbolized by their knowledge of sexuality. The ramifications of this knowledge, of the human couple being like God, are spelled out in the remainder of the narrative.

The Yahwist myth presents the particular social roles of the woman and the man in the final episode (3:8-24) to be the consequence of their new status of being "like God." Their social roles give content to the parallel relationships between *ha'adam* and *ha'adamah* and between *'ish* and *'ishshah*. These social roles embody the ancient Israelites' understanding of gender. They represent the normative social patterns of behavior for Israelite men and women. In other words, the first man's role as a farmer and the first woman's role as a mother symbolize the appropriate behavior for all Israelite men and women.

Yahweh institutes the woman's social role by declaring that he will increase her toils and pregnancies (3:16; Meyers: 99-109). Because the woman now has knowledge and an awareness of her sexuality, childbirth is possible. She will bear children, but such births will be painful. Her life will be filled with the labors that are characteristic of a mother and wife in ancient Israel. Yet the woman's status as mother will be dependent upon her husband. Because she is *'ishshah* who comes from *'ish*, her husband will rule over her. The context of procreation limits the extent and defines the purpose of the man's dominance. The woman's social task of bearing children is dependent upon the man; he will have control over her pregnancies. The woman's relationship to her husband is analogous to the man's relationship to the arable land. Although the man comes from the land, the arable land is dependent upon the man to bring forth vegetation. It will remain a barren desert without the man to till it and sow seed in it. Similarly, the woman's ability to bear children is dependent upon her husband, who must first impregnate her. The woman is like the land in that the fecundity of both is linked to the man's sowing of seed, but whereas the land had given birth to the first man due to Yahweh's activity, all future generations will be born from the woman. Rather than the arable land, the woman will be Eve, the mother of all living (3:20).

Although the Yahwist myth describes the woman's social role in relation to the man, the man's social role is described in relation to the arable land (3:17-19). The man's newly acquired knowledge and awareness of sexuality is expressed, not in terms of procreation, but in terms of agriculture. The man now has the knowledge to work the land, which is the purpose for which he was created. No longer will the man live off the fruit of God's garden. Through his toil and sweat the man will provide for his own subsistence, a task which is made more arduous because the land is cursed with no rain. The man will be like Yahweh in his social role of working the soil. Just as Yahweh planted a garden and caused trees to sprout up from the earth, the man will also bring forth life from the barren ground. Yet unlike Yahweh, the man's fate is linked to the arable land from which he came.

The ancient Israelites' understanding of gender is rooted in their particular understanding of the biological differences of sexual reproduction which is expressed through the metaphors and structure of the Yahwist creation myth. The man's birth from the ground, the woman's creation from and dependence upon the man, the association of the fruit of knowledge with sexual awareness, the parallel relationships between *ha'adam* and *ha'adamah* and between *'ish* and *'ishshah* and the woman's association with the arable land all serve to compare the process of procreation to agriculture. Just as a man sows seeds into the soil and thereby causes the arable land to produce vegetation, a man can sow his seed, semen, into a woman causing her to give birth to a child.

The man's role in procreation is metaphorically compared to the role of a farmer. As a father and a farmer, the man provides what is essential for life: seed and semen. Moreover, the man's semen, like seed, determines the character or quality of what will be produced; it contains all the essential characteristics of the child that will be born. The woman's role in procreation is compared to the land's role in agriculture. Like the soil, a woman nurtures to full development the seed that is planted within her. Although a man is dependent upon a woman for his own procreation, she contributes nothing essential to the makeup of the newborn child. The woman's role in procreation is wholly ancillary to the man's role.

GENDER AND HONOR

The Israelites' perception of the body and their concomitant understanding of gender had social implications for the gender roles of men and women. Their understanding of the body sustained a particular social structure, a structure of prestige, which was expressed through the fundamental social values of honor and shame. Honor was a person's claim to self-worth and the social acknowledgment of that claim, that is, honor was a person's public reputation, a person's prestige, which constituted his or her identity.

Shame was a person's concern for reputation. It was a positive value by which a person sought to maintain or protect his or her honor. Honor and shame belonged to both men and women and characterized their behavior as collective members of Israelite society and natural groups such as the family and the village. As individuals, however, men were associated with honor and women with shame. Prestige was a gendered structure. In ancient Israel the prestige of men and women was determined by the social construction of gender; it was rooted in the common Israelite understanding of the body, of the contribution of each in procreation.

Male honor was based on a man's ability to engender. It was symbolized by the penis and testicles, and also by the head and the face, and was an indication of his manliness and courage. Although the man had the power to create life from his seed, his honor, he did so externally to himself in the field of a woman. A man's honor was thus also dependent upon his ability to ensure that the child born was from his own seed. A woman, like arable land, represented an indiscriminate fecundity in which any man might sow his seed. Therefore, just as a farmer marks off land into a field and guards it against outside intrusion, an honorable man would cover and protect his wife, and his daughters and sisters by extension, and thereby bring order to her fecundity and safeguard the legitimacy of his paternity. Positive female shame, on the other hand, reflected a woman's ancillary role in procreation. It was symbolized by the hymen, and also by the veil, and it represented a woman's shyness, timidity, restraint, or sexually exclusive behavior. A woman would display honor by recognizing her position of shame and by acting accordingly. She would share in the honor of her husband by yielding to her husband's ordering of her sexuality; to do otherwise would be shameless. The sexual purity or exclusiveness of the woman was embedded in the honor of the man.

Because the Israelites' experience of their social world also shaped their perception of their bodies, social realities reinforced or challenged a person's gender identity. As long as a man displayed honor by fathering children, ensuring the sexual purity of his wife and daughters, and protecting his reputation, his social behavior affirmed his male gender identity. However, if a man was unable to maintain his honor against the encroachment of others, then he was shamed, that is, dishonored and disgraced. His behavior and shamed status called into question his masculinity. Because male gender identification and male honor were rooted in the active male sexual role, the loss of honor entailed a sexual reversal. By losing honor, a man has lost also his male gender identification. The shamed man has been symbolically penetrated like a woman, and is no longer considered a *real* man. Comparable ethnographies suggest that shamed men are feminized. They are perceived by others as effeminate or emasculated; symbolically, they have become women. Gender identification with women is less fragile. In a male oriented society like ancient Israel, a woman who acts like a man, that is, performs tasks usually taken care of by men, may often be admired or praised, as the biblical examples of the heroine attest. Yet she remains fully a woman, lacking the anatomical parts which are symbolic of manhood, and rarely is her femininity called into question.

GENDER AND THE HOUSE

The gendered division of honor and shame was replicated in the division of labor and the arrangement of space. Just as a man's honor was rooted in his ability to engender and a woman's shame was her recognition of dependence upon a man for procreation, so a man's social orientation was outward and a woman's orientation was inward. Because a woman was perceived to be indiscriminately fecund, her labor and space were ordered to ensure her exclusivity to a man. As a result, a woman modeled shame through her domestic roles, such as raising and educating children and managing the household economy (compare Prov 31:10-31). She carried out her tasks primarily in the home. Outside the home she displayed the honor of her husband and protected her own shame by limiting herself to public spaces dominated by female activities such as the women's market, the well, and public ovens. In contrast, men displayed their honor through work and public activity in space that was common such as the fields and industrial areas, city squares and gates, or exclusively male such as the temple and cultic areas.

The woman was symbolized by the house. Not only is the house the primary locus of female activity, it is homologous to the female body itself. Like the female body, the house is a bounded space with an entrance that is vulnerable to the encroachment of outsiders. It is a social space that a man marks off as belonging uniquely to himself, analogous to selecting a woman for a wife from the available virgin daughters of Israel. Like a wife, the house is sacred to the man, set apart from common, profane space. The house was the social replication of the female body, mirroring the symbolic relationship between the woman and the field. And just as with his field and his wife, the man's honor was symbolized by his house.

The homology of field, woman, and house is explicitly articulated in the Deuteronomic ideology of war. Because the ideology proclaimed that Yahweh would fight for Israel against its enemies, the size of the Israelite army was unimportant. As a result, certain men were excused from battle: the man who had built a new house, but had not yet used it; the man who had planted a vineyard, but had not yet enjoyed, that is, harvested, its fruit; and the betrothed man who had not yet consummated his marriage (Deut 20:5-7). Besides simply noting that a comparable relationship between a man and his field, his wife, and his house is highlighted in this legislation, the Israelite understanding of gender offers an explanation for why men in these particular situations were exempt from military service. What is critical in the case of each man is the incomplete nature of his actions where the commitment of his honor is concerned. In each case, the man had committed his honor, his manhood, without the sufficient opportunity for his claim to honor to be socially recognized. His manhood remained in the balance. Because his need to defend his honor was paramount, the man was freed from military service lest the battle deprive him of this right, and thereby deprive him of his honor. Elsewhere, the Deuteronomic legislation builds on this ideology by stating that the newly married man was exempt for one year from military or other public service (Deut 24:5). The man was given a year's reprieve in order to demonstrate his honor by impregnating his wife, an act which was comparable to enjoying the fruit of his field and living in his own house.

Because the house was symbolic of a woman's body, the boundary of the house was critical to the man's honor. The man must guard the entrance to his house, protecting the household from unwanted intruders. An outsider's unwelcome intrusion into the house threatened the household and brought shame upon the man of the house if not repelled. For this reason, a creditor who gave a loan to a man must wait outside the man's house to receive his pledge. He could not enter the house to take the pledge for himself (Deut 24:10-11). Such an act would have deprived the debtor of honor, and would have been symbolically comparable to raping the women of his house.

This symbolic relationship between a man's house and the women of his household is further illustrated by the Deuteronomic legislation concerning a man who charged that his wife was not a virgin at marriage. According to the legislation, if no evidence of her virginity could be found, the husband's charge was deemed true. The woman should be stoned to death by the men of the town at the entrance of her father's house because she had committed a shameful act by prostituting herself in her father's house (Deut 22:13-21). For our purposes, what is significant to note in this legislation is twofold. First, the daughter's crime, that she had sexual intercourse prior to marriage, and so shamed her father, was placed in her father's house. This was a symbolic identification rather than the geographic location of the crime. The sexual rights to the daughter belonged to the father to give as he saw fit; like a field, she was an economic resource of the household exchangeable through marriage. The sexual violation of his daughter, therefore, represented an unlawful invasion into the father's house. Second, the execution of the daughter should take place at the location which symbolized the daughter's crime. The daughter's vagina was symbolized by the entrance to her father's house. The participation of the men of the city in her execution further sanctioned and reinforced the sacred boundaries represented by the house and the women of the household.

GENDER AND THE CITY

Scholars have long noted that cities in ancient Israel, especially Jerusalem and Samaria, are commonly presented in the Bible with feminine images. The city is presented as a virgin daughter, a wife, a mother, a widow, and a whore. However, apart from drawing attention to the suitability of these feminine metaphors for the city in their particular contexts, scholars have rarely explained how the city as a personified woman fits into the ancient Israelite understanding of gender. I suggest that the city was perceived as a further extension of the symbolic replication of the female body on to the house. The city was the collective house of its citizens; it symbolized the body collective, the socio-political body. Like the family house, the city enclosed space exclusive to its populace; it was bound by a city wall with vulnerable entrances at its gates; and it symbolized the collective honor of its inhabitants.

The biblical texts provide scores of references to the Israelites' collective shame as a result of the people's defeat in battle by their enemies.

Although many of the references describe the Israelites' shame in terms of military defeat generally, without further elaborating on the defeat, a significant number of references connect shame to the invasion and destruction of the people's city. The book of Nehemiah, for example, presents the devastation of Jerusalem as the basis for the people's shame: the city is in ruins, the walls are broken down, and its gates have been burned. As a result, Nehemiah can address the populace, "Come, let us rebuild the wall of Jerusalem, so that we may no longer suffer disgrace" (Neh 2:17). Similarly, the book of Joel laments the shame of the people because Jerusalem is being invaded by a powerful locust army that cannot be stopped: Its warriors "leap upon the city, they run upon the walls; they climb up into the houses, they enter through the windows like a thief" (Joel 2:9).

Because the city was perceived as a female body, an assault against the city was like rape. It was an unwanted violation of the collective body; it was a penetration into the dominion of others; it was a defilement of sacred boundaries. The citizens of the city attempted to defend their collective honor by repelling the invasion, but the loss of the city in battle collectively shamed its populace in a way comparable to a man who is shamed by the rape of the women of his household. The people of the destroyed city were without honor; they were perceived as women, like the female city, that had been raped.

In the prophetic invectives against foreign cities this rape imagery for the destruction of the city is especially prominent. Nahum first challenged the honor of Nineveh by calling her a whore, but her defeat will seal her shame for she will be raped: her skirts will be lifted over her face to expose her nakedness and shame to the nations (Nah 3:5). Moreover, her populace would have no desire to defend their collective honor: her troops would be like women; her gates would be wide open inviting the rape from her foes (Nah 3:13). Jeremiah heralded the coming rape of Babylon, a rape so violent that she would be unable again to bear children, and all who pass by her would be appalled at her wounds (Jer 50:11-16). During this rape, the warriors of the city would have no strength to repel the assault; they would become like women (Jer 51:30). Second Isaiah also proclaimed Babylon's rape: Yahweh would uncover her nakedness and reveal her shame; Yahweh would exact vengeance without encountering any man to defend her honor (Isa 47:3).

GENDER, THE BODY, AND THE HEROINE

Scholars have noted that the heroine in the biblical tradition often acts contrary to gender role expectations. Although few in number, the heroine dominates the biblical stories in which she is presented. She leads her people into battle (Deborah), she single-handedly defeats her enemy (Jael), she saves her people from annihilation (Esther), she preserves the family lineage (Tamar, Ruth), and she undermines her husband's intentions (Rebekah, Abigail). Yet the subversive activities of the heroine were incorporated in texts which were produced by and for Israelite men. The gender role of the heroine, therefore, cannot be separated from the gender expectations of the typically male audience of the stories. I suggest that in the biblical narrative the heroine embodied the concerns and values of Israelite men. Having been repeatedly shamed by the dominant states around them through conquest and exploitation, Israelite men were symbolically like women. The heroine thus functioned as an appropriate symbol in response to this assault on their gender identification. The literary presentation of the heroine represented the Israelites' own desire to overpower their oppressors and regain their honor. This interpretation can be illustrated most clearly through an analysis of gender in the story of Judith.

In the thoroughly fictive book of Judith, Holofernes and his Assyrian army threaten to rape the virgin city of Bethulia, itself set at the entrance to the mountain pass to Jerusalem and the temple of Yahweh, the virgin daughter of Israel. The reason for this assault is stated at the beginning of the book. King Nebuchadnezzar had summoned his western vassals to assist him in his campaign against the king of the Medes, but all disregarded his summons. They shamed Nebuchadnezzar, their suzerain, by thinking lightly of him and sending his messengers back empty-handed (Jdt 1:7-11). In order to restore his honor, Nebuchadnezzar launched a campaign to destroy all those who had disobeyed his command and would not yield to him (Jdt 2:1-13). Through his general Holofernes, Nebuchadnezzar ravaged the peoples' lands, sacked their cities, and killed all who resisted (Jdt 2:21-28). Those who submitted to him were spared, but he destroyed their temples, thereby usurping the honor of their gods (Jdt 3:1-8). The Israelites, however, resisted the Assyrian invasion for the sake of Jerusalem and the temple of Yahweh. They stopped Holofernes and his army at Bethulia.

Bethulia, whose name is resonate with Hebrew *bethulah*, "virgin," embodies the honor of the Israelites like a virgin daughter embodies the honor of a household. If she is captured, all Judea will fall and the house of Yahweh, the temple in Jerusalem, will be plundered (Jdt 8:2 1). Suggesting that God has turned against them, the people of Bethulia demand that the rulers of the city surrender to the Assyrians (Jdt 7:23-28). They would rather suffer the shame of defeat than certain death. Judith, entering the narrative in this context, rebukes the city elders for their willingness to follow the people's demand (Jdt 8:11-17). The city cannot simply surrender to the Assyrians with impunity, for Yahweh's honor is also at stake. As a virgin city, Bethulia represents the sexual exclusiveness of the people, as a woman, to Yahweh. The people know and are devoted to Yahweh alone (Jdt 8:18-20). If, however, Bethulia surrenders to the Assyrian assault, as its populace suggests, she will betray her fidelity to Yahweh. Like a virgin who allows herself to be willingly seduced, she will be disgraced and treated like a whore (Jdt 8:22-23). Rather than surrender, Judith declares that the people should endure their suffering, for by her own hand God will deliver Israel.

Judith, whose name represents the people of Judea, more specifically symbolizes the virgin city. Like Bethulia, she is chaste, devoted exclusively to Yahweh. Moreover, just as Bethulia is threatened by the assault of the Assyrian army endeavoring to restore Nebuchadnezzar's honor, Judith is sexually threatened by Holofernes in his efforts to demonstrate his own honor. Male honor is displayed through sexual prowess, and Holofernes will display his manhood by sexually seducing Judith, a desire he had from the day she entered the Assyrian camp (Jdt 12:16). However, Holofernes' honor also *demands* that he seduce her. Judith's willingness to enter his camp, and even his tent, unprotected by a kinsman invites her own seduction. Holofernes would not be a *real* man if he passed over this opportunity. He would shame himself, and Judith could rightfully laugh at him (Jdt 12:12). So for honor's sake, Holofernes proceeds to seduce Judith, but loses his head in the attempt. Judith defends her honor by removing his honor, that is, his head. She symbolically castrates him, depriving him of his manhood. But at the same time, she removes the honor, the head, of the Assyrian army, bringing disgrace on the house of Nebuchadnezzar (Jdt 14:18), and thereby provides the means for the virgin city Bethulia to repel her rapist.

In defending herself against the assault of Holofernes, Judith acts like any honorable woman should. She also acts like a man when she speaks out against the elders of the city and takes the initiative to defend the people's collective honor. Their collective honor, symbolized by the virgin city itself, should be defended by the men of the city. Judith not only symbolizes the virgin city but also the men of the city. Her gender role reversal is made explicit in her prayer to Yahweh where she identifies with her ancestor Simeon. Just as Simeon took vengeance on the Shechemites for their rape of the virgin Dinah, she hopes to be used by Yahweh to crush the Assyrian threat (Jdt 9:2-10).

The Israelites' male gender role of defending their virgin city is appropriately symbolized by the woman Judith, for the people of Judea had been collectively shamed. They had been repeatedly defeated and victimized by powerful empires, and they remained in subjugation to them. The most notable assailant was Nebuchadnezzar himself, who not only raped the cities of the land, but also violated the very house of Yahweh. The people of Judea were like a woman, unable to repel her assailants. Yet Judith's heroic defense of the virgin city symbolized the hope of a shamed Israel. The people can overthrow their oppressors even as the woman Judith subdues her seducer. When the people remain devoted to Yahweh, their enemies can be struck down even by the hand of a woman.

The literary character of Judith and the populace of Bethulia illustrate in vibrant detail the thesis which we have been arguing throughout this essay: gender is socially constructed, and in ancient Israel gender roles were a social expression of the Israelites' understanding of their bodies in procreation. Shaped by their experiences of subsistence agriculture, the ancient Israelites perceived the male body to be the producer of seed and the female body to be like land, a depository for the seed. As the active agent in procreation, a man's gender role was characterized by honor, and he displayed his honor by ensuring the sexual exclusiveness of the women over which he had authority. When a man was unable to protect his wife or daughter, or when he himself was subdued by other men, that man was shamed. His male gender role was challenged, and he was perceived symbolically to be like a woman. The shame of a woman, on the other hand, was an expression of her ancillary role in procreation. Without possession of seed, a woman's gender role was both dependent upon and vulnerable to men. She had to submit to her father, her brothers, and finally her husband, lest any other man indiscriminately "sow seed" in her. These male and female social roles were replicated in gendered structures of space, the house, and the city. The body served as a gendered symbol of ancient Israelite society.

SOURCES

Bechtel, Lyn M.
1995 "Genesis 2:4b-3:24: A Myth about Human Maturation." *Journal for the Study of the Old Testament* 67: 3-26.

Delaney, Carol
1987 "Seeds of Honor, Fields of Shame." Pp. 35-48 in *Honor and Shame and the Unity of the Mediterranean*. Edited by D. D. Gilmore. Washington DC: American Anthropological Association.

Douglas, Mary
1966 *Purity and Danger: An Analysis of the Concepts of Pollution and Taboo*. London: Ark.
1970 *Natural Symbols in Cosmology*. New York: Pantheon.

Galambush, Julie
1993 "'*adam* from '*adama*, '*ishshah* from '*ish*: "Derivation and Subordination in Genesis 2.4b-3.24." Pp. 33-46 in *History and Interpretation: Essays in Honour of John H. Hayes*. Edited by M. P. Graham et al. Sheffield: Sheffield Academic Press.

Geertz, Clifford
1973 *The Interpretation of Cultures*. New York: Basic Books.

Gilmore, David D., ed.
1987 *Honor and Shame and the Unity of the Mediterranean*. Special Publication of the American Anthropological Association, 22. Washington D.C.: American Anthropological Association.

Hiebert, Theodore
1996 *The Yahwist's Landscape: Nature and Religion in Early Israel*. New York: Oxford University Press.

Lanser, Susan S.
1988 "(Feminist) Criticism in the Garden: Inferring Genesis 2-3." *Semeia* 41: 67-84.

Levine, Amy-Jill
1995 "Sacrifice and Salvation: Otherness and Domestication in the Book of Judith." Pp. 208-23 in *A Feminist Companion to Esther, Judith and Susanna*. Edited by A. Brenner. Sheffield: Sheffield Academic Press.

Matthews, Victor H. and Don C. Benjamin, eds.
1994 "Honor and Shame in the World of the Bible." *Semeia* 68 (Published in 1996).

Meyers, Carol
1988 *Discovering Eve Ancient Israelite Women in Context.* New York: Oxford University Press.
Oden, Robert A.
1981 "Divine Aspirations in Atrahasis and in Genesis 1-11." *Zeitschrift fur die alttestamentliche Wissenschaft* 93: 197-216.
Olyan, Saul M.
1996 "Honor, Shame, and Covenant Relations in Ancient Israel and Its Environment." *Journal of Biblical Literature* 115: 201-18.
Ortner, Sherry B. and Harriet Whitehead
1981 "Introduction: Accounting for Sexual Meanings." Pp. 1-27 in *Sexual Meanings: The Cultural Construction of Gender and Sexuality.* Edited by S. B. Ortner and H. Whitehead. Cambridge: Cambridge University Press.
Simkins, Ronald A.
1994 *Creator and Creation: Nature in the Worldview of Ancient Israel.* Peabody, MA: Hendrickson.
1994 "Return to Yahweh: Honor and Shame in Joel." *Semeia* 68: 41-54.
1998 "Gender Construction in the Yahwist Creation Myth." Pp. 32-52 in *Feminist Companion to the Bible (Second Series).* Edited by A. Brenner Sheffield: Sheffield Academic Press.
Trible, Phyllis
1978 *God and the Rhetoric of Sexuality.* Philadelphia: Fortress.
Yanagisako, S. J. and J. F. Collier.
1987 "Toward a Unified Analysis of Gender and Kinship." Pp. 14-15 in *Gender and Kinship: Essays Toward a Unified Analysis.* Edited by J. F. Collier and S. J. Yanagisako. Stanford: Stanford University Press.

By Grit and Grace:
Women and the Early Christian Frontier

Susan A. Calef

"History is lived in the main by the unknown and forgotten."

—Arthur M. Schlesinger, Jr., "Introduction," *Pioneer Women: Voices from
the Kansas Frontier*

Mention of America's western frontier conjures up in the imagination the
figures of Wild Bill Hickok and Buffalo Bill, Jesse James and General
Custer, cowboys and Indians, gunslingers and lawmen. Women, if visible
at all on this mindscape, are reduced to stereotype or myth: the notorious
Calamity Jane or the madam with a heart of gold exemplified by Miss Kitty
of Gunsmoke fame. Similarly, a litany of men's names dominates early
Christian history: Peter and Paul, James and John, Ignatius and Irenaeus,
Justin and Polycarp. Both histories amply illustrate Arthur Schlesinger,
Jr.'s observation, "Women have constituted the most spectacular casualty
of history."[1]

    If traditional historiography consigned women to the "dustbin of
history," modern social historians, determined to limn a more complete
picture, have devised techniques with which to achieve "the silent, mathe-
matical resurrection of a total past."[2] The women's movement and the
emergence of feminism in the 1960s, which made women a suitable subject
of study in all disciplines, have insured that women share in that resurrection. Indeed, scholars in various fields have been restoring women to the
historical record and to our imagination. Glenda Riley and Joanna Stratton,
for example, have recovered pioneer women of the prairie and plains, in the
process rectifying puerile stereotypes associated with the few who enjoy

name recognition, such as Calamity Jane and Annie Oakley, and chronicling the daily life of the anonymous majority.[3] Writing revisionist history is fraught with difficulty, of course. The crucial literary sources are androcentric (they assume the male is the norm), and elitist (they focus solely on the powerful few who dominated). They give the lion's share of attention, therefore, to what men, specifically the elite men of power, were doing. Material illuminating the lives of women is sorely lacking.

The paucity and nature of the sources, however, formidable obstacles though they may be, are not insurmountable. Scholars working on pioneer women in America have patiently unearthed enlightening sources penned by women themselves, a goldmine of information previously overlooked or dismissed; women's diaries, private letters, business correspondence. Historians of early Christianity are not as fortunate. Nowhere is the following observation regarding the challenges that early Christian scholarship faces more apt than when attention turns to women: "It is both our privilege and our accursed lot to work the flinty soil of a long-extinct and deeply reticent world ... a Christianity whose back is firmly turned toward us, untroubled by our own most urgent, and legitimate, questions."[4] The literary material is largely prescriptive, telling us more about an author's or culture's ideals than the reality of women's lives. Because women's own voices are nowhere to be heard, we cannot claim to recover the subjective experience of the women we seek to know.[5]

This essay will introduce readers to some of the early Christian women currently being retrieved by scholars, many of them women who, like those they study, have ventured into uncharted territory, a scholarly frontier of sorts, with all the attendant hazards and risks, all the excitement and challenges.[6] The women who pioneered America's plains set their faces westward and toward their future, vast stretches of land between them and their destination. As modern readers we set our faces to the past, almost twenty centuries stretching between us and our destination, the first century of the Christian movement, and eastward, to the Mediterranean basin, an equally vast expanse of earth and cultural distance between us and our faith-ancestors. This study will demonstrate that women were indeed active pioneers on the early Christian frontier, making contributions that until recently were left untold. Women may only now be making it into "History," the recorded past; but women were making "history" at the dawn of Christianity.[7] Then, as now, Christian life could not go on without them.

WOMEN ON THE EARLY CHRISTIAN FRONTIER

What can we know about early Christian women? Constraints of space require that this treatment of the question be limited to the earliest period of Christian history, the first century of the Common Era, for which the New Testament is our major informant. Extracting historical information from New Testament texts is not a straightforward procedure. Some texts are better suited to the task than others. Excavation through the multiple layers of tradition contained in the Gospels to determine what can be known about early Christian women requires far more space than is allotted here. The Pauline letters, which afford more direct access to the demographics of early Christian communities, including their women, will be our focus. From these letters and the Acts of the Apostles, one scholar has compiled a Christian "Who's Who?" of almost eighty persons, of whom approximately one-fifth are women.[8] These early texts provide tantalizing glimpses of the activities of those women who, together with their male counterparts, pioneered the settlement of a frontier of sorts, a Mediterranean basin previously unpopulated by Christians. Let us turn now to that "flinty soil," the Pauline evidence.

Generally, in the work of historical reconstruction descriptive references are considered more appropriate to the task than prescriptive. Prescriptive material, however, ought not be dismissed out of hand, for it too can provide a window onto the life of women in the Pauline communities. In the case of Paul's letters, we can imaginatively read between the lines to reconstruct the women and situations that his prescriptions aim to address.

1 CORINTHIANS

Paul's first letter to the Corinthians illustrates well the possibilities and challenges of the task. Although descriptive material is sparse, some of its ample prescriptive material proves to be a valuable source of information about women of the community. Ostensibly Paul writes in response to a letter the Corinthians sent him (7:1) seeking advice on various matters (chs. 7-15). In addition, a delegation, "Chloe's people," apparently has brought report of problems in the community (1:11). Chloe is one of two women named in the letter, along with Prisca (16:19); her mention apart from a man suggests that she is the head of her own household. Who her "people" are is not indicated. Most commentators suspect they are slaves or freed-persons of Chloe's household. The fact that Paul expects the name to be recognized by the Corinthians to whom he writes suggests Chloe was a figure of prominence in the community; she and her household were, perhaps, the nucleus of a congregation that met in her house. In any case, this brief mention introduces us, at the very least, to a woman who takes initiative on behalf of the community, seeking the counsel of its founder when divisiveness threatens its membership. Paul, it appears, does not disapprove of her initiative.

Information about anonymous women in the Corinthian community may be gleaned from Paul's comments about marriage and sexuality in chapter 7. His advice to persons married to a pagan spouse (7:12-16) is especially significant because it suggests the precarious situation that some early Christian women faced. Some non-believers, apparently, were not content to remain married to Christians and were treating the believing spouses with hostility. Although explicit reference to suffering is lacking, Paul's affirmation "for God called us to peace" (7:15) has been construed as implying strife between spouses.[9] This situation of mixed marriages seems to have raised for Christians the question whether they should divorce pagan spouses.

In Greco-Roman culture, mixed marriages would indeed have occa-sioned household strife, for it was expected that a wife accept her hus-band's gods.[10] Because references to male believers' entry into the church with their households suggests that wives usually shared their husbands' allegiances from the outset (Acts 18:8; 1 Cor 1:16), we may suspect that strife-ridden mixed marriages obtained more often when women were the believers in Christ.[11] In face of the pervasive cultural assumption that a wife's fidelity included acceptance of her husband's customs and religion, a woman's decision to become a Christian undoubtedly took tremendous initiative and courage. Her choice could cost a woman her marriage if the pagan spouse wished to divorce her, as our reading between the lines of 1 Cor 7:12-16 indicates. Although this would free her to marry a Christian, there were serious reasons why a woman might want to remain married, even to a non-believer. The financial loss that could be incurred was but one consideration. Because children belonged to their father according to Roman law, and would remain with him upon dissolution of marriage, divorce meant loss of her children and loss of the opportunity to evangelize them.[12] That a woman who converted without her husband also risked abuse is attested by references to pagan husbands' cruelty to their Christian wives, confirming that life in "a house divided" could be hazardous indeed.[13]

Her husband's hostility was not a woman's only worry. Women married to unbelievers also had to contend with intense public scrutiny. The scorn that could be directed toward a woman who dared to reject her husband's gods is revealed in Lucius Apuleius' memorable description of the marriage between a baker and the woman who worshipped "a God whom she called only." His invective heaps accusations upon her: "There was not one single vice which that woman lacked, but all crimes flowed together into her heart like into a filthy latrine; cruel, perverse, man-crazy, drunken, stubborn, obstinate, avaricious in petty theft, wasteful in sumptuous expenses, an enemy to faith and chastity."[14] In a society that put a premium on public reputation, slander such as this was daunting indeed.[15] Inasmuch, therefore, as early Christian women married to non-believers risked and even suffered much for their faith, they may be considered forerunners of the later women martyrs, Perpetua, Felicity, Blandina, Agnes. Unfortunately, unlike the martyrs whose deaths earned them a place of glory and honor in Christian memory, the anonymous women glimpsed here have been overlooked and forgotten.

Paul's position is that mixed marriages ought to be preserved if at all possible. The crux of his reasoning emerges in the question posed at the climax of his argument: "How do you know whether you will save your spouse?" (7:16). His hope that mixed marriages will produce new members for the church clearly envisages the evangelizing potential of household relations. Because traditionally both Greeks and Romans assigned the private space of the household to women, we may imagine that women were central to the evangelizing potential Paul had in mind. Within the domestic sphere a woman could touch the lives of the many members of the extended household: husband, children, slaves, freedmen, hired workers, even perhaps clients and business associates of the family, as well as tenants and partners in trade or craft. That women often brought the men of their families to the Christian faith is widely attested, first in the New Testament, which provides this testimony to women's role in the transmission of faith: "I am reminded of your sincere faith, a faith that lived first in your Grandmother Lois and your mother Eunice." (2 Tim 1:5).[16] The role of the woman evangelist glimpsed here expresses what anthropologist Jill Dubisch calls a "cultural acknowledgment of female power."[17] Although the power of these women was not granted authority, it was deemed effective: women could win their husbands, and Paul knew it.

Further information about women in Corinth can be gleaned from 1 Cor 11:2-16, a text on which an enormous amount of ink has been spilt. To date, a consensus about the exact nature of the behavior Paul targets has eluded scholarship. Is the issue women's head-covering (veils) or the hairstyles of men and women? Is Paul refuting the pagan practice of men covering their heads when sacrificing? Is he trying to control women prophets? Despite the tortuous reasoning and translation difficulties that leave us in the dark on the main issue, the text sheds light on our interest: women prayed and prophesied aloud in the Christian assembly (11:5). Significantly, Paul quibbles not with their right to do this but with the manner in which they do it.

Prophecy, which was considered a gift of the Spirit, flourished in the Church for centuries, including among women. No single individual or group could claim a monopoly on the gift, and conflicts arose between rival prophets. The book of Revelation, written in the late first century by a Christian prophet named John, reflects such conflicts. In it John admonishes the church at Thyatira for following a rival woman prophet. Claiming the authority of Christ for his own point of view, he smears his rival by the scornful epithet "Jezebel," evoking the treacherous queen of 1 Kings 16-21, and by the accusation that she teaches Christians to practice sexual immorality and to eat food sacrificed to pagan deities (Rev 2:18-20).[18] John's name-calling ought not obscure the fact that we have here evidence of the leadership of women in late first century Asia Minor.[19] His hostile caricature of her surely implies that she had enough of a following to pose a threat. Significantly, like Paul, John does not claim that the woman has no right to prophesy, nor does he question her right to teach; it is, rather, to the content of her prophecy and teaching that he objects.

One more passage of 1 Corinthians pertinent to our interest is 14:33b-36. The text reads,

As in all the churches of the saints, women should be silent in the churches. For they are not permitted to speak, but should be subordinate, as the law also says. If there is anything they desire to know, let them ask their husbands at home. For it is shameful for a woman to speak in church.

This stricture conforms to the societal injunction that women remain silent when in public space, the realm of discourse that belonged to men. Oddly, it appears to contradict 1 Cor 11:5, which assumes that women speak, pray, and prophesy, in the assembly. It also interrupts the flow of Paul's argument about prophecy (cf. 14:33 and 14:37). Several manuscripts place these verses after 14:40, indicating that ancient commentators already recognized these problems. As a solution, recent scholarship has proposed that the passage was not composed by Paul but is a later interpolation, introduced into the letter perhaps to bring it in line with the explicit prohibition against women teaching in 1 Tim 2:12.[20] If authentic, it suggests that some married women were speaking out in the assembly. The identity of the women and the character of their speech are clarified by the question Paul poses in hope of silencing them: "Or did the word of God originate with you?" The phrase "word of God" suggests the women were uttering inspired or ecstatic speech and, therefore, they were prophetesses entitled to weigh what was said and to ask questions.[21] In the absence of any reference to guiding leadership or a chairperson, which suggests the Pauline assembly met simply under the guidance of the Spirit, it is not difficult to imagine how ecstatic behavior could cause problems. The very nature of ecstatic experiences meant anyone could have them. In the Corinthian community apparently the Spirit, unconstrained by society's status- and gender-bound channels of authority, inspired the word of God in many, including women. Paul's call for silence and submission are his seemingly exasperated response to the "virtual cacophony of individual expressions" that resulted.[22]

PHILIPPIANS

Paul's letter to the Philippians, supplemented by the Acts of the Apostles, affords a glimpse of women in another community the apostle had founded. Acts informs us that many women were converted by Paul's gospel, among them one named Lydia "a seller of purple, of the city of Thyatira" (Acts 16:11-15, 40).[23] She was probably a freedwoman, as her name, the Lydian, indicates. Gathered with other women on the Sabbath, she was a "god-fearer," a gentile worshiper of the Jewish God. Upon hearing Paul's preaching, Lydia converted and was baptized along with her household. In the absence of any mention of a husband, we may surmise that she was the female head of her household. Luke also tells us that she welcomed the

Apostle and his associates into her home and that subsequently the church met in her house (16:15, 40). That Lydia owned a home large enough to accommodate guests and host a house church suggests she was a woman of some means. It is likely that her resources were related to her business; the purple goods in which she deals were a coveted luxury sold at high price in antiquity.[24] If the Lukan account is historically accurate, then the church at Philippi was founded among women, and it first met in the home of Lydia, an independent merchant woman with material and spiritual authority over her household.

The letter to the Philippians names two women, Euodia and Syntyche (4:2) who, if the information in Acts 16 about Lydia is trustworthy, follow in her footsteps in the Philippian church. Apparently, there is strife between the two, and Paul writes to urge them "to be of the same mind in the Lord" (4:2). Nothing in the reference itself allows us to determine the nature of the strife between them. We ought not assume it a case of petty personal disagreements. Strife between male co-workers was also a reality in the early mission. Paul, for example, had sharp disagreements with more than one associate, Barnabas, John Mark, and Peter, resulting in a parting of ways (Acts 13:5-13; 15:37-39; Gal 2:11-14). We know his rift with Peter was over the serious matter of table fellowship with Gentile believers. The case in Philippi, we may suspect, was no less serious. One commentator has offered the plausible suggestion that Paul's plea "be of the same mind" hints at what is at stake. According to Roman legal traditions, the equal partnership, into which the Philippians and Paul had entered was operative "as long as the partners are ... 'of the same mind' about the centrality of the purpose around which the partnership was formed in the first place."[25] That partnership was jeopardized by the strife between Euodia and Syntyche; hence, Paul's entreaty to "be of the same mind" reminded them of their original shared partnership and commitment to the gospel.[26]

Paul subsequently requests that an unidentified figure whom he addresses as "loyal companion" help these women. His request includes an explanation of why they deserve assistance: "they have struggled beside me in the work of the gospel together with Clement and the rest of my co-workers" (4:3). The image of struggling side by side as in an athletic contest affirms the equal footing on which these women work with Paul and other male workers and indicates they, too, are his co-workers. Elsewhere Paul uses the term "co-worker" to refer to itinerant workers who traveled to spread the gospel.[27] The use of the term here thus suggests

Euodia and Syntyche were a missionary team dedicated to gospel proclamation.[28]

Later evidence indicates that women continued to be active in the post-
Pauline churches of Philippi. The letter of Polycarp to the Philippians, for
example, provides evidence of an order of widows in the mid-second
century. Though the precise nature of their duties is not indicated, it is clear
these women were expected to live exemplary lives and offer public and
private prayers for all. The Acts of Paul, which includes a fragmentary
section dealing with Philippi, tells of a man named Longinus who orders
the death of his daughter Frontina when she is converted to a celibate way
of life by Paul's preaching. Although apocryphal acts such as this are
generally considered legendary, their portrayal of women indicates that an
ascetic form of Christianity was practiced and especially attractive to
women in and around Philippi in the late second or early third century.
Graves associated with two basilicas in Philippi bear several inscriptions
from the fourth to sixth centuries listing women as deacons and canonesses.[29] Unfortunately, we do not know the specific roles these women
played in church life.[30] If the church structure at Philippi was presbyteral,
as some have suggested, then female deacons and canonesses might have
been more important in these congregations than in others.[31] That women
played a significant role in the Philippian church for centuries is unsurpris-
ing in view of what we know of women's patronage and their civic and
religious activities in the region. Study of inscriptional evidence has revealed that well-to-do women maintained temples, sponsored festivals, and
acted as priestesses.[32] Given this cultural heritage, if it hoped to attract
these women, accustomed to prominent roles in pagan cults, it is unlikely
that the growing Christian community could deny them a comparable
prominence in their newly-adopted religion.

ROMANS

The most informative yet neglected testimony to the activities of women
in the Pauline communities is the list of greetings in Romans 16. Whether
this chapter actually belonged originally to this letter or to another is a
textual issue that need not concern us. Insofar as the chapter is considered
authentically Pauline and, therefore, reflects the life of Pauline communities, the textual issue does not affect what this chapter reveals about women

in first-century Christian communities. I assume the chapter is an integral part of the Romans letter.

Paul's opening commendation and long list of greetings includes some thirty names, of which eight are women: Phoebe, Prisca, Mary, Junia, Tryphaena and Tryphosa, Persis, Julia. In addition, two unnamed women are mentioned, Rufus' mother and the sister of Nereus, and we may suppose that still more women were among "the family of Aristobulus" (16:10), "the family of Narcissus" (16:11), and "all the saints" referred to in 16:15. We are told nothing more than the names of three of the women: the mother of Rufus (v. 13), Julia, and the sister of Nereus (v. 15).[33] Three other women are singled-out for their work or labor: "Mary, who has worked very hard among you" (16:6); "those workers in the Lord, Tryphaena and Tryphosa" (16:12); and "beloved Persis, who has worked hard in the Lord" (16:12). Paul uses the verb "laboring" (*kopiontes*) for various works in the missionary enterprise and the building up of the communities. According to 1 Cor 16:15, the co-workers and laborers are those who have "devoted themselves to the service (*diakonia*) of the saints." That the role of laborer was invested with authority is indicated by Paul's admonition to the Corinthians, "be subject to every co-worker and laborer" (1 Cor 16:16). Similarly, he urged the Thessalonians to "respect those who labor among you, and have charge of you in the Lord and admonish you; esteem them very highly in love because of their work" (1 Thess 5:12).[34] We may suppose that these women, whose work Paul deems worthy of mention, shared in the authority of such laborers.

Paul's references to three other women provide more detailed prosopographical information. Pride of place in the chapter is given to Phoebe of whom Paul writes, "I commend to you our sister Phoebe, a deacon of the church at Cenchreae, so that you may welcome her in the Lord as is fitting for the saints, and help her in whatever she may require from you, for she has been a benefactor of many and of myself as well" (16:1-2). Her mythological name suggests Phoebe was a Gentile, perhaps a freedwoman. In the absence of any mention of a husband, she, like Lydia, appears to have been independent of a patriarchal household. Phoebe is traveling to Rome, and Paul introduces her to the Roman Christians in the hope they will extend to her proper hospitality. His commendation probably implies that Phoebe has been entrusted with the task of carrying his letter to Rome. Thus, in his words, we glimpse a woman serving the church in an itinerant capacity.

Phoebe is recommended to the hospitality of Christians in three substantive titles, "sister," "deacon of the church at Cenchreae," and "benefactor of many and myself as well." Just as Timothy, similarly commended by Paul elsewhere (1 Cor 16:10-11), is called "brother" (2 Cor 1:1; 1 Thess 3:2; Phlm 1), Phoebe is called "sister." It is possible that the designation "sister," like "brother," meant nothing more than fellow Christian. However, given the evidence that brother was also used to refer to a relatively limited group of workers (e.g., Phil 4:21) who had the Christian mission and/or ministry as their primary occupation, we may assume that its feminine counterpart sister could also be used to refer to a missionary co-worker.[35]

Unfortunately, English translations of the text have tended to obscure the significance of the two additional titles ascribed to Phoebe. For example, when the first of them, *diakonos*, is used with reference to Paul or another male, commentators translate it "minister," "servant," "missionary," or "deacon." In the case of Phoebe, however, *diakonos* is often rendered "deaconess" and understood in terms of the later deaconess (*diakonissa*) whose position within the hierarchy of roles that eventually emerged was clearly subordinate and whose duties were gender-specific: caring for the sick and poor of her own sex, instructing women catechumens, being present at interviews of women with bishops, priests, or deacons, assisting at the baptism of women.[36] Phoebe, however, is termed *diakonos*, not *diakonissa*,[37] and in the earliest Pauline churches it is not apparent that the later development subordinating deacons to bishops had yet occurred.[38] We have no indication that her work was restricted solely to women. In the absence of evidence to the contrary, we should assume that at this early stage of the Christian movement the functions of male and female deacons or ministers were similar.

Pauline usage should be the determining factor in translation of such terms. Analysis of the terminology Paul uses for his circle of associates reveals frequent use of the term *diakonos* in tandem with co-worker (*synergos*) and worker (*ergates*), both of which refer to itinerant workers. The term is used more precisely with reference to preaching activity and also to those entrusted to teach the mysteries of God.[39] *Diakonos*, therefore, designates a special class of co-workers engaged in preaching or teaching as missionaries or as workers in local congregations.[40] In Phoebe's case, the possessive qualifier, "of the church of Cenchreae," suggests that she is a local leader rather than an itinerant missionary. Gal 6:6 implies that this type of worker deserved to be paid by the community. Therefore, since nothing in Paul's letters indicates that only men were real *diakonoi*, we may imagine that the deacon Phoebe was paid for her service.

The third title Phoebe bears, *prostatis*, is often translated "helper." This translation has the effect, again, of obscuring the significance of her activity and assigning her a subordinate role. In contemporaneous literature, the term often meant leading officer, president, superintendent. It is difficult, however, to see how this meaning could be intended since Paul claims that Phoebe was a *prostatis* of many and of himself. Another of its attested meanings seems far more likely, namely, *patrona*, patron or benefactor. The title suggests that Phoebe was a woman who had wealth at her disposal and acted as a patron of many Christians, including Paul. This rendering of the term is plausible, given what we know of women's patronage of groups in the Greco-Roman world.[41] Both private associations and Christian groups depended in part on the beneficence of wealthier persons, including women, whose patronage consisted in financial support, hospitality, and exerting influence on behalf of clients.[42] Apparently, Paul and many others stood in a patron-client relationship with Phoebe and, in accordance with the exchange law of Greco-Roman patronage, he requests that the Roman community provide her with whatever she needs during her stay as repayment for her benefactions.[43]

A further intriguing suggestion regarding what Paul requests on behalf of Phoebe is worth noting. A recent commentator contends that in her capacity as patron Phoebe had agreed to underwrite the mission to Spain, a project of vital significance to Paul and to the letter he is writing (Rom 15:24-5). The text of Rom 16 was written, then, in anticipation of her departure for Rome where she was to create the logistical base for the Spanish mission while Paul was delivering the Jerusalem collection. What Paul was requesting for Phoebe, according to this theory, was not simply the hospitality due a patron but also cooperation with her in the patronage that this mission would require.[44] The list of greetings that follows Phoebe's commendation ought then to be understood as comparable to "a roster of potential campaign supporters that political operatives bring into a city as they begin to establish a campaign for their candidate."[45]

Paul's commendation of Phoebe is followed by his greeting to Prisca, or the diminutive form Priscilla in Acts, one of the few women mentioned more than once in the New Testament. Not only Paul (Rom 16:3; 1 Cor 16:19) but also Luke (Acts 18: 2-3, 18, 26-27) and one of the Pastorals (2

Tim 4:19) preserve memory of her, always with Aquila, who is presumed to have been her husband. The remarkable fact that Prisca's name is mentioned before her husband's in four of these occurrences (Rom 16:3; 2 Tim 4:19; Acts 18:18, 26)[46] is generally interpreted as suggesting either her higher social status or her greater prominence in the Christian community.[47]

The couple appears in Acts 18 in the context of Paul's second missionary journey. There Luke tells us that in Corinth Paul encountered a Jew named Aquila, a native of Pontus, who had recently come from Italy with his wife Priscilla, because Claudius had ordered all Jews to leave Rome. Paul went to see them and, because he was of the same trade, tentmaker, he stayed with them and they worked together. From this we learn, first, that Priscilla and her husband were Jews and that they were Christians before meeting Paul.[48] When Claudius banished Jews from Rome they moved to Corinth where they accepted Paul as a co-worker in their trade of leatherworking or tent-making.[49] By the time Paul arrived, apparently they were well established in the city, had a house into which they welcomed him, and provided him with shelter and work.

The Lukan account further informs us about this couple in 18:24-26. After accompanying Paul to Ephesus where he took leave of them, Priscilla and Aquila encountered Apollos, an eloquent Jewish Christian from Alexandria, who spoke boldly in the synagogue (18:24-26) but apparently not accurately enough. "When Priscilla and Aquila heard him," Luke tells us, "they took him aside and explained the way of God to him more accurately" (18:26). Evidently, their instruction of Apollos was effective. Two verses later Luke reports a success for which the couple would seem to deserve partial credit: in Achaia "he [Apollos] powerfully refuted the Jews in public, showing by the scriptures that the Messiah is Jesus" (18:28). We meet here, then, an early Christian woman knowledgeable enough to correct the insufficient teachings of the learned Alexandrian.[50]

Paul's greeting of the couple in Rom 16:3-4 enables us to add four additional bits of information to the picture of Prisca sketched in Acts 18:1-28. First, Paul speaks of her and Aquila as "my fellow workers (*synergous*) in Christ Jesus." As already observed, this title indicates that she and her husband were itinerant missionaries. Their work as tentmakers likely underwrote the couple's missionary activities, while their missionary travels provided new venues in which to ply their trade. New Testament references that allow us to trace at least some of their movements attest the role of travel in their lives as missionary artisans: from Pontus to Rome, from Rome to Corinth, from Corinth to Ephesus, back to Rome. Part of their journeying was done as companions and fellow workers of Paul, but they also seem to have worked independently of him.

Second, Paul tells us they "risked their necks for my life," though we are told nothing of what this entailed. It is possible that it occurred during the riot that Paul's preaching caused at Ephesus (Acts 19:23-40).[51] Third, knowledge of their missionary work and of the risks they took on Paul's behalf evidently was widespread in the Gentile churches, for Paul subsequently declares that to them "not only I give thanks but also all the churches of the Gentiles" (16:4). Fourth, as in Ephesus (1 Cor 16:19), they hosted a church in their house in Rome (16:5). Unfortunately, we have little solid evidence regarding the relationship that obtained between Prisca and Aquila and those who met in their house, whether the host(s) enjoyed precedence and authority in the community. The answer depends on how Christians understood their organization. If as a household, then the head of the household would be expected to exercise authority over the group;[52] if as a voluntary association, structured according to the patron-client relationship, then well-to-do members who acted as hosts probably expected the community to return the favor in some way, for example, by bestowal of honor upon their patron(ess).

Still another woman of the Christian past deserves resurrection from the interment to which a scribal error consigned her for centuries. Verse 7 includes two names, the second of which could be either masculine (Junias) or feminine (Junia).[53] Until recently major translations rendered it Junias, despite the fact that to date the masculine name is unattested in Greek and Latin literature or inscriptions, whereas the feminine Junia is amply attested. In this instance the description of the two persons as "prominent among the apostles" seems to have been determinative of translators' decision. On the assumption that women could not be apostles, let alone prominent ones, they reasoned that the name had to be masculine. Recent scholarship, however, has accepted Junia as the preferred reading and regards the name Junias as a clerical error, introduced into the manuscript tradition by a scribe, probably on the assumption that women could not or should not be apostles. The recent rendering of the text enjoys the support of the earliest commentators on Romans. Origen of Alexandria, Jerome, and John Chrysostom all understood the name as referring to a woman.[54]

What does Paul's greeting tell us about her? He describes Junia and

Andronicus as "my relatives" or "my kinsmen," indicating that Junia, like Prisca, was a Jew. The last words of the verse, "they were in Christ before I was," indicate that she and her husband had become Christians before Paul, which would place them among some of the earliest believers. As Jews with Greek names, both may have been freedpersons. Junia and her husband are also called "apostles," a term which in Pauline usage designates a special class of *diakonoi*, deacons or ministers, those who do the same work of preaching and teaching but are distinguished by the claim of a direct, divine commission.[55] As its Greek derivation suggests, "one sent," the title refers to those sent forth as authorized evangelists.[56] We have here, then, another instance of the missionary partnership involving wife and husband, Prisca and Aquila, or same-sex pairs, Euodia and Syntyche, that seems to have been common practice among early Christians.

Paul singles out Junia and her husband as prominent or outstanding among the apostles. That is, he considers this woman and her husband outstanding within the larger circle of those called apostles. His approbation is probably based on their suffering imprisonment for the sake of the gospel, which he takes care to mention. It is well to recall that Paul understood the apostolic career, his own included, as a mimesis or imitation of the crucified Christ raised by God from the dead. The mark of true apostleship, in Paul's view, was not eloquent speech and mighty pneumatic displays but patient endurance of the hardships that missionary work could entail (1 Cor 4:8-13; 2 Cor 11-12). Junia and Andronicus, having suffered imprisonment, fulfilled these criteria and Paul singled them out as "outstanding among the apostles."

This seemingly innocuous list of closing greetings provides important evidence of the diverse roles of women in Pauline communities. Three of the four terms Paul uses elsewhere for himself and his male associates are ascribed to women in this text: "fellow-worker," Priscilla, Mary, Tryphaena and Tryphosa; "deacon" or "minister," Phoebe; "apostle," Junia. The fourth term, "brothers," implies the inclusion of women; and its feminine counterpart "sister" is used of Phoebe. The terminology, unfortunately, provides no precise information regarding the tasks attached to each role. Women's inclusion in the crucial tasks of the initial mission, however, seems to be taken as a matter of course. Like their male counterparts, women worked hard in the mission; and Paul saw fit to greet them by name just as he does the men.

CONCLUSION

Recent studies of America's western frontier have confirmed what many have suspected: brave, hardy, accomplished women made crucial contributions to its settlement. The majority of frontierswomen did not fill highly visible roles but quietly worked sixteen hours a day at tasks prescribed for them by traditional gender ideals: making food, clothing, and other essential goods; birthing and raising numerous children; acting as moral guides to family and friends. The churn, kitchen, and chicken house marked the boundaries of the immense workloads of most women. Numerous women also ventured beyond the confines of the domestic scene: some sought employment outside the home, entering the professions and politics; others spearheaded reform movements and community activities; still others acted and dressed like men.[57] In short, America's women pioneered the West in both conventional and unconventional ways.

Similar conclusions have been reached about the women who ventured onto what I have called the Christian frontier. According to Paul's letters and Acts, which provide a window onto the pioneer movement that settled Christians throughout the Mediterranean basin, women labored in the Lord in diverse roles, some quite conventional, others less so. The sheer weight of cultural tradition, including its longstanding gender ideals, gives us reason to suspect that most early Christian women, like their counterparts on the American frontier, made their contributions in conventional ways: caring for husband and children as wife and mother and dutifully managing the household. Conventional behavior, however, is by no means inconsequential behavior; nor should we assume that the denial of a woman's authority in relation to her husband eliminated female power. These women converts, by evangelizing their children and other members of the household, played a crucial role in the transmission of faith. Moreover, although it was exercised in the private realm, their power extended deeply into the public realm, contributing to the spread of a new religious movement that defied political authorities in its determination to worship the one God.[58]

Somewhat less conventional were those married women who dared to join the church without their husband's consent, a courageous initiative in view of prevailing cultural expectations. Within the precarious situation of the mixed marriage these women managed to wield influence on behalf of their new faith, becoming quiet evangelists of their households, even bringing unbelieving men to faith. Women who remained married to non-believers functioned as powerful mediators between church and world. Whether married to pagans or to Christians, women's conversion to a group branded a pernicious superstition surely exposed them to intense scrutiny and strife.

Other women, far fewer in numbers, I suspect, moved beyond the walls of their own homes and beyond the boundaries prescribed for them by the culture's gender code. We have glimpsed in Pauline texts women who headed households and brought their households with them into the church; others who gained prominence in the community through their patronage or their exercise of charismatic gifts; still others who traveled from city to city, accompanied by missionary partners. Some assumed in the churches the same roles as men: itinerant evangelist, prophet, teacher, deacon. They all broke new ground in venturing beyond the traditional understanding of female roles. Given the dominant gender ideal—that women be silent, modest, and confined to the domestic realm—how do we explain the fact that at least some Christian women moved beyond the boundaries their culture prescribed for them? A number of interrelated factors have been identified in answer to this question.

First, Paul's letters clearly attest that communities were focused in the homes of individuals whose houses were large enough to accommodate a gathering, and that Christians adopted relatively egalitarian familial terminology for members of the community, brothers, sisters, no fathers. Both realities almost certainly facilitated women's ability to stretch the boundaries of their roles. The location of early Christian churches within the private household, the traditional sphere of women, and the use of sibling terminology enabled early Christians to bring the public into the private sphere. The resultant blurring of boundaries between public and private permitted women to exercise power and public functions without explicitly challenging the traditional division of realms. It has been suggested that this ambiguous relationship between public and private in early Christianity may have been what allowed women married to unbelievers to join the church, since movement outside of one's house in the early church was essentially movement within a network of houses.[59]

Second, the emphasis on charismatic phenomena which were thought inspired by the Spirit also afforded women opportunities to exert influence and to experience prominence. That gifting Spirit was received in the baptismal ritual which included the statement made in Gal 3:26-28: "As many of you as were baptized into Christ have clothed yourselves with

Christ. There is no longer Jew or Greek, there is no longer slave or free, there is no longer male and female; for all of you are one in Christ Jesus." This remarkable assertion, which sets aside the ethnic, economic, and gender boundaries of the Greco-Roman world, may have served as the theoretical basis for Christianity's attractiveness to women and for a degree of liberty relative to the customary restrictions on women.[60] Add to this the conviction that "the present form of this world is passing away" (1 Cor. 7:31), a belief that may have fueled a radical disregard of worldly standards, and it is not difficult to understand how women could have ventured beyond traditional gender roles.

Third, a concomitant of early Christians' eschatological expectation of the imminent end was a preference for asceticism, including celibacy (e.g., 1 Cor. 7:1-7; 1 Tim. 4:3-5). The choice of celibacy, by severing identification with reproduction and childcare, freed women to assume new roles and statuses within Christian communities.[61] Finally, numerous studies have concluded that well-to-do women held offices in religious cults. Asia Minor, the locus of Pauline Christianity, seems to have been especially open to the prominence of women in public life, particularly in spheres in which civic and religious responsibility intersected. Since their culture and religion had socialized well-to-do women to assume important positions in civic life and religious institutions, when those women converted they undoubtedly expected to have the same influence in the Christian community.[62]

It is now a widely-acknowledged historical principle that women are systematically under represented in virtually all historical sources. We should not, therefore, assume that the women glimpsed in the New Testament accurately represent the proportion of women to men in first century churches or women's total contribution to the Christian movement. Unfortunately, due to the scarcity and androcentric nature of the sources, women's actual contribution remains largely lost. The flinty soil with which we labor yields but fragments of information that are the tip of the iceberg, only the most prominent women of the early Christian missionary movement visible on the surface, the unknown masses below. We can, however, gain an appreciation of their vital role from those fragments. Surely, neither the American nor the Christian frontier could have been settled without the admirable grit and elusive grace of women.

NOTES

1. Arthur Schlesinger, Jr., "Introduction," in Joanna Stratton, *Pioneer Women. Voices from the Kansas Frontier* (NY: Simon and Schuster, 1981), 11.

2. Ibid.

3. Glenda Riley, *Frontierswomen. The Iowa Experience* (Ames, Iowa: Iowa State University Press, 1981); idem, *The Female Frontier: A Comparative View of Women on the Prairie and the Plains* (Lawrence, Kansas: University Press of Kansas, 1988); Glenda Riley and Richard Etulain, ed., *By Grit and Grace: Eleven Women Who Shaped the American West* (Golden, Colorado: Fulcrum Publishing, 1997); Joanna Stratton, *Pioneer Women* (see n.1).

4. Peter Brown, *Body and Society: Men, Women, and Sexual Renunciation in Early Christianity* (New York: Columbia University Press, 1988), xvii. Brown further observes, "it is a dangerous illusion to assume that, in much of the evidence, the presence of women is even sensed by its male authors" (xvi).

5. The earliest Christian woman's voice we can recover is the martyr Perpetua, whose account of her trial is included in the Martyrdom of Saints Perpetua and Felicitas; for an English translation see Ross Kraemer, ed., *Maenads, Martyrs, Matrons, Monastics. A Sourcebook on Women's Religions in the Greco-Roman World* (Philadelphia: Fortress, 1988), 96-107. For sayings of the Desert Mothers dated to the fifth century, see Kraemer, *Maenads*, 117-24. On the few early Christian texts affording access to women's own voices and experience, see M. Alexandre, "Early Christian Women," in Pauline S. Pantel, ed., *A History of Women in the West, Vol. I: From Ancient Goddesses to Christian Saints* (Cambridge: Harvard University Press, 1992), 409-444, esp. 412. On the challenges of recovering and writing the history of early Christian women, see esp. B. Brooten, "Early Christian Women and Their Cultural Context: Issues of Method in Historical Reconstruction," in Adela Yarbro Collins, ed., *Feminist Perspectives on Biblical Scholarship* (Chico, California: Scholars Press, 1985), 65-91.

6. Among the most noteworthy pioneers on this scholarly frontier are Elisabeth Schussler Fiorenza, Bernadette Brooten, Ross Kraemer, Elizabeth Clark. Early Christian scholarship on women is indebted to classicists who have made enormous progress in recovering the women of ancient Greece and Rome. The literature and contributors are too numerous to cite; among the more noteworthy recent works see Sarah Pomeroy, ed., *Women's History and Ancient History* (Chapel Hill: University of North Carolina Press, 1991); Mary Lefkowitz and Maureen Fant, *Women's Life in Greece and Rome: A Source Book in Translation* (Baltimore: Johns Hopkins University Press, 1992); Pauline S. Pantel, ed., *A History of Women in the West, Vol. I: From Ancient Goddesses to Christian Saints* (Cambridge: Harvard University Press, 1992); Elaine Fantham et al., *Women in the Classical World* (New York: Oxford University Press, 1994).

7. On the distinction between History and history, see Gerda Lerner, *The Creation of Patriarchy* (New York: Oxford University Press, 1986), 4.

8. Wayne Meeks, *The First Urban Christians: The Social World of the Apostle Paul* (New Haven: Yale University Press, 1983), 55-63. Meeks' statistics exclude the Pastorals. For an annotated list based on Acts and all the literature ascribed to Paul, see E.B. Redlich, *St. Paul and His Companions* (London: Macmillan, 1913), 200-86.

9. See Margaret MacDonald, *Early Christian Women and Pagan Opinion: The Power of the Hysterical Woman* (Cambridge: Cambridge University Press, 1996), 192.

10. The Roman moralist Plutarch affirms, "It is becoming for a wife to worship and to know only the gods that her husband believes in, and to shut the door tight upon all queer rituals and outlandish superstitions" (*Moralia* 40D); cited in Meeks, *The First Urban Christians*, 25.

11. MacDonald, *Early Christian Women*, 191-92.

12. On women's responsibility for the religious education of their children, see Lilian Portefaix, *Sisters Rejoice: Paul's Letter to the Philippians and Luke-Acts as Seen by First-Century Philippian Women* (Stockholm: Uppsala, 1988), 33-36, 193-98.

13. 1 Clement 6.2-3; Tertullian, *Apology* 3; Pseudo-Clementine Recognitions 2.29. 1 Peter 3:1-6, probably composed in the late first century, also attests the precarious situation of Christian women in mixed marriages. For an enlightening discussion of the situation of this text, see esp. MacDonald, *Early Christian Women*, 195-204. On the threat that a Christian wife posed to a pagan family, hence, the hazards that the Christian wife had to endure, see Portefaix, *Sisters Rejoice*, 192-200.

14. See Apuleius, *Metamorphoses* 9.14, a text dated to the second century; translation by S. Benko, cited in MacDonald, *Early Christian Women*, 68. The phrase "a god called only" indicates that the description of the woman refers to either a Jewish proselyte or a Christian.

15. On honor and shame as pivotal values of the Mediterranean and, hence, biblical world, see the seminal work of Bruce Malina, *The New Testament World: Insights from Cultural Anthropology*, rev. ed. (Louisville: Westminster/John Knox, 1993); Ibid., "Honor and Shame in Luke-Acts: Pivotal Values of the Mediterranean World," in J. Neyrey ed., *The Social World of Luke-Acts: Models for Biblical Interpretation* (Peabody, MA: Hendrickson, 1991), 25-65; on the role these values played in relations between early Christians and their pagan neighbors, see esp. MacDonald, *Early Christian Women*, 27-30, 144-54, 162, 180.

16. Numerous patristic texts attest women's crucial role as transmitters of faith; see for example, the praise of Basil of Caesarea for his paternal grandmother who "had done battle, several times preaching Christ" while hiding in the mountains with her family during persecutions (Gregory Nazianzen, *Funeral*

Oration for Basil, 5.1); for additional patristic testimony see M. Alexandre, "Early Christian Women," 442-4.

17. Jill Dubisch, *Gender and Power in Rural Greece* (Princeton: University Press, 1986), 17-18. For an enlightening application of Dubisch's work to early Christian texts on women, see MacDonald, *Early Christian Women*, 42-7, 202-3.

18. On the nature of the controversial teachings associated with women prophets, see Adela Yarbro Collins, "Women's History and the Book of Revelation," *Society of Biblical Literature Seminar Papers* 26 (1987) 80-91.

19. Collins, "Women's History," 81, 83.

20. I am persuaded by Margaret Mitchell's rhetorical analysis that "the call to submission and silence is fully consonant and rhetorically consistent with the argument for inner-group concord," thus, that 14:33b-36 probably belongs to 1 Corinthians; see Mitchell, *Paul and the Rhetoric of Reconciliation: An Exegetical Investigation of the Language and Composition of 1 Corinthians* (Louisville: Westminster/John Knox, 1992), 280-83.

21. See Ben Witherington, *Conflict and Community in Corinth: A Socio-Rhetorical Commentary on 1 and 2 Corinthians* (Grand Rapids: Eerdmans, 1995) 287, who continues, "it is very believable that these women assumed that Christian prophets or prophetesses functioned much like the oracle at Delphi, who only prophesied in response to questions."

22. Mitchell, *Paul and the Rhetoric of Reconciliation*, 279.

23. Scholars agree that Acts, written in the mid-eighties, must be used cautiously in undertaking historical reconstructions. Its picture of the mission cannot simply be accepted as a direct, factual account. Feminist scholarship, while wary of Acts as a historical source due to its androcentric character, nevertheless acknowledges that it contains a significant slice of early Christian women's history, but insists that it must be read in conjunction with and augmented by other accounts, both Pauline and apocryphal (Ivoni Richter Reimer, *Women in the Acts of the Apostles: A Feminist Liberation Perspective,* Minneapolis: Fortress, 1995, 252, 259). Elisabeth Schussler Fiorenza maintains that "Acts probably reflects historical experience in stressing that women were involved in the Christian missionary movement at every stage of its expansion," but continues, "Acts is one-sided, however, in its presentation of the Christian missionary movement and of women's involvement in it. By stressing their status as prominent and wealthy, the author neglects their contributions as missionaries and leaders of churches in their own right," which, thankfully, are evidenced by the Pauline letters (*In Memory of Her: A Feminist Theological Reconstruction of Christian Origins*, New York: Crossroad, 1983, 167).

24. Juridical status, freeborn, slave, freedperson, did not automatically bestow a given socio-economic condition. Many freedpersons, for example, were relatively well-to-do business people and in a better economic position than many freeborn. Reimer, however, contests the current consensus that Lydia, as a purple dealer, was

well-to-do. Citing information about purple-dealers in antiquity, she maintains that Lydia's work was a "subsistence occupation for herself and her household" and "it is possible that there were slaves in Lydia's house; and it is probable that the income of her house made possible a better economic state of things than a lot of beggars. But still, as foreigners from the East who carried on a despised trade and also practiced the Jewish religion in that Roman colony, they belonged to the *plebs urbana*, the common people"; see Reimer, *Women in the Acts of the Apostles*, 98-112.

25. J. P. Sampley, *Pauline Partnership in Christ* (Philadelphia: Fortress, 1980), 62-3.

26. Schussler Fiorenza, *In Memory of Her*, 170.

27. E. Earle Ellis, "Paul and His Co-workers," *New Testament Studies* 17 (1971) 437-52, esp. 440-41.

28. Mary Rose D'Angelo, drawing attention to pairs such as Mary and Martha of Bethany, Tryphaena and Tryphosa, and Euodia and Syntyche, argues that pairs of female workers were part of early Christianity's leadership; see "Women Partners in the New Testament," *Journal of Feminist Studies in Religion* 6 (1990), 65-86.

29. Direkler, a basilica dedicated to St. Paul in the forum, and another, Extra-Muros, outside the walls, were built in the fourth century. The graves at these basilicas include references to two female deacons: Agatha buried with her husband John, and Posidonia buried with a woman canoness named Pancharia. Eight men were designated presbyters. Curiously, no evidence has been found for a bishop buried at Philippi even though the St. Paul basilica was associated with the bishop's palace in later years. See Valerie Abrahamsen, "Women at Philippi: The Pagan and Christian Evidence," *Journal of Feminist Studies in Religion* 3 (1987), 17-30, esp. 23; also H.W. Catling, "Archaeology in Greece, 1980-81: Philippi," *Journal of Hellenic Studies* 101 (1981), 34.

30. Letters 52 and 173 of Basil, dated to the late fourth century, are addressed to canonesses but shed little light on their roles. There is some evidence that female canons were responsible for burials. Canoness seems to be a specific position held by unmarried women in the post-Constantinian church. On the slim evidence see Abrahamsen, "Women at Philippi," 26.

31. As late as the fifth and sixth centuries, Philippi exhibits a certain amount of independence in its ecclesiastical structure. The evidence leads Abrahamsen ("Women at Philippi," 26-29) to conclude that the post-Constantinian churches at Philippi were administered primarily by male presbyters rather than bishops.

32. See Ross Kramer, *Her Share of the Blessings: Women's Religions among Pagans, Jews, and Christians in the Greco-Roman World* (New York: Oxford University Press, 1992), 80-92; Riet van Bremen, *The Limits of Participation: Women and Civic Life in the Greek East in the Hellenistic and Roman Periods* (Amsterdam: J.C. Gieben, 1996). On the role of women in the Diana cult at

Philippi, see Valerie Abrahamsen, "The Rock Reliefs and the Cult of Diana at Philippi" (Th.D diss., Harvard University, 1986; Ann Arbor, Michigan: University Microfilms).

33. Paul's peculiar reference to the mother of Rufus as "a mother to me also" suggests, perhaps, that this woman served as a benefactress to Paul.

34. The term co-worker or fellow worker does not mean that these women, or men similarly designated, were Paul's helpers or assistants. Only five coworkers, Erastus, Mark, Timothy, Titus, Tychicus, "stand in explicit subordination to Paul, serving him or being subject to his instructions"; see Ellis, "Paul and His Co-workers," 439.

35. Ellis, "Paul and His Co-workers," 446-48.

36. Assistance at baptism of women was one of their most important functions; therefore, when adult baptism became rare, the office of deaconess declined. See "deaconess" in *Oxford Dictionary of the Christian Church*, ed., F.L. Cross (New York: Oxford University Press, 1997), 455-56.

37. The term *diakonissa* was not used until the fourth century; see "deaconess," *Oxford Dictionary of the Christian Church*, 455-56.

38. A hierarchy of bishops, presbyters, and deacons first appears in the letters of Ignatius (*Magnesians* 2.1; 6.1) in the second century.

39. Ellis, "Paul and His Co-workers," 442.

40. Ellis, "Paul and His Co-workers," 441-2. Dieter Georgi argues that *diakonoi* and *episkopoi* are synonyms for missionary proclaimers and envoys in the early church (*The Opponents of Paul in the Second Corinthians*, Philadelphia: Fortress, 1986, 27-32). For discussion of the various titles and functions of Paul's associates, see esp. Ellis, "Paul and His Co-workers," 437-52; Meeks, *First Urban Christians*, 131-36; B. Holmberg, *Paul and Power: The Structure of Authority in the Primitive Church as Reflected in the Pauline Epistles* (Philadelphia: Fortress, 1978), 57-67.

41. See Ramsay MacMullen, "Women in Public in the Roman Empire," *Historia* 29 (1980), 211; also Van Bremen, *The Limits of Participation* (n.32 above); and Meeks, *First Urban Christians*, 24-5.

42. Meeks, *First Urban Christians*, 78.

43. Robert Jewett observes, "In light of this high social standing and Paul's relatively subordinate social position as her client, it is preposterous that translations like the RSV render *prostatis* as 'helper.'" ("Paul, Phoebe, and the Spanish Mission," in *The Social World of Formative Christianity and Judaism*, J. Neusner et al., ed. (Philadelphia: Fortress, 1988), 142-61, esp. 149-50. On patron-client relations, see Bruce Malina, "Patronage," in *Biblical Social Values and Their Meaning*, ed., John Pilch and Bruce Malina (Peabody: Hendrickson, 1993), 133-37; also H. Moxnes, "Patron-Client Relations and the New Community in Luke-Acts," in *The Social World of Luke-Acts. Models for Interpretation*, ed., J. Neyrey (Peabody: Hendrickson, 1991), 241-68.

44. Jewett, "Paul, Phoebe, and the Spanish Mission," 142-61, esp. 151-55.

45. Ibid. 153. Jewett's theory assumes that chapter 16 belongs to the letter to Romans. For a critique of Jewett and an alternative theory regarding Paul's recommendation of her as patron, see Caroline Whelan, "*Amica Pauli*: The Role of Phoebe in the Early Church,"*Journal for the Study of the New Testament* 49 (1993), 67-85. Whelan's theory assumes that the content of Rom. 16 is addressed to Ephesian, not Roman, Christians.

46. Text-critical study of the manuscript tradition of Acts 18: 1-28 has identified "an anti-feminist tendency" on the part of the Western reviser; see Bruce Metzger, *A Textual Commentary on the Greek New Testament*, 3rd ed. (New York: United Bible Societies, 1975), 466-67; also Reimer, *Women in the Acts of the Apostles*, 197-99.

47. In her study of epitaphs from three Roman families, Marleen Flory finds that when the name of a wife appears before that of her husband, it is generally because she has already been freed whereas her husband remains a slave; see her "Family and 'Familia': A Study of Social Relations in Slavery" (Ph.D. dissertation, Yale University, 1975), 8, 59-79. The fact that Phoebe worked manually with her husband (Acts 18:3) suggests that she neither outranked him nor had independent wealth. If Luke had known her to be of socially elevated status, he surely would have mentioned it in Acts, since he draws attention to women of distinguished status (Luke 8:3; Acts 17:4, 12); see Peter Lampe, "The Roman Christians of Romans 16," in *The Romans Debate*, ed., K. P. Donfried (Peabody: Hendrickson, 1977), 216-30, esp. 223. It seems more likely, therefore, that her greater prominence obtained in the Christian community (J. Murphy-O'Connor, "Prisca and Aquila, Traveling Tentmakers and Church Builders," *Bible Review* 8 (1992), 40-51, 62, esp. 42). C.E.B. Cranfield suggests that she was converted before her husband and perhaps brought Aquila to Christian faith; or that she played an even more prominent role in the life and work of the church than did her husband; see his *A Critical and Exegetical Commentary on the Epistle to the Romans*, Vol. II (Edinburgh: T. & T. Clark, 1979), 784.

48. Aquila, a Jew, could have acquired this Latin name, meaning eagle, in a number of ways. Upon being freed, slaves often added the name of their master to their own. It has been suggested that both Aquila and Prisca may have been freed slaves of the same Roman family; see Murphy-O'Connor, "Prisca and Aquila," 42-3.

49. The interpretive tradition from the early church is unanimous in the opinion that Priscilla, Aquila, and Paul worked in leather. In his *Salutate Priscillam et Aquilam*, John Chrysostom includes an extensive treatment of Rom. 16:3, emphasizing their work as artisans, their poverty, and their missionary work. Reimer observes, approvingly, that Chrysostom, unlike modern interpreters who separate the couple's preaching from their handiwork, holds together and praises both activities (*Women in the Acts of the Apostles*, 209).

50. It has been objected that women's contributions would have been severely hampered by their illiteracy. However, women would have had to acquire little if any literacy to be active participants in the transmission and interpretation of traditions about Jesus. It is widely acknowledged that the earliest believers in Christ relied heavily on oral tradition for the transmission of gospel tradition, and even their knowledge and use of Jewish Scripture may have been predominantly oral; see Ross Kraemer, *Her Share of the Blessings: Women's Religions among Pagans, Jews, and Christians in the Greco-Roman World* (New York: Oxford University Press, 1992), 144. John Chrysostom celebrated Priscilla's outstanding activity as a missionary artisan in his *Salutate Priscillam et Aquilam* 2.1. In contrast, Tertullian's praise of only Aquila probably represents an early attempt to demote Priscilla, and women who might be inspired by her precedent, from prominence (Reimer, *Women in the Acts of the Apostles*, 216).

51. On this hypothesis see Murphy-O'Connor, "Prisca and Aquila," 46-7.

52. Meeks, *First Urban Christians*, 76.

53. Depending on how it is accented in the manuscripts, Junian is either the accusative of the masculine Junias or the accusative of the feminine Junia; on the text critical options, see Cranfield, *Romans*, 788. On the history of interpretation of Rom. 16:7 see Bernadette Brooten, "Junia-Outstanding Among the Apostles (Rom. 16:7)" in *Women Priests: A Catholic Commentary on the Vatican Declaration* (New York: Paulist Press, 1977), 141-44.

54. Aegidius of Rome (1245-1316) is the earliest testimony to an understanding of the name as masculine; on this point see Bonnie Thurston, *Women in the New Testament: Questions and Commentary* (New York: Crossroad, 1998), 57.

55. Ellis, "Paul and His Co-workers," 444-45. In reference to his own apostolic labors Paul refers to himself as *diakonos* (1 Cor 3:5), thereby evidencing the close relationship between the two terms.

56. It is widely agreed that the term "apostle" did not represent an office in Paul's day. The title did, however, point to functions that carried authority in the Christian mission. Acts and the Pauline letters make no mention of formal offices in the Pauline communities but do attest a differentiation and development of roles which did not become fully institutionalized until the second century; see Meeks, *First Urban Christians*, 131.

57. Riley and Etulain, *By Grit and Grace*, ix-x.

58. MacDonald, *Early Christian Women*, 202-3, 248.

59. Ibid., 203.

60. The formula in Galatians does not indicate how such practice was translated into social life, either in the community or in Christians' relationships with those outside the community. Anthropological studies show that while ritualized reversal of or freedom from social roles and constraints is common in many rites and festivals, the reversal does not carry over into the social sphere. On this point see Pheme Perkins, *Ministering in the Pauline Churches* (New York:

Paulist Press, 1982), 59-60. However, there is also indication that in the case of groups maintaining a strong identity distinct from the larger society, some aspects of the liminal transcendence of societal barriers experienced in a ritual like baptism may linger in its daily life. Paul's letters, in fact, evidence confusion among various Pauline groups about the implications of being, after baptism, brothers and sisters of the one body; see Meeks, *First Urban Christians*, 160-1.

61. Kraemer, *Her Share of the Blessings*, 139, 150.

62. Schussler Fiorenza, *In Memory of Her*, 250; Kraemer, *Her Share of the Blessings*, 84-89.

The New Testament and Environmental Justice: A View from Luke

Dennis Hamm, S.J.

It may seem absurd, on the face of it, to claim that the New Testament has something to say that might help us address our contemporary ecological crisis. Mark knew nothing of the possibility of global warming. Matthew could not have imagined human participation in the extinction of species. Paul had no reason to concern himself about the wasting of rain forests. Nor could John imagine a human production of sulfur emission that would produce an acid rain damaging forests, lakes, and crops. In short, the early Christian communities had no way of anticipating patterns of human activity that would threaten the sustainability of the systems of what we have come to know as planet Earth.

On the other hand, two simple considerations demonstrate the relevance of the New Testament to the question of environmental justice. First, the authors of the New Testament presume the moral vision of the Hebrew Bible, which includes a strong message about human stewardship of the earth. Second, and more specifically, Jesus affirmed the ten commandments, whose proscriptions of idolatry, stealing, killing, and coveting have some bearing on the contemporary human interface with the rest of nature. The traditional summary of our biblically based ethic of the common good, namely, that the goods of the earth are meant by their Creator to meet the needs of all before they are considered the possession of any individual, is clear. As a New Testament scholar I am tempted to say, "What further need do we have to search Scriptures for ecological wisdom? We have all we need if we simply keep in mind the vision of the common good and the commandments: do not steal, do not kill, do not covet. Admittedly, the *solutions* will be complicated, multiple, and diverse, but the moral vision and principles, along with their biblical roots, are simple and obvious."

Having said that, however, I have to acknowledge that biblical scholarship does have something to offer in the current struggle for environmental justice. We can help people read the Christian Scriptures in the light of the full canon, retrieving the connections to the Hebrew moral vision. Such exegetical and theological elaboration can deepen and enrich the religious imagination in ways that promise to nurture prayer and worship and support the practical actions whose necessity is already obvious. My intention in this essay is to indicate some of the implicit creation theology contained in that part of the New Testament attributed to Luke, the Gospel of Luke and the Acts of the Apostles (hereafter Luke-Acts). I will do this in three parts. Part One will survey Luke's presentation of Creator and creation as mediated by his interpretation of Jesus' kingdom of God preaching. Part Two will give a close reading of two paradigmatic passages illustrating this Lukan creation theology, the portrait of community prayer and action in Acts 4 and the teaching on anxiety in Luke 12. Part Three will spell out some of the implications of this reading of Luke-Acts for promoting environmental justice in our day.

CREATOR, CREATION, AND THE KINGDOM OF GOD
IN LUKE-ACTS: LUKE'S ISAIAN LENS

Speaking of the Reign of God in the preaching of Jesus, commentators have rightly distinguished between a *sapiential* understanding of God's reign, God as perennial cosmic ruler, and the *apocalyptic* understanding of God's reign, God's special intervention in "the age to come." They rightly insist that Jesus' use of God's reign as a symbol owes more to the latter than the former.[1] As I hope to make evident, Luke understands Jesus to have been preaching and *inaugurating* the end-time intervention of God, always understood as the Creator, the Lord of Heaven and Earth. Contemporary readers can easily summon an abstract, philosophical image of God when they read "God" in the New Testament. However, when we pay attention to Luke's use of the Hebrew Scriptures or, more precisely, his Septuagint (Greek) version of the Hebrew Scriptures, we can see that Luke's image of God is far more specific than philosophical abstractions about the Deity.

This quick survey of Reign of God in Luke will basically follow the order of its narrative unfolding in the Third Evangelist's two-volume work. The first occurrence of Luke's presentation of Jesus' preaching the Kingdom of God is at Luke 4:43. The morning after his day of preaching and healing in Capernaum, when crowds try to prevent him from leaving them, Jesus says, "To the other towns also I must proclaim the good news of the kingdom of God [*euangelizasthai me dei t n basileian tou theou*], because for this purpose I have been sent." In our quest for Luke's image of the God who reigns, the Greek verb *euangelizomai*, a favorite of Luke's,[2] is important, for it sends us right to Isaiah. *Euangelizomai* is rare in the Septuagint, but it does occur six times in Isaiah, precisely in passages speaking of God imaged as king of the cosmos and reigning through liberating action. Take, for example, Isa 40:9-10:

> You who bring glad tidings [*ho euangelizomenos*] to Zion, go up on the high mountain; lift up your voice with strength, you who bring glad tidings [*ho euangelizomenos*] to Jerusalem. Lift it up, fear not. Say to the cities of Judah, 'Behold your God! [The targum, or Aramaic paraphrase used in the first century Palestine, adds here: "The kingdom of your God is revealed."] Behold the Lord! The Lord is coming with strength, and his arm is with power.

Here in Isaiah the specific manifestation of God's coming in power is the historical event of the return from the Babylonian captivity. But the context is clear that the one who comes in power is the Maker of Heaven and Earth (see the cosmogonic references to God as measurer of sea water, mountains; spreader of the heavenly vault, maker of the stars and the ends of the earth at 40:12, 21, 22, 26, 28).

The second passage is Isa 52:7. "I am present as a season of beauty upon the mountains, as the feet of one preaching glad tidings of peace [*euangelizomenou ako n eir n s*], as one preaching good things [*euangelizomenos agatha*]. For I will proclaim your salvation, saying, 'O Zion, your God shall reign [*basileusei sou ho Theos*]." We get an insight to the first-century understanding of these passages when we learn that the Targum, or Aramaic paraphrase of the Hebrew, adds to both of these passages the sentence: "The kingdom of your God has been revealed" (see Chilton, 59-60).

The final instance of the expression in Isaiah occurs in the passage Luke quotes in 4:18, namely, Isa 61:1. "The Spirit of the Lord is upon me because he has anointed me *to bring glad tidings* to the poor. He *has sent me* to announce liberty to captives, and recovery of sight to the blind, to let the oppressed go free, and to proclaim the acceptable year of the Lord."

Luke echoes this at 4:43. "To the other towns also I must *proclaim the good news of the kingdom of God*, because for this purpose I *have been sent.*" If the reader asks, "How does Jesus proclaim good news to the poor?," the text answers by narrating the healing of bodies, the deliverance of the demoniac at Capernaum, and the healing of Simon's mother-in-law and of those that were brought to him that evening at Sabbath's end, the only events that have happened between the inaugural preaching of 4:18 and the explicit reference to the kingdom of God at verse 43.

Once we are in touch with the Greek text of Isaiah, the version Luke used, it becomes evident that this prophet is Luke's preferred source for illustrating his understanding of God's action in the work of Jesus. Every commentator notes that the epiphany at the Jordan alludes to Isa 42:1 (see, for example, Fitzmyer, 1981: 486). What has been little noticed is the *cosmic context* of that first "servant song" and its importance to the theology of Luke. For the speaker of the oracle of Isa 42:1-4 is identified by the prophet as

the Lord God who made the heaven and established it, who firmed up [*stere sas*] the earth and the things in it, and gives breath to the people on it, and spirit to those that tread on it. I the Lord God have called you in righteousness and will hold your hand and will strengthen you. And I have given you for a covenant of a race, for a light of the gentiles, to bring the bound and those that sit in darkness out of bonds and the prison house.

In other words, the One who anoints Jesus with the Spirit is the maker of heaven and earth and the sustainer of all living things in creation. The Creator's intent is to make the anointed one an agent in the release of captives and a light to the nations. That Luke is conscious of this fuller context of the Isaiah passage alluded to in the Jordan scene becomes evident when we see the evangelist allude to that fuller context of this first servant song throughout the rest of his work. See Luke 2:32 and Acts 26:23 (alluding to Isa 42:6, "light of the nations"); Acts 17:24-25 (echoing Isa 42:5, God as maker of heaven and earth and giver of breath to all creatures); and Acts 26:18 (echoing Isa 42:7, opening the eyes of the blind). Luke understands the baptism and mission of Jesus as a fulfillment of Isaiah's promise of the saving work of the cosmic creator and underscores this interpretation in the summary of Jesus' ministry he presents in Peter's

speech to Cornelius in Acts 10:36-38. Peter speaks of God having proclaimed peace (that Isaian verb again, *euangelizomenos eir n n*) through
Jesus Christ (echoing Isa 52:7) and having anointed (*echrisen*) Jesus of
Nazareth with Holy Spirit and power (echoing Isa 61:1 and Luke 4:18
interpreting the Jordan experience of Jesus as call to prophetic mission).

Luke's presentation of the *verbal content* of Jesus' kingdom preaching
begins in earnest with the first beatitude of the Sermon on the Plain:
"Blessed are you poor, for the kingdom of God is yours." What, then, is
implied about the God of this kingdom in the remainder of the Sermon?
This God expects members of the kingdom to be nonviolent and gracious
to enemies, to beggars, to borrowers, and to thieves. Those that do so
become *huioi Hypsistou* ("sons of the Most High"), for he is kind
[*chr stos*] to the ungrateful and wicked. Be merciful just as your Father is
merciful [*oiktirm n*]." *Oiktirm n* can also be rendered "compassionate."
In the Septuagint it occurs in contexts describing the covenant love of God
(Exod 34:6; Deut 4:31).

That the image of God as father here likely refers to God as creator as
well as rescuer is suggested by the elaboration of the Q-saying about love
of enemies we find in Matthew 5:44-45, "But I say to you, love your
enemies, and pray for those who persecute you, that you may be children
of your heavenly Father, for he makes his sun rise on the bad and the good,
and causes rain to fall on the just and unjust." Here love of enemies is
imitation of the Lord of the sun and the rain, the Master of the cosmos, the
Creator. Luke's use of the Isaian image of God as the Creator who sustains
and rescues makes it plausible that he is drawing upon the same image as
Matthew's Jesus. Though the paternal image for God is rare in Isaiah,
occurring in just two passages, both of those passages call God "Father"
precisely in his capacity as the Cosmic creator who sustains his creatures
(Isa 45:10 and 63:16-64:8; 63:7: "Yet, O Lord, you are our father; we are
the clay and you the potter: we are all the work of your hands").[3]

The portrait of Jesus' followers in Luke 8 describes women who had
experienced the kingdom of God through being cured of evil spirits and
infirmities (as in 4:43); the practical outcome of their hearing the word of
God is their readiness to provide for the disciples "out of their resources"
(8:3). Luke 8 parallels Luke 3 in linking the image of "bearing fruit" with
meeting human needs out of the goods of the earth (food and clothing,
whose fiber comes from the earth). In 9:1-6, Jesus sends the Twelve to
proclaim the kingdom of God and to heal wherever they can find hospital-

ity. In the next scene, we have the return of the apostles and a gathering at Bethsaida, with Jesus teaching *about the kingdom of God and healing*, both elements unique to Luke's account of this Synoptic tradition. In other words Jesus is doing what he sent the apostles to do. The preaching of the kingdom of God is illustrated with the actions of healing and feeding. The disciples set the twelve loaves before the 5000 and all are satisfied, with twelve baskets of fragments left over.

In the mission of the seventy-two, the integration of the proclamation of the kingdom of God with healing, eating and hospitality becomes more explicit. Now healing becomes a *sign* of the kingdom and the rejection of their ministry also raises the prospect of divine judgment associated with the coming of the kingdom (10:11-16). The report of the seventy-two regarding the efficacy of their ministry issues in a prayer of praise from Jesus addressed to God as cosmic Lord, "Father, Lord of heaven and earth." Since the section on the seventy-two can be understood as a kind of flash forward to the life of the church, to be spelled out more completely in Acts (see Johnson, 1991: 170), it makes sense to see this prayer of Jesus as an articulation of post-Easter reality. This is evident in the statement "All things have been handed over to me by the Father," which sounds very much like the last supper discourses of the Fourth Gospel.[4] Thus in the mission of the seventy-two, the kingdom of God, inaugurated in Jesus' ministry, expresses the victory of the reign of the "Lord of heaven and earth" over the power of Satan. As in Isaiah, the Creator rescues his people.

It has been noticed recently that the first petition of the Lord's Prayer echoes Ezekiel 36 (Lohfink, 14-17). "Hallowed by thy name" (Luke 11:2) draws on the language of this prophetic oracle, which says, "I will prove the holiness of my great name, profaned among the nations, in whose midst you have profaned it," and then proceeds to elaborate just how that will occur: "I will put my spirit within you and make you live by my statues, careful to observe my decrees." As elaborated in Ezekiel, this renewal of the covenant life of the community will be accompanied by an ecological renewal: "I will order the grain to be abundant, and I will not send famine against you. I will increase the fruit on your trees and the crops in your fields; thus you shall no longer bear among the nations the reproach of famine" (Ezek 36:29-30). Thus, in its Ezekiel context, the first petition of the Our Father prays for the spiritual renewal of the community in a flourishing environment. Indeed, the expansion of the teaching on prayer in the verses that follow the Our Father speaks of the Father's gift of the

Holy Spirit as the ultimate gift, surely to be understood in Ezekiel's context of the restoration of the covenant community through the gift of God's own spirit.

Luke 11:7-20 pits the kingdom of God against the kingdom of Satan. Jesus' deliverance ministry is a sign of the presence of the kingdom of God: "If it is by the finger of God that I drive out demons then the kingdom of God has come upon you" (11:20, alluding to Exod 8:19). Strong language links Jesus' deliverance ministry with the inauguration of the kingdom of God. Luke relays two crucial kingdom sayings at 12:31-32: "First seek his [the Father's] kingdom, and these things will be added. Fear not, little flock, for it has pleased the Father to give you the kingdom." We shall give an extended treatment of these sayings below, for they are of special pertinence to our topic.

In Luke 13, concluding the episode of the Sabbath healing of the bent woman, we meet a cluster of four kingdom of God sayings touching both the *presence* of the kingdom, in the parables of the mustard seed and the leaven, and its *future*, in the scenario of the end-time banquet with Abraham, Isaac, Jacob, and the prophets, joined by people from all directions. Eschatological judgment enters the picture here: it takes repentance from evildoing to join the banquet. Lest the reader assume that the kingdom of God is exclusively other-worldly, the statement of 14:15 uttered during a conspicuously this-worldly banquet at which Jesus is present ("Blessed is the one who will dine in the kingdom of God"), and Jesus' response in the form of the parable of the Great Feast, show that the invitation to the end-time banquet is already out and the feast proleptically accessible.

Luke places the next kingdom of God saying (16:16) in the context of sayings and parables on the relationship between rich and poor and the right use of wealth: the Dishonest Steward (16:1-8), the poem about Mammon and God (vv 9-13), the excoriation of the Pharisees (here called "money lovers," vv 14-15), and the parable of Dives and Lazarus (vv 19-31). The kingdom saying in the midst of this material reads, "The Law and the prophets lasted until John; but from then on the kingdom of God is proclaimed and everyone is pressed to enter it (following Fitzmyer, 1985: 1117). It is easier for heaven and earth to pass away than for the smallest part of the letter of the law to become invalid" (16:16-17). The joining of these two sayings in this place points to the punch line of the Dives and Lazarus story, where Abraham says, regarding Dives' brothers, "If they will not listen to Moses and the prophets, neither will they be persuaded if someone should rise from the dead." This parable shows Jesus affirming the moral vision of Torah and Prophets that insists on the sharing of the Earth's goods to meet the needs of all. With respect to the immediate context, Isa 58:6-7 describes the situation of the Dives and Lazarus exactly: "This, rather, is the fasting that I wish ... Setting free the oppressed ... sharing your bread with the hungry, sheltering the oppressed and the homeless; clothing the naked when you see them, and not turning your back on your own."[5] Joining the end-time banquet is consequent upon one's entering the kingdom now through one's just use of material goods.

The latter half of Luke 17 deals with questions about the time and place of the coming of the kingdom. Asked by the Pharisees when the kingdom of God would come, Jesus replied, "The kingdom of God does not come *meta parat r se s,* and no one will announce, 'Look, here it is,' or, 'There it is.' For behold the kingdom of God is *entos hym n*" (Luke 17:20-21.) The interpretation of the Greek phrases is crucial here. *Parat r sis* is related to the verb *parat re* , which in the Greek of both Old and New Testaments always denotes a sinister kind of looking. It describes, for example, the voyeuristic spying of the elders on the bathing Susanna in Dan 13:12, 15, 16. Luke uses the word elsewhere to describe the spying out of the enemies of Jesus bent on trapping him in violation of the Law (see Luke 6:7; 14:1; 20:20). In the present passage, then, it would appear to refer to the uncommitted, calculating spying out of the Pharisees, who simply want to control Jesus rather take a stand on the truth of his identity and message. Though this kind of spying out does not perceive the kingdom, the kingdom of God is in fact *among* them. That preposition is best translated among rather than within (see Fitzmyer, 1985: 1161).

This question of the proper translation is no pedantic quibble. Translating *entos* as within has led generations of Christians to totally interiorize and spiritualize their understanding of the kingdom of God, as if were only a matter of acknowledging the presence of God within one's heart in the act of faith. The context suggests that the meaning is that the kingdom is here present in the person and work of Jesus, there to be known by those who, like the Samaritan leper of the previous pericope, acknowledge Jesus' identity and consequently come to know salvation (17:11-19) (see Hamm, 1994). The following speech on the "Day of the Son of man" (17:22-37) completes the thought by teaching that the kingdom of God already inaugurated in the person and work of Jesus will, at an unpredictable time, eventually issue in a definitive judgment of the world. Meanwhile, the disciple is to live according to the mysterious maxim: "whoever seeks to possess (*peripoi sasthai*, "to acquire for oneself") his life (*psyche*) will lose it, but whoever loses it will keep it alive" (17:33). In a moment we shall see that Luke has illustrated in the parable of the Rich Fool (in chap. 12) what it means concretely to try to possess one's life (or self).

This relationship of one's use of material goods to the kingdom of God is further elaborated in the cluster of five kingdom sayings in chapter 18. When the disciples rebuke people who bring little children to Jesus, he says, "Let the children come to me and do not prevent them; for the kingdom of God belongs to such as these. Amen, I say to you, whoever does not accept the kingdom of God like a child will not enter it" (18:16-17). With stunning simplicity, this last saying catches the two dimensions of the kingdom revealed thus far: (1) it is something already accessible now to the properly disposed, something already available for the childlike to accept; (2) it is something with a future culmination that such a person will eventually enter. This general principle is then illustrated in the pericope that follows, the encounter of the rich ruler with Jesus. Jesus tells the wealthy man that inheriting eternal life will require divestment of his possessions and following Jesus. That this talk of "inheriting eternal life" is another way of speaking of entering the kingdom of God is driven home in the three kingdom sayings in Jesus' instruction on riches and discipleship (vv 24-30). In Luke's version, the rich man does not go away sad as he does in Mark; he remains present for Jesus to address him directly with the saying, "How hard it is for those who have wealth to enter the kingdom of God. For it is easier for a camel to pass through the eye of a needle than for a rich person to enter the kingdom of God."

What follows is the episode of the healing of the blind beggar of Jericho and the story of Zacchaeus. Luke's artistry becomes evident in the way he tells the Zacchaeus episode. He makes a point of describing him as one having the childlike qualities of trying to "see Jesus who he is" and even scampering up a sycamore tree to get a good view. His childlike ability to take steps to see and to receive the presence of the kingdom in Jesus results in a conversion that expresses itself in a just realignment of his use of possessions, reimbursing those he has defrauded. Jesus affirms this by saying: "Today salvation has come to this house because this man too is a descendant of Abraham. For the Son of Man has come to seek and to save what was lost" (19:9-10) (on the question of whether this episode is indeed a conversion story, see Hamm, 1988).

The sayings at 19:11 and 21:31 tantalize the reader with statements affirming both the delay and the imminence of the Kingdom and set the reader up for the revelation that comes with the fourfold mention of kingdom in Luke's rendition of the Last Supper. At 22:29-30 Jesus speaks of not eating Passover until it is fulfilled in the kingdom of God and not drinking of the fruit of the vine until the kingdom of God comes. That raises the question of *when* this coming of the kingdom will occur, which is addressed in the verses that follow. Apart from the context of Luke-Acts, it might seem that this is a reference to the time of the Parousia. Yet the verses that follow indicate otherwise. "You have stayed with me during my trials, and I confer a kingdom upon you just as the Father has conferred one on me, so that you may eat and drink at my table in my kingdom; and you will sit on thrones judging the twelve tribes of Israel." Since this last statement occurs in a discourse against lording it over others, the judging in question cannot refer to some exercise of forensic authority. When these verses are read with a view to volume two, the Acts of the Apostles, against the background of Old Testament language, a different meaning appears. Jesus is referring to the apostles as judges in the Old Testament sense, the very sense indicated in the Book of Judges, an account of twelve charismatic leaders of the pre-monarchic Israel. The twelve tribes in question are the twelve tribes of the end-time restored Israel, the Jerusalem Christian community, for the Jerusalem community is interpreted as the end-time restoration of the twelve tribes and the risen Lord does indeed eat and drink with his disciples. In other words, these words of Jesus refer to the leadership of the twelve in the church (see Jervell). The church, then, is an expression of the kingdom of God under the Lordship of Jesus.

The last two kingdom statements of the Third Gospel sound both dimensions of the already/not yet theme: When the repentant criminal asks, "Jesus, remember me when you come into your kingdom," Jesus can affirm, "Amen, I say to you, today you will be with me in Paradise" (23:42-43). Then Joseph of Arimathea, described as good and righteous and waiting for the kingdom of God, expresses his character by daring to request the body of Jesus and donating his earthly possessions of a freshly hewn rock tomb and a linen shroud.

The eight scattered references to kingdom of God in Luke's second volume, Acts, are sparse, but enough to enable the conscientious reader to see that the kingdom inaugurated in the person and action of Jesus in volume one continues and expands in the creation and work of the church in volume two. Luke first summarizes the communication of the risen Jesus during the forty days after Easter by saying that he was "speaking about the kingdom of God" (Acts 1:3). He tells the disciples to stay in Jerusalem to "wait for the promise of the Father" and to "baptized in the Holy Spirit" (1:4-5). The risen Lord had already spoken of the "promise of [the] Father" at Luke 24:49. That the promise of the Father can be equated with the gift of the Holy Spirit is an identification already prepared for by 11:13, "... how much more will the Father in heaven give the holy Spirit to those who ask him?," and 12:32, "Your Father is pleased to give you the kingdom."

The apostles' question, whether Jesus was at this time going to restore the kingdom to Israel (1:6), refers to the expectation of Jewish apocalyptic. Note that Jesus does not dismiss the question as irrelevant; he reinterprets it. They will receive the power of the holy Spirit to be Jesus' witnesses from Jerusalem out to the "the ends of the earth" (v 8). The symbolic number twelve is restored through the choice of Matthias. On the Jewish feast celebrating the giving of the Law at Sinai, Pentecost, when Jews from "every nation under heaven," (Acts 2:5) gather in Jerusalem, they receive the Holy Spirit. Luke is careful to tell this episode in language that speaks of the Christian Pentecost experience as a reversal of the scattering of the Tower of Babel event, and therefore a fulfillment of the promise to Abram, to be a blessing to the nations.[6] That he wants the reader to understand these events according to Isaiah's vision of the Creator restoring his people through his Servant so that the servant people might be a "light to the nations" is demonstrated by his quotation of Isa 42:6 and 49:6 at Acts 13:47, Paul applying this mission to the work of himself and Barnabas, and 26:18-23, regarding the risen Jesus working through his church.

After Pentecost, the six further references to kingdom of God occur in statements about the proclamation of the good news by Philip to the Samaritans (8:12), Paul at Ephesus (19:8), at Miletus (20:25), and finally in Rome (28:23,31). Given the care with which Luke has constructed his narrative and given his cues to the Old Testament background, there can be no doubt that these references are meant to evoke all of the associations that have accrued to the phrase "kingdom of God" in the course of the Third Gospel: the Creator's rescuing work, begun in Jesus goes forward, under the guidance of the risen Lord, in the work of the church. To savor what this might mean more concretely regarding the human relationship to the goods of the earth, we shall look more closely at two paradigmatic passages: Acts 4:23-35, a community prayer and its aftermath and Luke 12:13-48, Luke's editing of Jesus' teaching on anxiety.

TWO PARADIGMATIC PASSAGES

Acts 4:23-35: The Creator saving through the Spirit-filled community: a paradigm of the coming of the kingdom.

The two cameo descriptions of the Jerusalem community life in Acts 2:42-47 and 4:32-35 have received plenty of attention from the post-biblical church, especially as models for monastic life. Read in their full context, however, they emerge as paradigms for understanding the life of the *whole church* within the theological vision of Luke-Acts. We shall focus on the second scenario (Acts 4:32-35) and read it as the culmination of an episode that begins at verse 23, which follows immediately after the healing of the man born lame and the inquest of Peter and John before the Sanhedrin:

> After their release they went back to their own people and reported what the chief priests and the elders had told them. And when they heard it, they raised their voices to God with one accord and said, 'Sovereign Lord, maker of heaven and earth and the sea and all that is in them, you said by the holy Spirit through the mouth of our father David, you servant: Why did the Gentiles rage and the peoples entertain folly? The kings of the earth took their stand and the princes gathered together against the Lord and against his anointed. Indeed they gathered in this city against your holy servant Jesus whom you anointed, Herod and Pontius Pilate, together with the Gentiles and the peoples of Israel, to do what your hand and [your] will had long ago planned to take place. And now, Lord, take note of their threats, and enable your servants to speak your word with all boldness, and you stretch forth [your] hand to heal, and signs and wonders are done through the name of your holy servant Jesus.' As they prayed, the place where they were gathered shook, and they were all filled with the holy Spirit and continued to speak the word of God with boldness.

The community of believers was of one heart and mind, and no one claimed that any of his possessions was his own but they had everything in common. With great power the apostles bore witness to the resurrection of the Lord Jesus, and great favor was accorded them all. There was no needy person among them, for those who owned property or houses would sell them, bring the proceeds of the sale, and put them at the feet of the apostles, and they were distributed to each according to need. Against the background of what we have already said about the kingdom of God in Luke-Acts, with its Isaian background, it should suffice to make eight observations regarding this excerpt from Luke's paradigmatic portrayal of the early church to show how it exemplifies the coming of the kingdom.

(1) This account of a community at prayer is not a transcription of a miracle of unified choral improvisation but a composition of Luke, in the manner of the other speeches in Acts, with Luke employing the convention of other Hellenistic historians, that is, creating a short cameo speech that embodies the historian's interpretation of what is going forward in the events narrated. It is therefore a paradigm, not a record.

(2) The prayer/speech is constructed according to what the Dead Sea scrolls have taught us to call the *pesher* format, that is, it presents an ancient text, here the opening verses of Psalm 2, and interprets that ancient text in the light of current or recent events.

(3) Strikingly, the community addresses God as cosmic Creator of the three-tiered universe of the Hebrew world view and of all that it contains. The title by which God is addressed, *despota* ("Master"), is a rare word for God in the New Testament, appearing elsewhere in the Gospels and Acts only at Luke 2:29 with the beginning of the *Nunc Dimittis*. Can we guess what lies behind Luke's choice of this title? It occurs in only one place in the Greek Pentateuch, at Gen 15:2, 8. Since this is the famous covenant promise to Abraham, it could well be the motive of the implied author to recall this passage, especially given the importance of the Abrahamic covenant in Luke-Acts.[7]

(4) How does this *pesher* work? Luke finds in the language of the first two verses of Psalm 2 a remarkable consonance with the developments leading to the death of Jesus. Acts 4:27 and 28 unpack the connections in reverse order, making a chiasm:

A "Why did the *Gentiles* [*ethn*] rage and the *peoples* [*laoi*] entertain
   folly?
   B The *kings* [basileis] took their stand, and the *princes*
       C *gathered* [*syn chth san*] together against the Lord and his

anointed [*christou*].

C' Indeed they *gathered* [*syn chth san*] in this holy city
        against your holy servant Jesus whom you *anointed*,
    B' Herod [a *king*] and Pontius Pilate [*a prince*],
A' together with the *Gentiles* [*ethnesin*] and the *peoples* [*laois*] of
    Israel."

(5) The implied reader, who would be tracking his application of Psalm 2 which was quoted and explicated, making no demands on memory, would at this point expect an application of the remainder of the Psalm, which goes on to threaten divine reprisal upon all those who dared to oppose the accession of the Lord's Anointed One. Rather than pray for divine power to show itself in reprisal, they pray for healing and boldness in preaching.

(6) In shape and content, the prayer echoes passages from the prophets. Commentators looking for an Old Testament model for this community speech/prayer have suggested Isa 37:16-20 (see, for example, Haenchen, 228). This is the prayer of Hezekiah, occurring in the historical appendix relating the invasion of Sennacherib. In response to the taunting letter of the Assyrian king, Hezekiah goes to the temple and prays to God "over all the kings of the earth" and as "maker of the heavens and the earth"; the prayer proceeds with a formula that can be paraphrased: "*in truth* they have done such and such ... *but now* show your power and save your people." That does indeed reflect the *structure* of the prayer of Acts 4, but the content appears to be influenced by another source, Jeremiah 39 (chapter 32 in the Hebrew Bible), verses 20-21.

The larger context in Jeremiah is that of the oracles of the new covenant of restoration. The immediate context is the narrative about the transaction in prison, in which the prophet, urged by a divine audition, purchases the family field in Anathoth from his cousin Hanamel. Jeremiah then prays, "Ah, Lord God, you have made heaven and earth by your great might, with your outstretched arm; nothing is impossible to you." The prayer then reviews God's continuing expression of mercy, moving seamlessly from creation to redemption: "You have wrought *signs and wonders* in the land of Egypt *even to this day*, and in Israel, and among the inhabitants of the earth; and you did make *for yourself a name, as at this day*. You did bring out your people Israel out of the land of Egypt *with signs, and with wonders, with a mighty hand*, and with a high arm, and with great signs; and you gave them this land" (v 21). It goes on to speak of

Israel's disobedience and the consequent punishing attack of the Chaldeans, of a divine oracle reiterating the promise that the Babylonian conquest will be followed by the full restoration of the people to the land, and of the renewal of the covenant meant to last forever (vv 36-41).[8]

The besieged Christian community of Jerusalem prays like Jeremiah by asking the Creator of heaven and earth to extend the divine hand in the "signs and wonders" of a new Exodus bringing liberation and restoration of the people, despite what the enemy has done in "the city." Here Luke reflects the union of creation and redemption that pervades his inherited Septuagint Greek Bible, especially in the Psalms, in Isaiah, and in Jeremiah. The experience of the early Christian community has led them to understand that the Creator redeems by extending the healing work of Jesus through them. The signs and wonders of the new exodus begun in his ministry continue through theirs.

(7) The outcome of the prayer is another Pentecost experience, an infilling of the Holy Spirit whose power is demonstrated in bold preaching and in a community life whose sharing of possessions fulfills both Hellenistic ideals of community life, "the community of believers was of one heart and one mind and no one claimed that any of his possessions was his own, but the had everything in common," as well as the Deuteronomic ideal of covenant life, "There was no needy person among them"; see Deut 15:4, 7, 1 (see Johnson, 1992: 86-87, 91).

(8) This convergence of motifs, Creator rescuing with the power of the Holy Spirit and creating a community that preaches boldly, heals, and shares goods, justifies our reading this passage as a paradigm of the unfolding of the kingdom of God in the life of the church. *Luke 12:13-48, Luke's setting of the Q preaching on anxiety.*

Now to the second example illustrating Luke's theology of kingdom, community, and the goods of the earth, Luke 12:13-48. First, a quotation of the core of the passage (vv 28-31):

If God so clothes the grass in the field that grows today and is thrown into the oven tomorrow, will he not much more provide for you, O you of little faith? As for you, do not seek what you are to eat and what you are to drink, and do not worry anymore. All the nations of the world seek for these things, and your Father knows that you need them. Instead, seek his kingdom, and these things will be given you besides. At first glance, no passage would seem less relevant to our ecological concerns. Though the teaching does deal with the relationship between humans and the environment, the earth provides the food and fiber to satisfy human needs, the words of Jesus appear to advise people not to worry about these things, to trust rather in divine providence. And yet, while this teaching might possibly be so understood when read in its Matthean setting, where it forms an important part of the Sermon on the Mount (Matt 6:25-34),[9] Luke's editorial framework helps the reader understand this teaching as an urgent call to responsibility, meeting human needs by properly stewarding the earth's resources.

Q material that Matthew places in his first and fifth speeches, the teaching on anxiety in Matt 6:25-33 and parables about watchfulness and faithfulness in Matt 24:43-51, Luke here gathers together in one place; and he frames and expands it with some of his own special material. He introduces the material with his parable of the Rich Fool (12:16-21), which provides a showcase example of how greed can spring from and foster a false interpretation of one's relationship to earth and community. For the landowner's greed, his effort to possess his life and his property for himself (Luke 17:33), works to sever all of his covenant relationships; his relationship with the *land* (the Creator's gift which itself produces the harvest), with the *community* (his monologue does not include the community for whose needs he is to steward the land), with *himself* (he addresses his *psych* in a possessive way that shows he does not understand even his own life as gift), and with the *Creator*, whose intervention at the end comes as a complete surprise. The saying about seeking the kingdom and all these other things will be added (v 30) is followed by another kingdom of God saying that is unique to Luke: "Do not be afraid any longer, little flock, for your Father is pleased to give you the kingdom." We know from the spelling out of the Father's gift of the kingdom in Acts that this entails the creation of the Spirit-filled community that uses the resources to meet the needs of all its members. The next verse makes that connection: "Sell your belongings and give alms. Provide money bags for yourselves that do not wear out, an inexhaustible treasure in heaven that no thief can reach nor moth destroy. For where your treasure is, there also will your heart be" (12:32-34).

The parables that follow in vv 35-38, the Vigilant and Faithful Servants, mirror the situation of the rich landowner in that he was subject to an unexpected visitation, the death for the landowner is mirrored in the return of the master for the steward (v 37), in the break-in of the thief for the master (v 39), and in the coming of the Son of Man for Jesus' audience (v 40). The parabolic expansion in vv 32-48 spells out the responsibility of the faithful steward as a matter of distributing food at the proper time (v 42). Conversely, the irresponsibility of the unfaithful steward is concretized as the abuse of persons and of food and drink (vv 45-46). This context makes it clear that the instruction about not worrying about what to eat, drink and wear, and seeking the kingdom of God have nothing to do with dropping out and everything to do with the responsible use of the goods of the earth in the context of community. The proper response to a provident Creator is sharing through almsgiving and a vigilant stewardship that manages the resources of food, drink, and fiber to meet the needs of all.

Luke has prepared the reader for this Creator-centered ethics by the saying, unique to this gospel, at 11:39-40: "… inside you are filled with greed and evil. You fools! Did not the maker of the outside make the inside too?" Here Jesus, and/or Luke, invokes the relationship of creature to Creator in function of his ethical exhortation. In this he is in the tradition of Isaiah who, in the midst of a similar set of six woes (Isa 5:8-22) directed against the arrogant, indulgent, and oblivious rich, says, "For they drink wine with harp and psaltery and drums and pipes, but they regard not the works of the Lord, and consider not the works of his hands" (Isa 5:12). They squeeze creatures dry for their pleasure but ignore the Creator, an acknowledgment that would surely lead them to act with justice. The money-loving Pharisees (see 16:14) are addressed in the same way, and with language that links them with the rich landowner: the word for fool is rare in the New Testament, appearing in the gospels and Acts only here and in the parable of the rich landowner. What the Pharisees are here accused of, greed of the most grasping kind, is precisely illustrated in the behavior of the landowner.

SUMMARY AND CONCLUSIONS
REGARDING ENVIRONMENTAL JUSTICE TODAY

First, let me summarize what this excursion into aspects of Luke's narrative has revealed regarding his vision of the relationship between God, Earth, and human beings. Luke's two-volume format afforded him an extraordinary range in which to spell out his vision. As a way of taking a sounding of this vision, we chose to follow his narrative development of the core symbol of Jesus' preaching, the kingdom of God. A good case can be made that the preaching of the historical Jesus was highly informed by the imagery of Isaiah. The Beatitudes, for example, find their home base in Isaiah 61 (elaborated in Hamm, 1990: 16-25).

When Luke provides his own narrative context to interpret the meaning of Jesus and his message of God's reign, he renders even more explicit its rootedness in the Isaian vision. This became evident in Luke's appropriation of Isaiah's special verb, *euangelizasthai* (to proclaim good news) and in his frequent quotation of and allusion to all parts of Isaiah, especially what we today call Deutero-Isaiah (Isa 40-55). This Isaian background makes it clear that the coming of the kingdom of God is the end-time action of the Creator of the cosmos whose continuing creation is now being manifest in a fresh way, beginning with the power of the divine Spirit in the life, death, and resurrection of Jesus, and continuing in the story of the church implicit in the Third Gospel and explicit in Acts. This fresh rescue action of the Creator shows itself in the formation of a community of transformed persons who express their conversion especially in their use of the goods of the earth to meet the needs of all. It would take a full commentary to spell this out, but we saw it demonstrated in our study of two sample passages, the cameo description of community at prayer and ministry in Acts 4 and in the framing and interpretation of the teaching on anxiety in Luke 12.

The outcome? Luke-Acts presents the kingdom of God as much a matter of this world as of the next. Through Jesus and a renewed Israel, the church, the Creator of the universe renews the divine covenant by changing hearts with the power of the Holy Spirit so that the renewed relationship to the rescuing Creator issues in a reordering of social relationships expressed in generalized reciprocity in the use of the goods of the earth to meet the needs of all.

PRACTICAL IMPLICATIONS
FOR ENVIRONMENTAL JUSTICE

Reading our Christian Scriptures without forgetting their Hebrew roots will heal an unnecessary, and biblically unwarranted, cleavage between creation theology and redemption theology. Reading Luke against the background of his Israelite sources shows that for him, as for his prophetic predecessors, it is the Cosmic Creator who rescues. What the Creator rescues is creation, through the conversion of the one species in creation that has the freedom to rebel against its Maker. If Scripture does not commit us to the *bio*centric vision of ecology, it does commit us to a *theo*centric vision that views the Earth as the Lord's and humans as stewards of the Earth's resources in the service of the common good. Luke stands firmly in this tradition. Although he does not explicitly use Paul's and John's new creation language to describe the church, he does describe the formation of the church and the conduct of its mission as the work of God the Creator. That privileged status of the church requires that the Christian community model in its own behavior and policies a use of the earth and its resources that is sustainable.

It might be objected that the ecological vision of Luke-Acts is confined to the Christian community and does not invite service of the larger human community, what Luke calls the *oikoumen* (see Luke 4:5; 21:26; Acts 11:28; 17:31; 19:27; 24:5). This objection overlooks the implications of other attendant themes in Luke-Acts. This community has the Isaian Servant's vocation of being a light to the nations; it implements the Abrahamic covenant which implies a fulfillment of the Noachic covenant between Creator and all human beings together with every living creature (Gen 9:9,12,15-17).

Some fundamentalist readings of some New Testament documents have led some Christians to social and political irresponsibility. Some reason this way: why work for nuclear disarmament if you understand the biblical symbol of Armageddon to refer to an inevitable nuclear holocaust? The theology of Luke-Acts gives a different interpretation of the Christian view of the last things. First-century Israelite expectations of the end-times have already been inaugurated in the first advent of Jesus and the emergence of the church; all four evangelists and Paul affirm this, each in his own way. While Luke affirms the traditions regarding personal and final judgment and a second coming of the Son of man, these eschatological realities serve to highlight the importance of one's stewardship of the resources of the earth (Luke 12 and 16).

One final consideration, regarding our conversation and collaboration with those who do not share our Christian faith. The wisdom-shaped cosmic christologies of Colossians, Ephesians, and John may well nurture the Christian vision of ecological justice, but our global ecological crisis requires the collaboration of persons living in all religious traditions. Though these traditions obviously vary in their assessment of the cosmological meaning of Jesus, they have in common some account of the relationship of the cosmos to its sacred Source. As we participate in the *interreligious* dialogue and action that our ecological crisis requires, we may do well to stress the Creator-centered theology to which Jesus pointed rather than to the Christ-centered cosmology that inspires the belief and actions of many within the household of Christianity.

SOURCES

The main sources for this study are the Greek text of Luke and Acts and the Septuagint. Translations of short citations are my own. The translations of fuller quotations are, for the New Testament, the New American Bible, and, for the Septuagint, the rendering found in *The Septuagint Version of the Old Testament and Apocrypha with an English Translation* (London: Samuel Bagster and Sons, n.d.). The following items represent the secondary literature cited in this essay.

Chilton, Bruce
    1984 *A Galilean Rabbi and His Bible*. Wilmington: Michael Glazier.
Fitzmyer, Joseph A.
    1981 *The Gospel According to Luke, I-IX*. Anchor Bible 28; Garden
        City: Doubleday.
    1985 *The Gospel According to Luke, X-XXIV*. Anchor Bible 28a;
        Garden City: Doubleday.
Haenchen, Ernst
    1971 *The Acts of the Apostles: A Commentary*. Philadelphia: Westmin-
        ster.
Hamm, Dennis
    1986 "Acts 3:1-10: The Healing of the Temple Beggar as Lukan
        Theology." *Biblica* 67, 305-19.
    1988 "Luke 19:8 Once Again: Does Zacchaeus Defend or Resolve?"
        Journal of Biblical Literature 197.3, 431-37.
    1990 *The Beatitudes in Context: What Luke and Matthew Meant*.
        Wilmington: Michael Glazier.
    1994 "What the Samaritan Leper Sees: The Narrative Christology of

Luke 17:11-19." *Catholic Biblical Quarterly* 56.2, 273-84.

Jervell, Jacob

1972 "The Twelve on Israel's Thrones." In *Luke and the People of God*, 75-112. Minneapolis: Augsburg.

Johnson, Luke T.

1991 *The Gospel of Luke. Sacra Pagina*, vol. 3; Collegeville, MN: Liturgical.

1992 *The Acts of the Apostles. Sacra Pagina*, vol. 5; Collegeville, MN: Liturgical Press.

Lohfink, Gerhard

1982 *Jesus and Community: The Social Dimension of the Christian Faith*. New York: Paulist.

Moxnes, Halvor

1988 *The Economy of the Kingdom: Social Conflict and Economic Relations in Luke's Gospel*. Philadelphia: Fortress.

NOTES

1. Some authors, notably J. Crossan and M. Borg, have recently argued that the historical Jesus preached only a sapiential eschatology, the ongoing reign of God as Lord of the cosmos, and that the apocalyptic dimension is the later elaboration of the New Testament church. My presentation concurs with J. Fitzmyer and R. Brown, who understand Jesus to have preached an apocalyptic Reign of the Lord of the cosmos.

2. The verb *euangelizomai* occurs not at all in Mark, only once in Matthew (11:5, the Q saying paralleling Luke 7:2, "the poor have the good news preached to them"), and 25 times in Luke-Acts.

3. Halvor Moxnes (1988: 34-35) describes the ethical vision of the Sermon on the Plain, as well as that of the rest of Luke-Acts, as a matter of seeing God as the ultimate Patron or Benefactor who frees the community of those who share this faith-vision to counter the culture around them by sharing possessions in the mode of "generalized reciprocity," that is, altruistic transactions based on knowing creation as pure gift to be shared as pure gift. The rest of the world operates according the "balanced reciprocity," attempting to reach equivalence in goods and services, and sometimes according to negative reciprocity, getting something for nothing.

4. The handing over to Jesus of all things is precisely what is announced in the Galilean resurrection appearance at the end of Matthew 28:28: "All power in heaven and on earth has been given to me." See also John 3:35; 17:2, where the

post-Resurrection perspective is retrojected into the story-line of Jesus' pre-Easter ministry.

5. Note that the phrase "setting free the oppressed" is interpolated into Luke's quotation of Isa 61:1 at Luke 4:18.

6. In addition to the reversal of the situation, Genesis 11 presenting a gathering of people of diverse languages who come to understand and Acts 2 presenting a scattering issuing in diversity and misunderstanding, note the play on the word group *syncheō/synchesis* (confuse/confusion). Whereas in the Babel episode God confuses (*syncheō*) their languages *lest* each understand/hear (*akouō*) his neighbor, in the Pentecost episode the people are confused *because* each understands/hears in his own language (Acts 2:6).

7. See also Isa 1:24 (*Kyrios ho despotes sabaoth*), whose context is divine judgment and restoration of the people, elaborated in the famous peace vision of Isaiah 2 (similarly 3:1; 10:33). Generally, the rare Septuagint uses of this title emphasize divine sovereignty (see Jer 1:6; 4:10; 15:11; Jon 4:3). This form of address enhances the sense of submission to the Creator of all.

8. The healing of the man born lame at the Beautiful Gate is interpreted by Peter's speech (Acts 3:12-26) as a sign of the beginning of restoration of all promised by the prophets and fulfilled in these days. Surely the passage from Jeremiah 31-33 is one of those passages referring to the restoration promised for these days (see Hamm, 1986).

9. Matthew's redaction of the kingdom saying finally forestalls the interpretation of these words as a summons to material irresponsibility. "But seek first the kingdom [of God] *and his righteousness,* and all these things will be given you besides" (Matt 6:33) Matthew's addition, "and his righteousness," makes it clear that this mandate is not about dropping out socially. It is about living the righteousness of the kingdom, which the rest of the gospel makes clear entails nonviolence, forgiveness, sharing, and meeting the needs of the poor. Thus, the advice about anxiety regarding what one will eat and drink is a call not to some kind of social quietism but rather to get one's priorities straight: living the righteousness of the kingdom will create a community in which the needs of all are met. All this Luke's context makes even more clear.

"What in the Church Is Going On?"
Or "Growing up Catholic in Lake Wobegon"

David G. Schultenover, S.J.

Most Americans have heard of Lake Wobegon, that mythical Minnesota town created by Garrison Keillor and situated, like the Garden of Eden, between two great rivers, the Mississippi and the Sauk. I grew up East of Eden, on the worldly edge of Lake Wobegon, where the Sauk empties into the Mississippi just across from St. Cloud. In fact, I could look out the upstairs window in winter when the trees were bare and see the St. Cloud Hospital, where my mother was for many years night superintendent, in the years when the night super did everything. She handled all the emergencies from Lake Wobegon.

I had ten siblings, until my brother just ahead of me sacrificed his infant life to political correctness, and we ended up with five boys and five girls. With such a tribe, you can imagine my mother's mantra was "What in the world is going on here? My stars!" Mom had a cosmic view of things. My Dad's mantra was "What in the hell is going on down there?," referring to the basement where all hell had indeed broken loose. Dad was cosmic too but in the obverse direction. He was infernal, Mom was celestial; that's how she made sense of the universe. She lived in eschatological hope. For Dad, there was no sense, life was hell. Mom went to church a lot, Dad only to make his Easter duty. For Mom, the Church was perfect and priests were oracles of truth, which explains why I became one. Dad was suspicious of priests long before they made good print. For myself, I settled into an anxious equilibrium between the two of them.

Both viewpoints on the Church are valid and true at the same time. Which means that the Church's reality east of Eden is ambiguous. And most people, if they be honest, feel ambivalent about growing up Catholic, or Lutheran, or Muslim, or whatever, even about growing up. We all wear the two-faced mask of Greek drama. We hold two antagonistic viewpoints together in tension.

What enables us to maintain two views in tension is the dominant story or myth by which we live our lives. Let me point to two dominant myths that are themselves contrasting: the first one is the last of the myths that introduce the book of Genesis and supply the reason for the promise to Abraham in Genesis 12, that he would become a great nation and a blessing to all other nations. "Once upon a time all the world spoke a single language and used the same words [my mother's eschatological reality]. But they became proud in their strength. They built a city and a tower to rival God. Then the Lord came down to see the city and the tower and said, 'Here they are, one people with a single language, and now they have started to do this; henceforth nothing they have a mind to do will be beyond their reach. Come, let us go down there and confuse their speech, so that they will not understand what they say to one another' [my Dad's profane reality]. So the Lord scattered them from there all over the face of the earth." That's the final myth that introduces the Torah. Life looks confused and desperate. It will take God's intervention, beginning with Abraham, to give people reason to believe that history has a goal, a point of ultimate resolution and reconciliation, a gravitation toward ultimate meaning, ultimate salvation.

The answering myth is in Acts 2: "While the day of Pentecost was running its course, they were all together in one place, visitors from all over the world, when suddenly there came from the sky a noise like that of a strong driving wind, which filled the whole house. And there appeared to them tongues as of fire which came to rest on each one. And they were all filled with the Holy Spirit and began to talk in other tongues. And they were utterly astounded and exclaimed, 'These men are Galileans, are they not? How is it that we hear them, each of us in our own native language, telling the great things God has done?' They were perplexed and asked one another, 'What can this mean?' Others said contemptuously, 'They are all drunk.' But Peter stood up with the Eleven and denied it." Ever after, Christians have taken wine with their meals. That was the Church's beginning, an auspicious beginning, arguing about spirits, in the Spirit, of course.

As long as the Church spoke one voice, she did just fine. But Pentecost meant that the good news was to be broadcast in and to all voices. As soon as the disciples took Pentecost seriously, they ran into naysayers who took literally the words of Jesus, "My mission is only to the lost sheep of the house of Israel" (Mt 15.24). This announcement sets up the problem experienced in Matthew's church up there in Gentile Syria. For whom does the Christian community exist? For whom is this good news of Jesus Christ? The question is resolved at the gospel's end: "Go therefore and make disciples of *all* nations; and lo, I am with you always, to the close of the age" (Mt 28.20). This is the promise to Abraham reconfigured for the Christian myth, which is not, as they say, "*just* a myth," but a *historicized* myth, the myth of God historically incarnate in Jesus of Nazareth and now living through his Spirit in the collective memory *of* the Church but *for* the whole universe.

What about *them*?, the Jewish Christians asked. The outsiders? The Gentiles? Those who don't even know let alone keep Torah? Who is Jesus for them? We know what he is for us; we figured that out by appealing to our Scriptures. But who is he for them? Is he for them what he is for us? And if so, how do we tell them that in a language they can understand? If we use *their* language, if we try to *translate* what Jesus means to us into *their* universe of discourse, will we be handing on the same Jesus? What will be gained, what will be lost in the translation? Does not God require *all* peoples to keep Torah? What after all *is* Torah? Is everything we have been taught Torah? The kosher kitchen rules? Circumcision? I mean, after all, that *is* the sign of Torah. Ah yes, said Paul to Peter at the Church's first Council, that is the sign of Torah, but has not Jesus crucified and risen abrogated *that* sign for the sign of the cross? Does not the sign of the cross supersede the sign of Torah? Has Jesus not, in fact, fulfilled the Torah and nullified the requirement to sign oneself by the old Torah? Is not the cross the sign of the New Torah? Are we not liberated by his Spirit, by the energy emanating from his cross and resurrection, to recognize him in the breaking of the bread and *not* in circumcision?

The Pentecost myth represents the Lukan community's effort to bridge a gap between Jews and Gentiles by annexing to the time-bound myth of God Incarnate, which ended with Jesus' death, a myth that would endure through all times and spaces, a myth that would speak not only to the House of Israel but to all houses everywhere. How is God incarnate in Jesus who died to remain with us to the ends of the earth? How is the promise to Abraham, that he would be a blessing for *all* nations, to be passed on to a new reality, a reality that attenuates the twelve tribes of Israel to all the nations of the world? As the early Church discovered, it would be through Jesus' Spirit, liberated by sacrificial death from constraints of space and time to enter into all times and all spaces. Through death Jesus would become existentially Emmanuel, God with us everywhere and forever. The myth of God Incarnate is subsumed into the myth of the Spirit of the Incarnate God circling the globe, suffusing the universe with divine energy, incarnating the love of God in all times and places.

THE EARLY CHRISTIAN APOCALYPTIC PARADIGM

To reach out beyond Judaism, the Church needed to shift into a new self-understanding, a new worldview. That shift, from a Jewish to a Gentile church, is now commonly referred to as a "paradigm shift."[1] You may be wondering what exactly a paradigm shift is. Thomas Kuhn, who gave this notion currency, defined paradigm as "an entire constellation of beliefs, values, techniques and so on shared by the members of a given community."[2] Now, it's one thing to define a concept; it's quite another to experience it and to have a feel for it. Paradigms are perceptual filters. They allow you to see some things but not others. They present for you your own world view. An analogy would be the "Magic Eye" illustrations printed in the comic section of Sunday newspapers and elsewhere. To the normal eye, these illustrations are merely two-dimensional. But if you stare at them a certain way, your perception suddenly changes and you now see three dimensionally what two dimensions prevent you from seeing. Married people experience a paradigm shift when their first child enters their lives. For a change to qualify as a paradigm shift, it has to alter one's entire world of perception.

The first paradigm shift in the Church's self-understanding meant breaking out of the cocoon of the Old Israel into the New Israel. It meant breaking out of the apocalyptic mode of early Christianity that expected the Second Coming within the lifetime of the first disciples. It meant breaking out of a strictly Jewish world view into a Greco-Roman worldview and language, into a culture that lived by different gods and myths.

The challenge became to translate the myth of God incarnate in Jesus and now present in his Spirit into the thought-forms of Greek-and Latin-speaking Gentiles. It meant doing what Paul first did when he debated with philosophers in Athens before the Court of Areopagus (Acts 17.16-32). "Some said, 'What can this charlatan be trying to say?'; others said, 'He would appear to be a propagandist for foreign deities.' This because he was preaching about Jesus and Resurrection. So they hauled him before the Court and said, 'May we know what this new doctrine is that you propound? You are introducing ideas that sound strange to us, and we would like to know what they mean.'" Note that the Athenians did not reject Paul because they didn't understand what he was saying or because it sounded strange. They were not convinced that they themselves had the complete and final answer. They were searchers. In fact, Luke continues, they had no time for anything but talking or hearing about the latest novelty. Then Paul stood up before the Court and said, "'Men of Athens, I perceive that in every way you are very religious. For as I passed along, and observed the objects of your worship, I found also an altar with the inscription, To an Unknown God. What, therefore, you worship as unknown, this I proclaim to you. The God who made the world and everything in it, being Lord of heaven and earth, does not live in shrines made by man, nor is he served by human hands as though he needed anything, since he gives to all men life and breath and everything ... yet he is not far from each one of us, for 'in him we live and move and have our being'; as even some of your poets have said: 'For we are indeed his offspring.'"

Needless to say, Paul did not convince everyone. In fact, for many generations to come Christianity would be considered merely a sect of Judaism and was intermittently persecuted. But, in time, Christianity's adaptability, its universalistic outlook, its power of appeal to searchers dissatisfied with all the other myths made it an attractive alternative for increasing numbers of the Roman Empire's leading citizens, so that, by the time of Constantine, it seemed a singularly shrewd idea to promote Christianity as the glue of his empire. Constantine himself was not baptized until his deathbed, but that didn't prevent him from doing all he could to bind the Church to the state by the closest possible ties: exempting clergy from taxation, massive funding of Church building, and co-opting Church leaders into positions of state leadership, as there was no separation between Church and State. Indeed, Constantine himself, even though not baptized, was considered the authoritative head of the Church. He called and presided over the first ecumenical council at Nicea. The bishop of Rome wasn't even at Nicea; he was represented by two priests. Why did Constantine call Nicea? Not because he was terribly disturbed about Arius' claim that Jesus was subordinate to the Father and therefore not fully divine, but because Arius was effectively and affectively splitting the Church, and a split church did not a unified empire make.

THE EARLY CHURCH HELLENISTIC PARADIGM

And so was ushered in the second major paradigm shift with its gains and losses. Among the gains can be listed the promotion of Christianity to the status of state religion, thus institutionalizing it, stabilizing it in creed, code, cult, and canon, and providing a vehicle of conversion of the West and perhaps eventually of the entire world to Christianity. But no gain is without its dark side. The practice of rule by ecumenical council presided over by the emperor established a style of governance that was both a strength and a weakness. The weakness was that dissent was often handled in a way that led to schism rather than to constructive dialogue. The interest of unity sometimes led to a demand for compliance rather than to the effort to incorporate the insights of opposing groups; and so it sometimes led to a win/lose schism rather than to a creative win/win resolution.

But even as the second paradigm was being born, seeds of the next were being sown. Constantine's decision to move the imperial seat from Rome to Byzantium, renamed Constantinople, was momentous for the subsequent development of the Church as Roman Catholic. His move left a power vacuum in the West, and the only suitable person to fill that vacuum was the bishop of Rome. To oversimplify: in the West only one person, the bishop of Rome, exercised both ecclesial and secular authority; in the East the Emperor did much the same, but with a subordinate bishop as nominal head of the Church. The upshot was that very soon the bishop of Rome was arguing with the bishop of Constantinople over church primacy, an argument that later mixed in different conceptions of the Trinity unacceptable to the East, and led to the Great Schism that remains to this day.

The gain for the West was that Roman Catholicism became the one and only religion. With the bishop of Rome claiming supremacy, political authority, no matter who exercised it, was always regarded as subordinate to and in the service of religious authority. The loss was that Eastern ways of thinking about God and grace were set aside for Western, more practical, legalistic ways, ways that reified grace, made it a substance that could be portioned, proportioned, value-assessed by days, and sold as indulgences to raise money.

Another gain was that the organization and style of governance developed by the secular Roman curia became the model for the Church. It was hierarchical, centrally controlled, and efficient for maintaining unity of belief and practice. The dark side became increasingly evident as the Catholic Church, under pressure of power struggles between emperors and popes, moved out of the Early Church Hellenistic Paradigm and into the new Medieval Roman Catholic Paradigm. The Holy Roman *German* emperors were increasingly usurping ecclesiastical power and controlling Church property by appointing their own bishops.

THE MEDIEVAL ROMAN CATHOLIC PARADIGM

The attempt to extricate the Church from control of the German emperors began under Pope Leo IX in 1048. Leo's first step in his strategy to reform and regain control of the Church was to impose celibacy on all clergy, for a celibate clergy would substantially vitiate the temptation to simony and other abuses. Leo's two executors were Hildebrand, who later became Gregory VII, and Humbert, who carried to Constantinople the excommunication of Patriarch Michael Cerularius in 1054, the event that sealed the break between East and West. The schism exposed the incompatibility between two church paradigms: the Early Church Hellenistic, in which the East continued, and the Roman Catholic Medieval, which became the established paradigm for the West into the twentieth century. Leo IX died in 1054 and his successor, Victor II, was the last pope to be nominated by a German emperor. Victor died in 1057 and was succeeded by Stephen IX, who was succeeded a year later by Nicholas II, the first pope to be crowned like kings and emperors, a symbol of the medieval paradigm with its monarchical papacy. In 1059 a Lateran synod under Nicholas II and Humbert established the college of cardinals as the exclusive organ for electing the pope, independent of interventions by secular powers. The college of cardinals also functioned as the principal advisory body for the pope and handled the most important functions of papal administration.

The election of Alexander II in 1061 marked a critical moment. Alexander, supported by his Chancellor Hildebrand, snubbed Emperor Henry IV by not bothering to solicit his support after the election, whereupon Henry appointed Honorius II as antipope. From this time on, centralization increased geometrically, as Pope Alexander and Chancellor Hildebrand countered imperial power by creating a network of papal legates to enforce reform decrees and confront the nobility with papal claims to territories. Increasingly, they appealed to that forged document, the Donation of

Constantine, to justify their claims. Alexander also renewed for Spain the promise made by John VIII in 878 to absolve the sins of troops who died defending Christians against Moslems. This was an important prelude to the crusades and papal militarism that began in 1095 with Urban II and sharply characterized the Medieval Roman Catholic Paradigm.

Hildebrand, elected Gregory VII in 1073, was the real architect of this paradigm. From 1049, when Leo IX appointed him administrator of the patrimony of St. Peter, he resolved to liberate the Church from control of the nobility. The single, most powerful instrument of that control had been "lay investiture," by which is meant the conferral of ecclesiastical office by lay nobility, a tool used by the nobility for gaining property and wealth. In the midst of Gregory's standoff with Emperor Henry IV featuring mutual depositions, Gregory drafted the most famous document of his papacy, the so-called *Dictatus Papae*, twenty-seven principles of papal primacy. They became the blueprint of the new paradigm that would reach its apogee with Popes Innocent III and Boniface VIII. Among the Dictates are these:

> The Roman pontiff alone is rightly called universal.
>
> He alone has the power to depose and reinstate bishops.
>
> His legate, even if he is not a bishop, presides at a council over all bishops and has the power to depose them.
>
> The pope has the power to depose, without a hearing, those who are absent [from a synod].
>
> The pope alone has the right, according to need, to make new laws, create new bishoprics, divide rich bishoprics or unite several poor ones.
>
> He alone may use the imperial insignia.
>
> All princes shall kiss the foot of the pope alone.
>
> He has the power to depose emperors.
>
> He has the right to transfer bishops from one see to another according to need.
>
> He has the right to ordain anyone from any part of the Church.
>
> No synod may be called general without his order.
>
> His decrees can be annulled by no one, but he can annul the decrees of anyone.
>
> He can be judged by no one.
>
> The important affairs of all churches are to be referred to the apostolic see.

The Roman Church has never erred and will never err to all eter-
nity, according to the testimony of sacred scripture.
By his command or permission subjects may accuse their rulers.
He can depose and reinstate bishops without calling a synod.
No one who does not agree with the Roman Church may be
regarded as a Catholic.
He has the power to absolve subjects from their oath of loyalty to
evil rulers.

Note that all of these dictates concern defining the power and authority of
the pope, no doubt for good reasons, but they also became the blueprint of
an absolutist papacy that Gregory himself did not realize. In fact, the same
Emperor Henry IV, whom Gregory excommunicated, then reconciled, and
excommunicated a second time, marched into Rome and enthroned his own
antipope Clement III, while Gregory fled into exile where he died. The
absolutist implications of Gregory's design remained to be realized in the
figures of Innocent III and Boniface VIII in just a little over a century that
saw 18 popes and 12 antipopes.

It was Innocent III who began to refer to himself not as vicar of Peter
but as the vicar of Christ himself. This concept burdened him with an all-
powerful position, which he described in a sermon as "between God and
man, under God and over man, less than God but greater than man, judge
over all and judged by no one (save the Lord)."[3] He strengthened and
extended papal primacy by strengthening canonical legislation which based
papal power on monarchical principles deliberately in accord with Roman
imperial law. The outcome was that he decisively institutionalized and cast
in law the monarchical papacy and the Medieval Roman Catholic Paradigm.

For Innocent and the canonical lawyers the role of the pope as monarch
rested on the claim to the "fullness of power" that descended from Christ
and inhered in the pope alone. This *plenitudo potestatis* distinguished the
pope from bishops and all other clergy. As the vicar of Christ has been
entrusted with the care of the whole Church, so he has a power that knows
no limits in canon law. He has the legal right to intervene in legal disputes
without recognizing the rights of lower courts and, in fact, is himself not
bound by law; as the highest lawgiver, he can dispense with the law under
certain conditions. Indeed, Innocent pointed out, the jurisdiction of the
entire hierarchy really flowed from the papal plenitude of power, for it is

the pope who summons all officeholders to a share in the care of souls. Bishops could say of themselves, therefore, as Innocent himself wrote, "Of his fullness we have all received."

Such a concept is far from the concept of bishop as it emerged in the early Church. It makes every bishop and ordained office holder little more than a papal deputy. When the First Vatican Council added to the papacy the exercise of infallibility, that only augmented the papacy's power. The Second Vatican Council attempted to redress the balance between bishops and pope by pointing out that bishops are heads of their local Churches by divine ordination, not by papal deputation.

Now all of this accumulation of power in the papacy carried with it a great deal of ambiguity. On the one hand, it enabled the Church to become the most far-reaching organization in the world and, therefore, a very powerful vehicle for the transmission of the gospel and that body of tradition so magisterially synthesized by Thomas Aquinas and the scholastics. The downside was, however, that the papacy laid itself open to abuse and corruption, as we see in the Renaissance popes, the Great Western Schism, and the Avignon papacy. During the Renaissance the papacy succumbed to human weakness, because there were no sufficiently powerful counter-institutions to check and balance it. In time, such powers would emerge in the secular world—economic, social, intellectual forces— to challenge the medieval ecclesiastical paradigm, forces that eventually led to a new paradigm, as the old grew increasingly dysfunctional and exploded in the Reformation over the sale of indulgences.

The sale of indulgences was merely the igniting incident. The mix that exploded was a long time in brewing. It began with the co-option of the gospel's spirit by Constantine, a co-option that led thousands to flee into desert monasticism as a protest movement. Monasticism and later religious life, such as the mendicants founded by Francis of Assisi, were all in one way or another efforts to purify and reform the Church.

The main problem, however, was cultural. The "same-size-fits-all" model of Church that worked in the Mediterranean world, so long as the Church was largely Mediterranean, would not work in the non-Mediterranean world. For the Mediterranean culture whose focus of personal identification was the group, the Medieval Roman Catholic Paradigm with its monarchical papacy and strict, hierarchical, authoritarian, male priesthood would be quite serviceable for centuries, although its dark side expressed itself clearly enough in the Crusades, the loss of the Eastern Church, the

Great Schism, the evils of the Renaissance papacy and the Inquisition. But for northern European cultures, whose focus of identification was not the group but the individual, it was only a matter of time before another paradigm would have to arise to challenge the Medieval Roman Catholic Paradigm.

THE REFORMATION PROTESTANT PARADIGM

The new paradigm began to take shape in the Mediterranean world itself, in the Italian Renaissance that discovered in pre-Roman Catholic Greek culture a standard to truth and beauty that predated Christianity and Church authority. It was the rediscovery of both artistic and intellectual beauty, of Greek philosophy and rationality unaided by revelation and Church doctrine. The Renaissance opened up a whole new world of investigation, validated not by external authority but by the internal authority of reason. Thus Humanism was born and flourished in the blossoming new university system and was supported by a new economic system based on money that gradually displaced the feudal system. These new movements served as plausibility structures to support the growing sense of individual identity over against group identity and that was much more congenial to the peoples of the north than of the south. If it hadn't been Luther, it would have been someone else. It was only a matter of time before some igniting moment would have marked the birth of a new paradigm.

The Reformation would not have happened if new social structures or plausibility structures had not already been in place to support the new paradigm. For many years already secular rulers in Germany and England had been eager to separate from Roman authority, and thus appropriate a substantial share of the Church's wealth and gain greater control over their own subjects. New capitalist structures favored individual possession of wealth, which in turn fostered independence of judgment. In education, universities were producing more and more educated laity who found themselves empowered not by external authority, ecclesiastical or royal, but by learning. Indeed universities were becoming an increasingly significant factor in the growing decentralization and democratization of authority. In Henry VIII's struggle with Rome over his divorce, it was to the universities that he appealed for support.

The Reformation Paradigm was not only about getting the Church back to the spirit of the Gospel. It was also about a return to the Gospel within the context of a different Church polity and structure, one that was de-Romanized, de-centralized, de-clericalized, and more compatible with the emerging new nationalistic and democratic cultural structures of northern Europe.

THE ROMAN CATHOLIC RESPONSE:
TRENT-REFORM OR COUNTER-REFORMATION COUNCIL?

Historians have debated for centuries whether the Roman Catholic response to the Protestant challenge, the Council of Trent, resulted in a Catholic Reformation or a Catholic Counter-Reformation. The truth is probably a bit of both. What the Protestants had hoped for, namely, the collapse of the Roman Church system, failed to materialize. Despite the loss of much of northern Europe, Roman Catholicism was able to regroup around the remaining territories of southern Europe, giving it a decisively Mediterranean stamp. One disastrous effect was the renewal of the Inquisition under Torquemada.

Trent also instituted wide-ranging reforms, establishing an impressive worldwide seminary system of schools in Rome for training foreign priests and future bishops. But just as important is what did not happen at Trent. The council did not reaffirm papal primacy and showed no interest in recognizing papal infallibility. Indeed, when leading German bishops and delegates from Protestant territories called for the council to reaffirm the resolutions of the Council of Constance that had defined the supremacy of the council over the pope, the papal legates deftly tabled that resolution, arguing that the council had to address the more burning issue of drafting decrees against the enemies of the Church.

The effects of Trent were enormous. Faith and theology, liturgy and canon law were unified as never before. The ultimate outcome, however, was that, despite Roman Catholicism's claim to universality, Trent made it into a confessional church over against other emerging confessional churches. We see this particularly with the promulgation of "The Tridentine Profession of Faith," the oath of allegiance to the pope, and the publication of the *Roman Catechism*.[4] Something else did not happen: the Church was unable to deal with the social-cultural roots of the differences. The Roman system was unable to embrace the implications of national cultures emerging independently of Rome, and it was not long before cultural/ religious dissonances expressed themselves in violence.

Wars of religion ravaged Europe for a century. Although they ended with the Peace of Westphalia in 1648, they resumed a century later with the French Revolution. The effect of these wars was that northern European culture, and the emerging American cultures, largely rejected religion and religious authorities as political players. The West began to develop without effective participation by Roman Catholicism, and modern culture began to emerge without much influence from Rome, because Trent had committed Roman Catholicism to a Church paradigm that was in eclipse rather than in renewal. The result was a negative hardening of the Catholic Church against dissent, whether within or without. The Church chose to close off dissenters and so was left alone in its own counter-Reformation and anti-modern paradigm.

THE ENLIGHTENMENT MODERN PARADIGM

The Wars of Religion left most religious authority bankrupt. Many of Europe's educated turned their allegiance to the only other authority at hand, namely, reason, and thus was born the Age of Reason or the Enlightenment which purged Christianity of incarnationalism and consigned God to the utterly transcendent. Western culture developed increasingly in a secular direction, independently of religious influence. If Rome was unwilling to be a partner in dialogue, Rome would be ignored altogether.

The nail in Rome's coffin was the French Revolution. The neuralgic point of the Revolution was the abuses of an absolute monarchy but, because the Church was wedded to the monarchy, when the monarchy was ousted so was the Church. The effect of the Revolution was cataclysmic. While it ended the Age of Reason, it was also in many ways the flower of the Age of Reason. A radical program of secularization ensued: Church property was nationalized; religious orders were suppressed; bishops and pastors were civilly elected; and the bishop of Rome was to have only a primacy of honor with no juridical authority over the Gallican Church.

Eventually the Revolution's de-Christianization effort spent its force and the Church fought back, but it was never again the same. Europe would never again return to a hierarchical society with an alliance of throne and altar, and programmatic secularization would continue unabated throughout the 19th and 20th centuries. Understanding the Catholic Church's reaction to the traumatic events of the revolutions of the 19th century is most important for understanding the developments in the Church's self-understanding right up to Vatican II.

The effects of the French Revolution on the Church's self-understanding were profound. The First Vatican Council and the definition of papal infallibility in 1870 probably would never have happened had it not been for the Revolution. Reason gave birth to Revolution, and the two combined to unseat religion and specifically Roman Catholicism from its position of cultural entitlement. The memory of a divided Church, a captive pope, of thousands of clergy exiled or executed, of a secularized state, and a hostile populace cast the Church into a reactive, siege mentality. Control of the Church and papacy by the temporal power had been greater during the revolutionary period than during any other period in the Church's history. Retaining the Papal States became, in the minds of many churchmen, the absolutely necessary means to guarantee some measure of the church's independence from secular rule. The loss of the Papal States to Italy in 1870, however, was a traumatic event from which the Church did not recover for at least two generations.

The effects of the French Revolution reached into all areas of human experience. It was not just ecclesiastical property that was secularized, but human thinking itself. As the European thought-world developed apart from religion, religion came to be seen as less and less necessary, more and more irrelevant, even retrograde. This secularization of thought increased as the scientific revolution passed into the industrial revolution, and humans increased their capacity to master their environment, all without appeal to God and religion. People began to explain even creation without God, and, in 1882, Nietzsche announced the death of God. As science and technology augmented human knowledge and domination, the desire for greater control in *religious* matters also increased. After all, religion is profoundly influenced by the culture in which it is embedded. People of faith began to seek the same kind of knowledge in religious matters as they sought in scientific matters. They subjected religion to the same tests of knowledge, and religion failed those tests, leaving increasing numbers of people despairing about the human ability to achieve certitude in religious matters. Thus scientific knowledge bred more doubts than certainties in the realm of religion.

The Church's bottom-line response to modern doubts was not to enter into dialogue but to insist on its own authority as a guarantor of certainty. Throughout the 19th century and into the 20th, time and again Rome summarily rejected every effort to accommodate liberal social and political movements. Gregory XVI rejected separation of Church and State, denounced liberty of conscience as sheer madness, and referred to freedom of the press as abominable and detestable. The opponents of liberalism, who saw the monarchical model for both Church and State as divinely ordained, wanted to return to the medieval model. They could see nothing good in liberalism and identified it with all the excesses of the French Revolution, so that by 1850 the Church throughout Europe was deeply divided between liberals and integralists, each group radically distrusting the other. In that atmosphere heresy hunting developed, and drove the Church into the so-called "Modernist Crisis" of 1890-1910.

As the Catholic Church attempted to restore the medieval paradigm in the face of the Reformation and Modern Paradigms, it isolated itself from the world. There were strengths in this isolation: a clear self-identity that served immigrant populations well, and a preservation of doctrinal and liturgical treasures. But the danger was that no one other than Roman Catholics would benefit from them, because the Catholic Church, reacting to trauma, had turned inward and away from the world.

THE CONTEMPORARY ECUMENICAL PARADIGM

Pope John XXIII understood this. He understood that the Catholic Church, in attempting to preserve the treasures of revelation, had buried them and was in danger of failing in its mission. He understood that to be faithful to its mission to be a blessing to all nations, the Church had first of all to affirm the world's natural goodness and acknowledge that God's grace works first of all in creation, including non-Catholic creation. He understood that the universality of God's grace, prior to any Roman Catholicizing of it, had to serve as the basis for dialogue. And he understood that dialogue was the absolute condition for sharing the Catholic Church's store of saving truth with the world.

The Second Vatican Council and its *Pastoral Constitution on the Church in the Modern World*, therefore, open with a paradigm-shattering declaration of love for the world.

The joys and the hopes, the griefs and the anxieties of all peoples of this age, especially those who are poor or in any way afflicted, these too are the joys and hopes, the griefs and anxieties of the followers of Christ. Indeed, nothing genuinely human fails to raise an echo in their hearts. For theirs is a community composed of human persons. United in Christ, they are led by the Holy Spirit in their journey to the kingdom of their Father and they have welcomed the news of salvation which is meant for every person. That is why this community realized that it is truly and intimately linked with humankind and its history (n.1).

The documents of Vatican II inaugurate a new paradigm. Let us call it the Ecumenical Paradigm. Why? Because the Roman Catholic Church recognized for the first time that it exists not *above* other human groups, religions, and Christian Churches, but in partnership with them. Partnership; there is something very consoling about that word. It requires generational Catholics to think of themselves very differently in relation to all the world's people who have been born non-Catholic. It requires, if we will truly engage in dialogue, a dramatic shift of posture, because authentic dialogue involves implications not congenial to the authoritarian worldview of the medieval paradigm. It means a presumption that the Catholic Church does not *existentially* realize the whole truth, that the Catholic Church's relationship to the whole truth is *eschatological*, that it humbly journeys into the truth, as does everyone in history. It means that every person and every group of persons organized in and around a belief system or paradigm has an angle on truth, an angle which could be of value to every other person willing to see truth from that angle. It means that truth is held in common and that we must search in common for common ground. It means an *a priori* mutuality among peoples and belief systems and a presumption of validity to the other viewpoints. It means a recognition of the incompleteness of one's own truth and empathetic entry into the other's point of view while suspending one's own. It means a willingness to embrace the other's truth and be changed by it, and a rejection of the position that one side has the final answer and engages in "dialogue" only to win the other side over.

This is a radically different posture from the authoritarian and imperialistic posture of the pre-Vatican II medieval Roman Catholic paradigm. Since the Second Vatican Council in the 1960s, Catholics have been experiencing serious head-butts between the old and new paradigms with attendant bumps and bruises and a good deal of hurt and confusion. What scares many is the danger of losing their grip on truth and certitude and, therefore, perhaps on salvation itself. Those who have been taking comfort in the preserve of Catholic doctrine are afraid that doctrine will be etherized into sheer relativity. No one, however, was ever saved by knowing the truth, only by doing it, at least if I read Matthew 25 and Luke's parable on the Good Samaritan correctly.

Perfect love casts out fear. What is needed is trust. Trust that the Holy Spirit was really at work in the Second Vatican Council and is really the author of this new paradigm for the Church. Trust that the Holy Spirit, God with us now as much as at the birth of the Church at Pentecost, will lead us into all truth. What emerges from the Council is that *all truth* will come to us only by sharing our truth with others and receiving their truth in return. It may well be that all truth is the truth incarnate in all peoples of the world, Muslims, Buddhists, Marxists, Lutherans, gays and lesbians, women, and men as well as in Catholics.

I know that song doesn't play well in Lake Wobegon where boundaries are clear and distinct, where "the women are strong, the men are good looking, and all the children are above average." But what if, just what if, we were to live by a fourth dimension, call it the dimension of Spirit, a discerning trust? What if by trust we were to lower our defenses and let the other in? We would, I believe, discover what Hopkins saw:

> I say more: the just man justices;
> Keeps grace: that keeps all his goings graces;
> Acts in God's eye what in God's eye he is—
> Christ—for Christ plays in ten thousand places,
> Lovely in limbs, and lovely in eyes not his
> To the Father through the features of men's faces.[5]

NOTES

1. The following analysis follows Hans Küng's enumeration of paradigm shifts in his *Christianity: Essence, History, and Future* (New York: Continuum, 1995). Küng has been using paradigm analysis since 1980. See his *Theology for the Third Millennium: An Ecumenical View* (New York: Doubleday, 1988); and his earlier *Paradigm Change in Theology*, ed. with David Tracy (New York: Crossroad, 1989;

German original published in 1986). John O'Malley and Karl Rahner antedated Küng's paradigm analysis: John W. O'Malley, S.J., "Reform, Historical Consciousness, and Vatican II's Aggiornamento," *Theological Studies* 32 (December 1971), 573-601 and "Developments, Reforms, and Two Great Reformations: Towards a Historical Assessment of Vatican II," *Theological Studies* 44 (September 1983), 373-406; Karl Rahner, S.J., "A Basic Interpretation of Vatican II,' *Theological Studies* 40 (December 1979), 716-27.

2. Thomas S. Kuhn, *The Structure of Scientific Revolutions*, 2d ed. (Chicago: University of Chicago Press, 1970), 175.

3. Cited in Küng, *Christianity*, 392.

4. Henricus Denzinger et Adolfus Schönmetzer, S.J., *Enchiridion symbolorum definitionum et declarationum de rebus fidei et morum* (Freiburg im Breisgau: Herder, 1963), 994-1000.

5. Gerard Manley Hopkins, *Poems and Prose*, selected by W. H. Gardner (London: Penguin Books, 1993) 51.

The Peril and the Promise of Patristic Exegesis

John J. O'Keefe

Those who pray the liturgy of the hours will, from time to time, meditate on nearly all of the psalms. If, as with me, the practice is somewhat irregular and fixed to one "hour" a day, the breadth of exposure declines somewhat. Even so, when prayed with the rhythm of the rising and the setting sun or with the regular passing of the seasons, the Psalms have a way of imprinting themselves in human memory and popping up, unexpectedly, to deepen the meaning of ordinary time. And so, a running stream encountered on a hike across the prairie may evoke the image of Psalm 42, "as a deer yearns for flowing streams, so my soul longs for you O God." A rural hike becomes sanctified and, in a way, Christianized, by its relationship to a remembered text. This ability of the Psalms to intrude on daily life is perhaps the last modern vestige of an ancient skill that came with the habit of memorization. For ancient Christians, the words of the scriptures were always near. The skill to read all of life in the light of the scriptures represents both the peril and the promise of patristic exegesis.

THE PERIL OF PATRISTIC EXEGESIS

As most modern students of the Bible are aware, ancient commentators were in the habit of ignoring history and indulging in flights of allegorization that appear outrageous to many modern readers. Because of this, the modern academic community has had little interest in early Christian interpretation of the Bible. As recently as 1985, when I began graduate studies, courses in patristics, monographs about patristics, and critical editions of patristic texts were virtually all focused on topics of doctrine. The patristic period served basically as a *preparatio* for systematic theology. Patristic scholarship tended to support this approach by offering a steady diet of studies dedicated to explication of doctrinal issues in the Fathers. Academic libraries are filled with books bearing titles that follow the formula, "doctrine so and so" in "author so and so." While many of these studies are good, the literary output of patristic authors gets distorted.

Scholarship surrounding the development of christological orthodoxy is a case in point. All modern theological studies of this question, even those that are in someway critical of traditional models, must engage the formulations of the Council of Chalcedon, which took place in 451 A.D. Patristic scholarship has greatly assisted systematic theologians in this process. Enormous amounts of scholarly energy have been invested in studying the fifth-century literature pertinent to this topic. One of the key figures in the ancient debates, Cyril of Alexandria, has had his doctrinal positions exposed in scores of monographs and academic articles over the past one hundred years or so. Cyril deserves this kind of attention. He was a brilliant theologian and a prolific writer. His total literary output fills ten volumes in Migne's *Patrologia*, a standard edition of patristic literature. This translates to thousands of pages of text. Yet, of those ten volumes, only three contain treatises that pertain directly to doctrinal concerns and a smaller number still are directly related to christology.

The majority of Cyril's work, including works now lost, was exegetical. From 412 A.D, the year of his appointment as bishop of Alexandria, until his death in 444, he produced massive commentaries on nearly every book of the Bible. In spite of this, scholars have produced only a few monographs and articles about his exegesis.[1] Cyril's case is hardly unique; all of the great patristic theologians, especially those writing in the fourth and fifth centuries, were engaged in exegesis. Most of that exegesis has never been edited, read, or studied by any modern person, except perhaps, by a scholar mining the commentaries for details that would illuminate a systematic question. The reason for this glaring omission can only be that patristic interpretation is so different from the standards of biblical interpretation embraced by today's academic community that these ancient works seem to be nothing more than curiosities, suitable for display in museums but not for use in church or academy. From a certain point of view they have nothing to offer; like many books from the past, they should be allowed to disappear.

The point is well taken. From the perspective of historical scholarship, patristic readings are often very odd indeed. For example, early Christian exegetes habitually linked the story of the Exodus and the crossing of the

Red Sea to the crossing from death to new life in baptism. Many Christians, of course, do not find this particular reading all that odd because it is still a theme that can be encountered in the Church at Easter time. Yet, there is no intrinsic link between the story of Exodus and the theology of baptism. Other exegetical moves, however, are not so familiar. The book of Malachi, for example, is a text not often read even in antiquity. The Septuagint version of 3:2-4 reads:

> He enters as the fire of a smelting furnace and as the lye of the washer; he will sit down, smelting and purifying as silver and gold, and will purify the sons of Levi. He will pour them out as gold and silver. They will offer sacrifices to the Lord in Justice, and the sacrifice of Judah and Jerusalem will please the Lord, as in the days of eternity and as in ages of old.

Contemporary Scripture scholars assure us this text is about the efforts of Israel to recover from the exile in Babylon; it has no direct bearing on Christianity. The ancients understood it differently.

When Cyril of Alexandria applied his exegetical talents to this text, he discerned a prophetic announcement of the Christian priesthood. Because of his deep familiarity with the Bible, he knew immediately that the "son of Levi" was a reference to the Levitical priesthood. He was trained to pay close attention to the tense of verbs.[2] In this case the phrases, "he *will* purify" and "they *will* be offering," seemed to indicate a prophecy. These kinds of clues, together with his theological conviction that the whole Bible was about Christ, led Cyril to offer this interpretation of the text:

> For we who have been called in Christ to perform sacred rites, approach [him] no longer through blood and smoke, nor do we offer to God lambs or kids, but rather we fulfill in the churches a holy and spiritual sacrifice, which is spiritually apprehended in Christ. When we bring forth [the offering] for the purpose of sanctity and even for participation in eternal life, like as choice incense, we offer him the sweet smells issuing from sacrificial rites. By sacrificing justice to him we have confidence that we will also be acceptable...Therefore, he said concerning those called in Christ to perform sacred rites that they will be better than the first ones [so called]. They will not slay sheep like them, nor defile the

altar by offering polluted bread, but they will offer God justice and the spiritual perfume of the evangelical polity in place of incense. For they celebrate the acceptable worship such that it in no way falls short of the sacrifices fit for the days of eternity, that is, for the life of the holy spirits in heaven, who pass unbroken days and ages.[3]

The modern reader will find Cyril's interpretation odd and perhaps even a little offensive. It is blatantly supersessionist, and he reads Malachi from the point of view of the ecclesiastical environment of the fifth century.[4] Cyril believed that the prophet had correctly predicted the replacement of the old Levitical priesthood with the new Christian priesthood and the old way of life based upon animal sacrifice with a new way of life based upon the just "unbloodied" sacrifice of the Eucharist. He is not an innovator here; these basic interpretive themes run throughout patristic exegesis from its very inception.

As a second example I point to a famous work of Gregory of Nyssa, *The Life of Moses*.[5] Gregory was one of the most important theologians of the patristic era, making significant contributions to the development of Trinitarian theology and laying the groundwork for subsequent reflection on the nature of the Christ. Yet, as an exegete, many would have difficulty taking him seriously. Despite its title, *The Life of Moses* is not a biography. It is, rather, an extended allegorical reading of Moses's life from the burning bush to the ascent of Mount Sinai. For Gregory, the events described in the book of Exodus encode a tale of spiritual realities that only the learned and the spiritually-minded are able to apprehend. Hence, the burning bush points secretly to the virginal life, the plagues in Egypt are obstacles to the virtuous life, and the wearing of shoes when departing from Egypt signifies the austere life of self-control "which breaks and prevents the thorns of sin from entering the soul."[6] Gregory's text goes on to discuss the ascent of the mind to God and the darkness of the apophatic vision as the true meaning of the Moses's ascent of the holy mountain. In all of this the historical Moses fades to insignificance and the story of the Exodus mutates from a tale of Israel's liberation into a treatise on the liberation of the Christian soul through a life of self-denial. Along the way Gregory squeezes in numerous reflections on Christian doctrine and practice. Such textual manipulation, odd as it may appear to us, raised few eyebrows in antiquity. It was simply taken for granted that the Bible, since it was a

Christian book, was about the Christian life.

My third and final example is surprising in a different way. In the second week of the Psalter the person at prayer encounters Psalm 29. This psalm includes the following verses:

> The voice of the Lord is over the waters;
> the God of glory thunders,
> the Lord, over mighty waters.
> The voice of the Lord is powerful;
> the voice of the Lord is full of majesty.
> The voice of the Lord breaks the cedars;
> the Lord breaks the cedars of Lebanon
> He makes Lebanon skip like a calf,
> and Sirion like a young wild ox.
> The voice of the Lord flashes
> forth flames of fire ...

One needs no formal training in Scripture to recognize in the Psalm a natural phenomenon with which all residents of the plains are well acquainted: this psalm is about a thunderstorm. Modern Old Testament scholars would appear to confirm the obvious when they confidently report that this psalm depicts YHWH's power over the Canaanite storm god.[7] Only the God of Israel had such power, so the message goes, and this God is deeply involved in the natural world; this is YHWH's thunder. Patristic exegetes did not see it this way.

One of the peculiar fascinations of many ancient exegetes was biblical chronology. They wanted to know the order of biblical events at a level of detail not provided by the Bible itself. The motives for this were not historical in the modern sense. Contemporary scholarship attempts to reconstruct what "really" happened behind the text. Ancient scholars accepted at face value the veracity of the biblical story. What troubled them were those places where the details were fuzzy. The Psalms presented just such a problem. According to ancient tradition they were the Psalms of David, so they had to be about David's life, or at least about things that David foresaw about Israel's future. Since the best sources for chronological information about David were the books of Samuel and Kings (1-4 Kings in the Septuagint), some ancient exegetes attempted to fit all of the psalms into this context. Hence, they argued, Psalm 29 refers to 2 Kings

19:35-36, which describes God's slaughter of an Assyrian army. The cedars of Lebanon are the army that is split by God's power. Other ancient sources see deeper meaning in this psalm. Theodoret of Cyrus, for example, argues that the Psalm is about the triumph of Christianity over paganism, and that the water anticipates the advent of holy baptism where God breaks the power of sin.[8] In any case, the meteorological interpretation that is so evident to the modern reader seems not to have occurred to these ancient interpreters. To us these interpretations seem profoundly strange and totally unhistorical.

It is, of course, possible to go on at length about varieties of ancient exegetical style and to multiply examples of interpretive oddities. At this point the perils of patristic exegesis should be obvious: the assumptions ancient interpreters made about the meaning of texts are fundamentally at odds with the most basic commitments of modern biblical interpretation. This deserves more explicit discussion.

From the point of view of contemporary historical scholarship, the examples of early Christian interpretation cited above contain nothing more than self-serving eisegesis. The commentaries containing these texts may be useful in illuminating details of Christian history, but they do not enhance our understanding of the Bible. Such an assessment stems from the particular commitments of contemporary historical criticism, which links closely the meaning of the text with the historical circumstances of its composition and the intention of the author. At the risk of stating the obvious, the exegete must labor to uncover the actual events to which a text points. The goal of biblical interpretation, then, is to recover as nearly as possible the original meaning and the original context of a given text. Ironically, the ancient texts themselves can actually hinder this process since they already insert a layer of interpretation between the event and the reader.

Nowhere is this tendency of historical scholarship more evident than in the work of the Jesus Seminar. According to the scholars involved in this project, the New Testament obscures rather than reveals the real Jesus. The historical Jesus must be reconstructed through the analysis of sources outside of the New Testament because the New Testament fundamentally distorts the message of Jesus in a direction favorable to the theological position of the early Christian community. While many within the guild of New Testament scholarship find the conclusions of the Jesus Seminar to be ridiculous and even self-promoting,[9] the basic assumptions behind the seminar's scholarship do, indeed, reflect the basic assumptions of modern criticism. The historical truth of Jesus and his original message is hiding in and behind the text and can be recovered only by means of historical analysis. Stated in another way, the holy grail of authentic Christianity lies with the message of the historical Jesus which, unfortunately, can be accessed only by trained specialists if it can be accessed at all.

From this point of view, patristic commentaries perpetrate a kind of naive distortion of reality. They take it for granted that the Bible cannot contradict itself and that the whole Bible is about Christ and the Christian dispensation in some way. Patristic authors display absolutely no awareness of layers of redaction and assume a continuous understanding of God from Genesis through revelation. They have no appreciation of the vast space of time separating Abraham, if he existed, from the communities of Paul, and they have the nasty habit of reading their own theological perspective into the text.

Two examples should suffice to make the point. In Genesis 1:26 God says, "let us make humankind in our image." Contemporary Old Testament scholars point out that this "us" indicates that ancient Israel conceptualized a kind of divine counsel rather than a single all-powerful deity. In contrast, patristic authors assume a univocal notion of God throughout the entire biblical text. They see in this "us" a hidden reference to the Holy Trinity that could only be discerned in the light of the revelation of Christ. They had no notion that monotheism developed over centuries. Proverbs 8:22 is a second example. "The Lord created me at the beginning of his work, the first of his acts of long ago. Ages ago I was set up, at the first, before the beginning of the earth..." Modern scholars point out that this text is simply a part of a reflection on the dignity and value of wisdom. In the fourth century, however, anti-Nicene theologians used this text to argue that the Son of God was less than the Father in the cosmic order. This protected God's monotheism, but clearly established Jesus as something less than God. Those who defended the theology of the Council of Nicaea, the theology that eventually became enshrined in the Nicene Creed, did not question the interpretive methods of their opponents. Instead, they found a way to read Proverbs 8:22, and other similar texts, so that it did not imply that the Son was created by God and, therefore, was less than God.[10]

From the perspective of modern historical scholarship, these patristic interpretations are not only strange but also wrong. Patristic exegesis runs the constant risk of distorting the record of the past and of perverting the very meaning of God's activity in and through the covenant with Israel.

The examples given above are but two from thousands of such historical distortions. Some early Christian interpretations are as innocuous as they are odd, such as the reading of Proverbs. Others, however, have had more destructive consequences. It was, for example, common for patristic authors to use the texts of the Bible as a tool of oppression. Augustine cited Luke 14:15-24, where the beggars are forced into the banquet, as a justification to compel schismatic Donatist north-African Christians to join the Catholic communion.[11] The tradition of suppressing dissent has a long history in the Christian church. Moreover, a particular reading of the mandate to become a eunuch for the kingdom (Matt 19:12) resulted in centuries of a tiered and stratified Christian society that exalted celibacy and, at times, belittled the life of the average married Christian.[12] Textual justification for the oppression of women was also easy to find.

Perhaps most devastating of all, however, has been the use of the Bible in a crusade against the Jews. From the patristic point of view, the Jews had lost the truth by their bull-headed rejection of Christ. They missed all of the biblical signs that pointed to Christ and were punished for their unwillingness to attend to God's new work for the salvation of humanity. As a result, God rejected them. The destruction of the temple and Jerusalem by the Roman army was concrete proof of God's displeasure. Typical of these attitudes is a text by Melito of Sardis written in the second century. Melito's treatise, the so-called *Peri Pascha*, is an allegorical reading of the Exodus.[13] The old Exodus from Egypt was a type of the new Christian exodus from sin. The Christian dispensation has replaced the Jewish one. Supersessionist themes are, of course, deeply rooted in the Christian tradition, but Melito reflects them with a harsh and bitter energy. "O lawless Israel," he writes, "what is this unprecedented crime you committed, thrusting your Lord among unprecedented sufferings, your Sovereign, who formed you, who made you, who honored you, who called you Israel.... You did not know, Israel, that he is the firstborn of God, who was begotten before the morning star ... who divided off the darkness ..."[14] Melitio's attitudes appear again and again in patristic commentary across a diverse range of textual materials.

The modern critique of these ancient authors and texts can and should be controlled. Ancient culture, after all, was not modern culture and we ought not to expect to find there either images of ourselves or reflections of our values. Ancient Christians were not feminists, they could not conceive of a religiously plural society, and they accepted without question a cosmos that was hierarchically fashioned. Moreover, patristic scholars point out that much of the vituperative energy directed against the Jews came from ancient rhetorical practices rather than from any kind of genocidal program.[15] In antiquity Christianity and Rabbinical Judaism were engaged in an exegetical struggle to determine the legitimate heir to the legacy of Israel. Insulting your opponent was a part of the ancient style and that style is reflected in this struggle. Still, while these historical nuances may help soften our assessment of the past, they do nothing to encourage an appreciation of early Christian exegetical methods. From the point of view of modern historical scholarship, patristic exegesis was too subjective, often reckless, and frequently dangerous. In part, and as a result of this attitude, many volumes of patristic exegesis lie unedited, unread, and unstudied in university libraries. What value could they possibly have?

THE PROMISE OF PATRISTIC EXEGESIS

Perhaps the best indicator of the promise of patristic exegesis is that this ancient approach to interpretation has not entirely vanished from the Church and that historical-critical exegesis has made little progress toward influencing popular piety. Patristic style survives both in preaching and in the spiritual tradition. Preachers commonly apply biblical texts to situations that range far beyond their historical context. Martin Luther King's speech declaring that he had been to the mountain top and seen the promised land directly evoked the power of the story of the Exodus and applied it to the struggle for civil rights in America. He thus Christianized the struggle by placing it in a biblical frame. Likewise, retreat directors in the Roman Catholic tradition frequently counsel their directees to meditate upon the scriptures to discover how the ordinary events of one's life can be illuminated and made meaningful by events and stories produced by a culture that vanished long ago. The road to Emmaus is not just a tale about the formation of early Christian community and the emergence of eucharistic theology; it is a tale about the way in which the contemporary believer can still encounter Christ in the breaking of the bread.

As with patristic exegesis, this kind of reading extracts meaning from the text that is not primarily historical. Indeed, this kind of reading actually makes it possible for the biblical text and the biblical stories to remain meaningful in the lives of believers. If the text were not in some way about us, it would cease to be a part of a living tradition; it would become an artifact. This, I think, is why the tradition of spiritual reading has endured in the churches and why historical-critical reading has made such little progress outside the academy. The first step, then, leading to a sense of the promise of patristic exegesis must be recognition that historical-critical exegesis has its own set of perils and cannot be the only path to uncovering the meaning of scripture.

In recent years many scholars have begun to express dissatisfaction with the results of historical investigation of the Bible. Historical-critical method, some would argue, claims more than it can deliver and produces results that are often at odds with the beliefs of the Christian community. Moreover, it tends to atomize the Bible into unrelated parts, has a simplistic understanding of the complexity of meaning, and has failed to deliver a message that has the power to sanctify and transform.[16]

In a way all historical scholarship claims more than it can deliver. The data of history is complex and difficult to interpret. Interpretations differ even when data is abundant; where it is scarce, conclusions are even more tenuous and subject to revision. This does not mean that all interpretations are equally valid, but it does mean that we must be careful not to claim too much for the results of our research. Recent discussions of the historical Jesus represent a clear instance of this problem. Jesus has been historically reconstructed as both Cynic sage and social revolutionary.[17] A more humble approach recognizes that there are severe and unsurpassable limitations on what we can know about the historical Jesus, and these limitations exist across the entire spectrum of biblical literature. Inquiry into the historical Jesus is a valid scholarly activity, but scholars can and often do present their own agenda as established fact.

A second powerful critique of historical-critical scholarship of the Bible is that it often produces results that are at odds with fundamental beliefs of the Christian faith. It may be that some of the beliefs of the Church should be revised in the light of historical insight, but this is not always clear. Critical scholarship, for example, rightly points out that the New Testament contains no specific Trinitarian theology and that few references to Jesus lead inexorably to the conclusions of the councils of Nicaea or Chalcedon. Some scholars, therefore, argue that both Nicaea and Chalcedon distort the theology of the New Testament. By implication, the beliefs and insights of generations of Christians are dismissed as naive and foolish. It is possible, however, to argue that both Nicaea and Chalcedon are, in fact, faithful readings of the New Testament. It may be true that, historically, the New Testament authors were not thinking about the Trinity. By insisting upon God's oneness, Jesus' lordship, and Jesus' saving death and resurrection, however, they set Christian theology inevitably on a path that would one day lead to the development of a more comprehensive doctrine of God. The Christian believer need not jettison core Christian commitments on the basis on a particular set of historical reconstructions. Lack of explicit Trinitarian thought in the New Testament does not negate the truth of later developments in Trinitarian theology.

A third critique of contemporary historical-scholarship is that it tends to atomize the Bible. Instead of being the story of God's faithful delivery of humanity from sin and death, the Bible becomes a collection of books by multiple authors written over many centuries and often teaching different and opposing doctrines. Examples of this are easy to find. Traditionally, the Christian Church has understood the suffering servant images in Isaiah as a prophetic reference to the Christ. Ancient Christians read the text this way without any sense of impropriety. In the light of historical scholarship, such a reading seems to be little more than wish fulfillment, and distorts fundamentally the intention of the author of Second or Third Isaiah. In the interests of historical accuracy, the Jerome Biblical Commentary, for example, separates Second or Third Isaiah from authentic Isaiah and places it next to the post-exilic books.[18] By implication the canonical arrangement of the text is at best naive and, at worst, historically inaccurate. Similarly, some contemporary historical scholars point out that the Christian reading of Genesis is seriously flawed.[19] Most Christians believe that death is the result of sin and that God originally created humans immortal. Christ, then, restored what was lost. Historical study, however, indicates that the text need not be read this way. It is possible to argue that humanity was not created immortal at all and that the link between sin and mortality theologically distorts the story of Genesis. Sadly, one of the primary culprits in the distortion was the apostle Paul who explicitly links sin and death.[20] In this case historical scholarship pits Paul against the Yahwist and removes a key theological link between Genesis, Paul, Jesus, and the entire Christian faith.

A fourth critique of historical-critical exegesis is that it tends to reduce meaning to the historical. Because the book of Genesis does not really historically link sin and death, then any reading that does link them is wrong. Scholars who have been influenced by contemporary literary and hermeneutical theory recognize more complexity in the way texts transmit meaning.[21] Historical reconstruction, many point out, never occurs in a value-free environment, and all writing of history is interpretation and bears the marks of the interpreters. Hence, as is the case with the Jesus seminar, all portraits of the historical Jesus, in some way or another, wind up resembling the modern authors who paint them. Other theorists suggest that the meaning of a text takes place in an encounter between a reader and the written word. The meaning that emerges from this encounter may not be the meaning intended by the author, but it is real, significant, and possibly true. From this point of view, Paul's reading of Genesis is legitimate and comprehensible only in light of the person he was as a follower of Christ. Genesis means more than its authors could have imagined.

Finally, historical-critical approaches to the Bible do not seem to be capable, on their own, of delivering a religious message powerful enough to help people lead transformed lives committed to God. On any given Sunday in any given church, one is not likely to hear the results of historical-study of the Bible preached. Occasionally preachers will consult a commentary to enrich their reflection on the Prodigal Son or the Good Samaritan, but historical insight is used here to deepen the drama and to show that these stories have abiding value for the individual Christian seeking to be conformed to Christ and to live as Christ lived. One will rarely hear that Paul misunderstood Genesis, that the Suffering Servant was not Jesus, that the story of Exodus has nothing to do with baptism, or that Paul's letter to Philemon was not written by Paul. Knowing the thoughts of the Yahwist, the history of the redaction of Isaiah, the details of Israel's history, and that there is pseudepigraphy in the New Testament does deepen our understanding of the history of the Jewish and Christian traditions, but it does not by itself deepen faith. Without nuance and theological reflection, these insights at best do nothing for the ordinary Christian. At worst they consign the Bible and the faith that accompanies it to the status of an ancient artifact, an interesting product of human culture, but not worthy of devotion and commitment.

I say all of this about historical-critical method not to argue that it is a waste of time, but to suggest that it is, like its patristic counterpart, subject to serious and real limitation. This methodology has played a part in what Hans Frei has called "the eclipse of biblical narrative." In a book by that title, Frei explains how modern assumptions about the world, including a robust historical consciousness, have contributed to a gradual alienation of believer from text.[22] In pre-critical times the reader could enter into the world of biblical narrative without mediation. Even though the Bible told tales of long ago and deeds long past, the reader did not experience the text as essentially alien, other, and in need of the mediation of historical commentary. The text was accessible directly to the reader. The rise of biblical criticism created the need for mediatorial interpretive schemes, and the heavy weight placed upon history was one such scheme. If, many scholars argued, the weight of revelation was shifted from the text to the events to which the text points, and if the truth of these events could be recovered, then biblical truth could be safeguarded. Frei explains that biblical criticism began as an effort to help the Bible and the Christian religion withstand the onslaught of criticism that came in the wake of a robust rationalism. This project, he argues, has failed in many ways. The history behind the text has proven to be impossible to recover and many of the primary truth claims of Christianity stand outside the reach of historical inquiry. The irony is that, at present, historical study of the Bible, which began as an effort to help faith, is often used to undermine traditional Christian claims.

Beyond the general tendency in some circles within the historical-critical guild to reconstruct an anti-Christian Christianity, there has been an even more pervasive negative effect. In today's seminary environment, while future preachers are trained according to the best methods of historical inquiry, they are not trained to recognize the limitations of this methodology and they are rarely exposed to alternative exegetical models. When they hit the street, so to speak, they quickly realize how difficult it is to preach the results of biblical criticism. Without resources, preaching degenerates to an uninspired and uninteresting pop homiletics that lacks biblical content. This is a serious crisis in many churches.

It is precisely in these areas of weakness that the promise of Patristic exegesis is exposed. Patristic commentary did avoid many of the difficulties into which modern exegesis has fallen. Patristic exegesis was rooted in the conviction that the Bible could not contradict the Christian faith, that the Bible was one unified story about God's redemptive work in Christ, and that meaning was more complex than the historical or the literal. Most importantly, Patristic exegesis delivered. It gave people a Bible they could imitate and follow. Patristic preaching might seem strange to us, but it was profoundly biblical and deeply persuasive.

The fundamental conviction of all ancient Christian exegesis was that the Bible could not contradict itself. This theological commitment was not embraced naively or without awareness of the problems it caused; patristic authors were not stupid. They, better than many modern readers, were painfully aware of problems in the narrative. They knew, for example, that Genesis contained two different accounts of creation and that the gospels contained different infancy stories. In spite of this, they defended the unity of the Bible over against, say, Gnostic efforts to excise the Old Testament from the canon and to homogenize the gospels. They also rejected the Syrian Diatesseron, which conflated the Gospels into one contradiction-free narrative, in favor of the complexity of the narrative diversity in four gospels. They did this because they were convinced that somehow God was revealed in the complexity and that problems of interpretation arose because of human limitation, not because of problems in the text. It did not surprise them that God would be difficult to understand or that God would be known in and though a complex textual tradition.

Second, patristic exegesis was profoundly convinced that Christ was the subject of Christian faith and that, in some way or another the entire story of Israel was the story of Jesus and the Church. This conviction did not come easily or naively. They knew and understood that Christ was not explicitly referenced in the Old Testament; they knew there were problems with textual transmission; they understood that prophets did not always see clearly what they were prophesying. Most patristic authors never failed to realize that the stories of the past referred to real events and real people.[23] Still, early Christian exegetes were so committed to the reality of Christ and to his transforming power that they made him, not history, the hermeneutical key to the scriptures. They argued, therefore, that certain things could be seen in retrospect, from the point of view of faith, that could not be seen from any other point of view. All of human history, all events of the past, in some way was leading to God's redemptive work. This, in my view, indicates a powerful commitment to the reality of God's presence in Christ.

Third, patristic authors recognized that texts had meaning at multiple levels. Even Origen, widely criticized in both the ancient and modern world for collapsing the meaning of biblical narrative into the spiritual at the expense of the literal, never totally denied the value of the plain sense and what it represented. It was part of the *lingua franca* of early Christian commentary to expose these various levels of sense and meaning.[24] The ancient world possessed a sophisticated and highly nuanced understanding of texts and the way to interpret them. It is the height of arrogance to dismiss the insight of ancient commentators because historical inquiry was not among their exegetical tools.

Most important of all is that patristic exegesis took place in an ecclesial context; it was done prayerfully. Most early Christian biblical commentators were bishops and most exegesis took the form of homily. Many ancient commentaries came into being as public lecture. The purpose of exegesis was to persuade and communicate to people the content and character of the Christian life and to do so through recourse to the rich textual tradition of the Bible. The homilies of the best patristic preachers are masterfully arranged exhortations rich in biblical allusion. These preachers created a Christian discourse, a kind of Christian rhetoric, that had the effect of gradually instilling in the hearer a Christian vision of the world. As Averil Cameron explains, this discourse was powerful enough to transform the religious identity of an entire culture and stamp forever the history of the West with Christian character.[25] Even modern readers, if they stay with the reading long enough and over enough time, can feel the effects of this discourse and be changed by it.

Patristic exegesis, then, offered a variety of readings that nourished Christian faith at multiple levels. In this, it was more successful than much contemporary interpretation. It is not possible, of course, for the modern person to simply jump over contemporary culture, ignore historical questions, and reintroduce patristic methodology. We cannot dismiss the conclusions of historical analysis simply because we do like them. Our culture is both burdened and blessed with historical consciousness in a way that ancient culture was not. Contemporary attempts to minimize the importance of history run the risk of becoming a new form of Gnosticsm.[26]

The claims that Christianity makes cannot be separated from real, concrete, historical events and located in the hearts of believers without risking a profound and dangerous subjectivity. Such an approach denies the incarnational claims that run to the heart of Christianity. Even though most patristic exegetes vigorously resisted Gnosticsm, there is a way in which their readings constantly threaten to shed their moorings in the concrete and float off into spiritual oblivion. Restored patristic biblical commentary will not by itself move the Christian community beyond the current exegetical conundrum. It can, however, suggest a way forward.

First, patristic commentary reminds us that the work of biblical interpretation is not just an academic enterprise. Interpretation has a place in the academy, but it belongs also in the churches. Interpretation that rises in the context of prayer and doxology is no less significant than interpretation that rises in the context of historical study. Second, patristic commentary can model a certain kind of humility that escapes many contemporary readers. For the ancients, when a reader encountered a difficult text, the problem was the reader not the text. There was a way in which ancient commentators were willing to submit themselves to the formative power of the text even when complete understanding eluded them. The principle that the Bible could not contradict itself certainly resulted in very odd readings at times, but it also ensured a willingness on the part of the exegete to wait for illumination. The lectionary system begs for this kind of attitude. When a pastor is asked to preach the readings, he must somehow fuse together texts that differ radically in their historical contexts and, through prayerful reflection, unify them into a word of God for those present to hear. There is nothing to prevent historical insight from playing a part in the formation of that word, but ultimately its formation is the work of the Holy Spirit.

Third, patristic exegesis offers the modern Christian reader dialogue partners from the past who attempted to live the Christian life faithfully. It is, in my view, a peculiar arrogance of our time to look upon the men and women of the past as stupid, ignorant, and foolish. Some manifestations of biblical criticism seem to suggest that Christian interpretation operated under a dark cloud of ignorance from the end of the first century to the dawn of enlightened historical study, and that interpreters of that period not only misrepresented the past but also distorted the message of Jesus. Surely it is true that every attempt to follow Christ in the time before the fulfillment of the promise is, in some way or another, a distortion of the message of Jesus. Our age is not exempt. I think we can and should affirm that those Christians who went before us reading and interpreting the Bible did pass on faithfully the message of salvation. Because of this, their insights have enduring value, not absolute value, but value that is worthy of our respect and attention. The exegetes of the past have the power to assist us in our own efforts and they can, at times, help us see our own arrogant presuppositions and move beyond them.

Finally, patristic exegesis reminds us that meaning is complex, and that there is no single way to read the Bible. This does not mean that all interpretations are equally good. David Koresh found meaning in the text, but we can fairly say that he was not a good reader. Assigning controls on reading is a difficult process that must draw upon all the tools that the Church has to offer, including historical study, Christian theology, and prayerful reflection. No single method can, by itself, encompass the whole of biblical faith. Patristic exegesis recognized this complexity in a way contemporary exegesis does not.

The promise of patristic exegesis, then, lies in its ability to critique the present and to suggest ways toward the recovery of a more integrated approach to scripture. Patristic exegesis can contribute to a renewal of Christian reading in which there is no longer a sharp divide between the reading of the Psalms as an example of Hebrew poetry and their reading as metaphor for life on the Great Plains. The word of God is more than enough for both.

NOTES

1. Good current bibliographies of scholarship on Cyril can be found in John McGuckin, *St. Cyril of Alexandria: the Christological Controversy: Its History, Theology, and Texts* (Leiden: Brill, 1996) and in Marie-Odile Boulnois, *Le Paradoxe Trinitaire chez Cyrille d'Alexandrie: herméneutique, analyses philosophique et argumentation théologique* (Paris: Institut d'Etudes Augustiniennes, 1994).

2. The impact of ancient rhetorical and grammatical training on the church fathers is well documented in Frances Young, "The Rhetorical Schools and their Influence on Patristic Exegesis" in *The Making of Orthodoxy: Essays in Honour of Henry Chadwick*, ed. Rowan Williams (Cambridge, 1989).

3. P. E. Pusey, ed. *Sancti Patris Nostri Cyrilli Archiepiscopi Alexandrini*, vol. 2 (Oxford, 1868), 601.24-602.4; 602.9-19.

4. The Church of early Christian Egypt is aptly described in C. Wilfred Griggs, *Early Egyptian Christianity to 451 C.E.* (Leiden: Brill, 1991).

5. Everett Ferguson and Abraham Malherbe, eds., *Gregory of Nyssa: The Life of Moses* (New York: Paulist, 1978).

6. Moses, 79.

7. *Gaudium et Spes*, 41; *Dei Verbum*, 201-03. These documents will be cited hereafter as *GS* and *DV* respectively.

8. Cf. Hans Joachim Kraus, *Psalms 1-59: A Commentary*, trans. Hilton C. Oswald (Minneapolis: Augsburg, 1988), 344-51.

9. J.P. Migne, *Patrologia Greca* 80, 1062-70.

10. Luke Timothy Johnson expresses this forcefully in *The Real Jesus: the Misguided Quest for the Historical Jesus and the Truth of the Traditional Gospel* (San Francisco: Harper, 1996).

11. These exegetical moves are discussed at length by R. P. C. Hanson in *The Search for the Christian Doctrine of God* (Edinburgh: T. & T. Clark, 1988).

12. Peter Brown, *The Body and Society: Men Women, and Sexual Renunciation in Early Christianity* (New York: Columbia University Press, 1988) offers a detailed analysis of the development of early Christian asceticism.

13. Stuart Hall, ed., *On Pascha and Fragments* (Oxford: Oxford University Press, 1979).

14. Melito, 82.

15. These issues are explored in detail by Robert Wilken in *John Chrysostom and the Jews* (Berkeley and Los Angeles: University of California Press, 1983).

16. An increasing number of books discuss this problem. For a particularly forceful statement in this direction see Francis Watson, *Text and Truth: Redefining Biblical Theology* (Grand Rapids: Eerdmans, 1996). Brevard Childs offers a more measured approach in *Biblical Theology of the Old and New Testaments: Theological Reflection on the Christian Bible* (Minneapolis: Fortress, 1993).

17. The history of the "quest" has been traced with interesting results by Charlotte Allen in *The Human Christ: the Search for the Historical Jesus* (New York: Free Press, 1998).

18. Raymond Brown, et. al. *The New Jerome Biblical Commentary* (Englewood Cliffs: Prentice Hall, 1988), 329-48.

19. Cf. James Barr, *The Garden of Eden and the Hope of Immortality* (Minneapolis: Fortress, 1992).

20. Cf. Romans 5-7.

21. Sandra Schneiders argues this point eloquently in *The Revelatory Text: Interpreting the New Testament as Sacred Scripture* (San Francisco: Harper, 1991). For a discussion of the sophistication with which early Christian authors approached a text, see Frances Young, *Biblical Exegesis and the Formation of Christian Culture* (Cambridge: Cambridge University Press, 1997).

22. Hans Frei, *The Eclipse of Biblical Narrative* (New Haven: Yale University Press, 1974).

23. For a good collection of essays on the topic of early Christian interpretation, see Paul Blowers, ed., *The Bible in Greek Christian Antiquity* (Notre Dame: University of Notre Dame Press, 1997).

24. The classic study is Henri de Lubac, *Exégèse Médiévale: Les quatre sens de l'écriture* (Paris: Aubier, 1959). An English translation has begun to appear: *Medieval Exegesis. Volume 1: The Four Senses of Scripture*, trans. Mark Sebanc (Grand Rapids, Michigan: William B. Eerdmans, 1998).

25. Averil Cameron, *Christianity and the Rhetoric of Empire: The Development of Christian Discourse* (Berkeley: University of California Press, 1991).

26. The German theologian Wolfhart Pannenberg recognizes this critical problem and attempts to account for it with a comprehensive theology of history. See his *Systematic Theology* published in English translation by Eerdmans Press.

The Joint Declaration on the Doctrine of Justification: An Outsider's View

Russell R. Reno

As an Episcopalian who wishes to take seriously the traditional Anglican claim that my Church is genuinely reformed and catholic, I have a special interest in Lutheran-Roman Catholic dialogue. Justification has been a crucial element of that dialogue and after the initial "getting to know you" phase in the decade following the Second Vatican Council, it has dominated the official discussion between Lutherans and Roman Catholics. By presenting a common understanding of justification for official adoption by Lutheran Churches and the Roman Catholic Church, the recently issued Joint Declaration on the Doctrine of Justification (JD) seeks to end the dialogue on justification and advance Lutheran and Roman Catholic relations to the next stage.

I do not plan to defend or criticize the JD on the substantive question of whether it gets justification right. My church has not been asked to adopt the JD, so I need not decide whether it brings Lutheran-Roman Catholic dialogue on justification to a successful end. That is for Lutheran member churches and Rome to discern. Instead, I want to analyze the JD in order to understand *how* it proposes consensus in doctrine. In the long run, the way in which the JD handles the problem of consensus and the role it establishes for doctrine will likely be as influential as its particular formulations. If adopted, the JD will set a pattern for future ecumenical proposals.

My argument will be that the JD offers a helpful way of approaching doctrine and the problem of consensus in doctrine, perhaps the only way in view of the theological constraints imposed by church division. To develop this argument, I will proceed according to the following outline. First, I will underline the complexity of the JD's proposal of consensus and indicate the way in which it invites criticism. Second, I will introduce the question of whether or not the JD's approach to consensus undermines or supports doctrine. Third, I will consider two instructive and, as I will suggest, unsuccessful criticisms of the proposed consensus. In conclusion, I will offer some sympathetic and programmatic remarks about the way in which the JD handles the problem of consensus in doctrine.

THE JD AND THE PROBLEM OF CONSENSUS

Wolfhart Pannenberg offers a useful distinction between "ecumenical mutuality" and "positive agreement" which helps clarify the internal complexity of the ecumenical process.[1] Mutuality involves recognition of doctrinal non-repugnance. This requires a negative consensus, an agreement that differences are insufficient to merit reciprocal condemnation or suspicion. According to Pannenberg, the Condemnations Report issued by the Ecumenical Study Group in Germany in the mid-eighties achieves a negative consensus.[2] The Report claims to show that the condemnations of the sixteenth century, in both Lutheran Confession and the Council of Trent, condemnations which have historically been thought to define the fundamental rationale for church division, either never did or no longer apply to the doctrinal traditions of Lutherans or Roman Catholics. In other words, on the question of justification, we need not assume antagonism.

A lack of mutual antagonism is not the same thing as substantive convergence and common vision, and for that reason Pannenberg distinguishes the ecumenical mutuality achieved by the Condemnations Report from positive agreement in doctrine. The Condemnations Report was very clear about its limited mandate. It was commissioned to consider the sixteenth-century condemnations with the goal of discerning whether or not Lutherans and Roman Catholics might achieve ecumenical mutuality (Pannenberg's terms) or a negative consensus (my term).[3] However, for full ecumenical progress, dialogue partners must do more than agree not to condemn; they must be able to identify a substantive convergence sufficient to count as a common understanding of the gospel. A successful conclusion to an ecumenical dialogue, therefore, requires a statement of positive consensus, and this turns out to be more difficult.

The earlier dialogue on justification manifests the difficulty of formulating a positive consensus which does not slide back into a negative consensus. Prior to the JD, the U.S. Common Statement on justification from the early eighties made the strongest statement of positive consensus. It affirms a common paschal core (§161), emphasizes the criteriological centrality of justification as the good news which frees us from sin and serves as the ultimate judge of "all our thoughts and actions, our philosophies and projects, our theologies and religious practices" (§162), and confesses a mutual failure to abide in purity of the gospel of salvation in Christ (§163). This convergence leads the Common Statement to conclude that the participants in the dialogue have reached "a fundamental consensus on the gospel" (§164). Here, then, we hear the note of positive consensus struck with a great deal of vigor.

Yet, at the outset of the Common Statement, the achievement of the dialogue is phrased differently. The Statement begins with a Christological agreement, but it continues with the observation that this Christological convergence "does not necessarily involve full agreement between Catholics and Lutherans on justification by faith ..." (§4). In view of this lack of full agreement, the Common Statement then formulates the ecumenical question in the negative. Do the remaining differences on the doctrine of justification, that is to say, the lack of full consensus or sufficient consensus to count as a common understanding, need to be church dividing (§4)? In this way, the introduction to the Common Statement seems to pose the issue of ecumenical consensus differently than the concluding declaration. Instead of positive convergence, the emphasis falls on showing that divergences are insufficient to be church dividing. To use Pannenberg's distinction, the Common Statement begins with the problem of ecumenical mutuality and ends with a statement of positive agreement.

The two senses of consensus at work in the Common Statement of the U.S. dialogue on justification epitomize a difficulty which runs through ecumenical dialogue in general and the Lutheran-Roman Catholic dialogue in particular. How are we to conceive of ecumenical progress or success? Should we think of this progress in terms of discerning and articulating a positive convergence? Or should we regard the primary ecumenical task as removing obstacles, showing how divergences are insufficient to warrant continued church division? Should we assess ecumenical documents according to the adequacy of their statement of consensus? Or should we judge each dialogue according to its ability to defuse and set aside differences?

As the culmination of the dialogue on justification, the JD rightly emphasizes both positive and negative consensus. Whenever it articulates its basic purpose, we hear the note of "common understanding." For example, at the outset of the document we read that the intention is "to show that on the basis of their dialogue the subscribing Lutheran churches and the Roman Catholic Church are now able to articulate a common understanding of our justification by God's grace through faith in Christ" (§5). This common understanding is expressed in a general formulation (§ 14-18) and is stated in five areas of traditional controversy. This emphasis on convergence sufficient to count as common understanding carries through to the conclusion of the JD. In the final section we read that "this declaration shows that a consensus in basic truths of the doctrine of justification exists between Lutherans and Roman Catholics" (§40).

Yet, even as the JD sustains this emphasis on positive consensus, the document is equally concerned to show that the very real differences and divergences "of language, theological elaboration, and emphasis" are "acceptable" (§40). In fact, when it directly engages the distinctive doctrinal traditions of the sixteenth-century Lutheran Confessions and Tridentine Catholicism, the real results of the ecumenical dialogue as summarized by the JD do not show convergence. Rather, the achievement of the dialogue is the discernment that the different treatments of justification in Lutheran and Roman Catholic doctrine are insufficiently divergent The emphasis falls on the statement of a negative consensus. Further, when the JD specifies the real consequences of its adoption by the appropriate ecclesiastical bodies, attention flows to the lifting of sixteenth-century condemnations (see §4 and §41). In this way, the consensus the JD articulates is complex. On the one hand it seeks to show a convergence sufficient to constitute a positive consensus, and on the other hand it hopes to demonstrate a negative consensus that remaining divergences are insufficient to undermine the positive consensus.

One need not be an enemy of ecumenism to find this complex statement of consensus perplexing. The JD sets out to show a convergence sufficient to constitute a common understanding of justification. This positive case for convergence, however, handles the familiar vocabulary regarding justification by negatively attempting to show divergence insufficient to undermine consensus. In areas of historic controversy, the discussion begins with a statement of positive consensus; but the classical vocabulary is kept at arm's length. When it is engaged, the attention turns to negative consensus. Given the shift from positive to negative consensus when handling historic controversy, what, we might ask, is the source of the common understanding? If every time the JD attends to the historic vocabulary of controversy the analysis shows insufficient divergence, then how can there be a genuine convergence? The JD does have a number of clear and helpful statements of positive consensus. But are they statements about justification or about Trinitarian and Christological consensus? If the latter is the case, then does the JD show sufficient convergence on justification, the ostensible matter at stake in the historic divisions of the sixteenth century?

THE ROLE OF DOCTRINE IN CONSENSUS

These are not idle or antagonistic questions, and more is at stake than the question of justification. Avery Dulles, a participant in the U.S. dialogue in the early eighties and a sympathetic reader of Reformation theology, is not persuaded. He does not think that the JD articulates a convergence sufficient to count as a common understanding.[4] Dulles points out that the distinctive vocabulary and practices which Roman Catholicism has traditionally associated with justification, for example, the notions of satisfaction and preparation for justifying grace, are not positively coordinated with Lutheran concepts and ecclesial practices. He allows that such a lack need not be church dividing in and of itself; he is persuaded by the element of the JD which focuses on articulating a negative consensus. However, the JD claims more; it asserts a positive consensus. And this claim troubles Dulles. "What," I can imagine him wondering, "is the source of this common understanding? If the distinctive features of Lutheran and Roman Catholic doctrine and discipline on the matter of justification are handled purely in the negative sense of non-repugnance, what is left to serve as the basis for a positive consensus?"

Dulles is more than unpersuaded, he is actively worried. "By prematurely declaring the process already accomplished," he writes, "we can easily drift into false complacency" (p. 220). This complacency is not benign. We live, Dulles observes, in a "climate of agnosticism and relativism," and our zeal for charity and mutual acceptance tempts us to downplay the authoritative and binding character of church doctrine (p. 220). For Dulles, the easy drift into I'm OK/you're OK ecumenism must be resisted. "One of the most precious things we have in common," writes Dulles, "may be our conviction that pure doctrine is crucially important and that ecclesial unity should not be purchased at the expense of truth" (p. 220). Ecumenical progress must be sought, but not blindly.

Here, Dulles strikes a note already present within the official dialogue. Wolfhart Pannenberg, one of the directors of the Ecumenical Study Group in Germany which produced the ground-breaking Condemnations Report, is just as emphatic as Dulles. However one judges the achievement of the Condemnations Report, Pannenberg certainly does not want us to conclude that the doctrinal traditions of Lutheranism and Roman Catholicism are a dead letter. As he writes, the great detail and complexity of the Condemnations Report grows out of the conviction that "the oppositions of the past must not be trivialized.... The claim of church teaching to abiding validity must not be neglected, notwithstanding present insights ..."[5] The Condemnations Report sought negative consensus, and this made an affirmation of historic doctrine easier to sustain than the project of articulating a positive consensus. Although it takes up the more strenuous task of stating a positive consensus, the JD reiterates Pannenberg's commitment to the importance of doctrine. "Like the dialogues themselves, this Joint Declaration rests on the conviction that in overcoming the earlier controversial questions of doctrinal condemnations, the churches neither take the condemnations lightly nor disavow their own past" (§7). Clearly, the JD does not wish to relativize doctrine. It seeks unity *in* doctrine, not unity *beyond* doctrine.

The suspicion remains, however, that the positive consensus proposed by the JD overwhelms the good intentions of the document writers and the dialogue participants. I think this suspicion is worth investigating. The move from ecumenical mutuality to positive agreement, from negative consensus to positive consensus, is crucial for the future of the ecumenical movement. Yet, as Dulles points out, the stakes are high, not only for the question of justification, but also for the ways in which late twentieth-century western Christianity understands doctrine and truth. If ecumenical progress sets aside historic doctrine in the purely negative demonstrations of non-repugnance, then ecumenism constellates with any number of cultural forces to drive a wedge between doctrine and truth. Doctrine becomes an impediment to be overcome rather than a source of insight with the power to express the truth of the gospel. I join Dulles in making the danger of a wedge between doctrine and truth my primary concern. Does the positive consensus expressed in the JD undermine or support the role of doctrine in our understanding of and witness to the truth of the gospel?

In order to ask this question effectively, I want to consider two objections to the JD, both of which argue that its positive consensus fails. Both objections are claims that the JD misconceives the nature of Lutheran doctrine and, therefore, severs the relation between doctrine and truth. These criticisms and their assumptions about the essence of doctrine will help us arrive at our own answer to the question of whether the approach to positive consensus in the JD undermines or supports the role of doctrine.

THE QUEST FOR EQUIVALENCE

Verbal agreement is the paradigm for positive consensus. Within ecumenical discussions, this expectation does not require saying the same words in the same way. Instead, a more sophisticated form of equivalence is at work. We know that, when you say "car" and I say "automobile," we need not fall into disagreement. Even though we use different words, the substitution of one word for the other renders no inference invalid or unsound. Everything I say about cars is true of automobiles. Here, then, we find a model for the kind of equivalence often at work in both the prosecution and assessment of ecumenical dialogue. A strong convergence is identifiable when the dialogue can demonstrate that one system of doctrine can accommodate the terminology of another. Ideally, a positive consensus would be demonstrated by showing how a common understanding of justification could be stated in both Tridentine terminology and the terminology of the sixteenth-century Lutheran confessions.

This expectation of equivalence seems to motivate Inge Lønning's objections to the JD.[6] As Lønning observes, the positive statements of consensus, both the general statement (§14-18) and the statements pertinent to areas of historical controversy (§19, 22, 25, 28, 31, 34, 37), are not formulated in the vocabulary of the Lutheran doctrine of justification or in equivalent terms. The general statement of positive consensus places justification within a super-ordinate trinitarian framework. This framework may be non-controversial, but it is not the standard way in which the Lutheran confessional tradition presents the meaning and importance of the doctrine of justification. Instead, the standard Lutheran and Roman Catholic ways of talking about justification are handled in the negative. All that is demonstrated is non-repugnance or divergence insufficient to undermine common understanding. For Lønning, however helpful the JD's formulations might be for new perspectives and insights into the context and significance of justification, they are not adequate statements of consensus. Regardless of our support of the ecumenical movement, we must judge the JD a failure.

For Lønning, the JD has not simply failed to show equivalence. He is worried that it, and the ecumenical dialogues leading up to it, have systematically evaded the task of showing equivalence in statements of positive consensus. Echoing Dulles' concerns, Lønning thinks that this evasion threatens to alienate Lutheranism from doctrinal authority and turn faith into a fuzzy sensibility. "In dealing with the contradictions of the doctrinal tradition," he writes, "the JD and its predecessor dialogue reports have depended upon the strategy of 'model building'" (p. 145). One often hears that the Lutheran doctrine of justification is, at root, an expression of the purity of the gospel, while the Roman Catholic understanding of justification emphasizes the fullness of God's gifts.[7] However helpful these models might be to orient discussion, for Lønning they cannot be substituted for close analysis of the linguistic particularity of the doctrinal traditions. Too often, he argues, divergences and even contradictions in the plain verbal sense of doctrine are interpreted "as expressions of different patterns of thought rather than as substantive theological positions ..." (p. 145).

The outcome is not just intellectual sloppiness. For Lønning, the drift away from the plain sense of doctrine has theological consequences. The abstraction of doctrinal statements into models or patterns of thought requires a fundamental distinction between "faith content" and "terminology"[8] which, for Lønning, is disastrous. As he questions,

How could "the faith content" of a doctrine be subject to communication apart from terminology employed? Is "the faith content" independent of the terminology employed in formulating the faith content, even in a consensus declaration intended to serve as a basis for binding doctrinal decisions? Does the faith content of a doctrine exist as such, in a shape which is weightless and without any kind of specific emphasis anywhere? (p. 146)

These are the questions which animate Dulles. If ecumenical consensus drives us away from the clear and vivid doctrinal anchors which historically have shaped our common faith and theological practice, then we become vulnerable to the subjectivist and relativistic spirit of the age. Doctrine becomes a resource for expressing the experience of faith rather than a norm for faithful speech and action. Further, the underlying religious ontology influences our relation to liturgy and scripture. An implicit distinction between terminology and faith content tempts us to think and act as though the particular linguistic shape and content of scripture and the ancient liturgies of the church have no essential relation to faith. Doctrine becomes detached from the truth of the gospel.

Lønning's criticisms of the JD are motivated, I submit, by a healthy worry. We should guard against tendencies which exacerbate an already widespread modern disregard for the particular linguistic shape of Christian truth. Even if the JD produces results which satisfy our desire for ecumenical progress, we should beware reasoning which make it easier to massage the recalcitrant objectivity of Christian teaching to satisfy other, less evangelical desires. The question is not whether we should share Lønning's larger concern about the dangers of detaching faith from the classical formulations which have defined the traditions of Lutheranism and Roman Catholicism. The important question is whether the demand for equivalence and the underlying assumptions about the propositional authority and efficacy of classical formulations can really protect us from a wholesale dismissal of doctrine. Does the kind of consensus which Lønning expects from ecumenical dialogue actually reinforce the central and formative role of inherited patterns of thought and action in the Christian life?

Unfortunately, the ideal of equivalence undermines rather than supports the role of doctrine in the life of the church. In spite of his desire to preserve the close link between doctrine and truth, Lønning's approach tends toward the opposite. The problem rests with the presumed propositional truth of doctrine which underwrites the ideal of equivalence. This assumption and the quest for ecumenical equivalence which it motivates ask doctrine to do something it cannot do, and the outcome is a dysfunctional view of doctrine which cannot help but undermine rather than upbuild the relation of doctrine to truth. The problem is not that Lønning is "propositional" and that this is, somehow, philosophically unsophisticated. The difficulties are concrete and practical.

The dialogues leading up to the JD illustrate the difficulty of relying on equivalence as the ideal of positive consensus. For example, the Condemnations Report shows the equivalence of "faith" in Lutheran talk about justification with the Roman Catholic use of "faith, hope, and love" in the Tridentine theology of justification. Because Luther was worried about works righteousness, he expanded the concept of faith to encompass the full scope of the human response to God. Because the Fathers at Trent were concerned about antinomianism and wished to express the full reach of divine grace, they insisted on the triad of faith, hope, and love. Nonetheless, the Condemnations Report suggests that the Lutheran conception of faith and the Catholic triad of faith, hope, and love are sufficiently similar to allow substitution of the one for the other without undermining the propositional logic of either Lutheran or Roman Catholic statements about justification. In this particular instance, no valid inference in one system of doctrine is rendered invalid by the use of the vocabulary of the other system.

Yet, as the dialogue points out, whether or not one chooses to use "faith" or "faith, hope, and love" influences the overall meaning of a doctrinal system. As the study observes, "we [do not] wish to restrict this difference to a *mere* (and hence fortuitous) choice of words. On the contrary, the difference reflects different concerns and emphases on which the practical Christian life and the self-understanding of Protestant and Catholic Christian's can depend."[9] In other words, even though one can substitute the Lutheran notion of faith for the Roman Catholic triad of faith, hope, and love without rendering any specific doctrinal statement invalid, both the sense of the words and the meaning of doctrinal statements changes. The network of doctrinal formulations about justification and their role in the formation of Christian identity in the two churches will necessarily change the meaning of the words to reflect precisely those concerns and emphases which led to the difference in the first place. Moreover, the semantic nuances of the singular "faith" or the triad of "faith, hope, and love" will necessarily shade the ways in which doctrine will influence the thought and action of those who accept their use as normative. In the process of ecumenical discussion, a close examination of the possibilities of verbal equivalence has demonstrated that doctrine cannot be understood as a logical system of inference based upon premises with semantically independent verbal senses. Whatever the importance of doctrinal terminology, it cannot be the importance of a verbal sense which could be mapped, word for word, onto an alternative terminology.

Some close reasoning captures the danger of insisting on a propositional view of doctrine in an ecumenical context. Consider this argument. God promises unity in Christ. If the results of the Condemnations Report are correct, particular propositions take on system-specific meanings and the goal of doctrinal equivalence is unattainable, which leads to a troubling disjunctive conclusion. Assuming, as does Lønning, that the truth of doctrine is propositional, either God's promise of unity cannot be fulfilled because it would be a unity outside the truth of doctrine or the truth of doctrine is not relevant to the fulfillment of God's promise of unity.

Here we have reached the real problem with a propositional view of doctrine. Surely God's promises are not in vain. We should be loathe, therefore, to conclude that the promise of unity cannot be fulfilled. Yet, if we agree with Lønning and Dulles that our relativistic age tempts us to disregard doctrine, then we should be equally unhappy to conclude that doctrine is irrelevant to the fulfillment of God's promise of unity. On the horns of this dilemma, if we sympathize with Lønning, we are tempted to insist that equivalence in doctrine really *is* possible and thus preserve the possibility of fulfillment of God's promise of unity through a unity in doctrine. However, as I have pointed out above, the current ecumenical dialogue, especially on the question of justification, has investigated equivalence with sufficient care to expose the possibilities and limitations of this approach. As a result, the disjunctive conclusion seems to be unavoidable.

Most of us are unwilling to believe that God's promises are futile. So, under the pressure of the disjunctive conclusion which flows from assuming a propositional relationship between doctrine and truth, we tend to push doctrine aside as irrelevant. If we have the kind of theoretical commitment to the verbal sense of doctrine which Lønning represents, we preserve and honor confessional statements. Yet, these statements of doctrine migrate to the margins of ecclesial life. We all too easily turn historical confessions into talismans of evangelical purity, detached from any particular habits of minds, patterns of speech, or expectations of behavior, so that our confidence in the purely verbal form becomes as magical as the most retrograde Tridentine confidence in the efficacy of the Mass. This is common. Surely we all know someone who is ardent on behalf of Lutheran identity, venerates the Book of Concord, but who preaches and counsels parishioners in a way utterly indistinguishable from the warm, experiential Calvinism which dominates conservative American evangelicalism. Intuitively, pastors and congregations feel that the truths of doctrine are irrelevant to the fulfillment of God's promises of new life in Christ. Preaching, catechesis, church policy, and moral decisions take place with doctrine very much on the periphery, the object of reverence but with no real role. In this way, Lønning's approach has the unsettling effect of encouraging just the complacent division of faith from confession which he fears.

Liberals have spent the last century trying to convince us that doctrine is, indeed, irrelevant. As propositions expressing an earlier stage of the church's experience of Jesus, the historical or cultural limitations of human language about divine truth burden doctrine with anachronism and human finitude. Right or wrong about the nature of doctrine, liberal theologians consistently have the advantage of accurately describing current ecclesial practice. Doctrine *is* largely irrelevant to current Christian leaders. Conservatives have reacted by insisting that the problem stems from a lack of faith and insufficient commitment to doctrine. Perhaps both are mistaken. Perhaps the irrelevance of doctrine is a consequence of viewing doctrine as a set of verbally clear and self-contained propositions. Perhaps we cannot resist the spirit of our age without altering our assumptions about doctrine and the way in which it forms us in the truth of the gospel. Perhaps we need to escape the disjunctive conclusion forced on us by the premise that God's promise of unity requires propositional equivalence in doctrine.

THE SEARCH FOR CONCEPTUAL CONVERGENCE

If we give up on equivalence as the true test of ecumenical consensus, we must turn away from a purely verbal or propositional view of doctrine. One alternative is to assume that the essential and authoritative force of doctrine is found in a distinctive conceptual scheme encoded into the verbal forms of historical confessions. We might say that doctrine is important because it outlines a certain model of the divine-human relationship, or that doctrine shapes our speech and action in a determinate way. Much of modern Lutheranism takes this approach.[10] According to one popular variant of this view, what is important about Lutheran teaching on justification is the Law/Gospel hermeneutic which conceives of the authority of Christ as promise and forgiveness rather than as law. Under the guidance of such a view, showing a positive convergence on the question of justification entails demonstrating that the Lutheran confessions and Roman Catholic doctrine outline similar conceptions of Christ's redemptive authority.

The emphasis on a doctrinal gestalt is the approach taken by the *Call for Discussion* (CFD) put forward by members of the faculty at Luther Seminary (ELCA) in St. Paul.[11] For the CFD the crucial issue in any assessment of the JD is "how 'grace' is understood" (p. 226). Addressing this issue does not involve demonstrations of verbal equivalence through a coordination of the vocabularies of Roman Catholic and Lutheran teaching. Instead, it involves the conceptual gestalt of the two doctrinal traditions. How exactly does Lutheranism conceive of the efficacy of divine grace? How does Roman Catholicism address the same question? And is there a positive convergence in these two ways of understanding the role of grace in the life of the believer?

For the CFD, Lutheran and Roman Catholic accounts of justification fall within the common Augustinian tradition of affirming the absolute priority of divine grace but, nonetheless, the two doctrinal traditions understand grace in quite different and even contradictory ways. Roman Catholic teaching depends upon a substantialist ontology, within which grace functions as a progressive causal power operating upon and transforming the soul of the believer from the outside (p. 226). In contrast, the Reformation promotes a relational ontology in which faith establishes a right relationship with God and neighbor. Far from allowing for a positive convergence, these two ontologies guarantee a profound divergence. For the Roman Catholic, the CFD insists, justification by grace will be understood as "a new quality imparted or infused into the soul," while in Lutheranism justification by faith will be understood as "sheer trust in God awakened by God's eschatological Word of promise." Precisely because the doctrinal gestalt shapes the entire outlook of a theological tradition, "these contrasting understandings of justification make all the difference for the actual exercise of the ministry of the gospel" (p. 227). The Roman Catholic gestalt of progressive transformation through the infusion of grace cannot help but transform Christ's power into an object or action which may be controlled by the church. In contrast, the Lutheran gestalt of relational transformation guarantees a self-critical focus on the event of God's eschatological promise of unconditional forgiveness.

On the basis of this approach to doctrine, the CFD observes that the JD disguises the real differences which separate Roman Catholicism and Lutheranism. The positive statements of consensus, it warns, are ambiguous, and when they are not ambiguous they tend toward the Roman Catholic substantialist view of grace and salvation. This is not, in the end, a matter of close textual analysis of the JD or the dialogues leading up to the JD. Indeed, the CFD notes that the very project of ecumenical declarations such as the JD, declarations which ask for official actions by ecclesial bodies to alter binding doctrine, is an intrinsically Tridentine project. "If justification is by faith in God's word of promise, then proclaiming God's living Word of promise, the actual delivery of the gospel in word and sacrament, is the highest exercise of authority in the church" (p. 229) In contrast, if one takes what the CFD assumes to be the Roman Catholic substantialist view, "then the highest authority in the Church will be a magisterium demanding obedience to the law ..." (p. 229). In other words, the essence of Lutheran doctrine, its distinctive gestalt, and ensuing hermeneutic, actually prohibits the authoritative articulation of doctrinal consensus and the official lifting of mutual condemnations, because just such activities focus our attention on ecclesial substances and turn us into Roman Catholics in disguise.

Whether or not we agree that Lutheranism rests upon a "relational ontology" or that Roman Catholicism depends upon a "substantialist ontology," we should acknowledge that the CDF offers an alternative to the propositional interpretation of doctrine which motivates the ill-fated quest for equivalence. Lutheran and Roman Catholic doctrines of justification are not significant in their purely verbal sense; the two traditions encode a shaping principle, an organizing idea, a determinate gestalt. A similar approach characterizes the Göttingen faculty's response to the earlier condemnations study. In that analysis of the ecumenical dialogue, doctrine is interpreted as disclosing a mode-of-being. Trent, according to the Göttingen analysis, defines doctrine through the use of condemnations, which creates a doctrinal system in which faith takes the form of law and "the truth thus made legal aims at obedience, at the subjugation to authority of the church which promulgates the law." In contrast, "by casting their teachings in positive and argumentative presentations, the Evangelical confessional writings aim at insight and understanding ... which can only be produced by God's Word itself."[12] The juxtaposition invites a standard contrast which reinforces, from the Lutheran side, the necessity of the sixteenth-century divisions. The Roman Catholic gestalt inevitably leads to a slavish and artificial obedience to human authority, yielding either hypocrisy or an afflicted conscience, while the Reformation gestalt shapes preaching and ecclesiastical discipline toward a free, critical, and personally meaningful faith.

However one's Reformation loyalties might be reassured by the CDF's conclusions, I hope that the free and critical Reformation conscience is unsettled by the ease with which a gestalt analysis of doctrine moves from characterization to caricature. By the time we get to the contrasts between Roman Catholic legalism and Reformation freedom we are a long way indeed from the verbal forms of the sixteenth-century confessions. This distance creates exactly the same problem as the propositionalist assumptions which motivate the quest for equivalence, namely, the increasing irrelevance of the historic confessions. However familiar might be the gestalt of Roman Catholic legalism and Reformation freedom, the actual content and complexity of the sixteenth-century confessions underdetermine these characterizations. Once analyzed, Reformation doctrine is overshadowed by the more decisive questions of Reformation ontology or hermeneutics. The danger is not that the outcomes might contradict our most dearly held beliefs; the problem with the CDF's approach is, rather, that it defines doctrine with a conceptualizing move. Gestalt analysis abstracts us away from the historically formative details and authoritative verbal forms.

Of course, the practitioners of this approach want to give us a second-order, big-picture view so that we can return to our confessional commitments with an enlivened sense of their meaning and purpose. This is an admirable goal, but the danger is that patterns of doctrinal analysis overwhelm these good intentions. If we are taught that a conceptual or ontological interpretation of doctrine defines the essence of our confessional identities, will we not gravitate toward the study of concepts rather than of the words and phrases of the historic confessions? Then, without even noticing, do we not find ourselves reading Hegel in order to understand the genius of the Reformation rather than re-reading the Book of Concord in order to understand the aspirations and failures of the Enlightenment? I raise these questions not to cast doubt on the reading of books devoted to concepts. Rather, I want to point out that a gestalt analysis which proposes to define the essence of a doctrinal tradition in abstract terms threatens to undermine the particular verbal sense of doctrine and render historic confessions a dead letter.

Just as in the case of the propositional view of doctrine, the danger's latent in the CDF's assumptions about doctrine are especially evident in the ecumenical context, for an objection to a proposal for church unity has a very different logic than criticism of a theological school of thought. Again, I offer a close argument to focus the logic of the problem. Christ commands us to be one. We cannot be one if we are divided in doctrine. Therefore, if we object to a proposal to fulfill Christ's command, it can only be on the basis of insight into the essential content of doctrine.

Since the CDF objects on the grounds of a meta-doctrinal analysis of the ontologies of Lutheran and Roman Catholic doctrines of justification, we must conclude that this kind of conceptual analysis captures the essence of doctrine and constitutes the basis of our encounter with the truth of the gospel. Thus, although proponents of conceptual analysis claim their approach as a second-order orientation to the first-order language of the doctrinal tradition, the logic of ecumenical proposal and objection void such a claim. Either the question of theological ontology is a school debate, in which case it cannot be the basis for church division, or it marks a division in the truth of the gospel, justifies church division, and constitutes a fundamental form of our participation in the gospel. Since the CDF seems to adopt the latter approach, to the extent that we are persuaded by its analysis we are also persuaded that conceptual decisions and choices in theological ontology are central to our response to the gospel. This strikes me as an extraordinarily dangerous assumption. The conceptualizing move carries us away from rather than into the details of Christian language and practice. It drives a wedge between the historic and verbal forms of doctrine and the truth of the gospel. Surely Lønning's worry, however ill-served by his own insistence upon propositional equivalence, should caution us against going down this road in our analysis of the JD.

POSITIVE CONSENSUS IN THE JD

I have surveyed the two criticisms of the JD's proposed consensus not because I think them foolish or ill-considered. Quite the contrary, I regard a concern about the verbal sense of authoritative doctrine crucially important in our highly subjectivist age. The Word of God cannot be a sharp and two-edged sword if we treat Church doctrine like a wax nose. Further, I think the effort to identify the conceptual shape of doctrinal traditions equally important if we are to do justice to the formative purpose of doctrine. Living doctrine *should* form our speech and action into an identifiable gestalt. In both respects, to preserve the verbal integrity and to do justice to the formative role of doctrine, the impulses behind the two lines of criticism of the JD are certainly healthy. The limitations of these criticisms rests in their singularity. Doctrinal meaning overflows its strict verbal sense and, if we insist upon propositional or verbal equivalence as a necessary condition for positive consensus, then we risk isolating doctrine and draining it of its formative power. But the formative power cannot be divorced from the verbal sense, and to define doctrine in terms of a conceptual scheme risks abstracting confessional identity from the very words and practices over which doctrine should exercise authority. Both approaches, if carried forward blindly, have the unintended effect of undermining rather than supporting the doctrinal tradition they hope to defend.

A better way to approach the JD is to drop univocal assumptions about doctrine and singular tests of doctrinal consensus. Doctrine has many forms and functions, and a positive consensus in doctrine will be multi-faceted.[13] The JD signals the internal complexity of the consensus which it claims to present. Not only does it clearly distinguish between positive and negative consensus but, within the notion of positive consensus, it suggests a number of different loci around which consensus has formed. The differentiation of the positive consensus tells us something important about the way in which the JD conceives of doctrine and its relationship to the truth of the gospel. We might categorize these different loci as biblical, trinitarian, sacramental, and pastoral; they constellate to give us a very rich understanding of the role of doctrine and the possibilities of positive consensus. I want to offer some observations about the biblical and pastoral loci of consensus. They both reinforce some of my conclusions about the limitations of the propositional and conceptual approaches to doctrine, and suggest a way forward to a more promising understanding of the relationship of doctrine to truth.

The key to the positive consensus in the JD is the convergence in biblical exegesis. No matter how highly we value doctrine, its authority stems from scripture, and one of its most important functions is to guide the interpretation of scripture. If scripture consistently yields results contrary to our understanding of doctrine, however, then we must either consign that doctrine to a corner of church history or revise our understanding of its true import. One of the most important results of the Second Vatican Council was the release of Catholic biblical studies from a rather slavish subservience to scholastic theology. As a result, Roman Catholic scholars have adopted the methods of historical inquiry which have dominated Protestant exegesis throughout this century, yielding a convergence in exegetical practice and interpretive results. The JD summarizes this convergence on the topic of justification in the Pauline letters, and this convergence has been the foundation for rethinking assumptions about the true import of the sixteenth-century doctrines.

This rethinking of sixteenth-century doctrine stems from more than a recognition of new opportunities latent in a material convergence in exegesis. Exegesis is embedded within the Christian system of thought and practice, and material changes in exegesis place pressure on other key elements of the Christian life. Again, some close inferences help expose the logic of the matter. Given that scripture is the *norma normans* of Christian thought and practice, there seem to be three possibilities when confronted with the emerging exegetical consensus on justification. Either the exegetical convergence is an illusion or the prevailing assumptions about the sixteenth-century doctrines are mistaken or those doctrines never were based upon scripture. The dialogue has assumed that the exegetical convergence is accurate and is unwilling to detach doctrine from scripture. Refusing those two alternative has disciplined the dialogue participants to subject their own confessional traditions to close scrutiny. If Protestant and Catholic exegetes can achieve a common understanding of justification, and if the sixteenth-century doctrinal statements are genuinely normed by scripture, then it must be possible to be faithful to those statements and to formulate a doctrinal agreement on justification.

This may strike some as disturbing, because it sounds as though we know where we are going and then bend words and patterns of doctrine to get there. This is an accurate perception and perhaps the discomfort is not altogether unhealthy. I want to point out, however, that both the propositional and conceptual approaches to doctrine leave open an implicit commitment to the third possibility in the threefold disjunction above. An insistence upon the verbal or propositional perspicuity of doctrine allows us to think that doctrinal meaning may be discerned and doctrinal authority applied without reference to scripture. If doctrinal truth is propositional, the sixteenth-century confessions can take on a life of their own and, instead of finding their authority in and through an ongoing exegesis which accepts the confessions as proper framework for scriptural reading and subjects them to ongoing exegetical testing, the confessions become incantatory. The same holds true for the conceptual approach. Although much more plastic than the propositional approach, the conceptualizing move tempts us to think that we have pierced the veil of scripture and secured a properly biblical anthropology or a relational ontology which allows us to apply the authority of scripture in a formal or conceptual way. At its most extreme, this can lead to the assumption that we know better than Paul what he meant by justification. With this approach, one can be uninterested in an exegetical convergence and scripture can easily become data to be interpreted rather than the most effective and enduring form of the gospel. However unsettling might be the JD's approach to doctrine, at least we should recognize that it avoids the danger of severing the relationship of doctrine to scripture which afflicts the propositional and gestalt approach.

A pastoral convergence parallels the biblical convergence and the common situations of Lutherans and Roman Catholics challenge our assumptions about doctrine. As doctrine serves to help us read scripture as exegetical changes force reexamination of doctrine, so also sustained changes in the challenges of pastoral work force reassessment. In the late twentieth century, western culture has become more thoroughly detached from its Christian heritage; the strong Augustinian atmosphere which characterized it has dissipated. We live in a profoundly antinomian age in which a preacher can no longer presume affliction of conscience or a sense of the curse of the law and, as a result, the questions which motivated debate about the doctrine of justification have subsided. No longer does the ordinary American wonder how and by what right he or she, as a sinner, might stand before God. Attentive pastors have shifted priorities accordingly.

Although this change in pastoral priorities is not as explicitly central to the JD as the exegetical convergence, it exerts a similar pressure on the dialogue. To the extent that doctrine in general and, for Lutherans at least, the doctrine of justification in particular, has a decisive role in the proclamation of the gospel and the guidance of believers toward discipleship, changes in pastoral practice must stimulate reassessments of the full import and consequence of doctrine. Here, the JD may be read as echoing a great deal of the modern theological impulse to meet the needs of modern man, and we are quite right to worry, along with Dulles and Lønning, that reassessment quickly becomes accommodation and capitulation to the spirit of the age. However, the defense of doctrinal truth through a reinforced commitment to the verbal sense runs the risk of detaching pastoral practice from doctrine, for it does nothing to bring pastoral practice back under the governance of doctrine. The conceptual approach appears to be better able to meet the exigencies of the age. Yet, in spite of the fact that a theological ontology is a useful way to order and shape a systematic theology, it has little influence over preaching and pastoral practice. The abstracting move all too easily turns doctrine into a slogan, justification is God's acceptance of the unacceptable.

The JD's general statement of a common Lutheran and Roman Catholic understanding of justification (¶¶14-18) responds to the increased pastoral irrelevance of the doctrine of justification by placing justification within a trinitarian framework (¶15). In so doing, it implicitly acknowledges that the doctrine of justification does not have an independent intelligibility as an articulation of the Christian gospel. This formulation of justification within a trinitarian framework stems from a shift in pastoral challenges; the articulation of the understanding of justification in a trinitarian framework repositions classical Reformation concerns to meet that pastoral challenge.

This response to changed pastoral challenges is further evident in the subtle and controversial treatment of justification as *an* indispensable criterion (¶18). Eberhard Jüngel has pounced on the implicit retreat from *the* indispensable criterion to *an* indispensable criterion.[14] He accurately senses that the JD's reexamination of justification constitutes a retreat from an earlier Reformation confidence that the doctrine of justification enjoys an evangelical immediacy. The question, however, is not whether the JD has demoted justification but whether contemporary Lutheranism has not already, in practice, treated the doctrine of justification as functionally irrelevant. If so, we ought to read the JD's articulation of common consensus as part of a larger effort among Lutherans and Roman Catholics to understand the doctrinal context for assumptions about our salvation in Christ in order to recover the role of justification as a living doctrine. What is important is that the JD guides this reassessment back into the trinitarian framework of the ancient tradition, a tradition which does have evangelical immediacy and spiritual pertinence.

These two aspects of the JD's effort to reestablish a connection between doctrine and truth, between doctrine and the scriptural witness to Christ, and between doctrine and the practical work of the Church, may entice, may provoke, may disappoint. Indeed, the very logic of doctrine and its relation to truth guarantees that the JD cannot fully persuade. Here, the difficulties are more than a matter of differences in doctrinal vocabularies (faith vs. faith, hope, and love) or in doctrinal Gestalts (substantialist ontology vs. relational ontology). The approach the JD takes to doctrine necessarily entails the articulation of an incomplete consensus. If doctrine is essentially embedded in the exegetical, sacramental, and witnessing practices of the church, then its full meaning and scope is only visible as a living doctrine, active in the expression and governance of the church's life. But there is no Church which could give life to the consensus articulated in the JD, for during the period of Christendom it is a consensus across division. For this fundamental reason, the positive consensus articulated in the JD is necessarily incomplete and inadequate. If doctrine is genuinely related to the truth of the gospel, and if the radiance of that truth is diminished by our inability to live in the unity of that truth, then any presentation of doctrine, such as that of the JD, will always be incomplete. Doctrine can only teach a truth visible and real. To the extent that Christian division makes the truth of our unity in Christ invisible and unreal, all doctrine, including the doctrine of justification, will be as much a matter of groping in the dark as a discernment of what is evident and plain for all to see.

My goal has not been to uncover defects or to defend the JD against material criticisms. I simply want us to acknowledge that, unlike the quest for equivalence or the comparison of conceptual schemes or gestalts, the JD's approach invites us to immerse ourselves in questions about the scriptural, pastoral, and concrete forms of doctrine which actually constitute our corporate and personal identities. This immersion supports rather than undermines the role of doctrine against the relativistic and subjectivist spirit of our age; it connects rather than separates doctrine and truth. However much we might fear that the JD is wrong about justification, we should be reassured that it proposes a consensus which in form if not content is worthy of affirmation. The JD's positive consensus is underdetermined by both the particular verbal forms of the historic confessions and the gestalts formed by those confessions. It is, nonetheless, formed under pressure from those aspects of the church's life, the scriptural word and pastoral practice, which have become alienated from doctrine. The outcome, however partially formed and inarticulate, is a treatment of the doctrine of justification which offers some progress toward the recovery of doctrine as indispensable to both our hearing and living the truth of the gospel.[15]

NOTES

1. "Can the Mutual Condemnation Between Rome and the Reformation Churches Be Lifted?" in *Justification by Faith: Do the Sixteenth Century Condemnations Still Apply*, Karl Lehmann, Michael Root, and William G. Rusch, eds. (New York: Continuum, 1996), 41-43.

2. The Report has been published in English under the title, *The Condemnation of the Reformation Era: Do They Still Divide?*, Karl Lehmann and Wolfhart Pannenberg, eds. (Minneapolis: Fortress Press, 1990).

3. Pannenberg insists that this limited objective be kept in view. He interprets a great deal of the criticism of the Condemnations Report as motivated by the assumption that the goal of the dialogue was to show positive consensus. For example, he considers Jörg Baur's criticisms and concludes that Baur misunderstands the goal of the Condemnations study. Although Baur formally acknowledges that the study did not aim to identify or articulate a positive consensus, Pannenberg thinks his criticisms are motivated by the assumption that the dialogue seeks just the sort of common understanding necessary for a positive consensus. Needless to say, if one assumes that the Condemnations Report sets out to achieve what it does not set out to achieve, then showing that the dialogue "fails" is rather easily demonstrated but fundamentally irrelevant. See Pannenberg's discussion of Baur's criticism in "The Doctrine of Justification in Ecumenical Dialogue," *Dialog* 31/2 (Spring 1992), 136-48.

4. "On Lifting the Condemnations," *Dialog* 35/3 (Summer 1996), 219-20.

5. "Can the Mutual Condemnations between Rome and the Reformation Churches Be Lifted?," 35.

6. See "Lifting the Condemnations: Does It Make Sense?" *Dialog* 36/2 (Spring 1997), 143-47.

7. See the U.S. Dialogue Common Statement, §120.

8. Lonning draws attention to the use of the term "faith content" in the JD. Though this term was in §5 of an early draft of the JD, it does not appear in the final version circulated to Lutheran World Federation members for acceptance.

9. *The Condemnations of the Reformation Era*, 52.

10. For a helpful characterization of some of the modern conceptual translations of the doctrine of justification, see George A. Lindbeck, "Article IV and Lutheran/Roman Catholic Dialogue: The Limits of Diversity in the Understanding of Justification," *Lutheran Theological Seminary Quarterly* (Gettysburg, PA) 61 (Feb 1981), 3-16.

11. "A Call for Discussion of the 'Joint Declaration on the Doctrine of Justification,'" *Dialog* 36/3 (Summer 1997), 224-20. The "Call" was formulated by six members of the Luther Seminary faculty: Gerhard Forde, Pat Keifert, Mary Knutsen, Marc Kolden, Jim Nestingen, and Gary Simpson.

12. "An Opinion on *The Condemnations of the Reformation Era*. Part One: Justification," *Lutheran Quarterly*, 5/2 (Spring 1991), 12, quotes in "The Call," 229.

13. See Harding Meyer, "Ecumenical Consensus," *Gregorianum* 77/2 (1996), 213-25.

14. See "Um Gottes Willen—Klarheit," *Zeitschrift für Theologie und Kirche*, 94/3 (Sept 1997), 394-406.

15. I would like to thank the staff of the Institute for Ecumenical Research (Strasbourg), and especially the Director, Michael Root, for inviting me to visit and use the fine library at the Institute. The substance of this essay grew out of the discussions and research there. I would also like to thank David P. Scaer for inviting me to address the Twenty-First Annual Symposium on the Lutheran Confessions at Concordia Theological Seminary in Fort Wayne. The topic he assigned, Lutheran-Roman Catholic dialogue on justification, provided the initial impetus for developing this essay. I delivered an earlier and defective draft of this essay at the Symposium, and I remain grateful for the indulgent attention of the gathered Lutheran Church Missouri Synod pastors.

Gambling with the Common Good: State Lotteries from the Perspective of Roman Catholic Social Thought

Julia A. Fleming

In 1992, Nebraska voters followed a trend first established nearly thirty years before by New Hampshire, and approved the institution of a state lottery.[1] Ticket sales began the following September, reaching the hundred million dollar mark in a little less than eighteen months.[2] These developments brought Nebraska onto a path already well-traveled by her sister states, for the great expansion in lottery growth occurred in the 1980s.[3] By 1988, two-thirds of the U.S. population lived in lottery jurisdictions, and the sale of tickets in that year totaled 14.9 billion dollars.[4] "Lottery revenues have risen more than 800 percent since 1982," reported PBS's *Newshour* in July of 1996.[5] Today over three-quarters of the U.S. states and the District of Columbia operate lotteries.[6] A product that was non-existent, and indeed illegal, less than forty years ago now represents a major American industry.[7]

Although New Hampshire's experiment ended a universal twentieth-century prohibition of lotteries in the United States, earlier generations had considerable experience with them, especially during the colonial period and the new nation's first decades. Such drawings financed not only the Revolutionary War effort, but various types of public works, including university and church construction.[8] These early lotteries were quite distinct from their modern counterparts, however, as Raymond McGowan explains:

> Once the good cause was completed, then the lottery ceased to exist. While the state needed the lottery to finance these projects, it did not depend on lottery proceeds to fund services that constituents expected the state to provide daily…. [Today] the causes that lottery proceeds support are activities that the state has traditionally funded and that the public expects the state to continue to fund.[9]

The modern state lottery has become a regular rather than an occasional source of revenue, a common rather than an exceptional experience.[10] Ironically, media coverage even brings the lottery home to people who live in non-lottery states, since televised images of drawings, winners, and long lines in convenience stores provide a type of vicarious participation. For better or worse, the lottery, in one way or another, is almost everywhere.

For Roman Catholic social ethics, the prevalence of the state-sponsored lottery should not become a *fait accompli*, which dissolves the ethical questions that its existence engenders. Granted that most U.S. states sponsor lotteries today, should they continue to do so? Does the lottery represent a legitimate governmental function, a contribution to the development of the common good, which includes the well-being of every member of society? This is the standard which Roman Catholic social ethics must use to evaluate state lotteries.[11]

THE STATE OF THE QUESTION

Within some religious traditions, an ethicist could resolve issues concerning the legitimacy of state-sponsored lotteries simply by invoking a universal prohibition against gambling. The Roman Catholic approach, however, includes no such prohibition. As the 1994 *Catechism of the Catholic Church* demonstrates, the traditional view holds that games of chance "are not in themselves contrary to justice," but "become morally unacceptable when they deprive someone of what is necessary to provide for his needs and those of others" (par. 2413).[12] When only surplus income is at stake, therefore, the choice to gamble is a matter of individual discretion rather than moral duty. The Roman Catholic lottery player might also appeal to the Pennsylvania Catholic Conference's statement that, if "properly controlled, gambling can have positive aspects such as the provision of legitimate recreation, the generation of funds for acceptable causes and in some cases the enhancement of local economies."[13] In his discussion of gambling, the noted conservative moralist Germain Grisez even describes a case of justifiable lottery participation.

> In certain circumstances, a gambling contract could be a morally acceptable investment vehicle. For example, a poor working-family, able to provide for current needs but unable to save significantly for the children's education or for retirement, might spend a small amount each week on a ticket in a state-run lottery, not choosing the high risk of losing, but only accepting it in the hope of winning enough to meet some of their future needs. For them, the lottery is a very high-risk investment, since no other investment they can make will serve their legitimate purpose.[14]

Acceptance of gambling, within due limits, as a matter for individual prudence, however, does not resolve the problem of state sponsorship of lotteries as a matter of social ethics. The state should not provide, much less, as in the case of lotteries, exercise a monopoly over, every activity in which individuals might choose to participate. Concerning this issue, the tradition's guidance is less explicit. One can certainly find Roman Catholic sources which treat state lotteries as legitimate, although sometimes their age casts doubts on their applicability to the modern situation.[15] The tradition, however, also contains comments like that offered by Bernard Häring:

> Public lotteries or open gambling only serve to whet the appetite and feed the passion for every form of gambling. In fact prohibition of immoderate and uncontrolled gambling is less convincing and effective if the state itself approves public games of chance provided it derives gain from them.[16]

Finally, in 1988, the bishops of Minnesota provided an important precedent by joining other religious leaders in issuing a statement on their state's proposal to institute a lottery—a statement which concluded that

such a policy was not in the state's best interests.[17] The tradition's resources for the assessment of state sponsorship, therefore, do not exclude
either answer, and require expansion.

Foundations for a more extensive analysis of state-sponsored lotteries
appear, not within explicit statements on the subject, but in the general
principles of Roman Catholic social thought. Such principles are certainly
useful for the consideration of general ethical questions about the lottery:
should the state devote time and resources to such a project? Does state
sponsorship encourage gambling? Does it promote the citizens' best
interests? Does it exploit the disadvantaged? Finally, does it encourage
belief in lucky numbers and other superstitions? However, the contribution
of Catholic social thought becomes particularly clear when one moves from
such issues to an analysis of the lottery's impact upon a community's moral
character. At this stage, insights from the Catholic tradition concerning
human nature as social, the meaning of the common good, the significance
of participation, and the development of virtue can ground a serious
critique of the state-sponsored lottery's legitimacy.

GENERAL ETHICAL QUESTIONS ABOUT THE LOTTERY

1. *Given that government cannot do everything, should state governments
spend their time and resources on lotteries?*

Ironically, during a period of national debate over the proper role of
government, when many candidates regarded its reduction as a an attractive
campaign pledge, voters and state officials nevertheless supported the expansion of governmental gambling monopolies. As Borg, Mason, and
Shapiro observe,

> ... state-operated lotteries were one of the fastest growing indus-
> tries in the United States during the 1980s.... It seems that while
> states were taking less responsibility for providing traditional
> services, they were taking more responsibility for providing
> gambling services![18]

One need not be a libertarian to ask whether this represents an appropriate
governmental function or a legitimate use of public resources, especially
since the development of contemporary lotteries "completely bypassed the

logical step of legalized, but unsponsored, gambling."[19] That more than three-quarters of the states now control monopolies over a once illegal product raises important ethical concerns about the purpose of government itself.

2. *Does state sponsorship of the lottery constitute state promotion of gambling?*

At the inception of its lottery, Missouri required the inclusion of the following statement within all lottery advertisements: "This message is for informational and educational purposes only. It is not intended to induce any person to participate in the lottery or purchase a lottery ticket." A drive to increase sales, however, eventually brought this obvious effort to distinguish state sponsorship from state promotion to an end.[20] Perhaps it was doomed from the beginning. No disclaimer could erase the effects of advertising a product which bears the state's name. Lotteries are particularly striking in this regard. As Rychlak points out, "Those states that have state liquor stores do not sell official state beer or whisky."[21]

Today, one would be hard-pressed to argue that states sponsor lotteries without promoting them.[22] Aggressive advertising efforts have become the lottery's *sine qua non*. In reference to the practices of the District of Columbia, Maryland, and Virginia lotteries, for example, the *Washington Post* discovered that these organizations "plow millions back into advertising campaigns, focus groups, polls, and sophisticated dissections of player psychology."[23] Indeed, lotteries actually spend a higher percentage of their total expenditures upon advertisements than do many other types of corporations.[24] "For better or worse," report Clotfelter and Cook, "most state citizens see lottery ads far more often than virtually any other message put out by the state."[25] Nor is such advertising the state's only vehicle for promoting its product, since drawings and other reports of the winning numbers represent a valuable form of free publicity.[26] In Nebraska, a web site, a magazine, and even a summer promotional tour carry the Lottery's message.[27] Tour Ambassadors sell tickets, rewarding the winners with opportunities for lottery hats, squeeze bottles, and other prizes, on display beside a Nebraska Lottery hot air balloon![28]

But what precisely do states promote when they promote their lotteries? In fact, they invite players to spend money in exchange for the chance to win money; in other words, to gamble. The incongruity of this effort becomes apparent when one compares it to public policy in other areas.

Recently great sums have been expended on advertising campaigns to dissuade drunk driving, drug abuse and high-risk AIDS behavior. At the same time, Congress has barred tobacco and liquor advertisements from television.... Obviously, the government believes these advertisements have an impact on society. Yet, when it comes to gambling, the state spends money *encouraging* high-risk activity.[29]

Clotfelter and Cook raise an excellent "test of the acceptability of the message of lottery promotion" by positing its inclusion within the public school curriculum. "It would be difficult, for example, to justify teaching children lessons such as 'Play your hunch. You could win a bunch.'"[30] Since no state could justify communicating such a message in the schools, its dissemination on the airwaves and other media seems distinctly problematic.[31]

Finally, if state-sponsorship of lotteries represents a promotion of gambling, then one must ask what values that promotion fosters. In "State Lotteries: An Issue for the Churches," Paul Minus argues, for example, that

Though it is not the business of government directly to "teach morals," its policies and programs inevitably promote some values and discourage others. A government lottery undermines values by which healthy communities are bound together. It feeds upon and nourishes greed. It encourages the individual to become so preoccupied with his own gain that he ignores the fact that his gain is the direct result of others' loss.[32]

George Will, working from a different perspective, worries that "aggressive government marketing of gambling gives a legitimizing imprimatur to the pursuit of wealth without work."[33] Such concerns highlight the significance of state sanction as a communication of social values.[34] In reference to the lottery, state-sponsorship may convey a message that the community would not explicitly endorse.

3. *Is a government which encourages citizens to participate in a lottery promoting their best interests?*

Most people who bet on the lottery will lose.[35] In the case of the large jackpots which gain so much media attention, the odds are literally millions-to-one against the individual ticket holder. It is fair to say, therefore, that, in promoting lottery play, the state encourages people to risk the loss of their investment.

For most people, of course, the entertainment value of the game seems to outweigh the pain of a lost wager. But inevitably, a certain number will risk more than they can afford, and perhaps even enter the ranks of problem gamblers.[36] Some of these players had developed gambling problems before their lottery participation began, and would continue to bet even if the lottery disappeared. Yet because the lottery offers a state-sponsored wager, readily available even to those who might be reluctant to patronize a casino or race track, it has the potential to involve persons unattracted to other types of gambling. With the lottery, the visit to a local gas station or convenience store can also become a betting opportunity. Rychlak argues that "... it is reasonable to conclude that lotteries have contributed to the spread of the gambling habit and to the spread of problem gambling to new demographic groups."[37]

Some states, including Nebraska, have attempted to address this issue by assigning a portion of the lottery's proceeds to the treatment of problem gambling.[38] But if one foresees that this negative social consequence will flow from the creation of a lottery, surely prevention is a better strategy than treatment after the fact. Otherwise, it appears that the state is treating a portion of its citizens as expendable: their anticipated misfortune is less important than the lottery's anticipated revenues. Those sacrificed include not only the bettors themselves, but also their families, creditors, and everyone else injured by the consequences of problem gambling. For the state, the choice to risk such consequences demands ethical reflection, and not simply assessments of expediency.

The source of the average lottery dollar is an important consideration in this regard. Although about half the adults living in a lottery state will participate during a given year, the bulk of the lottery revenue actually comes from a much smaller group: "the top 10 percent of players in terms of frequency account for 50 percent of the total amount wagered, while the top 20 percent wager about 65 percent of the total."[39] In other words, the lottery's most frequent players contribute as much to its revenues as do the other ninety percent of its participants combined. Their continued involvement is far more important to the lottery's success than the retention of the occasional ticket-buyer. If these heavy players are wagering more than they can afford to lose, then efforts to keep them in the game pose significant questions, as this passage from a recent *Washington Post* article illustrates:

> A Maryland Lottery consultant's 1994 report noted that "it will be critical to maintain [the state's] base" of heavy Keno players, who were described as "lower income, less educated [and the] heaviest minority" compared to more casual players. "Politically," the report added, "it could be difficult to defend promoting gambling to this segment.[40]

Such promotion is even more difficult to defend on moral rather than political grounds. If the core of heavy Keno players includes problem gamblers, it becomes virtually impossible. No responsible government should encourage destructive weaknesses in order to raise revenue.[41]

Finally, even for the most infrequent player, participation in the lottery comes at the expense of something else, although the person's financial status may render the wager's effects virtually invisible. "Because a consumer purchases a lottery ticket for one dollar," assert Borg, Mason, and Shapiro, "that is one less dollar that he or she will spend on some alternative good, pay in taxes, or save."[42] Lottery states must ask who benefits, and who loses, from that exchange. Would the citizens them-selves, other businesses, charitable organizations, or even state revenues, be better off if the state encouraged different uses of the lottery dollar?[43] Does the promotion of the lottery, when all is said and done, promote or damage the common good?

4. *Does the lottery burden the disadvantaged in order to raise revenue for the state?*

> In Chicago's saddest, roughest ghetto, high above filthy sidewalks, above windows that are dark, broken, or boarded, above shoeless toddlers wandering alone, above drug deals on the corner, there's a billboard that shows a huge Lotto stub. Its single line of boldface copy: "This might be your ticket out of here." (It does *not* say "But the odds are, literally, 12,913,583-to-1 against you.")[44]

Monsignor John Egan's eloquent statement reflects the most common ethical critique of the lottery, especially among those offered from a religious perspective; it takes advantage of the disadvantaged.[45] The judgment that "a lottery would appear to be especially burdensome to the poor" was apparently the Minnesota Church Leaders' major reason for opposing its establishment in their state.[46] From the perspective of Roman Catholic social thought, this is a particularly powerful claim, since Church teaching emphasizes the special responsibility for the poor which justice imposes upon society and upon government, as a crucial mechanism of social organization.[47]

In their analysis of lottery participation, Clotfelter and Cook provide some important data concerning the role of the disadvantaged. First, in contrast to other forms of gambling, rate of lottery play diminishes with formal education.[48] Second, although "absolute expenditures appear to be remarkably uniform over a broad range of incomes," the authors found that "as a *percentage* of household income, lottery expenditures decline steadily as income rises."[49] In other words, although the poor may not spend more money on the lottery than their more affluent neighbors, the wagers absorb a greater percentage of their income. Ten dollars devoted to the lottery has a greater impact upon the low wage-earner than upon those with high take-home pay. Finally, "members of certain groups are more likely to play lotteries and to play them heavily: males, Hispanics, Blacks, the middle-aged, Catholics, laborers, and those with less than a college degree."[50] Given these findings, it is difficult to contest the claim that, at the very least, lotteries represent a regressive means of supplementing state income.[51] A luxury product which proves generally more attractive to the less educated and to members of some minority groups represents a dubious form of state revenue-monopoly. "State government traditionally is seen as an institution to serve and protect rather than profit from its citizenry."[52] When the profit weighs more heavily upon the disadvantaged, the conflict with the state's *raison d'être* becomes particularly marked.

5. Does state sponsorship of the lottery encourage belief in lucky numbers and other superstitions?

This criticism applies to common practices currently employed by lotteries rather than to any imaginable form of lottery. Since any unrigged lottery represents a random drawing, every combination enjoys an equal chance of success, and there is no logical method for number selection which will increase one's chances.[53] A state lottery could certainly mirror this reality by assigning numbers on a random basis, and many lottery games do employ this procedure, or at least offer this option to the players. On the other hand, many lottery games also allow purchasers to select their own numbers, and even encourage players to do so. Lottery advertising often reinforces this tendency. Babington and Chinoy, for example, report that "to exploit superstitions, including widespread fears of failing to play a 'lucky' number every day, Maryland and other states deftly use supernatural themes in television commercials."[54]

At first glance, this may appear to be simple deference to a consumer whim. If people prefer to select their "lucky" numbers, why not encourage them to do so? Yet closer inspection suggests that the practice is less harmless, and even less innocent, than one might initially presume. The lottery enjoys state sponsorship; state advertising encourages citizens to participate in it. Should the same entity which educates through public service announcements advise its citizens that "your numbers are out there" or personify Lady Luck as the lottery's spokesperson?[55]

From a theological perspective, the idea of luck raises some interesting foundational questions about the nature of reality. What must the world be like in order for lucky numbers to exist, for dreams or experiences or birth dates to contain some clue about the results of a lottery drawing on a specific day? Does the concern of Providence extend so far, and on what basis does it offer hints of its intentions? That the vast majority of contemporary American believers in luck have never considered the theological implications of their view does not erase these questions's significance. In a sense, promotion of the idea of luck, even if it is only the byproduct of an effort to raise money, is a kind of secular evangelization.

One need not be a religious believer, of course, to find state involvement in such a practice objectionable. A skeptic might argue that belief in luck represents a superstition detrimental to an accurate grasp of reality. A pragmatist might explain that acting upon this belief could actually lessen a successful player's reward: since people tend to share the same lucky numbers, choosing such combinations creates "the prospect of a highly diluted prize."[56] However one identifies the harm, it is inappropriate for the state to reinforce it in order to raise revenue. Whether the intermediate goal of encouraging the belief in lucky numbers is consumer satisfaction or consumer anxiety,[57] the ultimate goal is gaining additional lottery dollars. To pursue it by nourishing an illusion may be acceptable for Madison Avenue, but it does not reflect the covenant between a public authority and the citizens it serves.

The preceding questions by no means exhaust the ethical problems which state sponsorship of lotteries engenders. Many of these issues hinge upon an interpretation of consequences, requiring the accurate analysis of complex data.[58] One can pose another type of question as well. How does a just community meet its financial needs? How do its revenue choices shape its moral character? Finally, what is the significance of lottery sponsorship for the development of civic virtue? In order to apply these concerns to the evaluation of state lotteries, one must first review the relevant foundational presuppositions of Roman Catholic social thought.

BACKGROUND FROM ROMAN CATHOLIC SOCIAL THOUGHT

"By his innermost nature man is a social being," proclaims *Gaudium et Spes*, "and unless he relates himself to others he can neither live nor develop his potential."[59] This statement expresses one of the most characteristic and foundational presuppositions of Roman Catholic social ethics: being human necessarily involves being-in-relationship. Even misanthropes committed to a flight from "civilization" cannot erase their knowledge of human language, concepts, and skills when they retreat into their caves. One may lament the communal orientation of human nature, but not escape it. We are social. The *I* necessarily exists in relationship to the *we*.

In light of this theological anthropology, a Roman Catholic approach requires no social contract theory to explain or justify the formation of human communities and the institutions which serve their development and maintenance, including government.[60] Such communities and structures instead represent a necessary consequence of human beings' social nature. As a result, the well-being of individuals, groups, and institutions is reciprocal rather than competitive. As *Gaudium et Spes* explains,

> Man's social nature makes it evident that the progress of the human person and the advance of society itself hinge on one other. For the beginning, the subject and the goal of all social institutions is and must be the human person, which for its part and by its very nature stands completely in need of social life. Since this social life is not something added on to man, through his dealings with others, through reciprocal duties, and through fraternal dialogue he develops all his gifts and is able to rise to his destiny.[61]

For Roman Catholic social ethics, the web linking individual, communal, and institutional welfare is the common good, "the sum of those conditions of social life which allow social groups and their individual members relatively thorough and ready access to their own fulfilment ..."[62] All elements of society, from individuals and groups to institutions, bear responsibility for sustaining the common good, which in turn nourishes their own welfare. One part of this responsibility is financial. To carry it out, individuals and groups contribute "their goods and their services as their rulers shall direct,"[63] while governments formulate and oversee the just distribution of benefits and burdens, including taxes.[64] Upon this ebb and flow of resources, depends the flourishing of the common good.

Though it is easy to confuse duty to the common good with self-sacrifice, Roman Catholic social thought instead emphasizes the benefits of that responsibility for individuals as well as for the entire community. Suffering for the good of the whole may occasionally prove necessary,[65] but a commitment to the common good is not a sentence to civic martyrdom. This duty, in fact, represents such a significant benefit to individuals that Catholic social teaching can describe it as a right. *Pacem in Terris* asserts that "man's personal dignity involves his right to take an active part in public life, and to make his own contribution to the common welfare of his fellow citizens."[66] *Economic Justice for All* actually ascribes this to social justice, which "implies that persons have an obligation to be active and productive participants in the life of society and that society has a duty to enable them to participate in this way."[67] Thus, those denied the chance to contribute to the common good have serious grounds for complaint.

When it comes to taxes, of course, this claim seems, at best, counter-intuitive. Many who cherish their opportunities to vote and to express their views freely would gladly surrender their right to make compulsory financial contributions to the common good. Even those who acknowledge their debt to publicly funded research, education, roads, fire and police protection, recreational opportunities, etc. may balk at interpreting the chance to pay taxes as a benefit rather than as a necessary evil. Ironically, however, the standard of living which a strong tax base can produce is not the only reason for identifying such contributions to the common good as benefits, in light of the Roman Catholic social tradition. After all, as previously noted, the common good allows persons and groups *"relatively thorough and ready access to their own fulfilment."*[68] Becoming a better human being is somehow at stake in this process of contribution to the common good. To understand why, it is helpful to consider Thomas Aquinas' ideas concerning virtue.

For Thomas, every virtue represents the "perfection of a power."[69] It is "a good habit, productive of good works."[70] To explain the presence of virtues, Thomas points to a number of causes. Sometimes a virtue represents a direct gift from God, who infuses it into the human person.[71] On other occasions, virtues develop from "certain naturally known principles of both knowledge and action, which are the nurseries of intellectual and moral virtues," although the aptitude for such growth varies among individuals.[72] Repeated action (habituation) is a mechanism of that development.[73] As a result of their choices, individuals shape not only external things, but also their own character.

Thomas acknowledges that, at one level, persons may possess some moral virtues while lacking others.[74] A strong habit of temperance, for example, could conceivably coexist with tendencies towards cowardice or miserliness. On a higher level, however, there is a definite connection between the virtues, so that a defect in one area inevitably affects the others. Imprudent persons, for example, may do brave things, but they cannot possess perfect fortitude, precisely because they lack the discretion which separates bravery from foolhardiness. Without the full range of moral virtues, those which are present are somehow incomplete. The person is virtuous in certain respects, but lacks some of the characteristics which define a virtuous character. Perfect moral virtue, Thomas reminds us, does not simply direct us towards correct choices; it "inclines us to do a good deed *well* ..."[75]

This insistence upon the connection between the moral virtues explains the following claim from Thomas' discussion of law. "Since then every man is part of the state, it is impossible that a man be good, unless he be well proportionate to the common good."[76] Persons lacking in civic virtues, no matter how well-developed their other capacities, are somehow deficient in the qualities which ground good moral character. To put it simply, to be a good person, yet a bad citizen, is a contradiction in terms.

Thomas' theory of virtues illuminates a critical theme in recent Catholic social teaching, participation, which *Octagesimo Adveniens* identifies as one of the most significant and pervasive contemporary aspirations.[77] "Such participation," insists *Economic Justice for All*, "is an essential expression of the social nature of human beings and of their communitarian vocation."[78] *Justice in the World* describes it as a right.[79] For those confused about the significance of that right, especially when it involves a right to pay taxes, Thomas' virtue theory provides a valuable piece to the puzzle. The chance to participate, to contribute to the common good of one's community, is an opportunity to develop one's own civic virtues. Just as no one becomes a virtuoso without spending hours in the practice room, no one can become a good citizen without participating in the quest for the common good. To rob persons of this chance strangles a vital element of their character. This is no less a form of marginalization than denying them the vote, freedom of speech, or material necessities.[80] Small wonder, then, that Catholic social teaching assigns participation such high value, treating it as a benefit as well as an obligation. *Gaudium et Spes* observes that "citizens ... should remember that it is their right and duty, which is also to be recognized by the civil authority, to contribute to the true progress of their own community ..."[81]

PARTICIPATION, CIVIC VIRTUE, AND THE EVALUATION OF STATE LOTTERIES

Imagine a utopian scenario: states develop a new lottery system which appeals primarily to the affluent, does not foster compulsive gambling or numbers superstition, flourishes without advertising, produces stable revenues without need for expansion, increases the profit of other businesses, encourages charitable donations, discourages illegal gambling, and avoids or even reverses all the other negative consequences commonly mentioned by lottery critics. Even in that idyllic circumstance, the importance of participation emphasized in Catholic social thought questions the wisdom of recourse to lotteries as a regular fundraising method. Lotteries circumvent the process by which individuals can develop civic virtues by contributing directly to the common good.

A governmental request to support the community with taxes acknowledges that the well-being of the community is each person's concern. Like a summons for jury duty, traffic tickets, and the ballot box, a tax bill represents a physical reminder of the moral responsibility that links all human beings. Contributions to the common good are not gifts to be made when we feel generous, but obligations that we owe to our fellow citizens as a matter of justice. Fulfilling these obligations, sharing in the development of the common good, enables us to improve not only our society but also ourselves. Participation can nurture civic virtues. Social beings require civic virtues if they are truly to be good persons. Character and common good thus remain inextricably intertwined.

One might argue, of course, that buying a lottery ticket is also a method of participating in the common good. On its web site, for example, the Nebraska Environmental Trust remarks that "people who enjoy the fun and excitement of the Lottery also know they are helping keep the state's earth, air and water clean for future generations."[82] Assuming that this assessment is accurate, however, the form of participation remains indirect, a side-effect of or secondary motivation in a decision to gamble.[83] For many, the contribution to the common good is probably incidental or even accidental.[84] Even if it produces the same dollar that a direct donation might, the subjective significance for the agent is not the same.

Lotteries are attractive to lawmakers because they enable them to obtain dollars without raising taxes.[85] Yet how a community acquires money is as important as its efficiency in revenue generation. If the projects which the lottery funds are essential to the common good, citizens deserve the chance to take responsibility for their community's welfare by funding them directly. If they are not, then the risks associated with the lottery outweigh the benefits of whatever luxuries it provides.

For states like Nebraska, the current economic situation provides a golden opportunity to reconsider the value of the lottery. If we cannot wean ourselves from lottery dollars in circumstances of surplus, when will we ever do so? Perhaps this is the time for the state to take another gamble, a gamble on civic virtue, the capacity of the citizens to recognize and embrace their right to contribute the common good. In the long run, that gamble might prove to be a very wise investment. As *Economic Justice for All* asserts, "the virtues of citizenship are an expression of Christian love more crucial in today's interdependent world than ever before."[86]

NOTES

1. Nebraska Lottery, "General Lottery Information," www.nelottery.com/geninfo.html., consulted June 9, 1998.

2. Idem, "Nebraska Lottery Milestones,' www.nelottery.com/hipoint. html., consulted June 9, 1998.

3. Richard McGowan, *State Lotteries and Legalized Gambling: Painless Revenue or Painful Mirage* (Westport, CT: Praeger, 1994), 16.

4. Charles Clotfelter and Philip Cook, *Selling Hope: State Lotteries in America* (Cambridge: Harvard University Press, 1989), 139, 237.

5. Spencer Michaels, "Betting on the Future," PBS *Newshour*, 15 July 1996 [Online *Newshour* Transcript] www.pbs.org/p1webcgi/fastweb?getdoc+newshour +newshour+3388+3+wAAA+gambling.

6. See McGowan, "Lotteries and Sin Taxes: Painless Revenue or Painful Mirage?," *America* 170, 30 April 1994, 4. See the figure given in McGowan, *State*, 18.

7. Some states, including Nebraska, had to amend their constitutions in order to establish their lotteries. See Nebraska Lottery, "General Lottery Information," and Ronald Rychlak, "Lotteries, Revenues and Social Costs: A Historical Examination of State-Sponsored Gambling," *Boston College Law Review* 34, (1992), 37-8, 47-8.

8. On the history of lotteries in the U.S., see Rychlak, 20-48; Clotfelter and Cook, 32-48, 235; and McGowan, *State*, 6-20.

9. McGowan, *State*, 18-19.

10. However, despite their success, lottery proceeds constitute only a very small percentage of state revenues. See Mary Borg, Paul Mason, and Stephen Shapiro, *The Economic Consequences of State Lotteries* (Westport, CT: Praeger, 1991), 48; and Clotfelter and Cook, 239.

11. See Pennsylvania Catholic Conference, "Criteria for Legislation on Gambling," *Origins* 24, no. 2 (1994), 223. This statement was issued in response to a proposal on riverboat gambling, not in reference to the lottery.

12. United States Catholic Conference, *Catechism of the Catholic Church*, English translation (Mahwah: Paulist Press, 1994).

13. "Criteria for Legislation on Gambling," 223.

14. *The Way of the Lord Jesus*, vol. 2, *Living a Christian Life* (Quincy, IL: Franciscan Press, 1993), 819.

15. See, for example, Francis Connell: "From the standpoint of divine law there is no objection to a governmental lottery for the raising of funds for a good purpose, such as the assistance of charitable institutions" (*Father Connell Answers Moral Questions* [Washington, DC: The Catholic University of America Press, 1959], 44). It is unclear whether Connell envisions a continuing or an occasional lottery, or whether he would regard the distinction as significant.

16. *The Law of Christ*, vol. 3, *Special Moral Theology*, trans. Edwin G. Kaiser (Westminster, MD: The Newman Press, 1966), 472. Häring also states that "sharing in the lotteries for charitable causes with proper motivation is a good work." In both cases, however, Häring is certainly not commenting on the contemporary situation in the United States.

17. Minnesota Church Leaders, "Lottery Called Not in State's Best Interest," *Origins* 18 (1988), 329-30. Though this statement addresses a particular situation, the arguments that it offers are general ones, rather than factors peculiar to the local conditions.

18. *Economic Consequences*, 3.

19. Rychlak, "Lotteries," 47.

20. Clotfelter and Cook, *Selling Hope*, 211.

21. Rychlak, "Lotteries," 76.

22. Indeed, the nature of the current system essentially requires states to increase participation in order to increase profits. Because they already enjoy a monopoly, most states cannot boost their revenues by increasing market share. See Clotfelter and Cook, *Selling Hope*, 187.

23. Charles Babington and Ira Chinoy, "Lotteries Win Players With Slick Marketing,"*Washington Post*, 4 May 1998, A1. For a very helpful discussion of lottery promotion, see Clotfelter and Cook, *Selling Hope*, 186-212.

24. Ibid., 240. "Lotteries devote about 2 percent of their total expenditures (including prizes) to paid advertising. This ratio is lower that the comparable ratio for corporations that provide amusement and recreation services but higher than those for all corporations in general and for corporations in the retail industry, and markedly higher than those for public utilities and other state-operated enterprises."

25. *Ibid.*, 199

26. Ibid. One can also obtain the results of most state lottery drawings online. See, for example, *USA Today*, "USA Today Lottery Results,"www. usatoday.com/leadpage/lottery/lotto.html. Updated daily.

27. The Nebraska Lottery's web site is available at www.nelottery.com. Its magazine is called the *Nebraska Lottery Digest Players Paradise*.

28. My colleague Susan Hellbusch of the Creighton University Communications Department provided the description of a Nebraska Lottery Summer Tour '98 event in Omaha. See also the online promotion of the tour on the Lottery's web site at "Summer Tour 98," www.nelottery.com/news/sumrtour.html., consulted June 11, 1998.

29. Rychlak, "Lotteries," 62.

30. Clotfelter and Cook, *Selling Hope*, 244.

31. All lottery states prohibit sale of tickets to minors. Ibid., 133-34.

32. *Christian Century* 90, 21 March 1973, 339.

33. "In the Grip of Gambling," *Newsweek* 113, 8 May 1989, 78.

34. State-sanction may be particularly important in influencing some persons' decision to gamble. See Clotfelter and Cook, *Selling Hope*, 191.

35. See Ibid., 119-20.

36. See Ibid., 123-127; Rychlak, "Lotteries," 64-71.

37. Rychlak, "Lotteries," 69.

38. Nebraska Lottery, "Beneficiary Funds,' www.nelottery.com/trustfnd. html., updated 17 March 1998.

39. Clotfelter and Cook, *Selling Hope*, 92.

40. Babington and Chinoy, "Lotteries Win Players," A10.

41. Though states raise revenue through sin taxes, they do not promote the use of alcohol and tobacco; hence these measures are ethically distinct from the lottery.

42. Borg, Mason, and Shapiro, *Economic Consequences*, 95.

43. See Borg, Mason, and Shapiro upon this point, particularly on the possible significance of lottery participation for contributions to charity. They also point out that lottery tickets are not subject to sales tax in many states (98-9).

44. John Egan, "State-Sanctioned Gambling is a Bad Bet," *U.S. Catholic* 62, November 1997, 25.

45. See Minus, "State Lotteries," 338; Byron Rohrig, "Lottery Foes Target Public Policy," *Christian Century* 104, 29 April 1987, 396-97; and Mitch Finley, "It's a Sin to Buy a Lottery Ticket," *U.S. Catholic* 55, September 1990, 13.

46. "Lottery," 329-30.

47. See, for example, *Economic Justice for All* (Washington: United States Catholic Conference, 1986), n. 16: "From the Scriptures and Church teaching, we learn that the justice of the society is tested by the treatment of the poor." This document will be cited henceforth as *EJFA*. See also Leo XIII, *Rerum Novarum*, n.38.

48. Clotfelter and Cook, *Selling Hope*, 97.

49. Ibid., 99-100.

50. Ibid., 100.

51. See *Ibid.*, 221-27; Rychlak, "Lotteries," 51-2, 72-4.

52. Babington and Chinoy, "Lotteries Win Players," A10.

53. Clotfelter and Cook, *Selling Hope*, 77.

54. "Lotteries Win Players," A10.

55. Ibid. The first is the slogan of Maryland Lottery; the second is a Virginia Lottery campaign.

56. Clotfelter and Cook, *Selling Hope*, 74.

57. Because some people fear the consequences of failing to play their lucky numbers on a regular basis. For further discussion, see Ibid., 89-90.

58. Is the lottery actually an efficient means of raising revenue? See, for example, Andrew Szakmary and Carol Szakmary, "State Lotteries as a Source of Revenue: A Re-Examination," *Southern Economic Journal* 61 (1995), 1167-81.

59. *Gaudium et Spes*, 12. Henceforth cited as *GS*.

60. On the origin of civil authority, see John XXIII, *Pacem in Terris*, 46-52. Henceforth this document will be cited as *PT*.

61. *GS*, 25.

62. *GS*, 26.

63. *PT*, 53.

64. See David Hollenbach, *Claims in Conflict: Retrieving and Renewing the Catholic Human Rights Tradition* (New York: Paulist Press, 1979), 147-51.

65. Military or alternative service is an obvious example.

66. *PT*, 26.

67. *EJFA*, 71.

68. *GS*, 26. Emphasis added.

69. *Summa Theologiae*, I-II, 55, 1. This document will be cited henceforth as *ST*. Aquinas divides the virtues into three categories, theological, intellectual, and moral. See I-II, 62, 2.

70. *ST*, I-II, 55, 3.

71. This is always true of the theological virtues; *ST*, I-II, 62, 1. See Q. 63, 3 in relationship to the infusion of moral virtues.

72. *ST*, I-II, 63, 1.

73. Ibid., 2.

74. *ST*, I-II, 65, 1.

75. *ST*, I-II, 65, 1. Emphasis added.

76. *ST*, I-II, 92, 1, *ad* 3.

77. Paul VI, *Octogesima Adveniens*, 22.

78. *EJFA*, 78.

79. Synod of Bishops (1971), *Justice in the World*, 18.

80. On the relationship of participation and marginalization, see *EJFA*, 77.

81. *GS*, 65, 2.

82. Nebraska Game and Parks Commission, "Nebraska Environmental Trust," www.ngpc.state.ne.us/admin/trust.html., consulted June 9, 1998.

83. Since prizes and operating expenses consume such a large percentage of lottery proceeds, state lottery tickets are a relatively inefficient method of contributing to worthy causes. In Nebraska, for example, state law requires that at least forty percent of the proceeds must be distributed in prizes, and the Lottery's web site states that its average rate is fifty-five percent (Nebraska Lottery, "General Lottery Information').

84. Of course, this is also true of the contributions to the common good which come from the tax payments of those who make them solely in order to avoid the penalties. However, one might argue that this represents a failure in education or socialization; society must teach people to understand what they are already doing. Moreover, if Aquinas is correct in his assessment of the effects of law, it is possible that the practice may eventually help them to understand its significance. See *ST*, I-II, 92, 1; 96, 2, *ad.* 2.

85. See Rychlak, "Lotteries," 48-54; Borg, Mason, and Shapiro, *Economic Consequences*, 47; Clotfelter and Cook, *Selling Hope*, 139-41, 159, 167.

86. *EJFA*, 66.

Theocentric or Anthropocentric?
Catholic Teaching on the Environment:
A View from the Great Plains

Roger Bergman

In the 1980s, the Catholic bishops of the United States twice made head-lines in the secular press with the preparation and publication of lengthy pastoral letters on issues of public concern and governmental policy: *The Challenge of Peace* in 1983 and *Economic Justice for All* in 1986. Over the last decade it has thus become increasingly disingenuous to speak of Catholic social teaching as the "Church's best kept secret."[1] That phrase might now more appropriately be applied to the Church's official teaching on the environment. The task I have set myself is straightforward. I will offer a brief overview, both historical and thematic, of magisterial teaching on the environment, comment on its two major documents and on the direction its further development might take, and finally, in light of this analysis, explore a regional bishops' statement and its application to a current vision of environmental renewal of a major area of the U.S. "Heartland."

ORIGINS AND THEMES

In what may have been a slip of the tongue, a U.S. bishop recently described our topic as "Catholic *social* teaching on the environment." Indeed, the earliest magisterial attention to the environment was deeply embedded in social teaching documents and perspectives. In the 1971 encyclical *Octogesima Adveniens*, also known as *A Call to Action*, Pope Paul VI included a brief paragraph headed "The Environment." The pontiff observes that "by an ill-considered exploitation of nature [man] risks destroying it and becoming in his turn the victim of this degradation." He continues. "This is a wide-ranging social problem which concerns the entire human family."[2] Paul VI's primary concern is with the impact on humanity, not on the degradation of nature itself.

In that same year, the Synod of Bishops published *Justice in the World*, remembered for its oft-quoted dictum that "action on behalf of justice and participation in the transformation of the world fully appear to us as a constitutive dimension of the preaching of the Gospel."[3] The bishops observe that

> men are beginning to...perceive that their resources, as well as the precious treasures of air and water—without which there cannot be life—and the small delicate biosphere of the whole complex of life on earth, are not infinite, but on the contrary must be saved and preserved as a unique patrimony belonging to all mankind.[4]

While this passage suggests a greater appreciation of ecology—nature is a "small delicate biosphere of the whole complex of life on earth"—the emphasis is still clearly on nature as resource for human society. A central note in Catholic teaching on the environment is here also sounded for the first time in such a context. The goods of this world have long been thought of as God's patrimony to all humanity, as our collective inheritance from the Creator, and therefore to be shared justly. This doctrine, however, takes on new meaning, as in this passage from *Justice in the World*, in the context of environmental degradation and crisis. The highly industrialized nations are assigned particular responsibility for the problem.

> ...such is the demand for resources and energy by the richer nations, whether capitalist or socialist, and such are the effects of dumping by them in the atmosphere and the sea that irreparable damage would be done to the essential elements of life on earth, such as air and water, if their high rates of consumption and pollution, which are constantly on the increase, were extended to the whole of mankind.[5]

This is an excellent example of the way in which the official teachers of the Church extend their social analysis to include environmental issues. This approach is developed by Pope John Paul II and the U.S. bishops in their major environmental statements of 1990 and 1991, respectively.[6]

POPE JOHN PAUL II

As early as his first encyclical, *Redemptor Hominis* (*The Redeemer of Man*), in the first year of his pontificate, the current Pope indicated the direction his later and fuller teaching would take by placing "the threat of pollution of the natural environment in areas of rapid industrialization" squarely in the context of that most fundamental of Christian doctrines, original sin. The Pope asks, rhetorically but passionately, with reference to such modern crises as pollution,

> Are we of the twentieth century not convinced of the overpower-
> ingly eloquent words of the Apostle of the Gentiles concerning the
> "creation (that) has been groaning in travail together until now"
> and "waits with eager longing for the revelation of the sons of
> God," the creation that "was subjected to futility [by Adam's
> sin]"?[7] Just as, in Catholic perspective, social problems are at root
> moral problems, so are environmental problems not only social but
> also moral. For those of us who have read Reinhold Niebuhr or St.
> Augustine this may not be a very hopeful or encouraging insight.
> It does, however, put Catholic environmental teaching very near
> the heart of Catholic doctrine generally. Concern for the environ-
> ment, then, cannot be divorced from the life of Christian faith.[8]

In *Redemptor Hominis,* John Paul II introduces another theme that any Christian teaching on the environment might feel compelled to address. It is ironic that perhaps the best known perspective on the relationship of Christian faith and ecological crisis is not that of the Catholic magisterium or other Christian theologians but rather of the medieval historian Lynn White. In a 1967 essay reprinted in 1971 under the title, "The Historical Roots of Ecological Crisis,"[9] White advanced the thesis that Christianity, "the most anthropocentric religion the world has seen[,]…by destroying pagan animism,…made it possible to exploit nature in a mood of indiffer-ence to the feelings of natural objects."[10]

> Somewhat over a century ago [White wrote 30 years ago], science
> and technology, hitherto quite separate activities, joined to give
> mankind powers which, to judge by many of the ecologic effects,

are now out of control. If so, Christianity bears a huge burden of the guilt.... For nearly two millennia Christian missionaries have been chopping down sacred groves, which are idolatrous because they assume spirit in nature."[11]

Somehow I do not think this is what John Paul II has in mind when he links the degradation of nature with original sin. Nonetheless, in *Redemptor Hominis* he at least indirectly takes up the challenge thrown out by White. Although he affirms "the superiority of spirit over matter,"[12] he also critiques the interpretation of the Genesis theme of dominion over nature that permits humanity to become "a heedless 'exploiter' or 'destroyer'" rather than "an intelligent and noble 'master' and 'guardian'" of the natural world.[13] This is the well-known image of the steward. As to the charge that Christianity is the most anthropocentric religion, one can imagine the Pope responding, "Hear, hear!"

On another challenge from White, John Paul II responded more affirmatively. A medieval historian proud of one of his own, White asks us to "ponder the greatest radical in Christian history since Christ: St. Francis of Assisi." "The key to an understanding of Francis," according to his scholarly champion, "is his belief in the virtue of humility, not merely for the individual but for man as a species."[14] Arguing that "we shall continue to have a worsening ecologic crisis until we reject the Christian axiom that nature has no reason for existence save to serve man [sic],"[15] White urges us to adopt a Franciscan humility instead. To that end, he "propose[d] Francis as a patron saint for ecologists."[16] Right on cue, in 1979, the first year of John Paul II's pontificate, and just a dozen years after White's proposal was first published in the journal *Science*, the Pope "proclaimed Saint Francis of Assisi as the heavenly Patron of those who promote ecology," explaining that Francis "offers Christians an example of genuine and deep respect for the integrity of creation."[17] Apparently for this Pope, champion of universal human rights, including "*the right to a safe environment*,"[18] and of a "due respect for nature,"[19] there is no contradiction between Christian anthropocentrism, Franciscan humility, and genuine regard for nature. That perspective, so contradictory to a critic such as White, is a key to understanding official Catholic teaching on the environment in these early documents.

Having suggested by looking at its beginnings some of the principal themes of this teaching, I would like now to focus on its single most important expression, John Paul II's World Day of Peace Message for 1990, titled *The Ecological Crisis: A Common Responsibility.* The message is of interest particularly because of its insistence on the order of nature and the disorder that human sin introduced into the world.

> Made in the image and likeness of God, Adam and Eve were to have exercised their dominion over the earth (Gen 1:28) with wisdom and love. Instead they destroyed the existing harmony *by deliberately going against the Creator's plan*, that is, by choosing to sin.[20]...When man turns his back on the Creator's plan, he provokes a disorder which has inevitable repercussions on the rest of the created order.[21]

Notice that the disorder is within humanity, that this disorder does indeed have repercussions for the natural world, but that God's good Creation retains its essential orderliness. This becomes clearer as the Pope observes that not just philosophy and science but also theology "speak of a harmonious universe, of a 'cosmos' endowed with its own integrity, its own internal, dynamic balance."[22] Because this is so *"we cannot interfere in one area of the ecosystem without paying due attention both to the consequences of such interference in other areas and to the well-being of future generations."*[23] While recognizing that, because of sin, "all of creation became subject to futility,"[24] the Pope insists that Creation itself retains its goodness, harmony, dynamism, balance, and innocence. It is as if John Paul II saw nature still fresh from the hand of God. It is as if, to speak mythologically, human civilization had not been expelled absolutely from the Garden, since the Garden itself, that is to say, nature, preserves something of its God-given beauty and wholeness despite the harm we do it. Indeed, says this hiking and skiing Pope, "our very contact with nature has a deep restorative power; contemplation of its magnificence imparts peace and serenity."[25] One cannot help but think of Gerard Manley Hopkins' poem "God's Grandeur" and its affirmation that "nature is never spent; There lives the dearest freshness deep down things."[26]

With such an explicitly *religiously appreciative* perspective on nature, John Paul II seems to be asking us to think of "original sin" more as an ongoing temptation to disorder in ourselves that expresses itself in our attitudes and actions toward nature, as well as toward one another, rather than as an ontological flaw introduced primordially and permanently into the created order itself. In John Paul II's perspective, Creation did not "fall" with humanity in the sense that it is not implicated in our guilt. Our *continuing* rebellion against the Creator's plan, as evident in our consumerism, our oppression of the poor, our unbridled technologies, the violence of our wars, is the sole source of nature's degradation. Despite humankind's destruction of the aboriginal harmony,[27] theology can still speak of a harmonious universe. To paraphrase Hopkins, nature bounces back. Creation still merits God's judgment as "good" in itself despite our inability to rise consistently and practically to such an appreciation. God's plan, of course, now includes redemption in Christ, and that redemption extends to nature through the due and renewed respect shown it by a redeemed humanity. This is the heart of the Pope's environmental teaching: the ecological order or dynamism imparted to Creation by God is still fundamentally intact and must be respected by God's human creatures. According to John Paul II, "respect for life and for the dignity of the human person extends to the rest of creation."[28]

U.S. BISHOPS

While the Pope's is the most significant example of Catholic environmental teaching, according to Drew Christiansen and Walter Grazer, editors of a recently published anthology on Catholic theology and the environment, forty-eight related documents have been promulgated by bishops' conferences or individual bishops around the world.[29] Every continent (except Antarctica) is represented. Six of these documents, as well as that of the Pope just discussed, are included in their book, biblically titled *And God Saw That It Was Good*. Although they are not all named, I presume the full list of 48 pastoral letters includes the following documents from the United States[30]: one by the bishops of Appalachia,[31] one by the bishops of the U.S. Heartland in 1980,[32] one by Bishop Anthony Pilla of Cleveland,[33] two by Bishop Michael Pfeifer of San Angelo, Texas,[34] and a particularly provocative statement by the Bishops of Florida titled *Companions in Creation*.[35] It would be a fascinating project to look at all of these documents systematically and comparatively, but in the remainder of this essay I can consider only *Renewing the Earth*, the 1991 pastoral letter of the United States Catholic Conference, and the 1980 letter of the bishops of the U.S. Heartland, *Strangers and Guests*. The USCC's 21-page document is the fullest treatment of Catholic environmental teaching of which I am aware, and is tellingly subtitled, *An Invitation to Reflection and Action on the Environment in Light of Catholic Social Teaching*. The heart of the bishops' letter is the development of seven principles drawn from the social teaching tradition. I will comment briefly on each of them.

First, the bishops, as it were, challenge the claim that Lynn White's charge of extreme anthropocentrism is a fair characterization of Christianity. Catholic tradition offers rather a theocentric and sacramental view of the universe. "Dwelling in the presence of God," say the bishops, "we begin to experience ourselves as part of creation, as stewards within it, not separate from it." The environmental movement, they observe, has "reawakened" appreciation of this Christian truth. The bishops set a high standard for human accountability. "Even as we rejoice in earth's goodness and in the beauty of nature, stewardship places upon us responsibility for the well-being of all God's creatures."[36]

This leads directly to the second principle, already mentioned as the heart of John Paul II's message: respect for life throughout creation. The bishops recall that God's covenant with Noah extended to every living creature. The ark, I am tempted to say, was the first endangered species act. This theme is picked up by no less an authority within the Catholic tradition than Thomas Aquinas, who wrote that the diversity of creation more perfectly represents the divine goodness "than any single creature whatever."[37] That last phrase pointedly precludes any crude anthropocentrism. We have come a considerable distance from Pope Paul VI's rather utilitarian call to protect nature a quarter-century ago. Now we are told that "it is appropriate that we treat other creatures and the natural world not just as means to human fulfillment, but as God's creatures, possessing an independent value, worthy of our respect and care."[38] I like to think of this as "the Noah principle."[39] The story of the ark is more radical than children's picture books might suggest.

The third principle is named, rather dramatically, the "planetary common good."[40] I find the bishops' extension of the central social teaching concept of the common good somewhat disappointing, especially after just having been encouraged to value all of God's creatures *in and for themselves*. The planetary common good, as the bishops envision it, refers more to global interdependence among humans than between *homo sapiens*, other species, and our common habitats. It seems obvious that a common good genuinely planetary would include the good of meadowlarks, prairie white-fringed orchids, and wetlands independent of their good for us humans. But in this passage the bishops do not make this explicit.

This means that the fourth principle, "a new solidarity,"[41] the duty specified by the universal common good, is not as new as one might hope. The solidarity we are here called to is essentially the same solidarity between the rich and the poor, the overdeveloped and the underdeveloped nations, which the Magisterium has been encouraging for decades, as in Pope Paul VI's 1967 encyclical *Populorum Progressio* (*On the Development of Peoples*) and in *Sollicitudo Rei Socialis* (*On Social Concern*), John Paul II's affirmation of his predecessor's letter twenty years later.[42] We have been called to demonstrate respect and care for other species, but not solidarity with them. Perhaps that would suggest something like an equality among God's creatures that the bishops understand to be out of step with Catholic tradition. But isn't it appropriate to speak of St. Francis' solidarity with non-human creatures?

The fifth principle, the universal purpose of created things, we have already mentioned. In *Renewing the Earth*, that purpose is defined in entirely utilitarian terms: "God has given the fruit of the earth to sustain the entire human family 'without excluding or favoring anyone.'"[43] While this is a radical *social* principle, it does not challenge our basic attitude toward the natural world as essentially a resource for human use. But might not the sacramental principle and the recognition that flows from it of the independent value of God's nonhuman creatures suggest *purposes* that go beyond social utility? Relatively few of those species led two by two[44] onto the ark had that kind of direct value to humanity, and some of them most of us would think of as possessing disvalue. Praise is due God for creating and preserving the mosquito, both pest and disease-carrier?

The sixth principle, the famous option for the poor incorporated into official Catholic social teaching from liberation theology, also remains deeply embedded in the anthropocentrism of that teaching.[45] The bishops point out that it is often "the poor of the earth...[who] suffer most directly from environmental decline," and who therefore "offer a special test of our solidarity." While we should wholeheartedly endorse the bishops' position that "solutions must be found which do not force us to choose between a decent environment and a decent life for workers,"[46] I regret that the bishops have not expanded the option for the poor to include the earth itself and its largely defenseless and increasingly dependent creatures. Surely this can be done without undermining the concept of *human* dignity and the preference to be shown toward vulnerable humans.

The seventh and final principle, authentic development, is the practical extension of the foregoing principles of Catholic social teaching. The sacramental view of the human person, the common good and the universal patrimony of creation, solidarity and the option for the poor, all these are summed up in the Church's insistence that economic development and social progress must be understood as more than material growth and the "accumulation of goods and services even for the benefit of the majority."[47] "Authentic development," say the bishops, "supports moderation and even austerity in the use of material resources...[and] ...encourages a balanced view of human progress consistent with respect for nature."[48] That last add-on and qualifier, "consistent with respect for nature," suggests how the Church is extending its social teaching to address the environmental crisis without consistently rethinking that teaching in any fundamental way.

As the subtitle of *Renewing the Earth* suggests, the bishops ask us to reflect primarily on the environmental crisis in light of Catholic social teaching, and only secondarily to reflect on Catholic social teaching or theology generally in light of the environmental crisis.[49] While the bishops invoke a theocentric and sacramental view of the natural world, their approach to it remains largely anthropocentric and utilitarian. They also acknowledge that "Catholic social teaching does not offer a complete environmental ethic" and is indeed a developing tradition in this regard,[50] and so invite "theologians, scripture scholars and ethicists to help explore, deepen, and advance the insights of our Catholic tradition and its relations to the environment and other religious perspectives on these matters."[51] I have indicated in this commentary, and in my title, "Theocentric or Anthropocentric?," at least one major direction this exploration might take.[52]

Perhaps Pope John Paul II's contrast of the resilient order and dynamic harmony still to be discovered within nature with the sin and disorder within humanity offers one possible guidepost for this exploration.[53] That makes for a provocative context in which to reexamine our traditional anthropocentrism, as does the Florida bishops' brief environmental statement, *Companions in Creation*, in which "a sense of solidarity and companionship with all creation" is explicitly invoked.[54] As both the Pope and Lynn White observe, some Franciscan humility seems called for on the part of *homo sapiens* if we are to live up to that self-designation.

AN EXPLORATORY CASE STUDY:
STRANGERS AND GUESTS

Ten years before the Pope's ecological homily and eleven years before the U.S. bishops' environmental teaching, seventy-two bishops representing forty-four Catholic dioceses and archdioceses and twelve states of the American Midwest published *Strangers and Guests: Toward Community in the Heartland: A Regional Catholic Bishops' Statement on Land Issues.*[55] Widely circulated throughout the region as a 29-page booklet, *Strangers and Guests* is essentially a defense of the traditional family farm against the encroachments of agribusiness and a plea for environmental responsibility from the perspective of a biblically-based ethos of stewardship. It is a representative document in that it does not offer theological or ethical innovation in light of environmental degradation. While noting that "Native Americans shared an attitude of respect for the earth and for all the natural world," and while acknowledging the extent to which "the face of the earth was transformed" by cultivation, fences, livestock, technology, and federal policies so that "the form of the land became shaped more by human hands than by nature,"[56] *Strangers and Guests* is not an ecologically or theologically radical document. On the contrary, the reiterated ideal of stewardship gives it a fundamentally anthropocentric perspective.

The bishops articulate that ideal in summary fashion as follows:

> The land is given by God for the benefit of all of humanity, as are the sun which lights and warms it, the water which refreshes it and the air which caresses it. All of these natural resources, vital parts of our natural, life-generating environment, must be conserved by us who are called to be God's stewards.[57]

Aware that "the land is living and helps provide life for *all* creatures,[58] the Heartland bishops nonetheless leave little doubt which of God's creatures are specially privileged:

> "The land is given by God for all *people*..."[59]
> "The land is God's gift for present and future generations of *humanity*."[60]
> "We must keep in mind the land's inherent status as a gift from God for the *human* family..."[61]

If we humans are the very reason for the rest of creation, then the non-human natural world is best understood as our communal resource, which, while ultimately belonging to God and demanding our wise and just stewardship, has no reason to exist on its own. This I take to be the defining element of an essentially anthropocentric view, no matter how often God's property rights are invoked. There is no explicit nor even implicit comment to the contrary in this rather lengthy text.

The bishops name ten "Principles of Land Stewardship," none of which is explicated in a non-utilitarian way, not even the first, which might seem to suggest a genuinely theocentric perspective:

> The land is God's;
> People are God's stewards on the land;
> The land's benefits are for everyone;
> The land should be distributed equitably;
> The land should be conserved and restored;
> Land use planning must consider social and environmental
>   impacts;
> Land use should be appropriate to land quality;
> The land should provide a moderate livelihood;
> The land's workers should be able to become the land's
>   owners;
> The land's mineral wealth should be shared.[62]

The emphasis is clearly on social justice rather than ecological integrity,[63] which I have demonstrated to be the emphasis of official church teaching since its inception in the early 1970s. What we have in *Strangers and Guests* is indeed Catholic *social* teaching on the environment, which I might characterize, I hope not too cynically, as enlightened self-interest. This attitude is clearly embodied in the bishops' contention that "as the earth's finite resources are used, provision must be made for people's future needs. The consumption patterns of the present generation must be adjusted so that future generations might also partake of the land's bounty."[64] Environmental stewardship, in other words, is social justice for humans not yet born. The fate of other species or of those complex inter-relationships of species we call ecosystems hardly enters the bishops' ethical radar.

But at least one of the Heartland bishops' stewardship principles, in addition to the first, might be developed in a more radical way than do the bishops themselves. I reproduce here almost their full explication of principle 7:

> *Land use should be appropriate to land quality.*
> The land should be utilized according to its "best and highest" use. That is, because land is a limited resource any determination of how a given portion of it will be used should take into consideration the quality of the land and how it might best serve the community as a whole. Prime farmland, for example, should not be used for an airport, a highway or a shopping center; *neither should range land be converted to farmland when such a conversion would severely deplete water reserves and destroy necessary soil cover....* In any case, since land is a community resource the way it is used should be based on a careful consideration of the various possibilities for its use and the short *and long term consequences* of each.[65]

Of course, much of the 12-state region the bishops describe as the "Heartland" was indeed rangeland for millennia before European settlers converted it into farmland, as the bishops themselves alluded to earlier in their statement, "the face of the earth was *transformed*." This principle of appropriate land use may have deeper implications than the bishops realize, especially for that area of the Heartland which overlaps the Great Plains, that enormous swath of grassland stretching from approximately the 98th meridian[66] on the east to the Rocky Mountains on the west. For the last ten or so years, perhaps no region of the country, with the possible exception of the old growth forests of the Pacific Northwest, has been so embroiled over exactly this question of appropriate land use. The question has been not only rangeland vs. farmland, but ranged by what, cattle or...*bison*, exotic imported European species or a species as indigenous to the place as its earliest prehistoric human inhabitants?[67]

In the last section of this essay, I wish to investigate the idea of a "Buffalo Commons" on the Great Plains in light of official Catholic environmental teaching, especially the underdeveloped theocentric/sacramental vision and "Noah principle" of *Renewing the Earth*, and the principle of appropriate land use of *Strangers and Guests*. That will require explicating the Buffalo Commons concept and bison ecology before exploring whether a more thoroughly theocentric environmental perspective might better respond to the ecological exigencies of contemporary human habitation on the Great Plains.

THE BUFFALO COMMONS

By the turn of the twentieth century, the great herds of American bison, estimated at as many as 60 million,[68] had been decimated by white hunters, and the species hovered on the edge of extinction. Today, estimates put the total number of bison as high as 200,000.[69] This resurgence of North America's largest animal (a bull may weigh as much as a ton[70]) as the eponymous linchpin of the emergence of a new environmental reality on the Great Plains, was first envisioned by two academics from the Eastern seaboard, Frank Popper, a land-use planner at Rutgers University in New Jersey, and Deborah Popper, a geographer now at the College of Staten Island/City University of New York. This husband-and-wife team had long puzzled over the fate of the Plains, the repeated boom-and-bust economic cycle with its accompanying in-and-out migration, as well as what has been described as the greatest environmental destruction on the continent.[71] Drawing on the imagery of scientist Garrett Hardin's famous, or infamous, invocation of "The Tragedy of the Commons," in 1987 the Poppers published a seminal essay in the journal *Planning*.[72] "The Great Plains: From Dust to Dust" offered this vision of the future of the arid American heartland:

> We believe that over the next generation the Plains will, as a result of the largest, longest-running agricultural and environmental miscalculation in American history, become almost totally depopulated. At that point, a new use for the region will emerge, one that is in fact so old that it predates the American presence. We are suggesting that the region be returned to its original pre-white state, that it be, in effect, deprivatized.[73]

Reciting a nearly biblical litany of blizzards and massive cattle loss, of droughts and the "mining" by irrigation of irreplaceable groundwater,[74] of plagues of locusts and crop disaster, of sodbusting and Dust Bowl, of boomtowns and ghost towns from the 1862 Homestead Act to the agricultural crisis of the 1980s, the Poppers foresee only more of the same "tragedy of the commons" for the future. On the Plains, as in Hardin's ecological fable, "individual short-term economic rationality...[has led] to collective long-term environmental disaster." Massive governmental programs to promote and buttress privatization on the Plains from the Homestead Act to contemporary agricultural support systems have proved largely ineffective at creating "a truly stable agriculture." Private interests have "overgrazed and overplowed the land and overdrawn the water" and overproduced in ways that cannot be sustained.[75]

The most intriguing response to this desolate view of the future, according to the Poppers, would be to restore the Plains to "the commons the settlers found in the 19th century." By 1987, potential elements of this vision had already been proposed, independently of each other and of the Poppers, by Bret Wallach, a geographer at the University of Oregon and a MacArthur Fellow, Charles Little, former editor of *American Land Forum*, and Robert Scott, of the Institute of the Rockies in Missoula, Montana. These elements include buyouts of farmers and ranchers by the federal government and restoration of their lands to native shortgrass prairie; expansion of the national grasslands and federally managed grazing and conservation districts; and the establishment of East African-style game preserves in cooperation with, rather than displacement of, large landholders.[76] At this "trial-balloon" stage in their thinking, the Poppers are boldly explicit that "the federal government's commanding task on the Plains for the next century will be to recreate the nineteenth century, to reestablish what we would call the Buffalo Commons." Creating "the world's largest historic preservation project, the ultimate national park," the authors admit, "represents a substantial administrative undertaking," and will require a new agency on the model of the Tennessee Valley Authority.[77]

Perhaps largely because of the activist role attributed to the federal government in this earliest articulation of their proposal, the Poppers were *personae non gratae* as they traveled the Great Plains to talk about their ideas in the late 1980s and early 1990s. Death threats were made and armed guards required.[78] In more recent treatments, the Poppers, no doubt chastened by such reactions, have been much less prescriptive and interventionist and much more descriptive and decentralized in their formulations of the Buffalo Commons. The emphasis now is not on what the government should do but what is in fact happening not only with but especially without government encouragement. In a recent tenth anniversary commentary on their "seemingly innocuous" but "surprisingly prophetic" essay anᵈ on the decade since its appearance, the Poppers assess the status not so much of the idea but of the reality, particularly on the Northern Plains, of the Buffalo Commons. Over this period, bison herds on public lands increased in size. "A noticeable number of Plains ranchers switched from cattle to buffalo and prospered economically and environmentally.... The buffalo market, which barely existed ten years ago, thrives while cattle (and sheep) markets keep slipping."[79] North Dakota has made substantial commitments to bison ranching and bison tourism.[80] Plains Indians formed the Intertribal Bison Cooperative, based in Rapid City, South Dakota, and now counting forty-two tribes as members. "The buffalo population on Indian land has tripled since 1992." The nation's leading private land-preservation organization, The Nature Conservancy, has for the first time purchased land on the Plains and restored buffalo to it.[81] Finally, remark the Poppers, various federal agencies have made moves that would at least indirectly facilitate development of a Buffalo Commons.[82]

While acknowledging that "no Plains locality has yet put the Buffalo Commons into effect," they observe that "the early-1990s hostility has ebbed somewhat" and that there is "a growing recognition that the idea makes ecological and financial sense—that it offers a plausible option for many places, especially if the other choices are casinos, prisons, hazardous waste, agribusiness or continued slow-leak decline."[83] The authors who first articulated the idea of the Buffalo Commons as a vision for ecological and economic sustainability on the Great Plains "confidently await the further return of the buffalo."[84]

BISON ECOLOGY

The Poppers, as land-use planners and geographers, especially in their early writing, took an historical rather than an ecological perspective on the Great Plains. Given the history of environmental calamity on the Plains under the regime of government-sponsored privatization, the Poppers recommended a return to the original commons predating white settlement. What they found in that retrospective view were enormous herds of buffalo. The answer to the Plains dilemma, therefore, was a renewed Buffalo Commons, a twenty-first century version of a nineteenth-century reality. The Poppers, that is, did not begin with a view of the buffalo, either nostalgic or ecological, and devise an argument along demographic and economic lines for the species' restoration. They have been social scientists first and environmentalists second.

This pattern, however, can be reversed, as has been done by Ernest Callenbach in *Bring Back the Buffalo! A Sustainable Future for America's Great Plains*. Callenbach, a well-known environmental author and editor,[85] makes a case for the restoration of the buffalo along ecological lines. A very brief rehearsal of that argument is necessary to an evaluation of the Buffalo Commons along the theocentric lines we are exploring.

"The ecological virtues of bison," according to Callenbach, "are exceptional."[86] The huge herds that roamed the Plains only a century and a half ago testify to the fact that "bison were perfectly adapted to life on the enormous grasslands of the continent."[87] "Grazing by millions of bison ... not only did not degrade the Plains but promoted coexistence and coevolution of animals and grasses in a remarkably rich and productive symbiotic relationship."[88] One of the reasons the Nature Conservancy restores bison to its prairies is that "the cropping of grasses by bison, who tend to bite off the top parts of the grass rather than tear away the near-ground growing shoots as do cattle and sheep, may aid the recovery of native grass species that cannot survive under livestock."[89] Bison are also easier on riparian areas than are cattle. According to Sharman Apt Russell, "unlike wild ungulates [such as bison], cows tend to stay near water, to wallow in it, to lounge on the stream banks, and to trample the same ground over and over,"[90] thus degrading both the soil and vegetation around the water and the quality of the water itself. Bison, on the other hand, are nomadic and wallow mostly in high and dry areas away from water.[91] For these reasons, Callenbach contends that "bison are part of the solution to erosion problems"[92] associated with cattle ranching in many Plains areas. The contention is that the restoration of buffalo to the Plains would be good not only for the buffalo but for the rest of the Plains ecosystem as a whole.

None of the advocates of the Buffalo Commons to whom I have been referring think of this restoration as a wholesale usurpation of farmers, ranchers, and rural settlements, nor of cattle, wheat, a domesticated short-grass, or corn, a domesticated tallgrass. On the contrary, environmental author Richard Manning sees it this way.

> Respecting the limits of the land would require a simple scaling back, a request that would not seem preposterous in light of nearly a century of grain surplus and waste. Pulling back would mean simply moving our most demanding activities east, cattle to wheat land, wheat land to corn land, grass to fill every hole left by the leaving.[93]

He might have also said, to begin this litany of enlightened human restraint, buffalo to cattle land, for elsewhere he presents the Buffalo Commons[94] as part of the restoration of the grassland that he sees as almost inevitable: "The grass will return. The question on the table is whether we can see this coming, accept it, and shape it."[95] The question now on the table of this essay is whether the Catholic Church on the Plains can see this environmental shift and renewal coming, whether it can and should accept it, and whether it should help to shape it. I believe the answer to each of these challenges is Yes, especially if the principles of Catholic environmental teaching which I have highlighted are the determining factors.

THEOLOGICAL RESPONSE TO THE BUFFALO COMMONS

What should the Catholic people of the Plains make of such a vision of the land they inhabit? If the Heartland bishops were to produce a twentieth anniversary commentary on *Strangers and Guests* in the millennial year 2000, what perspective should it take on the Buffalo Commons? What difference would it make if the theocentric/sacramental/Noah principles of *Renewing the Earth* were brought to the fore and developed as the deep background to the appropriate land use principle of *Strangers and Guests*? And what if all this were undertaken with a genuinely religious appreciation for the "dearest freshness deep down things" that seems to be an apt description of the deeply rooted[96] vitality of the once vast but now beleaguered, remnant American grasslands? In short, *should the Catholic Church take a friendly view of the Buffalo Commons?*

I have previously suggested that one crucial distinction between a genuinely theocentric and an actually anthropocentric perspective can be concretized in the Noah Principle, which values all species in and of themselves simply on the basis of their creation and salvation by God. The first covenant, we should remember, was made between God and Noah on behalf of *all* creation. Subsequent covenants do not cancel the first. We are aware today, of course, that creation is an ongoing, dynamic, evolutionary reality; species come and go as part of that dynamism quite apart from human intervention. Habitats themselves change as a result of wholly non-human factors such as climate change. All this suggests that humanity need not think about species preservation in absolutist fashion. But, at the very least, it should cause us to look on with alarm at the almost astronomically increasing *rate* of species loss caused by humans today. The preservation of the American bison, therefore, makes a *prima facie* moral claim on us. But an ark or zoo will not do. Although zoos may indeed function like Noah's ark to preserve species artificially in times of ecological crises, the point of the ark was to return all the species to their natural habitats once the crisis was passed. If bison as a species have a right to exist, then their habitat likewise has a moral claim on us. As Thomas Aquinas argued so pointedly, a diversity of creatures gives more glory to God than any single creature, humans not excepted, and that diversity requires habitat preservation and restoration, not simply better or bigger zoos.[97]

Is it too much to suggest that a Buffalo Commons on the Great Plains, however modest and gradually achieved and for whatever mixed motives, would be an expression of humanity's humble relatedness to the rest of creation and therefore an expression of a Creator-centered religious faith? If we are to take a truly sacramental view of creation do we not have to see God's hand in the creation of those awe-inspiring herds of bison that once ruled the Great Plains and that we can now see only in our imaginations? Might not the figure of Noah, that recovering addict to overconsumption of the fruit of the earth whose own redemption entailed responsibility and care for non-human creation, be a fitting saint for our ecological age, along with St. Francis, friend of the birds and the wolf?

If, as we know today, species depend on other species, as even prey depend on predators to maintain a healthy population, and on habitats, just as habitats depend on ecosystems, do we not have to think more radically about the land use principle enunciated in *Stewards and Guests*? What is the best and highest use of the Great Plains? It may seem contradictory to move from a strong affirmation of the avowedly non-utilitarian Noah Principle to such a question of use. But use that does not destroy but rather preserves and even restores would not necessarily admit of such a contradiction. Such *sustainable* use, indeed, is how we should now, in this ecologically threatened age, understand the biblical image of the steward and the steward's "dominion" over the Master's land, plants, and animals.

As the Florida bishops suggest, stewardship must now be understood as a relationship of companionship rather than heedless exploitation. The Buffalo Commons, however dramatic a departure from the history of recent human transformation of the Plains, is definitely not a call for wholesale human retreat. It is a call, in Richard Manning's language, for restraint and, in the language of the Heartland bishops, for a better and higher use of the Plains.

It is the audacious conclusion and claim of this essay that the restoration of the American bison to the Great Plains, as a necessary dimension of the ecological restoration of significant portions of the Plains themselves, in a new understanding of how the Plains can be more sustainably used for human benefit, would be an expression of praise and love and respect for God the Creator, who spoke to Job out of the whirlwind, to Noah above the roar of the flood, to Moses out of a bush, and whose cosmically creative power, Christians believe, was shared by Jesus the Christ. The Buffalo Commons, I would like to suggest, may be a guiding myth or metaphor[98] appropriate for our time, an ecological age, in this place, this particular sacred place, the Great Plains of North America.[99]

NOTES

1. *Catholic Social Teaching* (Maryknoll: Orbis, 1988), described as "the Cliff' Notes" on CST by Peter J. Henriot, one of its authors, was titled *Our Best Kept Secret* in previous editions.

2. David J. O'Brien and William A. Shannon, *Catholic Social Thought: The Documentary Heritage* (Maryknoll: Orbis, 1993), 273.

3. Ibid., 289.

4. Ibid., 289.

5. Ibid., 290.

6. John Paul II, *The Ecological Crisis: A Common Responsibility*; United States Catholic Conference, *Renewing the Earth*: both in Drew Christiansen and Walter Grazer, eds.,"*And God Saw That It Was Good": Catholic Theology and the Environment* (Washington, DC: United States Catholic Conference, 1997).

7. *Redemptoris Hominis*, 23. Henceforth cited as *RH*.

8. "Christians, in particular, realize that their responsibility within creation and their duty towards nature and the Creator are an essential part of their faith." John Paul II, *The Ecological Crisis: A Common Responsibility*, in "*Good*," 222.

9. In his *Dynamo and Virgin Reconsidered: Essays in the Dynamism of Western Culture* (Cambridge: MIT Press, 1971).

10. Ibid., 86.

11. Ibid., 90.

12. *RH*, 51.

13. Ibid., 47.

14. *Dynamo and Virgin*, 91.

15. Ibid., 93.

16. Ibid., 94.

17. "*Good*," 222.

18. "*Good*," 219 (emphasis in original).

19. "*Good*," 215.

20. "*Good*," 216 (emphasis in original).

21. "*Good*," 217.

22. "*Good*," 218.

23. "*Good*," 217 (emphasis in original).

24. "*Good*," 216.

25. "*Good*," 221.

26. The U.S. Bishops' document, *Renewing the Earth*, quotes this same Hopkins poem in its conclusion.

27. This aboriginal harmony, from a scientific, evolutionary perspective, is, of course, a myth. There was no Garden of Eden, no Golden Age, no time before the advent of mutability and death, in Darwinian perspective. So dynamic has the "balance" of nature always been, at least in cosmological perspective, that one might even ask in what sense we should use the word 'balance' in this context, suggesting as it does a stable equilibrium or "golden mean." As observed in *Gaudium et Spes*, "the human race has passed from a rather static concept of reality to a more dynamic, evolutionary one" (*CST*, 168). One wonders if Catholic theology has yet to incorporate this insight fully in this context. There can be no doubt that humankind increasingly accelerates this natural mutability. Species have become extinct since "the beginning," but never before at the rate induced by modern civilization.

28. "*Good*," 222.

29. "*Good*," 18, note 4. Since publication of "*Good*," "Care for the Environment: A Religious Act" [Origins 27 (April 9, 1998), 705-06] has been published with approval from the Vatican by the International Catholic-Jewish Liaison Committee.

30. Since the publication of "*Good*" in 1996, two other U.S. episcopal documents have appeared: "Life on the Land: A Call to Reflection and Action," by the Bishops of Ohio, *Origins* 27 (April 23, 1998), and "Reclaiming the Vocation to Care for the Earth," by the Bishops of New Mexico, *Origins* 28 (June 11, 1998).

31. "This Land Is Home to Me: A Pastoral Letter on Powerlessness in Appalachia," by the Catholic Bishops of the Region, in David J. O'Brien and Thomas J. Shannon, eds., *Renewing the Earth: Catholic Documents on Peace, Justice and Liberation* (Garden City, NY: Image Books, 1977), 472-515.

32. *Strangers and Guests: Toward Community in the Heartland. A Regional Catholic Bishops' Statement on Land Issues.* (Des Moines: National Catholic Rural Life, 1980).

33. "Christian Faith and the Environment," *Origins* 20 (November 1, 1990), 333, 335-38.

34. "What is Ecospirituality?" *Origins* 24 (February 23, 1995), 606-08.

35. Florida Catholic Conference, *Companions in Creation* (Tallahassee: 1991). I find this statement provocative because "companions" seems to be a "Franciscan" alternative or complement to stewards, the usual image or metaphor of human relationship to the rest of creation. See my discussion later in this chapter of stewardship as an ideal in *Strangers and Guests*.

36. *"Good,"* 232.

37. *"Good,"* 232.

38. *"Good,"* 232.

39. I did not invent the term. I first came across it in biologist David W. Ehrenfeld's "The Conservation of Non-Resources," *American Scientist* 64, 648-56. Ehrenfeld writes that "There is only one account in Western culture of conservation effort greater than that now taking place; it concerned endangered species. Not a single species was excluded on the basis of low priority, and by all accounts not a single species was lost.... [The Genesis story of Noah and the ark] is an excellent precedent.... Existence is the only criterion of value...and [this insight] by rights ought to be named the 'Noah Principle' after the person who was one of the first to put it into practice" 654-55.

40. *"Good,"* 232.

41. *"Good,"* 233.

42. Both encyclicals are included in *CST*.

43. *"Good,"* 233.

44. Or, in the lesser-known second version, in pairs or *groups of seven pairs*, respectively, of unclean and clean animals: see Genesis 6:19 and 7:2-3. One thinks of Matthew's analogous injunction to love one's enemies (5:44) "for he makes his sun rise on the good and the bad, and causes rain to fall on the just and the unjust."

45. See Leonardo Boff, *Ecology and Liberation: A New Paradigm* (Maryknoll, NY: Orbis, 1995) and Leonardo Boff and Virgil Elizondo, eds., *Ecology and Poverty: Cry of the Earth, Cry of the Poor* (Maryknoll, NY: Orbis, 1995).

46. *"Good,"* 234.

47. *"Good,"* 234.

48. Ibid.

49. For a provocative attempt to do just this, see Jane Blewett, "Social Justice and Creation Spirituality," *The Way* (January, 1989), 13-25.

50. "*Good*," 231.

51. "*Good*," 241.

52. Theologians who are exploring this avenue at book-length include Denis Edwards, *Jesus the Wisdom of God: An Ecological Theology* (Maryknoll, NY: Orbis, 1995), Sallie McFague, *The Body of God: An Ecological Theology* (Minneapolis: Fortress, 1993), and Rosemary Radford Ruether, *Gaia and God: An Ecofeminist Theology of Earth Healing* (San Francisco: Harper Collins, 1992). See the article by Michael J. Himes and Kenneth R. Himes, "The Sacrament of Creation," *Commonweal*, January 26, 1990, 42-9. See also, in "*Good*," articles by Clifford, Haught, Toolan, Irwin, Feiss, Hinze, Christiansen, and Blake.

53. Of particular interest might be the Pope's own apparent theological ambivalence toward the natural world. As pointed out above, he speaks in the same document of the destruction of nature's harmony at the hands of mythological humanity and of a still harmonious universe. I have offered one interpretation of this apparent contradiction, taking a cue from the sentiment expressed in Hopkins' "God's Grandeur": nature bounces back. More sustained examination of Christianity's perspective on the natural world is called for. In addition to the developing ecological theologies mentioned in note 52, see Paul H. Santmire, *The Travail of Nature: The Ambiguous Ecological Promise of Christian Theology* (Philadelphia: Fortress, 1985) for a retrospective view.

54. Companions in Creation, 3.

55. *Strangers and Guests.* The twelve states are Colorado, Illinois, Indiana, Iowa, Kansas, Minnesota, Missouri, Nebraska, North Dakota, South Dakota, Wisconsin, and Wyoming.

56. *Strangers and Guests*, 4, 5. Ernest Callenbach, in *Bring Back the Buffalo! A Sustainable Future for America's Great Plains* (New York: Island Press, 1966), 6, describes this "replacement of native grazing animals by imported livestock, the displacement of native grasses by European ones, the extermination of the predators who once performed crucial roles at the top of the Plains food chain,… the most stupendous transformation of a landscape that human beings have ever attempted."

57. *Strangers and Guests*, 28.

58. Ibid., 17. Emphasis added.

59. Ibid., 14.

60. Ibid., 15.

61. Ibid., 20. Emphasis added.

62. Ibid., 13.

63. I do not mean to suggest that there must necessarily be a tradeoff between social justice and ecological integrity, either at the theoretical or practical levels. As Bishop Michael Pfeifer has written in "What Is Ecospirituality?," "There is an

essential link between social justice and ecological integrity" (607). As I once heard it put, the earth can no longer afford the conspicuous consumption of the rich nor the desperate consumption of the poor. When, as in Brazil, for example, the rich allow vast amounts of prime land to lie fallow for investment and tax benefits, forcing the poor to farm marginal and highly erodible land, ecological harm cannot be countered without addressing the obvious economic disparities and political injustices which cause it.

64. *Strangers and Guests*, 15.

65. Ibid., 18.

66. The 98th meridian, which almost exactly bisects the 48 states as an east-west axis, marks the transition from what was once tallgrass prairie in western and southwestern Minnesota, all of Iowa, northwestern Missouri, and most of Illinois and Indiana, to the mixed-grass prairies covering all or nearly all of the Dakotas, Nebraska, Kansas, Oklahoma, and a large portion of north-central Texas. The determining factor, of course, is rainfall or the increasing lack of it as one moves west. The third grassland region is the shortgrass prairie, a narrower swath running immediately to the east of the Rocky Mountains from much of northern Montana almost to the Mexico border in west Texas and southeastern New Mexico. The Great Plains, then, are the semi-arid (less than 20 inches of rain annually) regions of the middle one-fifth of the 48 contiguous states characterized by shortgrass and mixed-grass prairie. The 98th meridian runs from just west of the intersection of the Minnesota-North Dakota-Canada borders to the southernmost tip of Texas, passing just west of Lincoln, Nebraska, and Oklahoma City before passing through Austin, Texas. Helpful maps are included in the books by Manning and Matthews cited elsewhere.

67. The ancestors of today's American bison are thought to have crossed the Bering Strait from Asia thousands of years ago.

68. Callenbach, *Bring Back the Buffalo!*, 9.

69. Ibid., 1.

70. Ibid., 10.

71. "Civilized man wrought more destruction on grassland than upon any other natural realm on the continent." Tom McHugh, *The Time of the Buffalo* (New York: Alfred Knopf, 1972), no page number given in the quotation in Richard Manning, *Grassland: The History, Biology, Politics, and Promise of the American Prairie* (New York: Penguin, 1995), 139.

72. Deborah Epstein Popper and Frank J. Popper, "The Great Plains: From Dust to Dust," *Planning*, vol. 53, no. 12 (December, 1987), pages 12-18. Reprinted in *The Best of Planning* (Chicago: American Planning Association, 1989), 572-77. Page numbers in subsequent notations refer to the reprint.

73. 73. Popper and Popper (1989), 572.

74. The Ogallala Aquifer, the huge underground lake on which much of the Plains sits, was reduced, in the portion under Kansas, from a depth of 58 feet in 1950 to 6 feet in 1987. Ibid., 574.

75. Ibid., 575.

76. Ibid., 576.

77. Ibid., 577.

78. For an engaging narrative of the Poppers' travels and travails, see Anne Matthews, *Where the Buffalo Roam* (New York: George Weidenfeld, 1992).

79. On a summer 1998 two-week trip through Buffalo Commons territory in Nebraska, Colorado, and Kansas, I ordered buffalo from menus of four very different restaurants. Buffalo meat is praised for being higher in protein and lower in fat and cholesterol than beef.

80. "The Bison Are Coming," *High Country News*, February 2, 1998, 15, 17. For example, the Konza Prairie, an almost 9,000 acre research preserve managed by Kansas State University near Manhattan, Kansas. See O.J. Reichman, *Konza Prairie: A Tallgrass Natural History* (Lawrence: University Press of Kansas, 1987).

82. Popper and Popper (1998), 17.

83. As a Nebraska resident since 1987, I can attest to both the attraction and repulsion each of these alleged economic stimulants have had for segments of the state's population.

84. Popper and Popper (1998), 17. It may be observed that the present status of the Buffalo Commons stresses buffalo over commons. Much of the resurgence of the buffalo must be attributed to private parties rather than to public entities, as the Poppers themselves suggest. The emergence of the Buffalo Commons, or at least the resurgence of the buffalo, thus does not necessarily depend on extensive deprivatization, as the Poppers once envisioned.

85. Callenbach is the author of *Ecotopia: A Novel About Ecology, People, and Politics in 1999* (Berkeley, CA: Banyan Tree Books, 1975) and *Ecotopia Emerging* (New York: Bantam, 1979) and for many years edited the Natural History Guides at the University of California Press.

86. Callenbach, *Bring Back the Buffalo*, 6.

87. Ibid., 11.

88. Ibid., 27.

89. Ibid., 24.

90. Sharman Apt Russell, *Kill the Cowboy: A Battle of Mythology in the New West* (Boston: Addison-Wesley, 1993), 21. Quoted in Callenbach, *Bring Back the Buffalo*, 30.

91. Ibid., 30. On the Konza Prairie, a former wallow can be found on the ridge of a hill high above a nearby stream.

92. Ibid., 22.

93. Manning, *Grassland*, 275.

94. Ibid., 266-268 and, on buffalo, *passim*. His book, dedicated to "bison, *for all that created them*, and for all they create" (my emphasis), quotes the voice out of the whirlwind in the Book of Job as one of its epigraphs, and demonstrates an appreciation of the religious dimension of environmental sensitivity: "In some real ways, the effort to re-find the landscape … is a religious quest, and it makes sense to consider it that way." 259.

95. Ibid., 268. Inevitable because "in thirty years, the Ogallala aquifer will be gone. In less time, saline seep and salinization, erosion, and nitrate pollution [from agricultural chemicals] will make huge areas of farmed land no longer farmable. Eventually American taxpayers will cut the flow of subsidies to crop agriculture and the drought cycle will deepen, probably spurred by global warming." 267-68. The subsidies are now being cut.

96. O.J. Reichman, *Konza Prairie*, 148, reports that a single rye plant, a domestic relative of grasses on the Konza tallgrass prairie, has 130 times as much surface area underground on its roots as above ground on its leaves and stems, and that big bluestem, one of the tallgrasses, may extend its roots as deep as twelve feet. Richard Manning, *Grassland*, 141, adds that "a square-yard chunk of big bluestem sod contains twenty-five miles of rootlets, root hairs, and roots." It is this underground life that enables grass to endure fire (and drought), and it is fire in turn that preserves grasslands against the encroachments of forbs (woody plants) and trees, with most of their biomass above ground. According to Manning, 102, 143, until improvements of the metal plow by John Deere and others in the early nineteenth century, it was this thick, deep, and otherwise impenetrable tangle of rootage that preserved the prairie from human transformation into farmland. Manning, 142, observes that "settlement was a war on roots."

97. Omaha's Henry Doorly Zoo, which has participated in an apparently successful program to return the black-footed ferret to the Great Plains, has recently opened a 360-acre Conservation Park and Wildlife Safari on the site of a former limestone quarry and farmland just off the interstate highway midway between Omaha and Lincoln. Here bison, antelope, elk, deer, wolves, waterfowl and other birds can be viewed in natural, fenced habitats. This ecotourist attraction is a glimpse of the Buffalo Commons and an example of how ecological restoration and commercial development can be harmoniously joined.

98. See Deborah E. Popper and Frank J. Popper, "The Case for Regional Metaphor as a Geographic Method: The Buffalo Commons and its Implications." Unpublished manuscript.

99. I would like to thank Frank Popper for his bibliographic help in preparing this chapter.

Magisterium and Conscience: Models of Discourse

Todd A. Salzman

As the tradition of the Catholic Church is a living tradition, so, too, are the relationships that structure that tradition living relationships. What this implies is that these relationships are renewed, revised, and sometimes even redefined in light of "the signs of the times."[1] In the modern Church, nowhere is this insight more in need of consideration and development than in the relationship between the Magisterium or teaching authority of the Church and the individual consciences of the faithful.

Pope Paul VI's encyclical *Humanae Vitae*, forbidding the use of artificial birth control, initiated reconsideration of this relationship. It raised a question for the relationship between conscience and the Magisterium: are Catholic Christians required to assent to every magisterial teaching without exception, even if in good conscience they do not agree with that teaching and have sound arguments to sustain their disagreements? Is assent unconditional or are there degrees of assent depending on the teaching and the authority proposing the teaching? At the heart of this question is the meaning and role of the Magisterium and its relationship to the individual conscience. Sparked in large part by the promulgation of *Humanae Vitae*, renewing, revising, or redefining this relationship has been the project of theologians in dialogue with the Magisterium, sometimes in a spirit of charity, sometimes in acrimonious debate and ecclesial censure.[2] In this essay, I will investigate the role and function of the Magisterium in relation to the individual conscience and present four different models of discourse between the two.

MAGISTERIUM: ITS DEFINITION, LEVELS,
AND ROLE IN THE CHURCH

The term 'authority' designates an asymmetrical social relationship between two parties built on mutual ideals, values, needs, expectations, and
responsibilities. Although authority can be based on power, which then
becomes tyranny, the power associated with a legitimate authority relies
upon freedom, intelligence, and commonality reflecting the concerns and
common bonds of the community, both from those in authority and those
under the authority.[3] Within the Judeo-Christian tradition, from its beginning, authority is an essential concept. God manifested God's authority in
and through creation and established a particular relationship with human
beings in the Garden of Eden. God further revealed God's authority to
Abraham and Moses in the Old Testament and, through Jesus the Christ,
extended to all people both that authority and the covenant which it
established. The gift of the Holy Spirit at Pentecost insured the continu-
ation of God's presence and authority within the Church, the new People
of God, and guaranteed abiding authority within the Church. That authority
has taken on different dimensions throughout the Church's history.

Only relatively recently has the teaching authority of the Catholic
Church been identified with "Magisterium" or "the Magisterium."[4] Magisterium refers to the pastoral teaching authority on "faith and morals"
exercised by Bishops in communion with the Bishop of Rome. As stewards
of the Spirit of Truth, those in authority do not create truth; they are searchers for truth and revealers of meaning discovered in truth. It is important to
consider the different levels of Magisterium and the different levels of
authority of their teachings. In light of these considerations the appropriate
response of the faithful to these teachings will become clearer. The Magisterium is commonly referred to as either extraordinary or ordinary and its
teachings are either infallible or non-infallible. Extraordinary Magisterium
is exercised in two ways. First, as defined by the First Vatican Council's
Pastor Aeternus when the Roman Pontiff speaks *ex cathedra* on faith and
morals, his statements possess the same infallibility the Redeemer willed
his Church to have.[5] The second exercise of the extraordinary Magisterium
occurs in council where Bishops and Pope in union profess solemn teachings of faith. In both cases the teachings are considered infallible, that is,
they are irreformable doctrines whose truth is guaranteed by the guidance
of the Holy Spirit and they require a religious assent of faith which is

absolute and certain.[6] Such weight is given to infallible teachings within the entire Catholic community that the exercise of this teaching authority is extremely rare.[7] Since the proclamation of the doctrine of papal infallibility in 1870, it has been exercised only by Pius XII in defining the Assumption of Mary. It has never been exercised in the area of morality. Though there is much discussion concerning the extraordinary Magisterium and, especially, the idea of infallibility as it pertains to the Pope, I am more concerned here with the non-infallible moral teachings of the ordinary Magisterium and their relationship to the individual consciences of the faithful.

The ordinary Magisterium is the day-to-day exercise of the Bishop's pastoral teaching mission throughout the world. It includes papal encyclicals.[8] Theologically speaking, the teachings of the ordinary Magisterium can also be infallible when certain conditions are fulfilled:

> Although the individual bishops do not enjoy the prerogative of infallibility, they can nevertheless proclaim Christ's doctrine infallibly. This is so, even when they are dispersed around the world, provided that while maintaining the bond of unity among themselves and with Peter's successor, and while teaching authentically on a matter of faith or morals, they concur in a single viewpoint as the one which must be held conclusively. This authority is even more clearly verified when, gathered together in an ecumenical council, they are teachers and judges of faith and morals for the universal Church. Their definitions must then be adhered to with the submission of faith.[9]

There are several important dimensions of these criteria that must be taken into consideration when discussing the ordinary Magisterium and infallibility. First, it is important to note that when Bishops make individual statements on faith and morals, such statements are not infallible. Second, Bishops teach infallibly when "they concur in a single viewpoint" or express "universal agreement" that a particular teaching of faith or morals is to be held definitively and absolutely. The phrase "universal agreement" narrows considerably the possibility that the ordinary Magisterium will issue an infallible statement.

First, in such questions "universal agreement" is not always an obvious matter,[10] especially with regard to questions of morality. Aquinas taught that the more one descends from first level principles, for instance, do good and avoid evil, to the concrete circumstances of a moral situation, the more ambiguous the applicability of the principle itself may become.[11] For example, the American Bishops' statement on the economy is based on a general principle of justice and is specifically directed towards North American democratic culture. Their application of the principle of justice will not function in the same way in a radically different social and cultural context. In what sense, then, can the Bishops ascertain "universal agreement?" It would seem that such agreement is limited to basic first principles whose specifics are historically, socially, and culturally bound. Second, consensus is either reflexive or non-reflexive. Reflexive consensus entails a conscious, theological investigation of a particular issue in light of "the signs of the times;" non-reflexive consensus may represent no more than a non-critical acceptance of something handed down from another age and having serious limitations in the current context.[12]

Given the importance of infallible statements for the salvation of souls, is it prudent to presume universal agreement among the Bishops without subjecting such teachings to dialogue and discussion? In other words, how can it be demonstrated whether or not Bishops throughout the world are in agreement unless they come together in council to discuss a particular doctrinal matter? In that case, such a teaching is not one of the ordinary but of the extraordinary Magisterium. Given the difficulty of meeting the criteria to pronounce an infallible doctrine outside the context of the extraordinary Magisterium, though theologically and logically such teachings are possible, they are indeed rare. These limitations notwithstanding, as the new *Code of Canon Law* explicitly states in relation to both the extraordinary and ordinary exercise of the Magisterium, "no doctrine is understood to be infallibly defined unless it is clearly established as such."[13] With regard to the ordinary Magisterium, I take this to mean that, if there is universal agreement among the Bishops, such agreement will be communicated in a clear, unanimous statement on a particular teaching's infallible authority. There has never been an infallible teaching made by the ordinary magisterium though, to repeat, logically such a teaching is possible.

If the ordinary Magisterium has never offered an infallible moral teaching, what then is the authority of non-infallible teachings of the ordinary Magisterium? First, a word about 'non-infallible.' Some theologians attempt to argue that 'non-infallible' is not a synonym for 'fallible.' They insist that, whereas 'fallible' is defined by the *Oxford English Dictionary* as "liable to be deceived or mistaken ... liable to be erroneous, unreliable," 'non-infallible' teachings "may well be infallibly true."[14] If we are to make any sense out of such an assertion, there is no way that we can rely strictly upon etymology. The dictionary does not define 'non-infallible,' but merely defines 'non' as 'not.' 'Non-infallible' is therefore, a synonym for 'fallible,' and to claim that non-infallible statements may well be "infallibly true" is a contradiction in terms. In what way, then, can one conceive of 'non-infallible' so that it is not a synonym for 'fallible'? It is important to distinguish between the non-infallible teaching itself which, by definition, may be mistaken, and the authority that teaches it. Because of the charism of the Magisterium to teach authoritatively Catholics respect this authority and presume that its teachings, including non-infallible teachings, are true not because of the teachings themselves but because of the authority that teaches them. This being the case, those teachings must always be investigated respectfully and with the sincere goal of more accurately defining or refining them. Such an investigation, however, may also reveal the deficiencies of a non-infallible teaching and show that it needs to be refined, redefined, or even abandoned.

Within the context of the teaching authority of the ordinary Magisterium, then, non-infallible teachings are those teachings that, though possibly needing reevaluation and redefinition in light of changing circumstances, scientific developments, or theological investigation, at the present time reflect an authoritative position of the Magisterium that must be considered by the faithful in the formation of their consciences. Such teachings warrant a presumption of truth among the faithful. Based on the promised guidance of the Holy Spirit, Scripture, and Church tradition, such teachings are to be given serious consideration by the Christian faithful. Nevertheless, they can be erroneous. Given this possibility of error, what is the authority of non-infallible teachings for the consciences of the faithful and what is the appropriate response of the faithful to those teachings?

Richard McCormick notes two extremes to be avoided when considering the authority of non-infallible teachings. The first is that the teaching is as good as the argument.[15] This position reduces such teachings to logical and rational exercises and denies the genuinely authoritative character of the magisterial charisma. The second is that the teaching is totally independent of the credibility of the argument.[16] In this case, the Magisterium becomes an arbitrary issuer of teachings without theological reflection.

These two extreme views on the authority of magisterial teachings indicate the need for a model of the Magisterium as learner-teachers.

As learners, the authentic Magisterium is continually searching for the fullness of truth in dialogue with Sacred Scripture, tradition, theologians, laity, other Christian denominations, non-Christian religions, and developments in the sciences. The learning function of the Church highlights the tentative nature of non-infallible teachings of the ordinary Magisterium. As learners guided by tradition and the Holy Spirit, the Magisterium also has the responsibility and authority to teach. The Bishops are "authentic teachers, that is, teachers endowed with the authority of Christ, who preach to the people committed to them the faith they must believe and put into practice."[17]

Endowed with the authority of Christ, Bishops possess the authority to teach. This authority is not in question here. What is in question is the authority of non-infallible teachings and the appropriate response of the faithful to them. Do non-infallible teachings require the same type of "religious assent" or "submission of will and intellect" as infallible teachings? To distinguish between the authority of non-infallible and infallible teachings is to distinguish also between the appropriate responses due those teachings by the faithful. The faithful must not treat infallible teachings as if they were contingent, non-definitive teachings open to revision and redefinition. To do so is to deny the authority of those teachings and to reject an essential "deposit of faith." Neither, however, are the faithful to treat non-infallible teachings as if they were definitive teachings essential to the "deposit of faith." To do so is to demean truly infallible statements and to give teachings greater authority then the Magisterium claims for them. The question remains, then, in the formation of conscience, what is the appropriate response of the faithful to non-infallible teachings of the ordinary Magisterium? Before answering this question, I will first investigate another authority within the Church's tradition, namely the authority of the individual conscience.

CONSCIENCE

Conscience is a complex notion in the history of Christianity. It is that dimension of the human person where God speaks to the individual and guides him or her in the discernment of moral truth manifested in moral judgment. The documents of the Second Vatican Council address the authority of conscience, the need for the formation of conscience, and the relationship between conscience and magisterial teaching. I will consider each of these in turn. *Gaudium et Spes* emphasizes that the pivotal point of its presentation will be the human person, "whole and entire, body and soul, heart and conscience, mind and will."[18] With its focus on the dignity of the human person and the authority of conscience as an essential element of that dignity, this document has had a profound impact on the way in which the relationship between conscience and authority is to be structured. A key paragraph of that text is the following.

> In the depths of his conscience, man detects a law which he does not impose upon himself, but which holds him to obedience. Always summoning him to love good and avoid evil, the voice of conscience can when necessary speak to his heart more specifically: do this, shun that. For man has in his heart a law written by God. To obey it is the very dignity of man; according to it he will be judged. Conscience is the most secret core and sanctuary of a man. There he is alone with God, whose voice echoes in his depths. In a wonderful manner conscience reveals that law which is fulfilled by love of God and neighbor. In fidelity to conscience, Christians are joined with the rest of men in the search for truth, and for the genuine solution to the numerous problems which arise in the life of individuals and from social relationships. Hence the more that a correct conscience holds sway, the more persons and groups turn aside from blind choice and strive to be guided by objective norms of morality. Conscience frequently errs from invincible ignorance without losing its dignity."[19]

This is a powerful statement on conscience that highlights many of its dimensions. First, though conscience does not formulate the divine law, which is from God, it enables human beings to discern that law and how it is to be applied in day-to-day moral judgments. Conscience could be seen as the gift of a *transcendent hermeneutic*. That is, God gives us not only law but also conscience to discern what the law entails and to apply the law in concrete moral judgments. "Good is to be done and pursued and evil is to be avoided" is the first precept of the natural law,[20] but when we descend into the particular circumstances of human behavior, that precept needs to be applied in a concrete situation. Conscience is God's gift enabling humans to make this application. Furthermore, it reflects the dignity of human beings, created in the image and likeness of God, to obey what conscience dictates.

Second, conscience is where humans are alone with God. Not only is conscience a gift for discerning the moral law and making moral judgments, it is also the place where God speaks to human beings. In theological history, spirituality and moral theology became somewhat independent after the council of Trent. One had little to do with the other. In the citation above, however, the unity between moral behavior and spiritual relationship with God is fully affirmed, and spirituality and morality come together in conscience. To discern the law written in hearts, we must listen to God's word by entering into relationship with God. Spirituality is the fostering of this relationship frequently, though not necessarily, manifested in the realm of concrete moral judgments. Conscience as defined reunites spirituality and morality, and testifies to the intrinsic relationship between the two.

Though nurtured and lived by individuals, spirituality and morality united in conscience are never individualistic. Spirituality, morality, and conscience are all necessarily communal by nature. Through spirituality and the manifestation of spirituality in words and deeds we interact with other human beings. To prevent an individualistic spirituality which, though an oxymoron, is a common temptation in America today, the paragraph goes on to emphasize the essentially social nature of conscience. "In fidelity to conscience, Christians are joined with the rest of men in the search for truth and for the genuine solution to the numerous problems which arise in the life of individuals from social relationships." In and through fidelity to conscience the human community as a whole can seek creative and genuine solutions to the problems that confront it. No human being is an island, and no individual possesses *the* truth, though individuals certainly have access to truth and reflect facets of it in their lives. Conscience and fidelity to conscience provide the human race with a compass on the journey towards truth.

Pope John Paul II's *The Splendor of Truth* affirms that, even when conscience errs due to invincible ignorance, it is still the ultimate guide for behavior. Even when conscience is in error due to invincible ignorance, men and women are morally obligated to follow their consciences. In so doing, conscience does not lose its dignity.[21] If conscience sincerely dictates a particular action which, objectively speaking, is wrong, for instance, to lie on a tax return in order to give extra money to charity, then, as long as the agent's ignorance is not due to her or his neglect in informing conscience, there is a moral obligation to follow it. Similarly, if a person believes that performing an act is wrong even when it is not, for instance, missing mass on Sunday to help a sick relative, he or she has a moral obligation to follow conscience and attend mass. In the case of an erroneous judgment of conscience due to invincible ignorance, there is no moral culpability.

In asserting the authority of conscience, the Catholic tradition maintains that this authority holds even in the case of invincible ignorance. A serious question, then, regarding conscience is what distinguishes invincible ignorance that maintains the dignity and authority of conscience from vincible ignorance that leaves conscience morally culpable? According to *The Splendor of Truth*, "Conscience, as the ultimate concrete judgment, compromises its dignity when it is *culpably erroneous*, that is to say, 'when man shows little concern for seeking what is true and good, and conscience gradually becomes almost blind from being accustomed to sin.'"[22] Vincible ignorance betrays a lack of concern for the proper formation of conscience. Invincible ignorance is the case in which, though one seeks what is true and good, because of circumstances beyond one's control one's conscience is unable to know the good and to do it. Vincible ignorance can be overcome by properly forming conscience, though this formation itself is a complex matter dependent upon multiple dimensions of the human person and her relationship to reality. These dimensions are vast and an investigation of them is beyond the scope of this essay, but one dimension of the formation of conscience must be considered, namely, the role of the Magisterium in the formation of conscience. "Christians have a great help for the formation of conscience *in the Church and her Magisterium*."[23] The *Declaration on Religious Freedom* details the role of the teaching authority of the Church for the formation of conscience.

> In the formation of their consciences, the Christian faithful ought carefully to attend to the sacred and certain doctrine of the Church. The Church is, by the will of Christ, the teacher of the truth. It is her duty to give utterance to, and authoritatively to teach, that truth which is Christ Himself, and also to declare and confirm by her authority those principles of the moral order which have their origins in human nature itself.[24]

Whatever other dimensions are essential for the formation of conscience, this paragraph clearly articulates the importance and necessity that
the Christian faithful "ought carefully to attend to the sacred and certain
doctrine of the Church" when forming their consciences. To confirm this
authority, the document further states that the Church is the teacher of the
truth. There are, of course, numerous senses of the word *Church*. Church
can refer to the authentic teaching authority of the Church, the Magisterium; it can also refer to Christian scholars and theologians, priests,
deacons, religious, and all the faithful. While all these senses of *Church* are
key to interpreting this passage, and indeed affect the perception of how to
interpret other passages that pertain to the authority of the Church, there is
a clear reference to the Magisterium as that authority which authentically
teaches the word of God and functions as the teacher of truth. I will return,
therefore, to the text previously cited from *Lumen Gentium* to see just how
non-infallible magisterial teachings are to inform the consciences of the
faithful and in what sense the faithful must assent to those teachings.

FORMATION OF CONSCIENCE
AND NON-INFALLIBLE TEACHINGS

The Second Vatican Council states that the faithful must show a "religious
submission of will and of mind ... in a special way to the authentic teaching
authority of the Roman Pontiff, even when he is not speaking *ex cathedra*"
or infallibly. They must also adhere to the teachings of the Bishops in faith
or morals "with a religious assent of soul."[25] The two key terms in these
texts, "religious submission" and "assent," can be interpreted differently
and can lead to fundamentally different models of the relationship between
the Magisterium and conscience. Two possible models will be considered.

The renowned ecclesiologist, Francis Sullivan, considers these two
phrases important in determining the appropriate response of the faithful
to non-definitive, non-infallible papal and conciliar teachings. In developing his position, he carries on a debate with Bishop Butler who also considers this question. Butler finds the term *obsequium*, rendered by both
Flannery and Abbott in the English translations of the Second Vatican
Council's documents as "submission," too strong. He notes that *obsequium*
is used three times in *Lumen Gentium* 25 for various levels of teaching.
First, of the response due the teachings of one's own Bishop; second, of the

response due the teachings of the Pope; and third, of the "submission of faith" due the dogmatic definitions of an ecumenical council. Butler insists on the different levels of authority in which the term is used, and prefers to translate *obsequium* as "due respect" when it is used of the response due non-infallible magisterial teachings.[26]

Sullivan, however, agrees with the English translations that render *obsequium* as *submission* for three reasons. First, he cites the authoritative Latin Dictionary of Lewis and Short that defines *obsequium*, from *obsequi*, "to follow" or "to yield to," as "compliance, yielding, consent, obedience, allegiance," "and not mere respect." Second, it is difficult to see how one could understand "religious respect of will and mind," whereas if *obsequium* is translated as submission, this phrase is comprehensible. Finally, while agreeing with Butler that there are certainly different degrees of *obsequium* required by the three kinds of Magisterium listed in *Lumen Gentium* 25, "they can all be understood as degrees of 'submission', but 'due respect' is certainly not the meaning of *obsequium* in the term *obsequium fidei*."[27] For Sullivan submission is a more accurate rendering of *obsequium*.

If *obsequium* is translated as submission, what does it mean for the faithful to give *obsequium religiosum* to non-infallible teachings of the Magisterium? Sullivan argues that it "means to make an honest and sustained effort to overcome any contrary opinion I might have, and to achieve sincere assent of my mind to this teaching."[28] There are two implications of this assertion. First, the interior assent to a proposition is a judgment of the mind and the proper object of the mind is truth. Authority alone cannot make a proposition true; it must demonstrate that it is reasonable to accept such a proposition. In the case of doubt among the faithful regarding a particular teaching, such reasonable arguments could demonstrate the truth of their assertions and dispel that doubt. The absence of such arguments may indicate that the assertion itself is questionable. Second, if Catholics have given

> "religious submission of mind and will" to the authority of the Magisterium, by making an honest and sustained effort to achieve internal assent to its teaching, and still find that doubts about its truth remain so strong in their minds that they cannot actually give their sincere intellectual assent to it, I do not see how one could judge such non-assent, or internal dissent, to involve any lack of

obedience to the Magisterium. Having done all that they were capable of doing towards achieving assent, they actually fulfilled their obligation of obedience, whether they achieved internal assent or not.[29]

Clearly then, though Sullivan prefers the stronger sense of *obsequium*, submission over respect, he recognizes that submission does not entail blind obedience. The opposite, in fact, is true. Authentic submission requires the commitment to attempt to come to a reasonable understanding of what the Magisterium teaches and to embrace that teaching. However, when one has made a conscious and sustained effort to understand the magisterial position and still finds the reasons either unconvincing or mistaken, then one has a moral obligation to follow one's conscience, even if this leads to dissent. By placing the locus of verification in the faithful, Sullivan is implementing a model of the relationship between conscience and the Magisterium, emphasized at the Second Vatican Council, that advocates active involvement and participation in conscience formation rather than blind obedience to authority. The credibility of the Magisterium in the eyes of the faithful comes not from authority as power demanding complicity; rather, it invites active participation and reflection encouraging the faithful to see for themselves the clarity of the truth the Magisterium is teaching. If such clarity is lacking, the assertion itself needs to be reformed, rearticulated, or redefined.

Butler also challenges the translation of the verb *adhaerere* in Flannery's *The Documents of Vatican II*. This verb, like *obsequium*, is used three times: of the response due the teaching of the local Bishop, the non-definitive teaching of the Pope, and the definitions of ecumenical councils. In each of these uses, the text refers to an obligation to "adhere" to the judgments made. According to Butler, the phrase "*et sententiis ab eo prolatis sincere adhaereatur*," which refers to the term's use in relation to the teachings of the Pope, is mistranslated by Flannery as "and sincere assent be given to decisions made by him." Butler's objection is to the use of the word "assent" to translate the term *adhaereatur*. Basing himself on Newman's idea that assent must always be unconditional, he argues that only infallible teaching demands unconditional assent. "Non-infallible teaching *cannot*, taken by itself, generate assent."[30]

Again, Sullivan disagrees with Butler's critique of the translation of the text on three counts. First, the only credible translation of the phrase *sen-*

tentiis sincere adhaerere is "to give one's sincere assent." Second, the Theological Commission addressed the question of the response called for by the non-definitive teaching of the Council and expressed that response in the following phrase, *"doctrinam excipere et amplecti"* which, according to Sullivan, can only mean "to give one's assent to the doctrine." Third, while it is the case that genuine assent, according to Newman, is always unconditional, it is foreign to Newman to assert that one can give one's assent only if the proposition has been infallibly arrived at. Assent can be unconditional even if the proposition to which one is assenting is not infallible.

Quoting Newman, Sullivan adds that unconditional means that "assent is an adhesion without reserve or doubt to the proposition to which it is given." Assent "stands for an undoubting and unhesitating act of the mind."[31] What Newman excludes from assent, then, according to Sullivan, "is any present *doubt* about the truth of what one affirms."[32] Sullivan further distinguishes between possibility and probability concerning undoubting assent to a proposition that is not considered infallible. Undoubting assent does not require that one exclude the possibility of error. All that is required for such assent is that one sees no probability that the proposition is erroneous. Sullivan concludes that "while the assent given to non-infallible teaching does not exclude the possibility that the proposition which one affirms might be erroneous, it can still be 'unconditional' in the sense that it is given without present doubt as to the truth of what is affirmed."[33]

Sullivan makes a strong case in defense of the English translation of the two terms. Nonetheless, it seems that both Sullivan and Butler, though differing in their conclusions regarding the etymology of the terms, could agree on the appropriate response of the faithful to non-infallible magisterial teachings. Both recognize that such teachings do not claim infallibility and are, therefore, open to exploration by all of the faithful including the Magisterium, even when there is submission or assent. Some further comments concerning these two terms and Sullivan's critique of Butler are necessary.

Regarding Sullivan's first point of contention with Butler, the translation of the term *obsequium*, it is interesting to note the translation in the new *Code of Canon Law*. Canon 752 reads as follows:

A religious *respect* of intellect and will, even if not the assent of faith, is to be paid to the teaching which the Supreme Pontiff or the college of bishops enunciate on faith or morals when they exercise the authentic magisterium even if they do not intend to proclaim it with a definitive act; therefore, the Christian faithful are to take care to avoid whatever is not in harmony with that teaching.[34]

The translators consciously chose the phrase "religious respect" for "*religiosum obsequium*," accepting Butler's translation over Sullivan's, Abbott's, and Flannery's. The official commentary on this canon, which received the *imprimatur* of the National Conference of Catholic Bishops signifying there is nothing in it harmful to faith or morals,[35] notes that "in the language of *Lumen Gentium* 25, the canon speaks of 'religious respect' as the proper response to what legitimate Church authority teaches in matters of faith and morals." It continues, "this is a general guideline which incorporates a healthy respect for and acceptance of sound teaching in the Church." The "religious respect" called for from the faithful in response to an exercise of the authentic Magisterium on non-infallible teachings is contrasted with the "assent of faith" demanded of the Christian faithful in response to the exercise of infallible teachings by either the extraordinary or ordinary Magisterium of the Church (Canon 750). The commentary adds that Canon 752 "carefully distinguishes this level of response from that described in Canon 750, namely a respect rather than the assent of faith."[36] Like Butler, then, the approved code renders *obsequium* as *respect* rather than *submission*. Canons 750 and 752 clearly distinguish between the type of response due various levels of magisterial teachings. Infallible teachings require "assent of faith," that is, certain and absolute assent; non-infallible teachings require "religious respect" which is neither certain nor absolute.

With regard to both *obsequium* and assent, we could argue for two basic senses in which the terms can apply to non-infallible teaching of the Magisterium and the authority they have in relation to the formation of conscience. Both terms can be taken in either a juridical, authoritarian, or responsible discernment sense. Taken in a juridical sense, *obsequium* and *adhaerere* evoke obedience to an *authoritative* teaching reflected by the terms 'must believe,' 'duty,' 'obligation,' 'blind obedience,' 'being bound.'[37] All of these terms imply constraint which may foster an infantile dependence on the part of the faithful towards the Magisterium. Responsible discernment evokes the mature exploration to discover the meaning and nature of faith in relation to magisterial teachings. Terms such as 'growth,' 'reflection,' 'discernment,' 'dialogue,' 'exploration,' reflect this sense of the two terms.

While both senses may lead to the same practical conclusions, namely, the faithful submit or assent to non-infallible magisterial teachings, the path to those conclusions differs fundamentally. In the juridical reading an unhealthy sense of dependency is created; Christian freedom and its call to discern truth challenges the individual to growth, insight, and understanding. Another fundamental difference between the two senses is that whereas there is no room in the juridical reading for responsible dissent, responsible discernment recognizes dissent as both a possiblity and an opportunity. It is a possibility because the creative freedom of both Magisterium and conscience is being encouraged to explore ever-new ways to communicate the gospel message. It is an opportunity because it can develop insight and understanding among all the faithful. In the juridical reading, opportunity is afforded only to one end of the spectrum, the Magisterium. These different senses of religious *obsequium* and *adhaerere* reflect different models of the relationship between conscience and the Magisterium.

MODELS OF THE RELATIONSHIP
BETWEEN THE MAGISTERIUM AND CONSCIENCE

Obsequium and *adhaerere*, their etymologies, and their authoritative claims on the faithful, evoke different models of the relationship between the individual conscience and the Magisterium. In this relationship, it is not a question of either/or, either conscience or Magisterium. It is a question of both/and, and of the emphasis given to each. Throughout tradition, characteristics that determine the nature of the teaching authority of the Church include the degree of tolerance for new ideas, the recognition and toleration of pluralism and the ideological challenges that it presents, the overall security of the authority that can dialogue about diversity without thereby feeling that its authority is being threatened, and the degree to which authority recognizes the working of the Holy Spirit in all the faithful.

Since a fundamental dimension of the formation of conscience for Catholic Christians is magisterial teachings, the Magisterium has a role not only in defining what is important for conscience formation but also in defining the appropriate relationship between conscience and the Magisterium. Those who wish to emphasize the Magisterium and its authority over conscience will focus on texts such as *Lumen Gentium* 25. Those who wish to focus on the role of conscience as the ultimate authority for the individual and his or her moral judgements will focus on such texts as *Gaudium et Spes* 16. Both are legitimate positions and both are supported by tradition. This reliance upon texts to argue for or against a particular dominance of either the Magisterium or conscience, thereby to justify one's own position, is not uncommon in debate over Christian dogma. Sacred scripture itself is most prone to such uses. What this implies is that a text is either underscored or downplayed in light of an overall reading of Scripture and/or Tradition, which will then define the relationship between conscience and authority.

A characteristic that frequently determines the autonomy and authority of conscience is how "freedom of conscience" is to be defined. Does this freedom mean freedom to assent strictly to what the Magisterium teaches with unquestioning submission or does it mean a respectful listening, along with the exploration and investigation of those teachings which may lead to a dissenting viewpoint? What is the Magisterium's view on dissent; what is its toleration of it? Also, from the perspective of individual conscience, has the individual taken an active role in forming her or his conscience? Is a person responsible for, and accountable to, the formation of conscience or is this viewed as unimportant? It could be reasonably argued that the freedom of the individual Catholic conscience, even the freedom for dissent, is in direct proportion to the responsibility the individual assumes for forming that conscience and investigating non-infallible magisterial teachings. Given the varied interpretations of the definition, role, and function of the authority of the Magisterium and of conscience, there are various models for this relationship throughout the history of the Church. In this section, I will investigate four different models.

The first model is strictly authoritarian and has dominated throughout much of the Church's history. According to this model, the Magisterium possesses the truth and passes that truth on to the faithful who submit unquestioningly. It is a descending, juridical model that puts conscience in the passive role of acceptance and adherence. Such a model functioned well at a time when the majority of the laity and a disproportionate number of clergy were uneducated. In this context, the faithful were dependent upon the hierarchy for clear and simple answers to complex questions, especially in the area of morality. Typically, the source for Church teaching would be a parish priest. Since he was the primary source of information on the teachings of the Church, his understanding of Church teaching would control the faithfuls' understanding. Since widespread accessibility to education in the world is a recent phenomenon, it is not surprising that the authoritarian model was the predominant model for the conscience-authority relationship throughout much of the Church's history. Given the change in culture, society, and history, however, we can legitimately ask if this is an adequate model for the twenty-first century Church?

The second model is that followed by the the current Magisterium. Though still authoritarian in tone this model is more parental, reflecting a parent-child relationship. In this model, the role and function of conscience is not only to accept magisterial teachings but also to assimilate and understand them. As the parent who teaches a child utilizes authority to insure obedience, so too does the Magisterium. While encouraging the faithful to understand and integrate doctrine, the parental Magisterium relies upon authority exercised through power and ecclesial censure to instill obedience. In this model, there is little room for dissent. The presumption of this model is hierarchical; the Magisterium possesses the deposit of faith and passes that deposit on to the faithful. There is no *meaningful* distinction between infallible and non-infallible magisterial teachings when it comes to the faithful's responsibility to submit unconditionally and unquestionably to those teachings. The model finds support both in *Lumen Gentium* 25 and, more recently, in Pope John Paul II's encyclical, *The Splendor of Truth.*

The Splendor of Truth asserts that "the task of authentically interpreting the word of God, whether in its written form or in that of Tradition, has been entrusted only to those charged with the Church's living Magisterium, whose authority is exercised in the name of Jesus Christ."[38] A central goal of the encyclical is to explain the authority of the Magisterium and its relationship to conscience. Authentically or authoritatively[39] interpreting the word of God is entrusted exclusively to the Magisterium which passes truth on to the faithful, who obey without question. The formation of conscience is dependent upon the teachings of the Magisterium.

The encyclical further notes that there is concern regarding dissent in the Church which is no longer "limited and occasional" but "an overall and systematic calling into question of traditional moral Doctrine." The attitude towards authority reflected by such widespread dissent views the Magisterium as "capable of intervening in matters of morality only in order to 'exhort consciences' and to 'propose values,' in the light of which each individual will independently make his or her decisions and life choices."[40] Such a state is unacceptable, the encyclical argues. Since the Magisterium is merely articulating truths which conscience should already possess, there is no question of a tension between teaching and the consciences of the faithful. If conscience does not yet possess this truth, or finds solid grounds for questioning it, then it is mistaken. Even in the case of a mistaken conscience, however, conscience does not lose its dignity if it is due to invincible ignorance.

The Splendor of Truth further exemplifies the parental model in its description of the role of the theologian in relation to the Magisterium. The teacher of moral theology has

> the grave duty to instruct the faithful—especially future Pastors— about all those commandments and practical norms authoritatively declared by the Church. While recognizing the possible limitations of the human arguments employed by the Magisterium, moral theologians are called to develop a deeper understanding of the reasons underlying its teachings and to expound the validity and obligatory nature of the precepts it proposes, demonstrating their connection with one another and their relation with man's ultimate end. Moral theologians are to set forth the Church's teaching and to give, in the exercise of their ministry, the example of a loyal assent, both internal and external, to the Magisterium's teaching in the areas of both dogma and morality.[41]

This paragraph, as the footnotes indicate, merely reasserts Pius XII's declaration in *Humani Generis*:[42] the role of the theologian is to justify and to explain the moral assertions of the Magisterium. There is no indication that a theologian's findings, based on scholarly research, scientific discovery, or changes in history, might uncover teachings that are in need of revision or redefinition and which may, therefore, cause dissent. Since there have been no infallible teachings in the realm of morality such incorrect teachings are possible. In fact, many theologians and educated faithful following their consciences have found the magisterial teaching forbidding the use of artificial birth control highly questionable and the arguments presented to sustain it unconvincing, unsubstantiated, and against the dictates of right reason. The highest virtue for both theologians and faithful in the parental model is obedience to the Magisterium.

A third model is the responsible-dialogical model. Within this model both the Magisterium and conscience have different perceptions of themselves and their relation with the other. First, the Magisterium recognizes its authority guaranteed in and through the guidance of the Holy Spirit. This authority, however, is neither static nor absolute. It recognizes the tradition of the Church as a living tradition and its understanding of truth as an evolving understanding. The pilgrim Church is on a journey towards truth, guided by the finite servants who occupy magisterial offices. The Magisterium, like any other human institution, is a fallible institution. Though the Holy Spirit's guidance is promised to it, the journey towards truth is more of a meandering than a straight path. Because of this, the Magisterium is constantly in need of discovering the most adequate way to communicate the "deposit of faith" in light of "the signs of the times." It carries on this search in dialogue with theologians, the faithful, other Christian denominations, non-Christian religions, science, culture, and changing experience in order to communicate the contents of ongoing divine revelation. Since it is finite, by definition, the Magisterium can never be absolute. Except for those teachings which are clearly defined as infallible, the Magisterium recognizes its own limitations, its need to search constantly, and its call to be open to the infinite number of ways God communicates to God's people.

This view of authority finds support in *Lumen Gentium*.

> The holy people of God shares also in Christ's prophetic office. It spreads abroad a living witness to Him, especially by means of a life of faith and charity and by offering to God a sacrifice of praise, the tribute of lips which give honor to His name.... The body of the faithful as a whole, anointed as they are by the Holy One ... cannot err in matters of belief. Thanks to a supernatural sense of the faith which characterizes the People as a whole, it manifests this unerring quality when, "from the bishops down to the last member of the laity," it shows universal agreement in matters of faith and morals. For, by this sense of faith which is aroused and sustained by the Spirit of truth, God's People accepts not the word of men but the very Word of God ...[43]

Within the responsible-dialogical model, conscience has a unique function and the person has a serious responsibility to form and inform conscience.

The presumption is that conscience is not a child in relation to the parental Magisterium. Conscience, rather, is a mature adult who, with deep respect, consults the Magisterium as a trusted friend and guide in spiritual truth. As in any mature adult relationship, there is a mutual respect between the two partners. While the presumption of truth is in favor of the Magisterium and its teachings, there is still the possibility for questioning and disagreement that does not destroy the relationship but provides the challenge and possibility of growth for both.

This model of conscience finds support also in *Dignitatis Humanae* 14. "The Christian faithful *ought carefully to attend to* the sacred and certain doctrine of the Church."[44] It is interesting to note that it was suggested that the phrase, "ought carefully to attend to," be emended to read, "ought to form their consciences according to," and that this suggestion was rejected by the Theological Commission. The Commission argued that "the proposed formula seems excessively restrictive; the obligation binding on the faithful is sufficiently expressed in the text as it stands."[45] Given what the Council had said elsewhere concerning conscience and its authority, it seems that the Theological Commission recognized that, while it is important for Catholics to give serious consideration to the non-infallible teachings of the Magisterium in the formation of their consciences, there are other sources which may come into conflict with those teachings. In such cases, a Catholic must presume in favor of the Magisterium unless there is overwhelming scientific or theological evidence, or a general experience of the Church that challenges those teachings. If such challenges develop overwhelming evidence against magisterial teachings, then dialogue must follow so that all the faithful, hierarchy, and theologians may come to a deeper understanding of the issues and discern the guidance of the Holy Spirit. This dialogue must reflect the Gospel charity that binds the community of believers.

In the responsible-dialogical model, then, there is a healthy and mutual respect between conscience and the Magisterium in the ongoing search for truth. This model is clearly formulated in *Gaudium et Spes*. Recognizing the needs of a credible Church in a culture of pluralistic ideologies, the document asserts that "all those who compose the one People of God, both pastors and the general faithful, can engage in dialogue with ever abounding fruitfulness. For the bonds which unite the faithful are mightier than anything which divides them."[46] The virtues in this model are responsibility for the formation of conscience, accountability of the Magisterium to those consciences, and respectful and charitable dialogue between the two in the ongoing search for truth and expression in the current socio-historical context.

A fourth model of the relationship between conscience and authority, the individualistic conscience, seems to be the concern voiced in *Splendor of Truth*. In this model, the voice of the Magisterium is seen as one among many competing and equal voices to which the conscience must give ear. It is up to the individual to decide what is or is not important for conscience formation. The Magisterium's concern with this model is that the individual's decision is not based on a sense of community guided by the Gospel imperative to love God, neighbor, and self; conscience formation here is guided by focus on the individual in isolation utilizing the principle of personal preference. Though a temptation in a pluralistic, secularized, individualistic society, this model is unacceptable for the Catholic Christian. The Magisterium is not just another authority for conscience formation; it is a *religious* authority. As such, it is to be trusted because Christ has promised that he will not abandon his Church to error.[47] Those who are in positions of authority within the Church have been promised the guidance of the Holy Spirit, and it is this fundamental truth that does not allow the individual conscience to view the authority of the Magisterium as but one authority among others. The individualistic model, though a temptation in our social, cultural, historical milieu, is not a viable option for Catholics.

Of the four models, the two which are most prevalent in the present climate of the Church are the parental and responsible-dialogical models. Both models function to maintain a balance of perspectives and to challenge the views of the other, lest one model presume that it holds the "definitive truth." Problems arise, however, when either model asserts the "moral high ground" and accuses the other of being morally inferior, less committed to the faith, or heretical in its assertions. In a pluralist Church where the interpretation of Revelation is a dynamic and ongoing process, there must be room for different models of interpretation. The two models can coexist in a healthy tension guided by charitable dialogue and an openness to the Holy Spirit, whose voice can come as easily from one camp as the other. As the faithful, theologians and the Magisterium continue to debate and discuss the relationship between the Magisterium and the individual conscience, let the words of the Second Vatican Council guide the ongoing dialogue: "let there be unity in what is necessary, freedom in what is unsettled, and charity in any case."[48]

NOTES

1. *Gaudium et Spes*, 41; *Dei Verbum*, 201-03. These documents will be cited hereafter as *GS* and *DV* respectively.

2. See most recently Pope John Paul II's addition of new norms to canon law. "The purpose of the new norms is to impose expressly the duty to preserve the truths proposed definitively by the Magisterium of the Church and to institute canonical sanctions concerning the same manner" (*Ad Tuendam Fidem*, *Origins*, 28 (July 16, 1998), 113.

3. Joseph Komonchak, "Authority and Magisterium," in *Vatican Authority and American Catholic Dissent*, ed. William W. May (New York: Crossroad, 1987), 103-05.

4. For an historical account of the evolution of the term 'Magisterium,' see Yves Congar, O.P., "A Semantic History of the Term 'Magisterium,'" in *Readings in Moral Theology No. 3: The Magisterium and Morality*, eds. Charles E. Curran and Richard A. McCormick (New York: Paulist, 1982), 297-313.

5. Heinrich Denzinger, *Enchiridion Symbolorum* (Fribourg: Herder, 1947, 26th ed.), 1839.

6. *Lumen Gentium*, 25. Hereafter cited as *LG*. DV, 48.

7. *The Code of Canon Law: A Text and Commentary*, ed. James A. Coriden, Thomas J. Green, and Donald E. Heintschel (New York: Paulist, 1985), 547.

8. Francis A. Sullivan, *Magisteruim: Teaching Authority in the Catholic Church* (New York: Paulist, 1983), 154-55.

9. LG, 25; DV, 48.

10. Daniel Maguire, "Morality and Magisterium," in *Readings in Moral Theology No 3*, 36.

11. *Summa Theologiae* I-II, 94, 4. Hereafter cited as *ST*.

12. Maguire, "Morality and Magisterium," 36.

13. *The Code of Canon Law*, c. 739, §3, 547.

14. William E. May, "Catholic Moral Teaching and the Limits of Dissent," in *Vatican Authority and American Catholic Dissent*, 95.

15. Richard A. McCormick, *Notes on Moral Theology: 1965 through 1980* (Washington, DC: University Press of America, 1981), 221.

16. Ibid.

17. LG, 25; DV, 47.

18. GS, 3; DV, 200-01.

19. Ibid., 16; DV, 213-14.

20. ST, I-II, 94, 2.

21. *Veritatis Splendor*, 62, 95. Hereafter cited as *VS*.

22. Ibid., 63, (emphasis in original).

23. Ibid., 64, (emphasis in original).

24. *Dignitatis Humanae*, 14. Hereafter cited as *DH*. DV, 694-95.

25. LG, 25; DV, 47-8: "Bishops, teaching in communion with the Roman Pontiff, are to be respected by all as witnesses to divine and Catholic truth. In matters of faith and morals, the bishops speak in the name of Christ and the faithful are to accept their teaching and adhere to it with a religious assent of soul."

26. B. C. Butler, "Infallible, Authenticum, Assensus, Obsequium: Christian Teaching Authority and the Christian's Response," *Doctrine and Life* 31 (1981), 82-87.

27. Sullivan, *Magisteruim*, 159.

28. Ibid., 164.

29. Ibid., 166. See Richard McCormick, *Notes on Moral Theology; 1981 Through 1984* (Lanham, MD: University Press of America, 1984), 191.

30. Butler, "Infallible," 83.

31. Sullivan, *Magisterium*, 160, citing John Henry Newman, *An Essay in Aid of a Grammar of Assent*, ed. N. Lash (Notre Dame, IN: University of Notre Dame Press, 1979), 148.

32. Sullivan, *Magisterium*, 160.

33. Ibid., 161.

34. *The Code of Canon Law*, c. 752, 548. Emphasis added.

35. See Charles E. Curran, "Authority and Dissent in the Roman Catholic Church," in *Vatican Authority and American Catholic Dissent*, 28-9.

36. *The Code of Canon Law*, 548.

37. Butler, "Infallible," 87-8.

38. *VS*, 27, 44 (emphasis in original omitted).

39. See Sullivan for his view that the correct interpretation of *authenticum* is authoritatively, not authentically, *Magisterium*, 26-8.

40. *VS*, 4, 8-9.

41. Ibid., 110, 165.

42. Pius XII, *Humani Generis*, *Acta Apostolicea Sedis* 42 (1950), 567-69.

43. LG, 12; DV, 29-30.

44. DH, 14; DV, 694-95. Emphasis added.

45. *Acta synodalia councilii oecumenici Vaticani II* 4/6 (Vatican City: Typis polygolottis Vaticanis, 1978), 769. Cited in Richard A. McCormick, *Notes on Moral Theology: 1981 Through 1984*, 191-92.

46. GS, 92; DV, 306. See also footnote 274 which points out the aim of Pope John to attain true dialogue, and Pope Paul's contribution that spelled out the nature and scope of such a dialogue.

47. Joseph Komonchak, "Authority and Magisterium," 110-11.

48. GS, 92; DV, 306.

Imaging the Formation of a Peacemaker: A Franciscan-Ignatian Dialogue

Joan M. Mueller

In the struggle to reconcile persons, cultures, and nations, Christianity claims it has something to say. When violence escalates, diplomacy fails, and systems theorists slink away, Christian pastors are often called upon and expected to be effective. The Christian theologian charged with the task of training pastoral persons to preach and teach finds little systematic work outlining Christian theologies of reconciliation. Historically, the soteriological focus has been placed upon recapitulation, atonement and, more recently, liberation. While the *Roman Rite of Penance* has a communal form of reconciliation, which is intended to address humanity.''s compliance with social sin,[1] pastoral application of the sacrament continues to emphasize individual rather than communal responsibility.

What might systematic theology have to offer Christian pastors called upon to be leaders in efforts of reconciliation? Are there historical figures who have survived war and violence, attempted reconciliation, and succeeded?

On the surface, successful instances of Christian reconciliation seem scanty. If Jesus tried to reform Judaism to avert disaster, his message of peace seems to have utterly failed. Early Christians proclaiming the peace of Christ were at times seen as enemies of the empire and were martyred for their trouble. Upon preaching to the Sultan, St. Francis returned from the Crusades distraught, sickened, and eventually stigmatized by his failure to reconcile the East and his own brothers. The evangelical fervor of primitive discipleship proposed by the Protestant Reformers reduced Europe to religious warfare and heresy. The reconciliation efforts of Archbishop Oscar Romero in El Salvador left him gunned down, his blood poured out while celebrating Eucharist.

The track record of Christianity appears easily summarized: reconcilers fail and often die. Accompanying these deaths, however, is a concept of resurrection. In one of his last sermons, Archbishop Romero expressed the Christian hope succinctly. Knowing that there was a contract out for his murder, he proclaimed: "If I am killed, I shall arise in the Salvadoran people."[2] In a country so torn by fighting that the emotions of the masses were sickened and numbed, Romero's was a strange hope. Even if Romero did arise in the Salvadoran people, what does this hope mean, and why might a theologian or anyone else care?

Elsewhere I have examined the role of forgiveness in the Christian experience of suffering and martyrdom.[3] The aim of this essay is to examine the identity and formation of the Christian peacemaker. In particular, I address the practical question: How might one outline the development of a Christian peacemaker? To formulate such an outline, I will study the journeys of two great and unique Christians, Francis of Assisi and Ignatius of Loyola.

Celano, Francis' first biographer, says of Francis' preaching:

In all his preaching, before he proposed the Word of God to those gathered about, he first prayed for peace for them, saying: "The Lord give you peace." He always most devoutly announced peace to men and women, to all he met and overtook. For this reason many who had hated peace and had hated also salvation embraced peace, through the cooperation of the Lord, with all their heart and were made children of peace and seekers after eternal salvation.[4]

While contemporaries focus on peace processes, medievals focused on a choice of Christian discipleship involving peacemaking. This peace was formed in the individual's heart and life, and then erupted into the greater society. Societies could be at peace when the holy person, the peace-filled person, was in their midst. Rather than degrees or certificates documenting skills and competencies, medieval peacemakers embraced a penitential program and struggled mainly with the violence and duplicity of their own hearts. Fidelity to the penitential program helped them evolve into disciples whose presence brought the grace of peace to those searching for it.

Given the duplicity of the human heart, the anger and at times rage within, and the difficulty of preaching anything not only with words but also with the integrity of one's life, how does Francis find the inner resources and confidence to consistently proclaim peace? A fallen knight, Francis, like Ignatius, begins his conversion wounded and disillusioned by war. As a result of disillusionment, both Francis and Ignatius seek remedy in the medieval penitential tradition,[5] a peace movement.[6] Both find in their penitential lifestyles[7] the grace to be at peace with themselves, others, and the cosmos. Might contemporaries discover in their legacies the path to peace?

A mutual reading of Ignatian and Franciscan sources is a better avenue for reconstructing medieval penitential foundations for a formative theology of reconciliation than an independent reading. Compared with Ignatius' *Spiritual Exercises*, Franciscan sources only sketch the penitential programs of Francis' early life. Franciscan literature, however, describes more fully the mature fruits of the penitential lifestyle. Held together, the Franciscan and Ignatian sources offer fuller insight into a program for the formation of pastoral peacemakers.

THE FRANCISCAN ROOTS OF IGNATIAN SPIRITUALITY

While the persons of Ignatius of Loyola and Francis of Assisi are often presented as polemic, the two have much in common. Ewert Cousins captures their similarity:

> Franciscans and Jesuits stand closer together than either group does to the Dominicans. This common ground is devotion to the humanity of Christ, which in each case flowered in meditation on the life of Christ. Both groups developed a Christocentric spirituality that looked back to the historical events of Christ's life as its point of departure. In this perspective, the Jesuits can be seen to be heirs of a tradition that was originally developed by the Franciscans in the thirteenth century, which was transmitted to subsequent centuries largely through Franciscan channels. Although Franciscan in origin and transmission, this tradition so permeated the religious sensibility of Western Christianity that it became a dominant feature of European culture as a whole.[8]

Ignatius himself admits Franciscan influence. In his *Autobiography*, he reports that, while he was recovering from his war injury, he sought some reading material, and was given a life of Christ and Jacobus de Voragine's *The Golden Legend*. He adds that his first understanding of the discernment of spirits came to him as a result of this reading:

> Nevertheless Our Lord assisted him, by causing these thoughts to be followed by others which arose from the things he read. For in reading the life of Our Lord and of the saints, he stopped to think, reasoning within himself, "What if I should do what St. Francis did, and what St. Dominic did?" Thus he pondered over many things that he found good, always proposing to himself what was difficult and burdensome; and as he so proposed, it seemed easy for him to accomplish it. But he did no more than argue within himself, saying, "St. Dominic did this, therefore I have to do it; St. Francis did this, therefore I have to do it."[9]

The Golden Legend's account of the life of St. Francis is filled with historical information, legends, and characteristic Voraginian interpretation. It is easy to see why Ignatius, the wounded soldier, immediately identified with St. Francis. Voragine writes, "Francis became a merchant and, until he was twenty years old, lived a vain and frivolous life. The Lord chastened him with the whip of ill health and quickly made a different man of him ..."[10]

The *Autobiography* reports further the content of Ignatius' imaginings.

> When he was thinking of those things of the world he took much delight in them, but afterwards, when he was tired and put them aside, he found himself dry and dissatisfied. But when he thought of going to Jerusalem barefoot, and of eating nothing but plain vegetables and of practicing all the other rigors that he saw in the saints, not only was he consoled when he had these thoughts, but even after putting them aside he remained satisfied and joyful.[11]

What is interesting about this account is that neither Voragine's life of St. Francis nor of St. Dominic present either saint as going to Jerusalem or as being vegetarians. Ignatius' imaginings were obviously affected by a legendary climate, reinforced more by his experiences of local penitential practices than by a careful reading of Voragine. That Ignatius' concept of the holy life had to do with making a pilgrimage to Jerusalem and with living a penitential lifestyle is articulated again in the *Autobiography*. "At this point the desire to imitate the saints came to him, though he gave no thought to details, only promising with God's grace to do as they had done. But the one thing he wanted to do was to go to Jerusalem as soon as he recovered, as mentioned above, with as much of disciplines and fasts as a generous spirit, fired with God, would want to perform."[12]

Ignatius does go to Jerusalem and encounters the Franciscans who take care of the sacred places. His zeal to see the holy sites concerns the Franciscans who worry that his indiscretions may precipitate his capture by the Turks and force the Franciscans to pay his ransom. The Franciscan provincial has to resort to threats.

> Ignatius frankly gave them to understand that even though the provincial thought otherwise, if there was nothing binding him under sin, he would not abandon his intention out of any fear. To this the provincial replied that they had authority from the Apostolic See to have anyone leave the place, or remain there, as they judged, and to excommunicate anyone who was unwilling to obey them; and in this case they thought he should not remain, and so forth.[13]

By 1523, the Franciscans were institutionalized, committed to their various ministries, and had little patience for individualized penitential zeal. Ignatius, on the other hand, was a man in his early thirties, whose youthful dream had been shattered. He discerned his second direction with mature care, if not with balanced prudence. Returning from Jerusalem he began his studies, modified his penitential lifestyle, and continued to discern God's will while praying the texts of the Gospel. His gift to the church, the *Spiritual Exercises*, records in manual form the basic outlines of the penitential program. While followers of Francis have to rely upon hagiography to piece together his penitential practices, Ignatius outlines the journey so that all might follow.

What is obvious in the journeys of both Francis and Ignatius is that neither undertook the penitential journey for the explicit purpose of becoming a peacemaker. Becoming something was not their objective. What both were searching for was a personal experience of Jesus Christ guided by the Gospels and the sacramental practices of the church. Through fidelity to this focus, they became peacemakers. Peacemaking was an outcome of discipleship. Francis states in Admonition XV. "Blessed are the peace-makers, for they shall be called the children of God (Matt 5:9). The true peacemakers are those who preserve peace of mind and body for love of our Lord Jesus Christ, despite what they suffer in this world."[14] The reason for preserving peace of mind and body is important. The medieval penitent was interested in relationship, not product; conversion was prized over success. The Christian who pursues the art of peacemaking for its own sake, will come up empty.

In *Admonition VII*, Francis describes the difference between the true disciple and the actor.

> The Apostle says: The letter kills, but the spirit gives life (2 Cor 3:6). Those are killed by the letter who merely wish to know the words alone, so that they may be esteemed as wiser than others and be able to acquire great riches to give to relatives and friends. In a similar way, those religious are killed by the letter who do not wish to follow the spirit of Sacred Scripture, but only wish to know the words and interpret them to others. And those are given life by the spirit of Sacred Scripture who do not refer to themselves any text which they know or seek to know, but, by word and example, return everything to the most high Lord God to Whom every good belongs.[15]

THE PENITENT AS CREATURE BEFORE THE CREATOR

How does one open oneself to the possibility of becoming a Christian peacemaker? Ignatius outlines his journey of discipleship in four dynamics which he terms *weeks*. The first begins with "The Principle and Foundation," an exercise which places the penitent as creature before the Creator. In pondering God's unconditional love and order, one discovers one's own apathy and disorder. Spiritual practices such as the conscious-ness examine, general confession, fasting, and other corporal penances are recommended. The meditations focus first on the fall of the angels, then on the fall of other people, and finally upon one's own sin. Ignatius carefully outlines for the penitent the application of the senses and of the imagination to the meditation material. Francis returns from war disillusioned, prays in caves, fasts, strips before the bishop, and puts on the garment of a hermit, but the further particulars of his spiritual journey are not fully revealed. Ignatius spells out his penitential journey in detail, allowing readers not only to observe it through his *Autobiography*, but also to experience the journey themselves through the *Spiritual Exercises*.

What cues can be drawn from Ignatius' *First Week* for the pastoral formation of a peacemaker? First, any penitential program must be rooted in the unconditional love of God and the reality of human creaturehood, the root of humility. Second, one cannot be a disciple, a Christian peacemaker, without addressing the reality of sin, particularly one's own. To be a penitent means that one searches one's heart and life meticulously, examining its nooks and crevices in order to access one's vulnerabilities.[16]

Ignatius needed to learn to balance the experience of God's love with this meticulous examination. To ponder sin without the experience of love leaves one with the burden of scruples. To fail to examine oneself honestly and meticulously sentences one to disillusionment. An unconscious do-gooder can be a dangerous person. To be a disciple of Jesus, to be a Christian peacemaker, means that one knows oneself as one is before God. Francis states in *Admonition XIX*: "Blessed is the servant who esteems himself no better when he is praised and exalted by people than when he is considered worthless, simple, and despicable; for what one is before God, that one is and nothing more."[17]

THE PENITENT AS DISCIPLE

Franciscan hagiography outlines Francis' life as the faithful following of Jesus Christ culminating in the stigmata. The portrayal of Francis as the *alter Christus* is intensified in the later lives, especially in 2 Celano and in the work of Bonaventure.[18] Exactly how the following of the Gospel is a map of discipleship is not systematically outlined in the Franciscan sources. Saint Clare describes the journey by means of three meditations on the mirror who Christ is:

> Look at the border of this mirror, that is, the poverty of Him Who was placed in a manger and wrapped in swaddling clothes.... Then, at the surface of the mirror, consider the holy humility, the blessed poverty, the untold labors and burdens that He endured for the redemption of the whole human race. Then, in the depth of this

same mirror, contemplate the ineffable charity that led Him to suffer on the wood of the Cross and to die there the most shameful kind of death.[19]

According to Clare, the Christian appropriates Gospel discipleship by contemplating the birth, public life, and crucifixion. Ignatius outlines the same contemplative program. In the *Second Week*, he reserves his exercises to meditations on the birth and public life. In the *Third Week* he outlines the discipleship needed to accompany Christ to his death.

One meditates one's way through the incarnation, nativity, baptism of the Lord, the call of the disciples, the Sermon on the Mount, the raising of Lazarus, and Palm Sunday. Other meditations can be added or subtracted as a director sees fit, but the basic idea is that the believer meditates with ever increasing intensity on the quality of discipleship. In the midst of these meditations, Ignatius inserts non-biblical exercises. Like Christ's prophecies of his own passion, the non-biblical meditations catch one short. Just as disciples become happy with their discipleship, a challenge is issued. They are invited to ponder what they really want in the following of Jesus, what kind of disciples they really are, and the quality of their humility. They are instructed to involve their physicality in discipleship through the application of the senses, and their everyday business is challenged in the process of making an election.

Election is core to the *Second Week*. In the following of Christ, one has to make decisions not only as to whether one will follow or not, but also concerning the character and quality of one's following. The Christian's following must be in line with her or his vocational identity making the self-knowledge of the *First Week* important. The depth of love is tested in the election process and will be more fully revealed in the *Third Week*.

THE PENITENT AS CRUCIFIED

It is particularly valuable in Ignatius' *Third* and *Fourth* Weeks to read the *Spiritual Exercises* and the hagiography of St. Francis in tandem. As disciples meditate on the passion of Christ, Ignatius asks them to pray for the following grace. "The third prelude is to ask for what I desire. Here it is what is proper for the Passion: sorrow with Christ in sorrow; a broken spirit with Christ so broken; tears; and interior suffering because of the great suffering which Christ endured for me."[20] This grace confounds the majority of retreatants. Why would anyone want to pray for the grace of sorrow, anguish, tears, and interior suffering?

Celano's description of Francis' desire before receiving the stigmata is similar. "Filled with the Spirit of God, he was ready to suffer every distress of mind and to bear every bodily torment, if only his wish might be granted, and that the will of the Father in heaven might be mercifully fulfilled in him."[21] Francis rises and takes the book of the scriptures from the altar. The passion of our Lord Jesus Christ was the first thing that met his eye, and that part of it that said he would suffer tribulation.[22] Francis opens the book two more times and this same message of suffering tribulation is confirmed. Celano reports. "Then the man filled with the Spirit of God understood that it was for him to enter the kingdom of God through many tribulations, many trials, and many struggles."[23]

Although primarily a legendary source, *The Little Flowers of St. Francis* gives an interesting account of Francis' spiritual preparation for the stigmata. Staged almost like Francis' annunciation, the story illustrates the desire for *Third Week* grace:

> The day before the Feast of the Cross in September, while Francis was praying secretly in his cell, an angel appeared to him and said on God's behalf: "I encourage you and urge you to prepare and dispose yourself humbly to receive with all patience what God wills to do in you." Francis answered: "I am prepared to endure patiently whatever my Lord wants to do to me." And after he said this, the angel departed. The next day ... , St. Francis prayed in this way: "My Lord Jesus Christ, I pray You to grant me two graces before I die: the first is that during my life I may feel in my soul and in my body, as much as possible, that pain which You, dear Jesus, sustained in the hour of Your most bitter Passion. The second is that I may feel in my heart, as much as possible, that excessive love with which You, O Son of God, were inflamed in willingly enduring such suffering for us sinners."[24]

Why would a Christian take Ignatius' suggestion and pray for the grace of sorrow, anguish, tears and interior suffering, or for Francis' grace of pain in soul and body and the heartache of love? Ignatius gives us a clue in one of his non-biblical meditations on three ways of being humble in the

Second Week. Regarding the third way of being humble, he says: "... in order to imitate Christ our Lord better and to be more like him here and now, I desire and choose poverty with Christ poor rather than wealth; contempt with Christ laden with it rather than honors. Even further, I desire to be regarded as a useless fool for Christ, who before me was regarded as such, rather than as a wise or prudent person in this world."[25]

It is possible to pray the scriptures of the passion with a *Second Week* grace and still be a good Christian.[26] One can look from afar, run away, even deny, and still be loved and forgiven during resurrection time. The Christian masses, for the most part, will not opt for radical solidarity with Christ. Yet, for anyone who wishes to become a peacemaker, who wishes that his or her ministry might possess a quality and an authority of one truly united with Christ, solidarity with Christ in Christ's passion is necessary. Every election brings with it both sorrow and joy. For Christians who choose to move out of the world of honor, glory, and riches and into a lifestyle of truth, peace, and respect for all, there will be ridicule, mockery, and trial. While the world of riches and honor might find them contemptible or might render them invisible, the religious world will find them dangerous and extreme. They experience in the *Third Week* not only the apathy of the rich but also the wrath of the religious. Since it is religion that introduced them to Christ and nurtured their journey, the wrath of their religious companions can be particularly devastating.

In embracing the crucified Christ, Franciscan sources consistently remind us that poverty and humility are necessary. Luxurious living and the following of the crucified Christ are difficult to reconcile in both the Franciscan and Ignatian minds. Asceticism by itself is not enough. The disciple also needs to be humble, to be who one is before God without the usual puffing up that is so much a part of having places of power and honor. Without this humility, even asceticism can lure one into haughtiness and violence. Peacemakers learn to make their home upon or under the crucifix. Because they are poor, they have nothing to defend; because they are humble, their self-esteem cannot be injured; because their joy is grounded in sorrow, it cannot be deflated; because they have embraced their Beloved who suffers pain and anguish, they take comfort in solidarity.

In the *Third Week*, love of God becomes love of neighbor. Christians can truly love others when their possessions, self-interest, and pride are given second place to the grace of solidarity. This dynamic is not totally alien to relational understanding. A parent stays with a sick child in a hospital room and sometimes sacrifices financial security, reputation, and opportunities, not because the child might not be cared for but simply to be with the child in his time of pain. In doing this, the parent chooses pain, suffering and heartache for the purpose of solidarity. Only love can explain such choices; only love can explain the prayers of Francis and Ignatius. Love can be expressed in ways other than solidarity, but the deepest love wishes to unite itself with the beloved.

FROM CRUCIFIXION TO REALIZED ESCHATOLOGY

While most might imagine the movement into poverty and humility as the most difficult dynamic of the penitential journey, the movement into peace and joy is even more challenging. When Christians have experienced a profound loss or grief, when they have been betrayed or have lost resources, friends, and even religious support, choosing joy and peace is a discipline. They have to find new reasons to hope, to love, and to trust. In doing so, they need to find new sources of joy and serenity. It is hard to get their minds around this new world. They find themselves on the road to Emmaus with profound disillusionment and disheartened questions.

Complicating this, eschatological peace and joy is a grace. The Lord rises in the Lord's time. Christians are not rescued from the depths of the pain, suffering, and at times even violence of the *Third Week* as soon as they grow tired. The solidarity embraced in the *Third Week* carves out the capacity for peace and joy. The Christian who has most profoundly understood, wept with, waited upon, and stood with the suffering, terror, betrayal, confusion, and anguish of the crucified Christ finds joy and peace in the resurrected vision. This vision is a strange one; Christ is not initially recognized; he comes and goes. He promises the Spirit, but leaves the disciple lonely. It is no wonder that many retreatants enter the *Fourth Week* wondering if the destination was worth the journey.

In the midst of meditating on the resurrected Christ, Ignatius asks the penitent to pray for this grace. "Here it will be to ask for the grace to be glad and to rejoice intensely because of the great glory and joy of Christ our Lord."[27] When contemplating divine Love, he recommends this grace. "Here it will be to ask for interior knowledge of all the great good I have received, in order that, stirred to profound gratitude, I may become able to love and serve his Divine Majesty in all things."[28] The *Exercises* end abruptly here, leaving the follower to flounder in this new land of resurrection with the still poignant wounds in heart, mind, and body. Ignatius hints that the heart should be filled with joy and gratitude, but the writer who laid out careful meditations and exercises for opening self up to the desired grace now suddenly leaves with only the barest instructions in a strange land.

Here the Franciscan sources are most helpful. Franciscan writings and hagiographical sources portray what it is like to live as a human being with the limitations that humanness implies, the beginnings of eschatological joy and peace, presented as both a task and a grace. Celano insists that Francis maintained peace and joy and describes how he did it:

> The saint, therefore, made it a point to keep himself in joy of heart and to preserve the unction of the Spirit and the oil of gladness. He avoided with the greatest care the miserable illness of dejection, so that if he felt it creeping over his mind even a little, he would have recourse very quickly to prayer. For he would say "If the servant of God, as may happen, is disturbed in any way, he should rise immediately to pray and he should remain in the presence of the heavenly Father until he restores unto him the joy of salvation. For if he remains stupified in sadness, the Babylonian stuff will increase, so that, unless it be at length driven out by tears, it will generate an abiding rust in the heart."

He adds further illustration of Francis' insistence upon preserving spiritual happiness:

> So much, however, did he love a person who was full of spiritual happiness that he had these words written down as an admonition to all at a certain general chapter. "Let the brothers beware lest they show themselves outwardly gloomy and sad hypocrites; but let them show themselves joyful in the Lord, cheerful and suitably gracious."[29]

According to *The Mirror of Perfection*, 96:8-9, there are some behaviors that do not signify spiritual happiness. "It should not be imagined that Francis, who loved mature and reputable behavior, wished this happiness to be shown in levity or vain words, for these things are not evidence of spiritual happiness but of vanity and folly."[30] *The Mirror* contains some practical advice as to how one might possess and preserve spiritual happiness:

> He used to say, "... since this spiritual joy springs from the cleanness of heart and the purity of constant prayer, it must be your first concern to acquire and preserve these two virtues, so as to possess this inward joy that I so greatly desire and love to see both in you and myself, and which edify our neighbor and reproach our enemy. For it is the lot of the Devil and his minions to be sorrowful, but ours always to be happy and rejoice in the Lord."[31]

Christians are able to invite the grace of resurrected joy by keeping their hearts clean through constant prayer. *Admonition XVI* demonstrates that these two elements are connected. "Blessed are the pure of heart, for they shall see God (Matt 5:8). The truly pure of heart are those who despise the things of earth and seek the things of heaven, and who never cease to adore and behold the Lord God living and true with a pure heart and soul."[32] The one who is pure of heart fosters a spirit worthy of eschatological glory and engages in constant prayer.

THE FORMATION OF THE PASTORAL PEACEMAKER

What might this introduction to reading the *Spiritual Exercises* in conjunction with Franciscan sources teach us about the formation of a pastoral peacemaker? Three points might be made. First, the goal of all Christian discipleship is the following of Jesus Christ, not the attainment of an ideal. Christians become peacemakers because Jesus was a person of peace. Generously embracing gospel discipleship, while developing peacemaking skills and strategies is core to what makes the Christian an effective peacemaker. Second, in accepting discipleship Christians suspect that their peacemaking will be challenged, ridiculed, and even undermined by good people. They need, therefore, to surrender their anger, frustration, and rage at the foot of the cross, begging for Christ's forgiveness and mercy. The road of discipleship is a path that shatters illusions and delusions. Christian peacemakers are bearers of reality precisely because they are who they are before God, nothing more and nothing less. Third, the gift of peace is both a grace and a task of living the constant worship and innocence of eschatological glory. To enter into the poverty and humility of crucifixion without keeping firm faith, constant prayer, and a tender heart is to subject oneself to violence without hope. The peacemaker enters into Francis' *Canticle of the Creatures* in union with the crucified Christ. Infirmity, tribulation, and the need for forgiving others are accepted as part of the human condition. "Praised be You, my Lord, through those who give pardon for your love and bear infirmity and tribulation. Blessed are those who endure in peace for by You, Most High, they shall be crowned."[33]

Francis and Ignatius became peacemakers because they committed themselves radically to following Jesus Christ. In doing this, they became peaceful with the glories and limitations of the human condition. Their relationships with others projected the peace that was rooted in their hearts, a peace whose maturity inspired others to peace. Franciscan and Ignatian penitential formation, while not always guaranteeing successful peacemaking, encourages the evangelical honesty of Christian reconciling efforts and the integrity of the peacemaking character.

NOTES

1. See Annibale Bugnini, *The Reform of the Liturgy 1948-1975*, trans. Matthew J. O'Connell (Collegeville: The Liturgical Press, 1990), 664-83.

2. Reported by José Calderón Salazar, Guatemalan correspondent of the Mexican newspaper *Excelsior* as taken from a telephone interview with Romero two weeks before his death. Quoted in James R. Brockman, *Romero: A Life* (Maryknoll, NY: Orbis Books, 1990), 248.

3. See Joan Mueller, *Is Forgiveness Possible?* (Collegeville: The Liturgical Press, 1998).

4. 1 Celano 23:74-75. Passages from *First and Second Celano* used in this essay are taken from Marion A. Habig, ed., *St. Francis of Assisi: Writings and Early Biographies* (Chicago: Franciscan Herald Press, 1973).

5. For further information on St. Francis as a penitent and on the early Franciscan penitential movement see Raffaele Pazzelli, *St. Francis and the Third Order* (Chicago: Franciscan Herald Press, 1989), 87-154. Ignatius' *Autobiography* [9] states: "From this lesson he derived not a little light, and he began to think more earnestly about his past life and about the great need he had to do penance for it. At this point the desire to imitate the saints came to him, though he gave no thought to details, only promising with God's grace to do as they had done." The *Auto-*

biography [12] states Ignatius' intent was to be a penitent and to attach himself as an oblate to a monastery, a common penitential lifestyle. "And taking stock of what he might do after he returned from Jerusalem, so he could always live as a penitent, he thought he might enter the Carthusian house in Seville, without saying who he was, so that they would make little of him; and there never to eat anything but plain vegetables." In *Ignatius of Loyola: Spiritual Exercises and Selected Works*, ed. George E. Ganss, S.J. (New York: Paulist Press, 1991). All further references to the *Autobiography* will be taken from this volume.

6. Those who declared themselves penitents could not pursue military careers, bear arms, participate in military endeavors, or take oaths of loyalty to feudal lords or to civil authorities. The *Memoriale Propositi* for Franciscan penitents of 1228 reads: "All are to refrain from formal oaths unless where necessity compels, in the cases excepted by the sovereign pontiff in his indult, that is, for peace, for the faith, under calumny, and in bearing witness." Pazzelli, *St. Francis and the Third Order*, 134.

7. Pazzelli outlines the disciplinary elements of the penitential lifestyle: (1) a characteristic dress; a habit of penance; (2) dedication to a charitable works mostly in hospitals, pilgrim hostels, and leprosaria; (3) prayer; (4) norms for continency, usually absolute for single penitents and periodic for the married; (5) prohibition to engage in certain types of public entertainment, dances, and banquets; (6) prohibition to serve in public offices; (7) ineligibility for military careers, Ibid., 39-40.

8. "Franciscan Roots of Ignatian Meditation," in *Ignatian Spirituality in a Secular Age*, ed. George P. Schner (Ontario: Wilfrid Laurier University Press, 1984), 51-2.

9. *Autobiography*, 7.

10. Jacobus de Voragine, *The Golden Legend: Readings on the Saints*, Vol. II, trans. William Granger Ryan (Princeton: Princeton University Press, 1993), 220.

11. *Autobiography*, 8.

12. Ibid., 9.

13. Ibid., 46.

14. The *Admonitions* of St. Francis are found in *Francis and Clare: The Complete Works*, ed. Regis J. Armstrong, (New York: Paulist Press, 1982), 25-36. All further references to the *Admonitions* will be taken from this volume with inclusive language added. For further commentary on *Admonition* XV see: Theo Zweerman, "Jesus' Word: 'Blessed Are the Peacemakers' In the Interpretation of St. Francis," *Greyfriars Review* 9:1 (1995): 39-60.

15. Armstrong, *Francis and Clare*, 30.

16. Rule I:14 of Ignatius' *Rules for Discernment* addresses the need to understand one's vulnerabilities: "To use still another comparison, the enemy acts like a military commander who is attempting to conquer and plunder his objective. The captain and leader of an army on campaign sets up his camp, studies the

strength and structure of a fortress, and then attacks at its weakest point. In the same way, the enemy of human nature prowls around and from every side probes all our theological, cardinal, and moral virtues. Then at the point where he finds us weakest and most in need in regard to our eternal salvation, there he attacks and tries to take us." See the *Spiritual Exercises* [327], in *Ignatius of Loyola: Spiritual Exercises and Selected Works*. All further references to the *Spiritual Exercises* will be taken from this volume.

17. Armstrong, *Francis and Clare*, 33.

18. Noel Muscat, *The Life of Saint Francis in the Light of St. Bonaventure's Theology on the Verbum crucifixum* (Rome: Editrice Antonianum, 1989), 240-49.

19. From the *Fourth Letter of St. Clare of Assisi to St. Agnes of Prague* [19, 22-3], in *Clare of Assisi: Early Documents*, ed. and trans., Regis J. Armstrong, OFM Cap (St. Bonaventure, NY: Franciscan Institute Publications, 1993), 50-51.

20. *Spiritual Exercises* [193].

21. 1 Celano 92:20-1.

22. 1 Celano 93:24.

23. Ibid.

24. *The Little Flowers of St. Francis* is found in Habig, *St. Francis of Assisi*, 1448.

25. *Spiritual Exercises* [167].

26. For more on the dynamics of grace within the experience of *Spiritual Exercises*, see my article, "The Suscipe Revisited," *Review for Religious* 53 (1994): 534-43.

27. *Spiritual Exercises* [221].

28. Ibid., [223].

29. 2 Celano 125:1-6.

30. *The Mirror of Perfection* is found in Habig, *St. Francis of Assisi*, 1103ff.

31. Ibid., 95:9.

32. Armstrong, *Francis and Clare*, 32.

33. Translation taken from Ibid., 39.

Becoming One in the Spirit:
An Ecumenical Approach to Spirituality

Richard J. Hauser, S.J.

While teaching in our graduate program in Christian Spirituality I had an eye-opening experience. Among the 24 students enrolled in my course "Discernment of Spirits: Theory and Practice" were seven ordained Protestant ministers, two Lutherans, two Presbyterians, a Methodist, a Baptist, and a member of the United Church of Christ. I am used to having Protestants in my classes, but confess that the number and variety of denominations represented by the ordained ministers was intimidating. I asked them to let me know whenever I began talking in a way that sounded alien to their traditions. Rarely did anyone admit to being alienated; problems always involved terminology rather than fundamental theological concepts. The course went superbly and I am still reflecting on the implications for spirituality of this experience.

Over the years I have given presentations on spirituality to clergy and congregations from a variety of Protestant traditions. Several years ago I was invited to give a weekend workshop on discernment of spirits to the leaders of the religious judiciaries of the state of Iowa. Some twenty bishops, presbyters, and presidents attended this gathering. At no time did we encounter major theological disagreements on my topic. Within the past two years I had been privileged to give three extended weekend presentations to Lutheran clergy, twice with the Lutheran bishop of Nebraska present. Again, no problems arose. Annually I give workshops on spirituality to Protestant congregations, and I have often found myself joking with my Protestant audiences that they are more receptive to my insights than Roman Catholic audiences.

My experience leads me to assert that as far as spirituality is concerned, the Reformation conflict between Catholics and Protestants is over, at least for the main-line Reformation churches. This bold assertion is defensible only when Catholic spirituality flows from the renewed theological insights of the Second Vatican Council, which transformed my approach to spirituality. My transformation occurred through my understanding and appropriation, for the first time in my life, of the role of the Holy Spirit in Christian spirituality. Unknowingly, I was simultaneously echoing the classical Reformation themes of *Sola Gratia* and *Sola Scriptura*. These two terms imply, respectively, that the initiative for justification and all good works comes from the prior action of God's grace and that the foundation of every Christian belief must be contained in Scripture. It has been my experience that the renewed theology of the Holy Spirit speaks directly to both concerns.

This essay presents an approach to personal prayer and discernment of spirits compatible for Protestants with Reformation insights and for Catholics respecting the renewed theology of the Holy Spirit of the Second Vatican Council. My remarks fall into three parts—The Holy Spirit: Second Vatican Council and Reformation Themes; The Holy Spirit and Personal Prayer; and The Holy Spirit and Discernment of Spirits.

THE HOLY SPIRIT: SECOND VATICAN
COUNCIL AND REFORMATION THEMES

The Second Vatican Council profoundly affected many areas of Roman Catholic theology and practice, one of which is spirituality. To grasp the effect on Roman Catholic spirituality, it is necessary to understand the shifts in theological models of Church and of the self. Without these shifts in models, the ecumenical dimension of spirituality simply would not have been possible. I will describe these shifts and reflect on their relationship to classical Reformation themes in light of a renewed understanding of the role of the Holy Spirit.

The first theological shift relates to the understanding of the Church. In recent decades Roman Catholics have witnessed two differing, though complementary, models of Church. Each model assigns a distinctive role to the Holy Spirit. Since I am a Roman Catholic, I understand Church primarily in the context of my own tradition, but I have learned my insights are also applicable to Protestant traditions. In the first model the Holy Spirit is present in the Church, but the Church is seen primarily as an institution governed by hierarchical authority, for Catholics, priests, bishops, pope.

The Holy Spirit guides the institution through the hierarchy, which, especially through the local priest, guides the people. In the second model, the Second Vatican Council model, the Holy Spirit is present in the Church, the People of God, the entire community of believers united in one Body of Christ. While continuing to guide the Church corporately, the Holy Spirit also guides the members individually. The following excerpts from Chapter One of the *Dogmatic Constitution on the Church* highlight this truth elegantly:

> The Spirit dwells in the Church and in the hearts of the faithful as in a temple (cf. 1 Cor 3:16; 6:19). In them he prays and bears witness to the fact that they are adopted sons (cf. Gal 4:6; Rom 8: 15-16 and 26). The Spirit guides the Church into the fullness of truth (cf. John 16: 13) and gives her a unity of fellowship and service. He furnishes and directs her with various gifts, both hierarchical and charismatic, and adorns her with the fruits of His grace (cf. Eph 4: 11-12; 1 Cor 12:4; Gal 5: 22).

In order that we may be unceasing renewed in Him [Jesus] (cf. Eph 4: 23), He has shared with us His Spirit who, existing as one and the same being in the head and in the members, vivifies, unifies, and moves the whole body.[1]

This renewed Roman Catholic model of Church flows from Scripture, from the Old Testament model of the People of God and from the Pauline model of the Body of Christ. It is fully compatible with the *Sola Scriptura* theme of the Reformation. Both Catholics and Protestants agree that according to Scripture the Church, constituted by all those in whom the risen Jesus lives through faith and baptism, should not be solely identified with a hierarchical structure. Reformation theologians had bristled at a prior Roman Catholic model of the Church which reflected the hierarchical strata of medieval society and thereby undermined the full participation of every baptized Christian into the Body of Christ. Luther's famous *Treatise on Christian Liberty* presents his view that the priesthood of all believers flows from their baptism and relationship with Jesus:

> Now just as Christ by his birthright obtained these two prerogative [priesthood and kingship], so he imparts them to and shares them with everyone who believes in him.... Hence all of us who believe

in Christ are priests and kings in Christ, as I Pet. 2:9 says: "You are a chosen race, God's own people, a royal priesthood, a priestly kingdom, that you may declare the wonderful deeds of him who called you out of darkness into his marvelous light."[2]

While differences between Catholic and Protestant views of the Church remain, the Second Vatican Council's understanding of the Church as the People of God and the Body of Christ is much more compatible with a Protestant model of church than the hierarchical model.

NEW TESTAMENT MODEL OF THE SELF: THE SELF-IN-GOD

The second shift in models for Roman Catholics relates to the understanding of human nature that flows from the New Testament. Catholics are discovering anew a central element of the New Testament message: the role of the Spirit within the self. Before the Second Vatican Council an appreciation of this role was virtually absent from consciousness; after the Council it dominates consciousness. During the early seventies, when I was working on my doctoral dissertation in theology, I finally began grasping the role of the Spirit. The plethora of books on the Spirit and spirituality in the seventies is an indication that I was not alone. What is the role of the Spirit within the self?

Treatment of the role of the Spirit in the Christian community must begin with the Last Supper discourse. Jesus is comforting his disciples, having told them of his imminent departure. "But now I am going to the one who sent me, and not one of you asks me, 'Where are you going?' But because I told you this, grief has filled your hearts. But I tell you the truth, it is better for you that I go. For if I do not go, the Advocate will not come to you. But if I go, I will send him to you" (John 16: 5-7). He assures them it is better for them that he goes; the Spirit he sends will take his place, guiding and strengthening them in their mission. This union with Christ through the Spirit is the condition for apostolic effectiveness. The Gospel could not be clearer. "Remain in me, as I remain in you. Just as a branch cannot bear fruit on its own unless it remains on the vine, so neither can you unless you remain in me. I am the vine, you are the branches. Whoever remains in me and I in him will bear much fruit, because without me you can do nothing" (John 15: 4-5). Jesus' prediction is fulfilled at Pentecost when the Spirit vivifies the community. The Acts of the Apostles gives witness to the working of the Spirit in the apostolic Church. Note the difference in the disciples before and after the coming of the Spirit.

Among New Testament writings the epistles of Paul are a most eloquent witness to the power of the Spirit, a power he received only after his conversion to Christ at Damascus. For Paul belief in Jesus and the subsequent infusion of the life of the Spirit is the source of all power. It is a new principle of life, a new creation. Paul contrasts it with the flesh and its tendency to sin. But you are not in the flesh; on the contrary, you are in the spirit, if only the Spirit of God dwells in you. Whoever does not have this Spirit of Christ does not belong to him. But if Christ is in you, although the body is dead because of sin, the spirit is alive because of righteousness. If the Spirit of the one who raised Jesus from the dead dwells in you, the one who raised Christ from the dead will give life to your mortal bodies also, through his Spirit that dwells in you" (Rom 8: 9-11).

Pope John Paul II's 1986 encyclical *Lord and Giver of Life* reflects the Second Vatican Council's emphasis on the centrality of the grace of the Spirit in Christian life. It succinctly summarizes the connection between redemption by Jesus and sanctification by the Holy Spirit. "The redemption accomplished by the son in the dimensions of the earthly history of humanity—accomplished in the 'departure' through the Cross and Resurrection—is at the same time in its entire salvific power transmitted to the Holy Spirit: the one who 'will take what is mine'..."(n.22). We adequately understand the Christian view of the self only when we understand the role of the Holy Spirit; redemption is brought about by the Spirit.

This renewed approach to the understanding of the Spirit in the self relates directly to the Reformation theme of justification by grace through faith *Sola Gratia*. The Protestant reformers, Luther in particular, had bristled at the implications triggered by the famous controversy concerning the selling of indulgences, which seemed to imply that Christians are justified by good works and not by grace through faith. In the *Treatise on Christian Liberty* Luther presents his view on justification by grace through faith:

Since, therefore, this faith can rule only in the inner man, as Rom 10 says, "For man believes with his heart and so is justified," and since faith alone justifies, it is clear that the inner man cannot be justified, freed, or saved by any outer work or action at all, and that these works, whatever their character, have nothing to do with the inner man.... Wherefore it ought to be the first concern of every Christian to lay aside all confidence in works and increasingly to strengthen faith alone and through faith to grow in the knowledge, not of works, but of Christ Jesus, who suffered and rose for him, as Peter teaches in the last chapter of his first Epistle, I Pet 5:10. No other work makes a Christian.[3]

Without the movement of faith through grace in the self, which is identical with the movement of the Holy Spirit, there are no salvific movements within the self. The Christian's initial justification as well as all subsequent movements of sanctification flow from grace, flow from the Spirit. Though the language is different, the foundational concept behind justification by grace through faith and the salvific power of the Holy Spirit is analogous.

One note on the activity of the Spirit in the self is important for Catholics and Protestants. The Holy Spirit joins our human spirit; it does not replace it. We humans enjoy three modes of activity flowing from the three dimensions of our being—body, mind, spirit. It is helpful to imagine three concentric circles: the center is the spirit, the middle is the mind, the outer is the body. Every human activity engages all three levels. Our physical and psychological activities are obvious to all. But what are our spiritual activities? The spiritual level is the level on which we choose whether or not to respond to the Spirit. The Holy Spirit joins our human spirit, initiating within us the desire for goodness, without which we would not even have the desire. Responding to the Spirit then transforms the other levels of our being, the physical and the psychological. The Spirit is the principle for all Christian life. Catholics traditionally have called this indwelling of the Spirit sanctifying grace.

The view of the self just described is contrary to popular conceptions. Most of us live within a model of the self that I call the Western model, the model that dominates my approach to God and that of many of my Catholic brothers and sisters. It is also operative in the so-called Puritan Ethic, the belief arising from Calvinist origins that material prosperity is a reward from God for hard work. In this model God is solely transcendent, in heaven, and so not dwelling within the self through the Spirit. Since God is in heaven God cannot be the initiator of good actions. Though the Western model duly acknowledges that we are made to know, love, and serve God in this life and will, therefore, be happy in the next, it gives God no prior role in these actions. It grants only that God rewards us with grace, and perhaps material prosperity, in this life and with eternal life in the next. This model violates the foundational Reformation principle of *sola gratia* because it erroneously assumes that we are the initiators of our own good deeds.

This Western view of self is taken not from the New Testament but from our culture. Our view of the self tends to be secular and individualistic; we do not recognize God's presence within us influencing our behavior. At best we give intellectual assent to the notion that through baptism we receive grace, but do not understand that God's presence has implications for our daily motivation. Our culture is capitalistic. We give financial rewards based on performance; we presume God gives spiritual rewards the same way, rewarding the just with grace, and perhaps also material prosperity, and withholding these rewards from the unjust. Our culture is individualistic. We prize independence, eschew dependence, and find dependence on God's grace demeaning. Without giving it much thought we presume we earn our salvation as we earn everything in life by our own hard work.

CHRISTIAN SPIRITUALITY: RESPONDING TO THE SPIRIT

The third shift of Roman Catholic models concerns spirituality itself. It presumes the Second Vatican Council models of Church and self in which the Holy Spirit is central. Four statements regarding spirituality get to the heart of the shift in models. I am presenting these statements to highlight the contrast with the previous Roman Catholic understanding of spirituality.

First, Christian spirituality is other-centered, centered on God and our neighbor. We are called to work with Christ for the Kingdom by loving and serving God and our neighbor. I like Luke's presentation of the two great commandments. "Teacher, what must I do to inherit eternal life?" Jesus said to him, "What is written in the law? How do you read it?" He said in reply, "You shall love the Lord, your God, with all your heart, with all your being, with all your strength, and with all your mind, and your neighbor as yourself." He replied to him, "You have answered correctly; do this and you shall live" (Luke 10: 25-28). The questioner is concerned with being saved and inheriting eternal life and Jesus' answer is framed in terms of loving God and others. Jesus responds with the parable of the Good Samaritan to illustrate what he means by loving your neighbor as yourself. Previous approaches to spirituality often seemed more self-centered than other-centered. We were concerned with earning grace and getting to heaven, saving our souls. Jesus seems to say, "Don't worry about saving your soul; just love and serve God and others and all will be fine." The operative question becomes how can I help others, not how can I be saved?

Second, Christian spirituality is action-centered. Matthew's Last Judgment scene is a dramatic reminder of the criteria for final judgment. "He will place the sheep on his right and the goats on his left. Then the king will say to those on his right, "Come, you who are blessed by my Father. Inherit the kingdom prepared for you from the foundation of the world. For I was hungry and you gave me food, I was thirsty and you gave me drink, a stranger and you welcomed me, naked and you clothed me, ill and you cared for me, imprisoned and you visited me'" (Matt 25:33-36). Recall the king's response to their puzzlement concerning when they fed and clothed him, "Amen, I say to you, whatever you did to one of these least brothers of mine, you did for me" (Matt 25:40). Previous approaches to spirituality seemed more concerned with fidelity to prayer and sacraments than to service of others; they seemed prayer-centered rather than action-centered. We evaluated the quality of our Christian life by fidelity to prayer and sacraments. The Gospel's witness that Jesus expressed his intimacy with his Father through a regular rhythm of prayer, in solitary places, in synagogues, in the temple. This prayer provided the foundation for his ministry; from it he seemed to receive light and strength. The goal for Jesus, however, was fidelity to the mission he received from the Father. The Second Vatican Council restored the role of service to Christian spirituality. We are disciples of Jesus to the extent we labor with him for our neighbor, especially for those most in need. Ministers of the Church fulfill Jesus' injunction through official commitment to service to the Church and to the Kingdom.

Third, Christian spirituality is concerned with the quality of heart underlying our actions, both our prayer and our service. Prayer and service that no not flow from the heart do not fulfill Jesus' commandment to love. The Gospels present Jesus as having the most difficulty with the Pharisees who perfectly fulfilled all the commandments. He refers to them as whitened sepulchers. Externally they kept the commandments, internally they violated the very essence of the commandments, love. Paul gives a summary of the qualities of heart that mark the presence of the Spirit: love, joy, peace, patience, kindness, generosity, faithfulness, gentleness, self-control (Gal 5:22). He contrasts these with those marking the Spirit's absence: immorality, impurity, hatreds, rivalry, jealousy, outbursts of fury, acts of selfishness, dissension, occasions of envy (Gal 5:20). It is good to recall Paul's classic expression of the two contrary desires we all experience, one from the Spirit, the other not:

> I say, then: live by the Spirit and you will certainly not gratify the desire of the flesh. For the flesh has desires against the Spirit, and the Spirit against the flesh; these are opposed to each other, so that you may not do what you want. But if you are guided by the Spirit, you are not under the law. Now the works of the flesh are obvious: immorality, impurity, licentiousness, idolatry, sorcery, hatreds, rivalry, jealousy, outbursts of fury, acts of selfishness, dissensions, factions, occasions of envy, drinking bouts, orgies, and the like. I warn you, as I warned you before, that those who do such things will not inherit the kingdom of God. In contrast, the fruit of the Spirit is love, joy, peace, patience, kindness, generosity, faithfulness, gentleness, self-control (Gal 5:16-23).

Previous Catholic approaches to spirituality often seemed more concerned with the external performance of actions than with the quality of heart underlying them. Indeed, we usually examined our consciences in terms of sinful actions performed or omitted. For instance, we focused not on whether we hated our neighbor but on whether we performed hateful actions. Likewise, we focused on whether we fulfilled our Sunday mass obligation by being physically present at Mass; our dispositions were almost irrelevant. This particular shift is central to discernment of spirits, which looks primarily at the quality of heart.

Fourth, Christian spirituality is a response to the Spirit. This statement implies that the focus has shifted from responding to external written laws and commandments to responding to the internal law of the Spirit written on our hearts. These two laws usually coincide but the real Christian challenge is not simply conforming to external laws, which is relatively easy, but conforming to the internal law of the Spirit. Paul teaches his Jewish communities that they have been freed from subservience to the former Mosaic laws and are now called to respond to an inner law, "But now we are discharged from the law, dead to that which held us captive, so that we serve not under the old written code, but in the new life of the Spirit" (Rom 7:6). This truth also highlights the inadequacy of the Western model understanding of good deeds as self-initiated and emphasizes the scriptural teaching that all good deeds are Spirit-initiated.

Two final notes related to this truth are significant. First, love in us originates with God in us. When we live in love we live in God; it is that simple. The power to love derives ultimately from the Spirit sent by God to take Jesus' place. John's teaching is clear and bold. "Beloved, let us love one another, because love is of God; everyone who loves is begotten of God and knows God. Whoever is without love does not know God, for God is love.... Beloved, if God so loves us, we also must love one another. No one has ever seen God. Yet if we love one another, God remains in us, and his love is brought to perfection in us"(1 John 4:7-8, 11-12). Second, we can trust our inner selves because at our center we have God's Spirit to guide us. Previous approaches to spirituality did not adequately acknowledge the Spirit's presence. Commonly they taught that the self cannot be trusted because of fallen human nature and inherited original sin. This inherited brokenness so dominated our consciousness that we undervalued the power of redemption from sin. Since we could not trust this inner self, it became necessary to look outside ourselves for external guidelines. Treatments of discernment fully acknowledge sinfulness and brokenness; indeed, they examine the quality of heart for signs of this sinfulness. They also acknowledge redemption; grace in us is stronger than sin in us and we can, therefore, trust our inner selves.

I believe this renewed understanding of spirituality is compatible with classical Reformation *sola gratia*. Perhaps the most troublesome theological difference between Protestants and Catholics has been the relationship between grace and works. Catholics, misunderstanding their own tradition, have tended to emphasize the centrality of good works; Protestants have emphasized the centrality of grace. Yet grace was at the heart of every action in the Catholic tradition and good works are central to Luther's theology because they are the necessary fruit of faith. Luther's *Treatise on Christian Liberty* emphasizes that, though we are justified by grace through faith, good works are an integral result of this justification.

The following statements are true: "Good works do not make a good man, but a good man does good works; evil works do not

make a wicked man, but a wicked man does evil works." Consequently it is always necessary that the substance or person himself
be good before there can be any good works, and that good works
follow and proceed from the good person, as Christ also says, "A
good tree cannot bear evil fruit, nor can a bad tree bear good fruit"
(Matt 7:18). Our faith in Christ does not free us from works but
from false opinions concerning works, that is, from the foolish
presumption that justification is acquired by works. Faith redeems,
corrects, and preserves our consciences so that we know that
righteousness does not consist in works, although works neither
can nor ought to be wanting ...[4]

John Dillenberger, in *Martin Luther: Selections from His Writings*, presents
Luther's position succinctly. Both faith and works remain central. "In faith,
man stands before God in the light of grace. For him, even at his best, there
is no other possibility. Hence for Luther, good works are not determinative
of one's relation to God: they follow from faith as day follows night, as
good fruit comes from a good tree. Where there are no works, there is no
faith; the seriousness and joy of belonging to God are not known."[5]

Though doctrinal differences remain concerning the relationship
between grace and works, the renewed theology of the Holy Spirit seems
to be bridging the gap between Catholic and Protestant positions. Pope
John Paul's affirmation that the initiative of God through the Holy Spirit
is essential for all good works is similar in intent to Luther's justification
by grace through faith. Both Catholics and Protestants acknowledge that
separating grace from works is contrary to the Gospel; both acknowledge
that faith *and* works are central to living the Gospel. This makes it possible
to have a common discussion on two spiritual disciplines, good works, such
as personal prayer, and discernment of spirits.

THE HOLY SPIRIT AND PERSONAL PRAYER

I believe my Protestant audiences have been comfortable with my presentations on spirituality because I address foundational Reformation concerns
of *Sola Scriptura* and *Sola Gratia*. In addition I believe they have been
comfortable because both the Second Vatican Council and the Reformers
have similar theologies of the Holy Spirit. In both Catholic and Protestant

traditions the Holy Spirit is simply the sanctifier. The Third Article of the Creed in Luther's *Large Catechism* of 1559 summarizes the Lutheran belief:

> As the Father is called Creator and the Son is called Redeemer, so on account of his work the Holy Spirit must be called sanctifier, the One who makes us holy. How does this sanctifying take place? Answer: Just as the Son obtains dominion by purchasing us through his birth, death, and resurrection, etc., so the Holy Spirit effects our sanctification through the following: the communion of saints or the Christian church, the forgiveness of sins, the resurrection of the body, and life everlasting. In other words, he first leads us into his holy community, placing us upon the bosom of the church, where he preaches to us and brings us to Christ. All this, then, is the office and work of the Holy Spirit, to begin and daily to increase holiness on earth through these two means, the Christian church and the forgiveness of sins.[6]

The Westminister Confession of Faith of 1647 adapted by the Presbyterian Church gives an especially apt teaching on the necessity of the Holy Spirit in sanctification and for all good works:

> The Holy Spirit, whom the Father is ever willing to give to all who ask him, is the only efficient agent in the application of redemption. He regenerates men by his grace, convicts them of sin, moves them to repentance, and persuades and enables them to embrace Jesus Christ by faith. He unites all believers to Christ, dwells in them as their Comforter and Sanctifier, gives to them the spirit of Adoption and Prayer, and performs all those gracious offices by which they are sanctified and sealed unto the day of redemption.[7]

Their ability to do good works is not at all of themselves, but wholly from the Spirit of Christ. And that they may be enabled thereunto, besides the graces they have already received, there is required an actual influence of the same Holy Spirit to work in them to will and to do of his good pleasure; yet are they not hereupon to grow negligent, as if they were not bound to perform any duty unless upon a special motion of the Spirit; but they ought to be diligent in stirring up the grace of God that is in them.[8]

Since Catholics and Protestants share a common tradition about the necessity of the Holy Spirit in our sanctification, we share the belief that the fruitfulness of every spiritual discipline such as personal prayer is in direct proportion to our openness to the Holy Spirit. This Spirit will give us the desire for personal prayer and sustain us in responding to this desire. In an open discussion with Lutheran pastors, one pastor admitted he had always been uncomfortable with the idea of setting time aside for personal prayer. It seemed, he added, like the practice bordered on the heresy of works righteousness, that is, righteousness earned through good works, not gifted by grace through faith. In the ensuing discussion he realized that since the very desire to pray comes from the Spirit, the practice is fully in accord with justification by faith through grace. He resolved to put time into his daily schedule for personal prayer; prior to this time his personal prayer consisted, he said, totally of prayers of petition.

PRAYING IN THE SPIRIT

Let me relate my experience of learning to pray in the Spirit. I was teaching as a young Jesuit at a mission in South Dakota. Our life was very difficult. Regular Order included rising at 5:00 a.m. and retiring after the students were asleep around midnight. We were expected to do an hour of meditation before 6:30 mass in the Mission Church. Eventually sheer physical exhaustion drove me to begin sleeping late, getting up only in time for mass. Daily meditation had always been presented to me as essential for living the Jesuit life, so I experienced continual guilt for skipping it. Every evening after the students had quieted down in the dorms I walked down the highway under the stars, often for over an hour. I recall being discouraged and lonely and pouring out my heart to God. I also recall returning from these walks peaceful, feeling close to Christ and wondering how I could survive without these walks. My conscience continued to bother me for skipping daily meditation, but one night I had a startling realization: I was not skipping daily meditation, I was doing it at night! I was walking down that highway each night to be with the Lord, not to fulfill a religious obligation by dogged determination and conscientious efforts to think about God and Christ. I had discovered a rhythm of being totally open to the Spirit. I had learned to pray.

I receive requests to give talks on prayer. Usually I am instructed that the group would like some practical methods for improving the quality of their prayer. I am uncomfortable with the assumptions behind these requests. My own experience tells me that praying involves more than the determination to pray and conscientious use of methods, which I had been doing for years before my breakthrough at the Mission. My experience tells me that prayer happens best when we find a time and place that enables us to be in touch with God's Spirit and with our own deepest selves. At that moment God's Spirit joins our spirit and we truly pray from our hearts. In this context Paul's remarks about God's Spirit aiding our prayer make great sense. "The Spirit too comes to help us in our weakness. For when we cannot choose words in order to pray properly, the Spirit himself expresses our plea in a way that could never be put into words, and God who knows everything in our hearts knows perfectly well what he means, and that the pleas of the saints expressed by the Spirit are according to the mind of God" (Rom 8:26-27).

How then do we respect the initiative of the Spirit in our personal prayer? We are called to live and to pray within the Scriptural Model of the Self, not the Western Model. I understand prayer as the movement of the heart toward God under the influence of the Holy Spirit. It is a movement of the heart; no heart movement, no prayer. It cannot be identified either with words we say or with thoughts we think. Indeed, prayer need not be accompanied by words or thoughts. In Christian tradition the deepest prayer transcends both. The movement can occur only when we are under the influence of the Holy Spirit. We have seen that Spirit abides with us as a permanent indwelling gift of God. Though the Spirit is always present, we are not always in touch with that presence. In prayer we set time aside to allow God's Spirit to join our spirit and to raise our hearts to God.

In prayer the movement of the heart under the influence of the Spirit is ultimately toward God, towards the Father and towards Jesus. Just as Christian theology sees the Spirit as the bond of union between the Father and the Son in the Trinity, so the Spirit is our bond of union with the Father and Jesus. We pray with, not to, Mary and the saints; we pray with them to the Father and Jesus. The Spirit unites us with the entire communion of saints which exists in a continual movement of love and praise to the Father and Jesus. Under the Spirit's influence the deepest yearnings of our hearts, united with those of the saints, our privileged intercessors, move toward communion with God. It is impossible to imagine Mary's not wanting to unite us more deeply to her son and to our Father.

Christians must pray, for in prayer we experience our deepest identity. Often we erroneously assume that we pray simply to seek specific favors from God. Deeper reflection reveals, however, that what we are really seeking is a confirmation of God's love for us. Though we may be led to prayer to seek specific favors, as we continue praying we eventually realize that our deepest need is for God's presence and support. The Spirit transforms our initial desires in a way that is not unlike Jesus' transformation in Gethsemane. Jesus begins by seeking to have the chalice of suffering removed, but concludes by yielding to God's presence and surrenders to God's will. I believe I experienced this same type of surrender during my nightly walks at the Mission. I wait expectantly for a similar renewal each Advent.

The key to praying well is discovering conditions that best facilitate the movement of the Spirit. The time, place, and setting for prayer are important; we choose the best available time, place and setting. For me at the Mission it was late at night walking down a highway, definitely not early in the morning when I was half-asleep. The following conditions and methods best facilitate my own daily response to the Spirit in personal prayer. Everyone's conditions and methods will be distinctive, related to their personality and schedules. First the time. After rising, showering, and shaving, I light a candle before my prayer wall. I spend 60 to 90 minutes in spiritual disciplines. I begin by journaling with a cup of coffee beside me. Journaling clears my head and allows me to process what has built up in my psyche, matters which could emerge as distractions in personal prayer. Often journaling provides the topic for the subsequent prayer. Then, putting the coffee aside, I move to the morning office. After completing the office, I move to personal prayer for the last 20 to 30 minutes. I never rush, spending as much time as is needed on each movement of my prayer.

Next the place. I pray in my own room, in a chair, facing my prayer wall, next to a large window with an eastward exposure overlooking the secluded garden mentioned above. The chair is upholstered and comfortable, but supports me firmly in an upright position. I place all the materials I need, my journal, a Bible, the daily office and meditation books related to the liturgical season, on a side table beside the chair. I love this room; it is away from my office. The window, open in warm weather, gives direct access to the sights and sounds of the garden and to the warmth and light of the rising sun. My prayer wall is hung with favorite icons, prints, and crucifixes gathered over the years and arranged for the different liturgical seasons and feasts. I occasionally use musical tapes as background. The physical setting, the time, place, furniture arrangement, is key. The regular rhythm of entering this environment at this time each day not only establishes the conditions for facilitating the Spirit but often promotes immediate communion with the Lord. Given the desire for communion with God, praying can be simple: just find the right time and place and go there regularly.

METHODS FOR PERSONAL PRAYER

Use of prayer methods may also help or hinder the movement of the Spirit. Many of us pray using the method of Lectio Prayer. In Lectio Prayer we chose an aspect of God's word to focus our attention, and then we wait, listen, and respond to the word of God under the influence of the Spirit. This method is based on the conviction that God is present and can speak to us through the word, which has manifold meanings. God is present in the scriptural word, traditionally the most helpful starting point. God is also present in the *created word*, which focuses on God's presence in creation, the beauty of nature. God is also present in the *existential word*, which focuses on God's presence in events or relationships. Any aspect of creation or embodiment of creation, images, poetry, music, is a word of God and starting point for prayer because God is present in all aspects of reality and uses them to bring us into communion: "Creation proclaims the glory of God."

The Christian tradition affirms a wonderful truth: by focusing on the word of God we can be led by the Spirit to the highest levels of communion with God. This tradition, enshrined in Benedictine spirituality, describes internal transformation as moving from thinking (*meditatio*) about God's presence in the word, to praying (*oratio*) to God about our reactions to this presence, to resting (*contemplatio*) in God's presence without thinking about God or consciously praying to God. Guido II, a twelfth century Carthusian abbot, gives the classic expression of the internal dynamic of this prayer.

You can see ... how these degrees are joined to each other. One precedes the other, not only in the order of time but of causality. Reading (*lectio*) comes first, and is, as it were, the foundation; it provides the subject matter we must use for meditation. Meditation (*meditatio*) considers more carefully what is to be sought after; it digs, as it were, for treasure which it finds and reveals, but since it is not in meditation's power to seize upon the treasure, it directs us to prayer. Prayer (*oratio*) lifts itself up to God with all its strength, and begs for the treasure it longs for, which is the sweetness of contemplation. Contemplation (*contemplatio*) when it comes rewards the labors of the other three; it inebriates the thirsting soul with the dew of heavenly sweetness. Reading is an exercise of the outward senses; meditation is concerned with the inward understanding; prayer is concerned with desire; contemplation outstrips every faculty.[9]

The goal of the process is contemplation which outstrips every faculty and rests in communion with God. Our activity recedes; God's increases; God holds us to God's Self with little or no effort on our part.

For me two other methods of prayer complement Lectio Prayer. Centering Prayer is based on the truth of God's presence in the center of our being, beyond the level of thoughts and desires. It presumes the Scriptural Model of the Self. I find it most helpful when the Spirit brings me to the contemplation mode of Lectio Prayer. After I have reached a level of interior quiet I experience no need to verbalize thoughts and desires to God and am drawn by the Spirit simply to rest in the Lord. To symbolize my intention I choose a favorite appellation for God, such as 'Father,' 'Abba,' 'Jesus,' 'Lord,' repeating my prayer word only when distractions arise. The rest of the time I simply sit in faith before the Lord. The method, taken from the fourteenth-century English classic *Cloud of Unknowing*, is more useful for those who have been praying regularly. In this method the Spirit holds us in communion with God without the mediation of thoughts and desires.

The assumptions and dynamics of Mantra Prayer are similar to Centering Prayer. In Mantra Prayer we also respond to God directly, without reflection on God's word. Having reached a level of interior quiet, we sustain our prayer not by a word but by a mantra. Most mantras have four phrases; we slowly repeat the mantra, coordinating its four phrases, indicated below by asterisks, with our inhaling and exhaling. Most, though not all, authors suggest coordination with breathing. The desert fathers preferred: "O God * come to my assistance * O Lord * make haste to help me." The most famous mantra in the Christian tradition, however, is the Jesus Prayer which arose with the Greek Fathers in the fifth century: "Lord Jesus Christ * Son of God * have mercy on me * a sinner." I frequently recast scriptural passages into mantra form. Among my favorites: "The Lord * is my shepherd * there is nothing * I shall want;" "You are my servant * whom I have chosen * my beloved * with whom I am pleased;" "I am the vine * you are the branches * without me * you can do nothing." Mantra Prayer enters the Christian tradition in the fifth century in the *Conferences* of John Cassian.

When thoughts arise in Centering or Mantra Prayer the practical advice for handling them is simple: resist no thought, react to no thought, retain no thought; simply return to the prayer word or mantra. Thoughts have a positive quality to them because as we let them pass we are evacuating from our psyches obstacles to the contemplative communion with God; they are actually part of the purification process. Handled well, they move us toward interior silence which outstrips every faculty.

I use Mantra Prayer frequently. When I have reached a state of interior quiet I often choose a favorite mantra to focus my attention. This minimizes my interposing thoughts between myself and God and enhances my receptivity to God's drawing. I often use three methods of prayer in one period. I begin with Lectio Prayer by reflecting on some blessing or need in my daily life; after I have reached a certain quiet, I move to Mantra Prayer and allow a favorite mantra to sustain my attention; finally, as I reach a deeper quiet I drop the mantra and move to Centering Prayer and allow my prayer word to signify my intention to be totally present to God.

THE BEST METHOD OF PRAYER?

There is no best way to pray; whatever works is best. Since the goal of all prayer methods is communion with God and since only the Spirit can bring about this communion, our role is discovering conditions that facilitate the movement of the Spirit for us. Communion remains a gift. I once believed, erroneously, it was my conscientious use of a particular method that *guaranteed* good results in prayer. Through trial and error we discover how

best to be open to God. Robert Frost's little poem "Not All There" catches
the challenge for praying well.

> I turned to speak to God
> About the world's despair;
> But to make bad matters worse
> I found God wasn't there.
>
> God turned to speak to me
> (Don't anybody laugh);
> God found I wasn't there—
> At least not over half.[10]

The following are some additional reflections on what helps me pray; I am
not presenting them as ways everyone *should* pray.

My starting point for prayer is usually my life, the existential word of
God as I am experiencing it. I have had little luck, and in the past wasted
much time, forcing myself to reflect on meditations, written by others,
unrelated to my daily life. I believe that through the Spirit God's self is
continually manifested in all creation and history and in my life. I choose
some aspect of God's word from my previous day, a person or event. I
bring the matter to mind and begin focusing my attention upon it. I put
distractions aside as they occur and attempt to keep my mind gently on
God's word. I wait in God's presence, listen to God's speaking through the
word in my heart and respond in any way the Spirit moves. The Spirit
directs my attention to the word (*lectio*); transforms my mind and prompts
suitable thoughts about the word (*meditatio*); transforms my will and
prompts suitable desires and affections about the word (oratio); and leads
me to rest in God's presence beyond thoughts and desires (*contemplatio*).
I believe that listening to God is a better metaphor for the prayer process
than the traditional speaking to God. We speak only in response to the
Spirit and only after we have listened.

Frequently after lighting my candle, settling into my prayer chair,
sipping my coffee and journaling, I find myself already held to God by God
with no further effort needed on my part, so I stop journaling: I am already
centered; no method is needed. I have developed a facility for being drawn
by the Spirit into communion by the regularity of being present to God each
morning at this time and in this place. The setting has not only prepared me

for praying but has actually induced it. Perhaps my journal recordings have brought to mind some blessing, some word of God, from the previous day. The blessing becomes the occasion, the sacrament, for awakening consciousness of God and for resting gratefully in the presence of God. The Spirit moves me from gratitude to communion and contemplation. All I know is that I have no desire either to reflect upon or pray over the blessing and that perhaps the journaling has recalled a need. The need then becomes the occasion for awakening consciousness of dependence on God and resting in silent acknowledgment of my helplessness without God. At this point I often use Mantra Prayer and then Centering Prayer to sustain my attention.

Occasionally my attention is caught unexpectedly by some aspect of the garden outside my window. I see the sun rising through the trees, I hear a song of a bird or rustle of leaves, I smell the fragrance of the garden and feel the wind on my face. I have no desire to continue reflecting or praying; I find myself held by God to God; I am centered. Nature has become the sacrament occasioning communion with God and contemplation. Again Mantra Prayer or Centering Prayer may help me sustain attention.

Frequently my attention is caught by one of the icons or prints on my prayer wall. My favorite images include a print of a fourth-century sculpture of the Good Shepherd, the Vladimir Madonna, Fra Angelico's Annunciation. I also rotate favorite works of art relating to the current liturgical season; I believe the Spirit offers graces to help savor the season. Each season finds me anticipating and responding anew to my favorite art works: for Christmas Gorgione's "Adoration of the Shepherds," for Lent Perugino's "Crucifixion," for Easter Fra Angelico's "Noli Me Tangere." For Advent Edward Hick's "Peaceable Kingdom" seems to evoke best my yearning for a fuller coming of the Lord to the human family and to my life. I find myself held by God to God through these images often with no desire to think about them; I am centered. The images have become sacramentals occasioning communion with God and contemplation. Again, I may move from this Lectio Prayer on the word of God to Mantra Prayer to Centering Prayer.

We may arrive at prayer preoccupied and discouraged by the events of our day. We dare to hope again for a better life and a better world through a fuller opening to God's presence. In prayer we seek to experience again the truth of Augustine's famous dictum, "Our hearts are restless until they rest in Thee." Sometimes, in the stillness of our prayer, we are touched in the center of our being and taken out of time and beyond the ability of words to explain; God holds us to God's Self. It is the experience of T.S. Eliot's "still point of the turning world."

> Neither movement from nor towards,
> Neither ascent nor decline. Except for the point, the still point,
> There would be no dance, and there is only the dance.
> I can only say THERE we have been: but I cannot say where.
> And I cannot say, how long, for that is to place it in time.[11]

We have experienced Immanuel, God-with-us.

THE HOLY SPIRIT AND DISCERNMENT OF SPIRITS

I am frequently asked why discernment of spirits has assumed such major importance in Roman Catholic spirituality in recent years and was all but missing in earlier discussions before the Second Vatican Council. We have already seen the answer to this question. Discernment of spirits presumes that God deals directly with us. Not until the Second Vatican Council did Catholics have models of the Church, the self, and spirituality that assumed that God, in the Spirit, deals directly with individual believers. Reformation models have always assumed this direct personal presence; the Protestant principle asserts this unmediated direct relationship between the believer and God.

I am a Jesuit priest. I have to acknowledge that in my own Jesuit formation, largely before the Council, I received no introduction to discernment. This is strange since our founder, Ignatius of Loyola, is the source of most current discussions of discernment with the "Rules of the Discernment of Spirits" found in his book the *Spiritual Exercises*. In an oft-quoted statement from the *Exercises*, Ignatius exhorts those giving them to others to stay out of the way and allow the Creator to deal directly with the creature. "Therefore, the director of the *Exercises*, as a balance at equilibrium, without leaning to one side or the other, should permit the Creator to deal directly with the creature, and the creature directly with his Creator and Lord."[12] Ignatius was arrested by the Inquisition three times for such statements because of their Protestant ring.

The Ignatian spiritual vision is distinctive. It is a spirituality for people living active lives in the world who seek God in ordinary daily actions. To foster the realization of Ignatius' vision of finding God in daily life, he suggested appropriate spiritual practices or exercises. The heart of these practices are his Examination of Conscience and Rules for the Discernment of Spirits. Ignatius was acutely aware from his own tempestuous past, thirty years as a warring, romancing Spanish courtier, that every human heart has two contrary movements, one from the good spirits and the other from the evil spirits. He learned that to grow in union with God we must learn to recognize and respond only to the movements of the good spirit, the Holy Spirit, and to distinguish or discern those from movements of the evil spirits. Since finding God in daily life was his goal, he applied discernment of spirits to ordinary daily actions. He, therefore, suggested daily periods for examination of conscience that focused upon inner motivation.

The practice of discerning movements from the evil spirit from movements from the good spirit is built into the thought of the Reformers. The phrase *simul justus et peccator* sums up the human condition; we are simultaneously saints and sinners. Because we have received God's grace through faith we are saints; because of the sinfulness remaining within us we are sinners. Luther's *Commentary on Galatians* expresses the classic tension:

Let no man marvel therefore or be dismayed, when he feeleth in his body this battle of the flesh against the spirit: but let him pluck up his heart and comfort himself with these words of Paul: "the flesh lusteth against the spirit" ... and "These are contrary one to another, so that ye do not those things that ye would." For by these sentences he comforteth them that be tempted. As if he should say: it is impossible for you to follow the guiding of the Spirit in all things without any feeling or hindrance of the flesh; nay, the flesh will resist: and so resist and hinder you that ye cannot do those things that gladly ye would.... Therefore when a man feeleth this battle of the flesh, let him not be discouraged therewith, but let him resist in the Spirit, and say: I am a sinner, and I feel sin in me, for I have not yet put off the flesh, in which sin dwelleth so long as it liveth; but I will obey the spirit and not the flesh ...[13]

RECOGNIZING GOD IN DAILY LIFE

We find God in daily life to the extent that we recognize and respond to God's Spirit in our hearts. Not every movement within our hearts, however, can be trusted, we have spontaneous inclinations not only toward good, from the Holy Spirit, but also toward evil, not from the Holy Spirit. Traditionally we call the sources of evil inclinations or temptations the "capital sins": jealousy, envy, anger, hatred, sloth, lust, drunkenness. Honesty compels us to admit that in a typical day we experience much evidence of these inclinations; some days we may experience our hearts as more inclined toward evil than toward good. For conscientious Christians the key question becomes "What criterion can we use to recognize the Spirit's movements within our hearts?"

I have developed a criterion for recognizing the Spirit's movements that focuses on the direction of our hearts: to the degree our hearts are moving toward the desire to love and serve God and others, we are under the influence of the Spirit; to the degree our hearts are moving away from this desire, we are not. This criterion for recognizing the presence of the Spirit relates to our inner experiences, to our quality of heart. We know that external actions can be performed with little or no love and, therefore, cannot be in themselves accurate indications of the presence of the Spirit. The question then becomes which of our inner experiences, imagining, thinking, desiring, feeling, become the best criteria for discernment? The desire to love arising with us is the basic criterion for recognizing the transformation of our inner experience by the Holy Spirit. The theological reasoning behind this truth is simple: we can make no movement toward good, toward God, or others in love by our own initiative. Since the desire to love and serve God and others is definitely a movement toward good, it cannot come from our initiative; it must come from the Spirit, "without me you can do nothing!"

Desire is a more reliable criterion for recognizing the Spirit than feelings or inner peace. Feelings are ephemeral; feelings come and go but desire remains. We may wake up sick one morning and not feel like serving God and others, but we can still desire to serve. Desire is even a more reliable criterion than inner peace. We may experience a period in life dominated by sadness from troubled relationships or discouragement from failure in work. Our *habitual* inner peace may be lacking yet we "hang on" to the desire to love and to serve. When inner peace is absent and we still desire to serve the Lord, it is comforting to realize that we are indeed responding to the Spirit. It should be noted, however, that normally inner peace will accompany our desire to serve. Paul reminds us that "the fruits of the Spirit are love, joy, peace, patience, kindness, generosity, faithfulness, gentleness, self-control"(Gal 5:23).

Service is also central. The two great commandments of love given by Jesus center on service; we demonstrate our love for God by loving our neighbor. This love (*agape*) is situated primarily in the will; it requires us to move through life willing our neighbor's well-being. It counters the temptation to move through life with an individualistic, self-centered attitude. Since this desire is situated in the will, it need not be accompanied by feelings of affection. We are commanded to love everyone irrespective of personal feelings, even our enemies. Our love is to be like God's love, universal care and concern. Only because the Spirit of God is within us can we love like God with a love expressed by deeds. Luke's gospel gives us the Good Samaritan story to illustrate what Jesus meant. Matthew's gospel gives us the Last Judgment scene, "I was hungry and you gave me food, I was thirsty and you give me drink" (Matt 25:35). Those who were saved were not aware of serving God in their neighbor, but this did not matter to the Son of Man: "Whatever you did for one of these least brothers of mine, you did for me" (Matt 25:40).

RESPONDING TO OBSTACLES TO THE SPIRIT

Awareness of the quality of heart underlying our daily actions is the key to finding God in daily life. Normally when we are moving toward the desire to love and serve God and others we experience a quality of heart marked by the fruits of the Spirit, love, joy, peace, and patience. Our hearts are aligned with our deepest selves and the result is interior peace. Normally when we are moving away from the desire to love and serve God and others we experience a quality of heart marked by inner restlessness and anxiety. Our hearts are no longer aligned with our deepest selves and we experience disorientation.

My short-cut to discerning the presence or absence of the Spirit is becoming more aware of my different moods: in a good or peaceful mood the Spirit is usually present, in a bad or anxious mood the Spirit is usually not present. When my daily life is not marked by inner peace but rather by restlessness and anxiety, I must be careful. A quality of heart marked by anxiety is a red flag telling me something is amiss and should be checked out. It is a clue that my heart may not be responding fully to the Spirit because the fruits of the Spirit are not present. In short, I am in a bad mood. Over the years I have become better at recognizing these moods. The restlessness prompting me to examine my moods then becomes a grace because it calls me, if necessary, to realign my heart with the Holy Spirit.

A further clarification on moods is important. I am connecting good and bad moods with the presence and absence of the Spirit. By a good mood I mean simply a feeling state transformed by the Spirit that supports the desire to love and serve God and others; by a bad mood I mean a feeling state that is not transformed by the Spirit and does not support the desire to love and serve. We all know the difference that being in a good mood makes for living our day. There is an intimate correction between our moods, thoughts, and actions. When our mood is peaceful our thoughts tend also to be peaceful and our actions reflect this peacefulness; when our mood is anxious our thoughts tend to be anxious and our actions reflect this anxiety. The following guidelines are short-cuts to developing the skill of recognizing the Spirit in daily life.

First, be aware of situations causing bad moods. The place to start is our daily schedules. What daily activities do we approach without the desire to love and serve God and others? These situations may relate to our family lives or our work lives; what daily activities do we dread? Chances are we approach these parts of our day in bad moods. Next we should review our relationships. What people tend to get to us, in our homes, neighborhoods, or workplaces? Chances are we approach these people with bad moods. Finally, what other areas of our lives habitually irritate us, parish governance, community or national politics, sports? In addition to these daily occurrences we all experience bad moods during periods of special stress caused by such things as sickness, death, job threats, financial need.

Second, replace bad moods with good desires and respond to the good desires. Recall that the most reliable sign of the presence of the Spirit is the desire to love and serve. We want our actions to flow not from the bad mood but from the good desire. When we replace the bad mood with a good desire and respond to the desire, we are doing all in our power to align ourselves with the action of the Holy Spirit. The mood may not change, but we are comforted by the knowledge that our deepest identity flows not from our moods but from our desires. Having replaced the bad mood with the good desire and responded to that desire, we have done all we can to align ourselves with the Spirit. Often I find my inner peace restored immediately.

Third, examine the causes of the bad moods and resolve to deal with them appropriately. It is important to know the causes in order to apply the right remedies for dealing with bad moods. For instance, if the cause relates to the physical dimension of our being, we must deal with it on that level. We all know the effect physical exhaustion and illness can have upon our moods. If the mood flows from our psychological dimension, we deal with it differently. Does my mood flow from some area of my life that preoccupies me and causes me special stress, for instance, worry about my family, my job? Finally, does my mood flow from a spiritual need? Perhaps we have not been faithful to our rhythm of spiritual activities and are living alienated from our centers. We want to readjust these daily rhythms to be more faithful to being with the Lord. Often bad moods are caused by all three dimensions. We are preoccupied with major tasks; we ignore our physical and spiritual needs to fulfill these tasks. We need to reinstate a daily rhythm that facilitates living in tune with the Spirit.

BECOMING ONE IN THE SPIRIT

The prayer of Jesus at the Last Supper in John's Gospel should give us Christians pause. "I pray not only for them, but also for those who will believe in me through their word, so that they may all be one, as you, Father, are in me and I in you, that they also may be in us, that the world may believe that you sent me" (John 18:20, 21). Jesus prays for us! As Christians we are called to be one with one another in Christ even as the Father and Jesus are one. Granted, we are more one today than at any time since the Reformation, but we are far from fully one. Sadly, there are places in the world where Christians kill one another because of their differences. Only the Holy Spirit can overcome our divisions and make us one. Our oneness, Catholics, Protestants, all Christians, grows in proportion to our response to the Holy Spirit.

Becoming one with one another assumes we have become one with Christ. Living our baptismal vocations and truly becoming the Body of Christ for and in our world demands we know Christ intimately. Only the Holy Spirit can lead us to this oneness with Christ, a oneness imaging Christ's own communion with his Father and impelling us to exclaim with

Paul, "It is no longer I who live, but Christ who lives in me" (Gal 2:20). Experiencing oneness with one another in Christ becomes a lifelong vocation for Christians. I believe daily rhythms of personal prayer and discernment of spirits are essential. In prayer we open ourselves to be drawn by grace into communion with Christ and in discernment of spirits we examine all our daily actions in the light of this experienced communion with Him.

We know that through our openness to the Holy Spirit the Father will give us this gift of oneness; God does not ask what God does not give. With Augustine's confidence we pray: "Ask what you will, but give what you ask!" With Jesus we ask to become one flock with one shepherd.

I am the good shepherd, and I know mine and mine know me, just as the Father knows me and I know the Father; and I will lay down my life for the sheep. I have other sheep that do not belong to this fold. These also I must lead, and they will hear my voice, and there will be one flock, one shepherd (John 10:14-16).

NOTES

1. *Lumen Gentium*, 17; *Dei Verbum*, 21-22.

2. John Dillenberger, ed., *Martin Luther; Selections from His Writings* (New York: Anchor Books, 1961), 63.

3. Ibid., 56

4. Ibid., 69, 81.

5. Ibid., xxix.

6. Theodore, G. Tappert, ed. and trans., *The Book of Concord: The Confessions of the Evangelical Lutheran Church* (Philadelphia: Fortress Press, 1959), 415, 418.

7. *The Constitution of the Presbyterian Church (USA): Part I: Confessions* (New York: Office of the General Assembly, 1983), Chap. IX, 3.

8. Ibid., Chap. XVIII, 3.

9. Edmund Colledge and James Walsh, eds. and trans., *Guido II: The Ladder of Monks and Twelve Meditations* (Kalamazoo: Cistercian Publications, 1981), 79-80.

10. Robert Frost, *Complete Poems of Robert Frost* (New York: Holt, Rinehart, and Winston, 1964), 408.